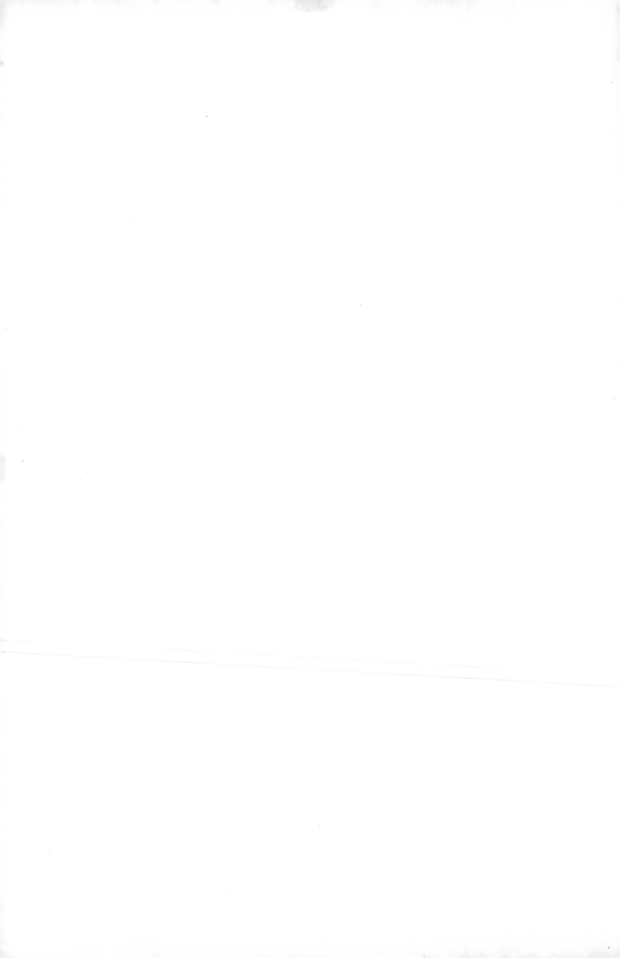

UNDERSTANDING AND TREATING ANXIETY DISORDERS

UNDERSTANDING AND TREATING ANXIETY DISORDERS

AN INTEGRATIVE APPROACH TO HEALING THE WOUNDED SELF

BARRY E. WOLFE

American Psychological Association · Washington, DC

Published by
American Psychological Association
750 First Street, NE
Washington, DC 20002
www.apa.org

To order
APA Order Department
P.O. Box 92984
Washington, DC 20090-2984
Tel: (800) 374-2721; Direct: (202) 336-5510
Fax: (202) 336-5502; TDD/TTY: (202) 336-6123
Online: www.apa.org/books/
E-mail: order@apa.org

In the U.K., Europe, Africa, and the Middle East, copies may be ordered from
American Psychological Association
3 Henrietta Street
Covent Garden, London
WC2E 8LU England

Typeset in Goudy by Stephen McDougal, Mechanicsville, MD

Printer: Edwards Brothers, Inc., Ann Arbor, MI
Cover Designer: Naylor Design, Washington, DC
Technical/Production Editor: Devon Bourexis

The opinions and statements published are the responsibility of the authors, and such opinions and statements do not necessarily represent the policies of the American Psychological Association.

Library of Congress Cataloging-in-Publication Data

Wolfe, Barry.
    Understanding and treating anxiety disorders : an integrative approach to healing the wounded self / Barry E. Wolfe.—1st ed.
        p. cm.
    Includes bibliographical references and index.
    ISBN 1-59147-196-6
    1. Anxiety. 2. Anxiety—Treatment. 3. Eclectic psychotherapy. I. Title.

RC531.W64 2005
616.85'2206—dc22   2004025351

British Library Cataloguing-in-Publication Data
A CIP record is available from the British Library.

Printed in the United States of America
First Edition

CONTENTS

PREFACE

I began work on this book over 15 years ago. At that time, my two major professional activities included my position as a program manager for psychotherapy research grants at the National Institute of Mental Health (NIMH) and my role as a part-time private practitioner. During a long career at the NIMH, anxiety disorders and their treatment eventually became my primary focus of research grant administration. As I sought to integrate my clinical experience with the findings of the research literature, my therapeutic interests also evolved into a specialty in the treatment of anxiety disorders. Thus, a process of cross-fertilization developed over time in which my knowledge of the cutting-edge developments in the treatment of anxiety disorders informed my clinical interventions in my private practice.

As I attempted to apply the mainstream treatments for anxiety disorders, my clinical experience pointed up the weaknesses in the usefulness of research findings to inform my psychotherapeutic efforts. This book emerged out of a struggle to reconcile the disparities between my clinical experience and my extensive knowledge of the research literature on the treatment of anxiety disorders. This struggle has led me to develop an integrative etiological and treatment model for this class of disorders.

This book, therefore, takes as its point of departure the mainstream view of anxiety disorders and their treatment. The mainstream view suggests that anxiety disorders, which are descriptively classified as a syndrome manifesting a cluster of anxiety symptoms, can be treated by both psychosocial and pharmacological means. These treatments have been standardized and empirically tested. Yet it became my conviction based on my clinical experience that the mainstream view of anxiety disorders is limited in (a) its conceptualization of the disorders, (b) the etiological models that have been proposed, (c) the treatments that have been developed, (d) the questions that have been researched, and (e) the methodologies proposed to research these questions. What has been developed are a number of effective treatments for the symptoms of anxiety disorders. But these treatments and the premises on which they are based tend to ignore the connections between anxiety symptoms and the intrapersonal, interpersonal, family, cultural, and ontological issues that are more often than not connected to the manifestation of these symptoms.

There are, in fact, several existing yet evolving perspectives on anxiety and its disorders, including the psychoanalytic, cognitive–behavioral, experiential, and biomedical perspectives. Each of these perspectives has something important to contribute to our understanding and treatment of anxiety, but none holds a monopoly on truth or efficacy. The fact that no single orientation seems to provide a sufficient theory of—or treatment for—anxiety disorders suggests that it may be time to develop an integrative perspective on these disorders. An integrative perspective is one that can borrow the best constructs, treatment strategies, and specific techniques from the various existing treatment perspectives to enhance understanding of—and the efficacy of treatments for—anxiety disorders.

The original scope of this book was to develop an integrative treatment model for phobias. The work scope expanded to include other anxiety disorders. But my ambitions did not stop there. It is the aim of the book to present a relatively unified theoretical integration of the existing perspectives on anxiety and to show how the integrative treatments selected flow from the theoretical premises regarding the anxiety disorders. The focal point of this theoretical integration is the concept of *self-wounds*, which in the most general sense is defined as difficulties and dysfunctions in the experiencing of the person's self or identity. I arrived at this notion only after repeated observations of the fact that the implicit meaning of anxiety for most patients with anxiety disorders whom I treated is that they are about to face an unbearable catastrophe to their physical or psychological well-being. The two integrative models that are presented within (i.e., etiology and treatment) are designed to capitalize on the very real contributions to our knowledge made by each of the existing perspectives on anxiety disorders while minimizing their limitations.

ACKNOWLEDGMENTS

This book could not have been written without the loving as well as critical support of friends, family, and colleagues. Among my colleagues I must list my teachers, particularly Morris Parloff who explicitly and implicitly taught me much about how to think and to communicate my ideas. I often have been tempted to emulate his elegant and witty prose but knowing that I could never reach his level, I was forced to develop my own style. With respect to therapy, Rudy Bauer stands out for teaching me the power of experiential techniques in psychotherapy.

Next I thank my colleagues and friends in the Society for the Exploration of Psychotherapy Integration (SEPI). Although I cannot mention all of them, I must mention Marv Goldfried and Paul Wachtel, the true founders of the psychotherapy integration movement, and Diane Arnkoff, Carol Glass, and George Stricker who with Marv, Paul, and I make up SEPI's Steering Committee. It has been an honor to work with all of you all of these years.

Thanks also go to those colleagues who have read parts of this book and have generously given of their wisdom. Thank you Marv, Paul, and George. I also thank Tom Borkovec, who read earlier portions of the book and saw the links to his own seminal work on the worrying process, and Michael Mahoney, who has often encouraged me to infuse my writing with my humanity as well as my critical analyses. I again want to thank Morris Parloff for his thoughtful and penetrating questions that he always sweetened with his overly generous praise of my work.

I want to extend special thanks to the two book representatives of the American Psychological Association (APA) who were instrumental in helping me bring this project to its fruition. First I thank Margaret Schlegel, who initiated my association with APA Books and was very helpful to me during the early stages of the book's preparation. Then I want to thank Susan Reynolds for her patience and skillfully timed inquiries that catapulted me to the final stages of the book. In addition, I want to thank Ed Meidenbauer, the development editor for APA, who was enormously helpful during the review and revise phase of the book. To the two anonymous peer reviewers go many grateful thanks for their comments that also helped to significantly improve the final product.

I also thank my former students who midwifed various stages in the birthing of this book. They include Leila Bakry-Becker, Sherry Benica, Lindsey Daniels, Joseph Grillo, Phyllis Jensen, Hany Malik, Amy Nowlin, Frank Ouseley, Phillip Pearlman, Tammy Redman, Patti Sigl, and Victor Welzant. Special thanks go to all my patients who showed such courage in facing the internal and external sources of their terror.

I give further thanks to my children, Tammy Goldberg and Neal Weiner, whose bountiful love is matched by their copious intelligence. Tammy, who is herself a therapist, often lent a willing ear to my seemingly interminable cogitations.

Finally, I thank my wife, Annette, who was unflagging in her love and support throughout the arduous process of this overdue book. Although psychology is not her field, her creativity, which graces her every endeavor, is legendary. Her ability to think out of the box in matters both practical and intellectual as well as her natural gift for human empathy resulted in her asking the most penetrating questions about a large range of issues discussed in this book. It is to her that this book is lovingly and gratefully dedicated.

I

FOUNDATIONS FOR UNDERSTANDING ANXIETY

1

INTRODUCTION

The most beautiful thing we can experience is the mysterious. It is the source of all true art and science.

—Albert Einstein (1930)

A number of years ago, a young man came to see me for the treatment of his bridge phobia. For several years, Trent was unable to cross long and high bridges without extreme anxiety. In most instances, he avoided such bridges entirely. If it were absolutely necessary for him to cross a bridge he would do it, but in a state of absolute terror. Because imaginal and in vivo exposure therapy had been blessed by the research literature as the most effective treatments for simple (now called *specific*) phobia, I began Trent's therapy with these treatments. Typically, I begin with imaginal exposure because it is both better tolerated initially than in vivo exposure and because imaginal exposure serves as a behavioral rehearsal of the in vivo therapy.

During the imaginal therapy, it became clear that a chief anticipatory fear for Trent was that when he reached the peak of the bridge, he might lose control and throw himself over the rail. This fear is a rather common one experienced by individuals with height phobias, particularly those persons with a fear of crossing high bridges. I asked him to remain with the frightening scene for as long as he could tolerate. At one point, I asked him to imagine himself doing exactly what he feared—hurling himself over the rail. I further asked him to pay attention to whatever thoughts or feelings automatically arose as he imagined himself plummeting to his death.

Trent began to experience a deep sense of despair about his life. Imagery relating to the experienced deficiencies in his life came pouring out of him. A central theme that emerged from this montage of painful images was his inability to find a suitable mate. As he further elaborated this theme, he began to document specific lacks in his personality that made it unlikely that he ever would find such a mate. Trent's painful indictment of his own personality segued into an intense fear of "dying before I have even lived." As he allowed himself to experience this fear, he began to cry. This process of allowing himself to experience these feelings moved him completely out of a state of severe anxiety into a state of extreme sadness. This sadness seemed to be clearly connected to his very negative and painful perspective on his self, which he believed prevented him from creating a meaningful and satisfactory life for himself.

The revelation of Trent's dysfunctional self-beliefs was one of the earliest hints that I received in my work with individuals with phobia that their phobias may be connected to deeper issues relating to the way in which they experience their self (Wolfe, 1989). Second, it was apparent that some intense and painful emotions seemed to lie just beyond the phobic fear and that Trent was unable to experience and articulate these feelings because of the phobic anxiety—that is, until he allowed himself to experience the anxiety fully.

Moreover, the exposure therapy produced some definite improvement in the bridge phobia but was by no means a sufficient intervention. We combined the behavioral therapy with an exploratory psychotherapy that simultaneously addressed the phobic symptoms and the presumed underlying issues. Over time, it began to be apparent that a felicitous synergy existed between the two treatment modalities. As Trent saw that he could gain some control over his phobic symptoms by means of the behavioral therapy and thereby expand his life choices (by crossing bridges rather than taking a more circuitous route), he gained confidence in his ability to remedy the other deficiencies in his life. As he began to achieve some success in his life in general with the help of the exploratory psychotherapy, he allowed himself to tolerate more discomfort in his quest to completely overcome his phobia.

The appearance of catastrophic imagery as a consequence of imaginal exposure therapy turned out not to be an isolated occurrence. With regularity, imaginal exposure elicited images of catastrophe associated with the experience of extremely painful emotions. The imaginal scenes that spontaneously arose would typically find the patient in a powerless position, about to be humiliated or badly harmed by the phobic object. There was, for example, the individual with a driving phobia who recaptured, in a state of almost unbearable rage, the trauma of being kidnapped as a 4-year-old child by her own father and placed in a strange house for a year; the individual with a public speaking phobia who, from childhood onward, experienced the constant hostile criticism of his father that led him to doubt his very obvious intellectual competence; the individual with a severe rodent phobia whose imagery revealed that her horror at the inexplicable cruelty that human beings inflict on one another had been displaced on rats as a way of preserving her belief in the basic decency of human nature; the individual with agoraphobia whose imagery revealed a bipolar fear that, on the one hand, found him in a state of terrified isolation when he achieved his desperately sought-after freedom and, on the other hand, found him in a state of horrified confinement whenever he achieved his just as desperately sought-after security; the patient with panic disorder who, through constant exposure to frightening body sensations (i.e., interoceptive exposure), began to sob hysterically as he recaptured memories of painful neglect by—and disillusionment with—his parents; and the patient experiencing generalized anxiety disorder who with the aid of Wolfe's focusing technique (Wolfe, 1992, 2005; see also Appendix) began to experience the implicit meaning of his anxiety—an intensely painful self-perception that he was basically mentally ill, an opinion frequently reinforced by his mother. Finally, there was the patient with obsessive–compulsive disorder who eventually realized that he equated sexual and selfish thoughts with mistakes he committed earlier in his life that he now believes will either shorten his own life or seriously harm his family.

As my patients and I explored their catastrophic imagery, we found either that they were recapturing long-forgotten traumatic events in their own history or that these images were constructed prototypes that symbolized the sense of helplessness, powerlessness, and doom originally experienced much earlier in their lives. These powerful and emotion-laden insights were not powerful enough to cure the phobia, but they did provide patients with the awareness of a connection between issues with which they have struggled often for most of their lives and their contemporaneous phobia. However, exposure-based behavioral therapy rarely cured the phobias. I was not seeing the rapid reduction or elimination of phobic symptoms in 60% to 70% of the cases I treated as I was led to expect by the research literature (Barlow & Wolfe, 1981). In my 25 years of experience with over 300 patients with anxiety disorder, I found that exposure therapy led to the rapid reduction of symptomatology in approximately 30% of the cases.

Typically, however, patients experienced at least three other outcomes with exposure therapy: (a) they found the treatment too frightening, however gradually it might be conducted, and were not able to complete it; (b) they experienced symptomatic relief that did not last; and (c) they were able to reduce their avoidance behavior but continued to experience substantial anxiety whenever they confronted their feared object or situation. This apparent ceiling effect with certain patients with a phobia suggested that other issues must be directly connected to the phobia that required treatment before the phobic symptoms can further improve. In other words, for the patients I see in my private practice, the previously named simple phobias were not so simple.

As the serendipitous discovery of catastrophic imagery with painful emotions became a routine occurrence in my treatment of phobias, I was increasingly struck by the irony that unconscious conflicts were being elicited by a therapeutic approach that denied their existence. Of course, this was not new. Feather and Rhoads (1972a, 1972b) demonstrated something like this phenomenon over 30 years ago when they attempted to use systematic desensitization to previously elicited unconscious fears. Even before that, Stampfl and Levis (1967) highlighted the importance of psychodynamic issues in the development, maintenance, and treatment of phobias. These unconscious issues, which invariably related to a felt threat to the self, clearly had to be addressed along with the symptoms of a given phobia. My growing conviction that something more was required in the treatment of phobias than the highly touted and often very useful behavioral therapy led me to consider the implications of this conviction for my conception of specific forms of psychopathology and their amelioration. If something more was required in the treatment of a specific disorder, then something more (or at least something different) was probably required in my conception of the disorder being treated.

As I continued to explore the frequency with which these same issues were raised in the treatment of other anxiety disorders, I began to see that an eclectic conception and treatment were going to be necessary for many patients who met the *Diagnostic and Statistical Manual of Mental Disorders* (4th ed.; *DSM–IV*; American Psychiatric Association, 1994) criteria for social phobia, panic disorder with and without agoraphobia, generalized anxiety disorder, and obsessive–compulsive disorder. With many such patients, the initial, imaginal exposure therapy uncovered catastrophic imagery associated with painful emotions that together were experienced as primal threats to their self-esteem and sense of identity.

My own leap to eclecticism, I suspect, is no isolated occurrence in this field. Many, if not most, psychotherapists of every orientation have experienced the same need for something more or something different in their treatment of specific patients. In fact, I contend without fear of contradiction, that every psychotherapist, whether working within a psychoanalytic, cognitive–behavioral, or humanistic–experiential framework, eventually encounters a significant number of patients who cannot be helped—fully, or at all—by his or her preferred mode of treatment. When confronted by a difficult patient who seems refractory to treatment, many—if not most—therapists become eclectic practitioners. Therapists freely borrow techniques from other therapy orientations to deal with specific troublesome issues in the therapy. As M. B. Parloff (personal communication, June 7, 1985) has stated, "Most therapists are eclectic either by design or by default." They do so without relinquishing either their primary therapy orientation or their identity as a practitioner of that therapeutic perspective. But these efforts are typically unsystematic and often quite in violation of the theoretical premises that initially guided their conception of the patient's problems and approach to the course of therapy. These sobering treatment failures and mismatches between theoretical assumption and clinical observation have been the germinating spores of a new movement within the field of psychotherapy—the psychotherapy integration movement.

PSYCHOTHERAPY DESEGREGATION

As more and more practicing therapists and therapy researchers experienced this paradigm strain (Goldfried & Padawer, 1982), they began to see less reason for maintaining the sectarian boundaries that had grown up around the different approaches to psychotherapy. Articles increasingly appeared in the literature questioning the need for such barriers. This trend was initially framed in terms of a desired rapprochement between psychoanalysis and behavioral therapy (Goldfried, 1980; Wachtel, 1977). These two approaches were chosen for special attention because they represented the two most dominant theoretical orientations in the field of psychotherapy and because pundits from these two therapy orientations often were the most vitriolic and vociferous critics of each other's approach to the conduct of therapy (Carrera & Adams, 1970; Eysenck, 1960; Salter, 2000; Wolpe, 1958). The desire for rapprochement eventually evolved into an interest in psychotherapy integration.

The growing interest in breaking down the sectarian barriers that existed among the various therapy orientations—a process that Paul Wachtel (personal communication, March 10, 1986) once labeled *psychotherapy desegregation*—eventually led to the formation of the Society for the Exploration of Psychotherapy Integration (SEPI) in 1983. SEPI was predicated on the conviction that no therapy theory, therapeutic strategy, or therapist possesses a monopoly on psychotherapeutic truth, wisdom, and efficacy. Since its inception, SEPI has grown into a truly international organization, with over 700 members in 25 countries.

The guiding premise of SEPI and of psychotherapy integration, more generally, is that the complexities of clinical practice seem to demand an integrative approach to the treatment of many, if not most, emotional and behavioral disorders. Since the formation of SEPI, literally hundreds of books and thousands of articles have been published on the topic of psychotherapy integration. SEPI also sponsors its own journal, the *Journal of Psychotherapy Integration*. In the two decades since SEPI's creation, three distinctive pathways to psychotherapy integration have been formulated with increasing clarity, and each has acquired its fair share of enthusiastic adherents. These pathways are *technical eclecticism, common factors approach*, and *theoretical integration*.

Technical eclecticism involves the selective combination of specific intervention techniques, which are combined without much concern regarding the underlying theories that have generated these techniques. This highly pragmatic strategy attempts to systematize the process of selecting combinations of treatment interventions tailored to the specific and idiosyncratic characteristics of the patient (Beutler, 1983; Beutler & Clarkin, 1990; Lazarus, 1992).

The common factors approach focuses on specific aspects of psychotherapy shared by all or most of the different therapy orientations. This approach is based on the conviction that positive outcomes obtained by different forms of psychotherapy may result more from the factors that unite the various therapy traditions than from those factors that differentiate them (Weinberger, 1993).

Finally, theoretical integration is based on the notion that common factors and the eclectic combination of techniques from different traditions should eventually lead to the development of an emergent unifying conceptual framework for psychotherapy (Wachtel, 1991; Wolfe, 2000).

PSYCHOTHERAPY INTEGRATION APPLIED TO A SPECIFIC CLASS OF *DSM* DISORDERS

This book attempts to marry two of the most significant trends in the field of psychotherapy: the integration of psychotherapy and the treatment of specific *DSM*-defined disorders. Most work in the field of psychotherapy integration has not focused on the application of an integrative psychotherapy to a specific class of disorders. Instead, the work has centered primarily on generic issues in psychotherapy integration. For my work, I selected anxiety disorders not only because of my extensive experience in their treatment but also because they seem quite amenable to the development of an integrated psychotherapy. All anxiety disorders possess a number of sharply delineated symptoms that are as clearly observable to the therapist as they are painful for the patient. These symptoms typically compel an initial focus of treatment and yet, in most cases, they are connected to tacit issues that go to the core of the patient's being.

In the course of developing my own treatment for the anxiety disorders, I began to explore and discover the potentially promising ideas and procedures from psychoanalytic, behavioral, cognitive, and experiential therapy orientations that would directly contribute to a more comprehensive and durable amelioration of the symptoms and their underlying tacit issues. This review suggested that the extant therapies tended to focus on a primary target of change: The behavior therapies focused on behavioral change. Cognitive therapies focused primarily on cognitive changes, whereas experiential therapies tended to focus on corrective emotional experiences. Psychodynamic therapies attempted to focus on both cognitive and emotional changes but a greater emphasis was placed on cognitive change. In any case, all three targets of change seem to be necessary foci of a comprehensive treatment of anxiety disorders.

In addition, I have experimented with ways in which pharmacotherapy and an integrative psychotherapy can be usefully combined. This has been particularly useful for patients who either feel the need for medication or feel too frightened to undertake the rigors of a psychologically based treatment without it. However, I view this combination as treatment integration rather than as psychotherapy integration, and the former is therefore not a major focus of this book.

AN INTEGRATIVE ETIOLOGICAL MODEL

The primary purpose of this book is to present an integrative perspective on anxiety disorders. This perspective includes two integrative models, an integrative conception of the etiology of these disorders, and an integrative psychotherapy for anxiety disorders. The etiological model begins with the *DSM–IV* classification of anxiety disorders. Although the *DSM–IV* is perhaps the place to start, its symptom-focused conception of anxiety disorders is insufficient to address the many issues that have arisen in clinical practice. In its effort to define the observational lowest common denominator, the *DSM–III* (American Psychiatric Association, 1980), the *DSM–III–R* (American Psychiatric Association, 1987), and the *DSM–IV* have primarily honored the cognitive–behavioral and biomedical perspectives on these as well as other disorders. I therefore found myself with a similar and parallel task of exploring the etiological conceptions of anxiety and its disorders extant in the psychoanalytic, behavioral, cognitive, experiential, and biomedical perspectives.

An integration of the various theoretical models of anxiety disorders and my clinical experience convinced me that anxiety possesses both explicit and implicit meanings to the patient, and both have to be addressed. Whereas the explicit meanings often involve secondary anxiety reactions that the patient experiences in relation to his or her perception of being anxious, the implicit meaning usually involves a feared catastrophe to the self. A deeper understanding of these fears suggested that they are based in unbearably painful ways of viewing one's self (i.e., defective, unlovable, or worthless). I have labeled these painful perceptions of self as *self-wounds*. These subjective impressions are as relevant to an understanding of the generation and maintenance of anxiety as are the natural science-based causes of anxiety disorders. Therefore, at a broader theoretical level, an understanding of the causes of anxious behavior needs to be integrated with an interpretive appreciation of the individual's reasons for his or her behavior.

AN INTEGRATIVE PSYCHOTHERAPY FOR ANXIETY DISORDERS

Healing self-wounds, the ultimate goal of my integrative psychotherapy, is predicated on prior symptom-focused treatment. The symptoms of an anxiety disorder are addressed first because patients typically come to therapy seeking symptom relief. It is at the very least respectful to try to accommodate a patient's self-selected goals for therapy. Thus I typically begin with a symptom-focused treatment that helps the patient gain a sense of control over his or her anxiety. I choose the treatment on the basis of an assessment of the patient's most comfortable area of functioning, which I call the patient's *access point*. Some patients are action oriented and therefore prefer behavioral interventions. Others are more cognitive in orientation and thus initially prefer cognitive interventions. A few prefer emotion-focused treatments because they are more comfortable with emotional expression. Over time, however, each target of change is addressed because a comprehensive treatment for anxiety disorders necessarily involves behavioral, cognitive, and emotional changes. The concept of an access point, however, allows a flexible, individually tailored psychotherapy that integrates elements from the major therapeutic orientations.

A RESEARCH-INFORMED PSYCHOTHERAPY

Much has been written of late of the need to place treatment interventions on a better empirical footing. A decade ago, Division 12 (Society of Clinical Psychology) of the American Psychological Association launched a Task Force to develop criteria for establishing empirically validated treatments and to encourage clinical practitioners to use only treatments that would qualify in terms of these criteria (Chambless, 1996; Chambless et al., 1996; Task Force on Promotion and Dissemination of Psychological Procedures, 1995). The name of this trend has evolved from *empirically validated treatments* to *empirically supported treatments*, to its current iteration, *evidence-based treatments*. Whatever the name, the qualifying psychotherapies were determined primarily by randomized clinical trials. These investigations were designed to evaluate the relative efficacy of manualized psychotherapies applied to homogeneous groups of individuals who meet criteria for a particular *DSM*-defined disorder. The initial assumption was that an evidence-based treatment could be directly applied to real-world patients. Several investigators took issue with this assumption (e.g., Borkovec & Castonguay, 1998; Messer, 2001). Goldfried and Wolfe (1996, 1998) have suggested that this trend is only the latest example of a historically strained alliance between clinical researchers and practitioners.

The integrative models presented here are works in progress and I hope that these too will eventually be empirically demonstrated to add to the present compendium of treatment approaches for anxiety disorders. However, it is my conviction that the actual practice of this integrative treatment model cannot be completely evidence-based as that term is currently defined. Instead, I view this psychotherapy as research-informed rather than evidence-based. By research-informed I mean the following: I do value research and attempt to apply its findings to the development of my integrative model; however, much of the necessary evidence is not available and is likely not to be available for a substantial period of time. Accordingly, I attempt to use research findings as far as they will take me and then supplement with my clinical experience. I revisit this issue in chapter 11.

The integrative models that have been developed thus far have borne the clear imprint of my original orientation. Treatment interventions from other orientations have been assimilated into my original theoretical framework (Lazarus, 1992; Gold & Stricker, 1993; Wachtel, 1997). Messer (1992) has labeled this approach to model building as *assimilative integration*. I recently argued that assimilative integration represents the current state of the art in terms of developing a theoretically coherent model of psychotherapy integration (Wolfe, 2001b). I hope that the field will eventually develop an emergent theoretical model that reflects many of the existing therapy traditions without being beholden to any one of them, in terms of language, concept, clinical strategy, or techniques (Goldfried, 1980). I hope that the reader finds what lies within to be a successful beginning step toward such an emergent model.

The book is divided into three parts. Part I develops a foundation for understanding anxiety and its disorders. Chapter 2 provides a summary account of the evolution of the classification system for anxiety disorders, culminating in the current *DSM–IV* description of the disorders under consideration. Chapter 3 concerns another evolution, that of the various existing theoretical perspectives on anxiety. I present brief accounts of the evolution of the psychoanalytic, behavioral, cognitive–behavioral, experiential, and biomedical theories of anxiety and anxiety disorders.

Part II concerns the synthesizing and evolution of an integrative etiological model of the anxiety disorders. Chapter 4 explores the ideas from each perspective that are included in the etiological model as well as the rationale for their selection. The methodology includes the abstraction of the factors common to all theories of anxiety and then the selection of certain etiological ideas over others. This selection process is based on both research data and clinical experience. Chapter 5 presents yet another integration, a synthesis of the various extant models of the self. This synthesis presents some consensually validated ideas about the nature of positive self-knowledge. This model necessarily serves as a normal baseline to help the reader locate the difficulties and deficiencies in self-experiencing that constitute the core issues of an anxiety disorder. With the model of the healthy self as a reference point, chapter 6 presents the integrative etiological model for anxiety disorders, which contends that in the general case, anxiety disorders are based in extremely painful self-wounds. In chapter 7, the model is described for each of the specific anxiety disorders under consideration, including the variables and issues that appear to differentiate one anxiety disorder from another. The third and final part of the book shows the synthesis and evolution of an integrative psychotherapy for anxiety disorders. Chapter 8 begins a consideration of an integrative treatment model. The process of developing an integrative theory of treatment follows a path similar to that of the previous development of the etiological model of anxiety disorders. The common and differentiating factors of the various therapeutic perspectives on anxiety are analyzed and synthesized into an integrative model of psychotherapy for anxiety disorders. In addition, I also show that this treatment model can be derived directly from the etiological model. However, the specific interventions that are used include variations of interventions from the four psychotherapy traditions. Chapter 9 provides a formal presentation of the integrative treatment model. Chapter 10 applies the treatment model to the same prototypical cases of specific anxiety disorders that have been described in chapter 7. These case illustrations elaborate the issues involved in the application of this integrative psychotherapy. A final chapter involves an evaluation of the current status of the two integrative models. It acknowledges the need for empirical verification of the models, but I provide some suggestions for a research program that goes beyond the clinical trial methodology for evaluating the treatment model. In addition, I discuss the planned expansion of the model to other disorders such as posttraumatic stress disorder and mood disorders. I hope that through this volume, an integrative model of the etiology and treatment of the anxiety disorders will advance the breadth, depth, and duration of positive benefits of therapy.

2

ON THE NATURE AND CLASSIFICATION OF ANXIETY

There are more things to alarm us than to harm us, and we suffer more in apprehension than in reality.

—Seneca (1st century A.D.)

No one who ever has been tormented by prolonged bouts of anxiety doubts its power to paralyze action, promote flight, eviscerate pleasure, and skew thinking toward the catastrophic. None would deny how terribly painful the experience of anxiety can be. The experience of chronic or intense anxiety is above all else a profound and perplexing confrontation with pain. It is ironic that the defining characteristic of anxiety for virtually all theorists is that it is an extremely painful and alarming anticipation of future pain (e.g., Barlow, 1988). "If we expect to suffer, we are anxious," said Charles Darwin in the first scientific consideration of anxiety ever published; "if we have no hope of relief, we despair" (Darwin, 1872/1965, p. 176). Patients often report that once they allow themselves to experience the situations they fear will cause them catastrophic pain, they find that the anticipatory anxiety was more painful. That an extremely painful experience is often an attempt to cope with an imagined experience of pain is but one of the many mysteries surrounding anxiety and its disorders.

Is anxiety identical to fear? Although Sigmund Freud (1926/1959) believed that the two emotions were not identical, many behaviorists used the terms interchangeably (e.g., Mowrer, 1939). For Freud, fear possessed a specific referent, whereas anxiety often did not. Anxiety in S. Freud's original theory was an automatic biological product of undischarged tension (1894/ 1962b). His second and more psychological theory of anxiety viewed it as a signal to the ego of dangerous internal impulses that are anticipated to bring external retaliation (1926/1959). Today, the consensus view in psychoanalysis is that fear pertains to real dangers, whereas anxiety is based on unconscious fantasies or imagined dangers that stem from childhood (Michels, Frances, & Shear, 1985).

As previously mentioned, behaviorists used the terms *fear* and *anxiety* interchangeably to describe a learned drive whose reduction served as reinforcement for the learning of new habits (Mowrer, 1960). A. T. Beck and Emery's cognitive perspective views anxiety as an emotional process that accompanies the perception of danger. Fear, in contrast, is viewed as a cognitive process, which involves the intellectual appraisal of a threatening stimulus; anxiety is the emotional response to that appraisal (A. T. Beck & Emery, 1985).

Barlow (2000), who is identified with the cognitive–behavioral tradition, has based his view of anxiety on the latest research information on emotion. Fear, he argued, involves the direct and immediate perception of a present danger. Anxiety involves a sense of uncontrollability regarding an anticipated danger. In fact, he preferred the term *anxious apprehension* as a more precise rendering than anxiety for "a future-oriented mood state in which one is ready or prepared to attempt to cope with upcoming negative events" (Barlow, 2000, p. 1249).

The biomedical perspective views anxiety as a normal response to the perception of danger that has been primed by evolution. Anxiety becomes problematic only when its neurobiological substrate malfunctions (D. F. Klein, 1993). Experiential theories view anxiety as based in a vital sense of threat to a person's subjective well-being (May, 1979; Wolfe & Sigl, 1998).

EVOLUTION OF THE CLASSIFICATION OF ANXIETY DISORDERS

Any classification scheme highlights certain features of reality and de-emphasizes or ignores others (Blashfield, 1991). Although the fourth edition (text revision) of the *Diagnostic and Statistical Manual of Mental Disorders* (4th ed., text revision; *DSM–IV–TR*; American Psychiatric Association, 2000) currently serves as the epitome of psychiatric classificatory wisdom, a brief excursion into the history of the classification of the anxiety disorders plainly reveals which realities of this class of mental disturbance have been emphasized, which have been de-emphasized, and which are now totally ignored. Prior to the publication of the *DSM–I* (American Psychiatric Association, 1952), most mental health practitioners subscribed to a classification scheme influenced by a broadly based psychosocial model of psychopathology. The psychosocial model of mental illness encompassed a synthesis of Freud's theory of personality and intrapsychic conflict and the environmentally based views of Adolph Meyer (Wilson, 1993). The assumptions of the psychosocial model were

> (1) that the boundary between the mentally well and the mentally ill is fluid because normal persons can become ill if exposed to severe-enough trauma, (2) that mental illness is conceived along a continuum of severity—from neurosis to borderline conditions to psychosis, (3) that an untoward mixture of noxious environment and psychic conflict causes mental illness, and (4) that the mechanisms by which mental illness emerges in the individual are psychologically mediated (known as the principle of psychogenesis). (Wilson, 1993, p. 400)

What is particularly noteworthy for the present discussion is that the model underlying the classification of mental illness highlighted the diagnostic task of understanding the meaning of symptoms in terms of their underlying psychogenic causes. The task of treatment then was to undo the psychogenic cause rather than to change the symptom directly.

The influence of the psychosocial model could be seen on the classification of the anxiety disorders as well. Two kinds of anxiety disorders had been delineated by Freud: anxiety neurosis and anxiety hysteria. The distinction between the two was based on the theoretical premise that one class of anxiety disorders was apparently rooted in psychogenic causes, whereas the other class presumably was not (1894/1962a). Anxiety neurosis was further differentiated in terms of the acute or gradual nature of its onset. If the disorder had an acute onset, it was termed *panic anxiety* or *panic attack*. If the onset to the disorder was more gradual, it was usually labeled *free-floating anxiety*. And if the anxiety became chronic, it was diagnosed as *neurasthenia* (S. Freud, 1894/1962b). By the time the *DSM–I* was published, however, the two kinds of anxiety disorders were placed under the category of psychoneurotic disorders. The influence of the classificatory ideas of Adolph Meyer could also be seen in the *DSM–I*. Because he believed that most mental illnesses were reactions to biopsychosocial events, the term *reaction* is found throughout the *DSM–I*. Thus the two disorders of anxiety neurosis and anxiety hysteria were called anxiety reaction and phobic reaction.

The *DSM–I* diagnosis of phobic reactions possessed many of the same diagnostic features that characterize phobias today, but it also included the etiological hypothesis that they were rooted in unconscious conflict, and that psychological defense mechanisms were presumed to mediate the processes linking the conflict with the phobic object or situation (Pasnau, 1984).

The *DSM–II* (American Psychiatric Association, 1968) retained much psychoanalytic thinking regarding the etiology of anxiety, phobias, and panic. The role of unconscious conflicts and psychological defenses was readily apparent in the classification of anxiety disorders. However, the term *neurosis* was uniformly substituted for *reaction*. Thus phobic neurosis, as defined by the *DSM–II*, was characterized by an intense fear of an object or situation that the patient consciously recognized as harmless. Phobias were based in fears displaced to the phobic object or situation from some other object of which the patient was unaware.

By the time the third edition of the *DSM* was to be published, the embarrassing unreliability of psychiatric diagnosis was evident to any knowledgeable mental health practitioner or researcher. To address these diagnostic deficiencies, the Task Force on Nomenclature and Statistics shifted to an allegedly atheoretical, descriptive approach to classification. The strategy was to eliminate etiological hypotheses from the definitions of specific disorders and present instead a descriptive classification system that, as much as possible, defined clinical syndromes on the basis of observable symptoms (Spitzer, 1980). In fact, the *DSM–III* (American Psychiatric Association, 1980) represented a sea change in classification philosophy. It reactivated the descriptive classificatory strategy of Emil Kraepelin (Kraepelin & Diefendorf, 1904/1907). Kraepelin believed that all mental illnesses were based in brain diseases, but because the state of scientific knowledge was such that the ultimate causes of mental illnesses still were beyond the reach of medical science, he adopted an approach to the description of mental illnesses that focused on the course and prognosis of a given disease. As Kihlstrom (2002) pointed out, Kraepelin's belief that mental diseases emanating from the same causes would produce the same symptoms paradoxically justified diagnosis on the basis of symptoms. However, it was always Kraepelin's hope and belief that the diagnosis of mental illnesses would eventually be based on the underlying brain disease causing the presenting symptoms—that is, diagnosis should include symptoms and their underlying causes.

The assumptions on which the neo-Kraepelinians based their contrasting philosophy of diagnosis and classification of mental illness in almost every instance reversed the psychosocial assumptions that underlay earlier editions of the *DSM*. Instead of viewing mental illness as based in psychosocial processes, they viewed them as medical diseases. Instead of conceptualizing mental illnesses in terms of a continuum, they conceptualized them in terms of discrete categories. Instead of relying on clinical inferences to understand the meaning of symptoms in terms of their underlying psychogenic causes, this approach was based on diagnostic algorithms that specified objective rules for combining symptoms to reach a diagnosis (Klerman, 1978).

According to the developers of the *DSM–III*, the clinical manifestations of each disorder are "described at the lowest order of inference necessary to describe the characteristic features of the disorder" (Spitzer, 1980, p. 7). Research evidence was supposed to replace "armchair" clinical speculation as the basis for defining criteria sets for each mental disorder. Published in 1980, the *DSM–III* represented a dramatic departure from its taxonomic predecessors.

In terms of content, the most notable and controversial change was the deletion of the term *neurosis*. Many lamented this change. For example, Frances and Cooper (1981) argued that a psychiatrist required both descriptive and dynamic classification schemes, lest some crucial information be lost (e.g., the patient's typical patterns of intra- and interpersonal functioning). Spitzer, the chairperson of the Task Force on Nomenclature and Statistics, defended the decision to remove the term *neurosis* by contending that the mental health field lacked a consensus with respect to its definition. Spitzer reported that the task force did agree on the small concession of including the term *neuroses* in parentheses after the categories of phobic disorders and anxiety states. Barlow (1988) pointed out that, apart from the lack of definitional consensus, there were several other reasons for the deletion of the term *neurosis*. The concept of neurosis appeared to the framers of *DSM–III* to be overly broad, difficult to measure reliably, and lacking heuristic value for research on classification.

The *DSM–III*, *DSM–III–R*, and *DSM–IV* on Anxiety Disorders

This change in classification and diagnostic philosophy had a profound effect on the way in which anxiety and its disorders were conceptualized, classified, and diagnosed. In the *DSM–III*, anxiety disorders were defined as a class of mental disorders in which

> anxiety is either the predominant disturbance as in Panic Disorder and Generalized Anxiety Disorder, or anxiety is experienced if the individual attempts to master the symptoms, as in confronting the dreaded object or situation in a Phobic Disorder or resisting the obsessions or compulsions in Obsessive-Compulsive Disorder. (American Psychiatric Association, 1980, p. 225)

By the time the third edition was revised (*DSM–III–R*; American Psychiatric Association, 1987), anxiety disorders were defined as those in which the characteristic features are symptoms of anxiety and avoidance. The document goes on to spell out the minor variations in appearance of anxiety symptoms and avoidance that together characterize the specific anxiety disorders themselves. The *DSM–IV* (American Psychiatric Association, 1994) does not even spell out a definition for this class of disorders but instead lists the 12 specific anxiety disorders that fall in this class of mental disorders and the cluster of symptoms associated with each.

In addition to its focus on symptoms, the now enshrined descriptive approach to diagnosis led to other shifts of emphasis in the classification of the anxiety disorders. Specific problems or major features of anxiety disorders that had been underemphasized in the *DSM–II* became the basis for *DSM–III* categories (Barlow, 1988). In the *DSM–III*, two major categories of anxiety disorders were defined—phobic disorders and anxiety states—a distinction that oddly mirrored S. Freud's early distinction between anxiety neurosis and anxiety hysteria. In anxiety states, anxiety was considered the predominant disturbance, and it included, among other anxiety disorders, panic disorder and generalized anxiety disorder. In phobic disorders, anxiety is experienced if the individual attempts to master his or her symptoms. Agoraphobia was listed under the phobic disorders in the *DSM–III*, which included social and simple phobia as well. Panic disorder, by contrast, was listed under anxiety states and was conceptualized as a disorder independent from that of agoraphobia with panic attacks.

The *DSM–III* classification of agoraphobia, on the one hand, and panic disorder, on the other, represented the existing status of an ongoing dispute between behavioral and biomedical conceptions regarding the nature of these disorders. During the 1970s, behavioral theorists conceptualized agoraphobia as a disorder constituted by three coequal elements: phobic avoidance behavior, panic attacks, and anticipatory anxiety. In treatment, behavior therapists tended to focus more on phobic avoidance and anticipatory anxiety than on panic attacks (Goldstein & Chambless, 1978). Biomedical theorists, heavily influenced by the work of D. F. Klein (1981), conceptualized panic disorder as a discrete disorder, which appears in its own right for the first time in the *DSM–III*. Through his research on the efficacy of pharmacological agents with anxiety disorders, D. F. Klein had found through what he has called *pharmacological dissection* an experimental basis for distinguishing panic states from more generalized anxiety. The prototypical finding was that the antidepressant imipramine could block panic attacks without significantly affecting generalized anxiety. Although this distinction came under significant question (Barlow, 1988), panic disorder eventually came to be seen as the primary disorder, with agoraphobic avoidance behavior viewed as a secondary consequence of the fear of future panic attacks. This reconceptualization of panic and its relation to agoraphobia was codified in the *DSM–III–R*. Consequently, three closely related but distinguishable disorders were described in the *DSM–III–R*: panic disorder with agoraphobia, panic disorder without agoraphobia, and agoraphobia without a history of panic disorder (American Psychiatric Association, 1987). These three disorders were retained in the *DSM–IV*. However, by the time the *DSM–IV* was published in 1994, it was recognized that panic attacks and agoraphobic symptoms occur in the context of several other anxiety disorders as well. Consequently, criteria sets for both classes of symptoms are listed separately from the previously mentioned, closely related disorders. This particular change reflects the prevailing view that agoraphobia is not by itself a disorder that is independent of panic attacks or paniclike symptoms. With these changes, the subordination of agoraphobia to the phenomena of panic is now complete.

Panic disorder also underwent an evolution from the *DSM–III* to the *DSM–IV*. In the *DSM–III* the criteria for panic disorder included at least three panic attacks in a 3-week period. Each attack had to be characterized by at least 4 of 12 mostly somatic symptoms. There was no requirement that the person had to exhibit a fear of subsequent attacks or a fear of bodily sensations. The *DSM–III–R* delineated two alternate paths to a diagnosis of panic disorder. The panic attack criterion was changed from three panic attacks in a 3-week period to four attacks in a 4-week period. However, if the individual also worried fearfully about the occurrence of future attacks, then a single panic attack was also sufficient for the diagnosis of panic disorder. With the publication of the *DSM–IV*, the fear of future panic attacks became an integral criterion in the diagnosis of panic disorder. Now the diagnosis of panic disorder required repeated, unexpected panic attacks and persistent anxiety regarding future attacks (McNally, 1994).

The *DSM–III*, *DSM–III–R*, and *DSM–IV* on Phobias

Phobic disorders were defined in the *DSM–III* in a way similar to that of the *DSM–II*, except without the psychoanalytically based etiological hypothesis. The essential feature of a phobic disorder is "a persistent and irrational fear of a specific object, activity, or situation that results in a compelling desire to avoid the dreaded object, activity, or situation (the phobic stimulus)" (American Psychiatric Association, 1980, p. 225). In the *DSM–III*, there were three classes of phobic disorders: agoraphobia, simple phobia, and social phobia. Social phobia was defined as a persistent and irrational fear of, and a compelling desire to avoid, a situation in which others expose the individual to possible scrutiny and fears that he or she may act in a way that will be humiliating or embarrassing.

The *DSM–III–R* removed the categorical distinction between anxiety states and phobic disorders. In addition, as mentioned, agoraphobia was grouped with the panic disorders rather than considered a separate phobic disorder. The definitions of simple and social phobia in the *DSM–III–R* remained essentially the same. In the *DSM–IV*, simple phobias were renamed specific phobias and, for the first time, subtypes of specific phobias were defined, including animal type, natural environment type, blood-injection-injury type, and situational type. Also included was a miscellaneous subcategory, other type, which includes such phobic stimuli as

> the fear or avoidance of situations that might lead to choking, vomiting, or contracting an illness; "space" phobia (i.e., the individual is afraid of falling down if away from walls or other means of physical support); and children's fears of loud sounds or costumed characters. (American Psychiatric Association, 1994, p. 407)

DSM–III, *DSM–III–R*, and *DSM–IV* on Generalized Anxiety Disorder

As with panic disorder, *generalized anxiety disorder* (GAD) was first defined in the *DSM–III*. In previous editions of the *DSM*, the phenomena associated with GAD were collectively labeled *anxiety neuroses*. In the *DSM–III*, GAD was primarily a residual category to be used when other anxiety disorders had been excluded. Hence there was much disagreement about this poorly defined disorder. In this edition, GAD was characterized as a disorder of persistent anxiety of at least 1 month's duration. The focus, however, was mostly on the somatic indications of anxiety such as motor tension and autonomic hyperactivity. In addition, the criteria set included apprehensive expectation and vigilance and scanning. By the time the *DSM–III–R* was published, the definition had altered somewhat. GAD then referred to unrealistic or excessive anxiety and worry about two or more life circumstances such as worries about money or about the well-being of one's children for a period of at least 6 months. The previous criteria of motor tension, autonomic hyperactivity, and vigilance and scanning were retained. In the *DSM–IV*, an effort was made to distinguish more clearly the boundary between this disorder and normal worry. The criterion "The person finds it difficult to control the worry" (American Psychiatric Association, 1994, p. 435) was added as was the requirement that three or more of the following six symptoms accompany the anxiety and worry: restlessness, easily fatigued, difficulty concentrating, irritability, muscle tension, and sleep disturbance.

DSM–III, DSM–III–R, and DSM–IV on Obsessive–Compulsive Disorders

The criteria set for obsessive–compulsive disorder remained virtually the same in the *DSM–III*, *DSM–III–R*, and *DSM–IV*. Only minor wording changes were made.

ADVANTAGES AND DISADVANTAGES OF THE *DSM* CLASSIFICATION SYSTEM

The alleged advantages of the *DSM–III*, *DSM–III–R*, and *DSM–IV* are increased specificity in the classification of mental disorders, greater precision in the description of "narrower, more manageable categories," (Barlow, 1988, p. 324) an increased likelihood of obtaining interobserver diagnostic agreement, and an increased likelihood of serving as an important heuristic for research on the classification of mental disorders (Barlow, 1988). Moreover, they provide a common language for clinical practitioners to use in communicating with one another about the difficulties experienced by their patients.

But these advantages are obtained at some cost. The chief disadvantage of the classification system underlying the *DSM–III*, *DSM–III–R*, and *DSM–IV* is that it results in a severe narrowing of the areas of clinical concern

(Wilson, 1993). Wilson (1993) has suggested that the "psychiatric gaze" has been narrowed in three ways:

> (a) there has been a loss of the concept of depth of mind, including the unconscious; (b) the consideration of time has been sharply limited. That is, there is a lack of the developmental perspective, which forecloses our understanding of symptoms in the context of a developing life; and (c) Finally, and most importantly, there has been a constriction in the range of what we as clinicians take to be clinically relevant, a narrowing of the content of clinical concern. . . . The emphasis on careful description [of symptoms] fosters the confusion of the easily observable with the clinically relevant. (p. 408)

The first of these narrowings, the phobic avoidance of unconscious phenomena, has prevailed in the development of later editions of the *DSM* despite the fact that unconscious processes increasingly have become an important focus of empirical research on basic cognitive and emotional processes (Kihlstrom, Barnhardt, & Tataryn, 1992). In reaction to the undeniable deficiencies of psychoanalytic theory, behavioral and biological investigators, particularly those who were most influential in the development of the *DSM–III*, have concluded that virtually no research evidence is available to support the relevance of unconscious phenomena to the acquisition and maintenance of the symptoms of the various mental disorders, including the anxiety disorders (Barlow, 1988; D. F. Klein, 1981). Yet it is becoming increasingly clear, even to many clinical investigators from the behavioral tradition who formerly eschewed them, that tacit processes do operate in human behavior and experience, particularly in the formation and maintenance of phobic and other anxiety disorders (A. T. Beck & Emery, 1985; Bowers & Meichenbaum, 1984; L. S. Greenberg & Safran, 1987). Both clinical and experimental evidence support the reality of unconscious processes, although significant debate continues over just how much influence these processes wield and whether verifiable unconscious processes include unconscious motivations (Greenwald, 1992).

One of the difficulties in uncovering the unconscious associations of anxiety symptoms is the fact that these associations are initially unknown to therapist, patient, and clinical investigator alike. They are not likely to be ascertained at the usual time of clinical assessment in a typical research project. The implicit meaning of anxiety symptoms typically becomes clear only in later therapy sessions, after much work has been done in solidifying the therapeutic relationship. Furthermore, clinical evidence suggests that special techniques may be required for uncovering the unconscious meanings of anxiety symptoms, techniques that can be effective only after the therapeutic alliance has been solidified (Wolfe, 2005). I describe several such techniques later in this book. Both the typical foci of the assessment instruments used in research studies of anxiety disorders as well as the timing of those assessments ensure that the unconscious meanings of a patient's anxiety symptoms will remain undetected.

Wilson's second point, the lack of a developmental perspective in the *DSM*, again relates to the problem of meaning. Patients become anxious about many issues, which vary in terms of their level of development. The meaning of panic or anxiety will be different for a young woman who experiences a panic attack on being jilted for the first time in her life than it would be for a woman in her late thirties whose panic attacks are connected to yet another unsuccessful relationship. The freshly jilted young woman may fear that she is unlovable, but the older woman who has been abandoned by yet another man may implicitly fear that she will spend the rest of her life alone. Both women may have panic attacks because they are alone, but differences in their developmental histories (and therefore in the way they construe the meaning of the loss) will possess different implications for treatment. Therapy that helps them become free of panic attacks will neither address nor solve the underlying issues that appeared to be generating them.

Wilson's third point, the narrowing of the content of clinical concern, has a number of different implications in the context of the current discussion. First is the de-emphasis of an interpersonal focus in the *DSM*. In the year before its publication, McLemore and Benjamin (1979) published a critique of the forthcoming *DSM–III*. They argued that there was much support for the contention that "the most useful aspects of psychiatric diagnosis are psychosocial in nature and that most diagnoses of 'functional mental disorders' are made, albeit implicitly, on the basis of observed interpersonal behavior" (p. 17). From the vantage point of the author's perspective, the de-emphasis again relates to the problem of meaning. The interpersonal meanings of the symptoms of the various anxiety disorders are virtually ignored by the later editions of the *DSM*. Because there is much variability among individuals with the same anxiety disorder with respect to the interpersonal significance of anxiety symptoms, there is a loss of valuable information that may relate to the possible interpersonal antecedents and consequences of anxiety symptoms. One patient's panic attacks may be associated with the fear of being thought of as incompetent or pathetically weak in relation to his colleagues, whereas another's fear may relate to expressing her rage at her spouse for fear of his retaliation. These interpersonal issues do matter, and although it is possible to reduce a person's panic attacks with a symptom-focused treatment, such treatment likely will not solve the associated interpersonal dilemmas.

All of these deficiencies point in the same direction: the failure to focus on the personal meaning of the symptoms of anxiety. Symptom cluster descriptions ignore the issue of meaning of the symptoms to the patient. There are in fact two kinds of meaning that anxiety symptoms typically possess for the patient. There are the as-yet-unarticulated meanings, which I call the preconscious or implicit meanings of anxiety. In addition, however, anxiety symptoms possess other meanings for the patient, once he or she becomes aware that he or she is anxious. Once patients begin to speculate about the possible catastrophic meaning of their anxiety symptoms, their anxiety rapidly increases. Patients with panic disorder, for example, become afraid because they are anxious—the fear-of-fear process (Goldstein & Chambless, 1978).

Another issue relevant to the meaning of symptoms is the fact that the criterial symptoms of a particular anxiety disorder can vary in meaning for different individuals diagnosed with the same anxiety disorder. Phobias, for example, may include a variety of different fearful meanings associated with the same specific phobia. In their study of 56 individuals with a flying phobia, for example, W. A. Howard, Murphy, and Clarke (1983) uncovered a variety of different fears associated with the fear of flying. Just over half (51.8%) reported primarily being afraid of a crash, but substantial minorities of the sample reported four other fears as their primary fear: the fear of heights, the fear of confinement, the fear of instability, and the fear of panicking. A smaller percentage feared losing control in front of other people. Of course, this study dealt just with meanings that were conscious. Often, however, it is the unconscious or preconscious meanings that differ in individuals diagnosed with the same nominal phobia. There is suggestive evidence that this may be the case for many specific phobias (Wolfe, 1989). Differences in the source fear for a given simple phobia may have differing etiological and treatment implications. Thus a DSM–IV diagnosis of specific phobia may actually provide little information.

Comorbidity represents a further issue in which the avoidance of the meaning dimension has consequences. It is the exception rather than the rule that a patient presents with a single anxiety disorder without the complications of other symptoms or disorders. The more typical clinical picture of a patient meeting criteria for a specific anxiety disorder is that he or she also is experiencing many symptoms associated with several different disorders, including other anxiety disorders, affective disorders, somatoform disorders, and personality disorders. The anxiety disorder may be a discrete disorder, one that is integrally related to other disorders, or an expression of a more pervasive emotional disturbance. The narrow focus of the DSM–IV can easily mislead the clinical investigator in his or her effort to understand the broader pattern of psychopathology that is evident in the patient with anxiety disorder. The DSM–IV attempts to address this problem somewhat with its multiaxial approach to classification. Thus, comorbidity with other Axis I as well as with Axis II disorders can be discerned. But this system sheds little light on the interconnections among anxiety and other disorders. A focus on the meaning of the symptoms of an anxiety disorder, however, can help the clinician assess the relationship of anxiety symptoms to other symptoms and problems that the patient may be expressing or exhibiting. Different treatment implications may become apparent depending on whether comorbid disorders are discrete entities or interconnected by recurrent, disturbing meanings. For example, I once treated a woman in her 40s who met criteria for both social phobia and depression. Her sensitivity to rejection by men produced both fear of social encounters and despair over being alone. The interpretive thread that connected both disorders was her despair over never having been chosen and her fear of future rejection. In such a case, therapies that would attempt to treat these two problems as discrete disorders have less chance of being successful than one that would confront the interpretive theme directly and explore her experience of romantic relationships.

ANXIETY DISORDERS AND THE PROBLEM OF MEANING

A perspective that takes both experience and meaning seriously will produce a different conception of the nature of anxiety disorders. If the focus is on human beings as meaning makers, as entities that experience meaning immediately and directly as a result of their interactions with the world as well as their second-order evaluation (cogitation) of these immediate meanings, then it is possible to view anxiety disorders in the broadest sense as primarily disorders of anticipated catastrophic meanings. The symptoms of anxiety typically serve as a signal of something dangerous in one's experiencing that is felt to be fundamentally threatening to one's self. I spell out this conception in much greater detail later. For now, I argue that the current system for the classification of anxiety disorders is quite limited. The current edition of the *DSM* requires practitioners to pay too high a price in understanding of and ability to treat the psychopathology associated with—and underlying—anxiety disorders, because insufficient attention has been focused on the patient's implicit construals of his or her experience. Paying closer attention to the subjective experiences of patients with anxiety disorders will yield more understanding of the nature and treatment of these disorders as well as the interplay of biological, cognitive, behavioral, and affective factors in the acquisition and maintenance of these disorders. But before I present an integrative model of the etiology of anxiety disorders, I first consider the etiological hypotheses of the several extant theoretical models of anxiety and its disorders.

3

PERSPECTIVES ON ANXIETY DISORDERS

The deficiencies in our description [of the mind] would probably vanish if we were already in a position to replace the psychological terms by physiological or chemical ones.

—Sigmund Freud (1920)

In this chapter, I briefly consider five theoretical perspectives that have contributed significantly to an understanding of anxiety and anxiety disorders: psychoanalytic, behavioral, cognitive and cognitive–behavioral,[1] experiential–existential, and biomedical. Within each perspective, I consider the same four questions: (a) What is the nature of anxiety and its disorders? (b) What are the factors and processes associated with the development of an anxiety disorder? (c) What factors contribute to the maintenance of an anxiety disorder? and (d) What factors determine which anxiety disorder is manifested?

THE PSYCHOANALYTIC PERSPECTIVE

The evolution of S. Freud's thinking on anxiety reflects, on the one hand, his belief that the psychological level of explanation would eventually

---

[1] I have grouped together the cognitive and cognitive–behavioral points of view even though they have different theoretical roots and in some instances different theoretical ideas. In the specific context of anxiety disorders, their similarities far outweigh their differences.

be reduced to neurobiological laws, and on the other, his inability to transcend his psychological metaphors. In the spring of 1895, S. Freud began work on his *Project for a Scientific Psychology*. He was explicit about the goal of this work, which was to reduce the laws of the mind to the laws of neurophysiology (S. Freud, 1895/1966). As Sulloway (1979) has documented, S. Freud's biological reductionism was an abiding philosophic postulate throughout his entire career. And although his later writings appeared to place an exclusive focus on the individual's perception of meanings, it was always implicit that these perceptions were based on more fundamental transactions taking place in the individual's biological systems. The *Project* was eventually abandoned uncompleted, but S. Freud never abandoned the biological underpinnings of his theory (Sulloway, 1979).

What Is the Nature of Anxiety?

S. Freud's commitment to biological reductionism was explicit in his first theory of anxiety in which the experience of anxiety is cast entirely in energic metaphors. The mental apparatus is conceptualized as an energy-based system, one that regulates psychic energy derived from instinctual drives. This energy-regulating system functioned according to two principles: (a) the principle of homeostasis, in which a steady state of low energy was the constant goal of the organism, and (b) the pleasure–unpleasure principle, which referred to increases and decreases of sexual tension.

At the same time, S. Freud's early views on anxiety were based on clinical observations. He observed, for example, anxiety neuroses in women who were unable to directly discharge sexual energy (i.e., in virgins, widows, and newlyweds, as well as in women who were abstinent or whose husbands experienced a sexual dysfunction; S. Freud, 1894/1962b). Anxiety, therefore, for S. Freud, was a product of incompletely repressed sexual energy that had been blocked from being discharged. This partially repressed libido would undergo an automatic transformation to anxiety, "as wine to vinegar" (S. Freud, 1905/1975, p. 224). Even his initial distinction between normal and neurotic anxiety was couched in the language of biology:

> In the neurosis, the nervous system is reacting against a source of excitation which is internal, whereas in the corresponding [normal] affect it is reacting against an analogous source of excitation which is external. (S. Freud, 1894/1962b, p. 112)

In S. Freud's second theory, developed in 1926, anxiety was conceptualized in psychological rather than in biological terms and therefore was more concerned with the meaning of anxiety. Anxiety was now conceived of as a signal of dangerous unconscious impulses that are anticipated to bring about retaliation. One of the advances of this new theory of anxiety is that it highlighted a capacity for anticipating events. This theory of anxiety could now explain such phenomena as apprehension, dread, or the sense of impending doom, for which the first theory could not adequately account.

The new theory also made it possible for a more psychological distinction to be made between anxiety and fear. Fear, S. Freud argued, is based on current real dangers, whereas anxiety is based on imagined dangers, which had their origins in childhood. Although fear and anxiety can be distinguished, they often occur together. For example, a person afraid of expressing legitimate anger at his or her boss out of fear of losing his or her job may also be experiencing castration anxiety. In fact, realistic fears are often exaggerated by neurotic anxiety.

How an Anxiety Disorder Develops

In contrast with the earlier quantitative theory of anxiety, the new theory emphasized different sources of anxiety-evoking danger situations associated with different developmental stages. Included in developmental progression were the following:

- fear of being overwhelmed by traumatic excitation from without or from within,
- fear of loss of the object of primary care and attachment,
- fear of loss of the object's love,
- fear of castration or other bodily punishment or hurt,
- fear of superego, conscience, or social condemnation, and
- fear of abandonment by the powers of fate.

These danger situations, which are often connected to unconscious wishes, trigger anxiety that, in turn, leads to a defensive response that attempts to reduce the anxiety. Anxiety symptoms occur when defense mechanisms fail to completely solve the underlying conflict.

Thus S. Freud had delineated the basic psychoanalytic paradigm with respect to emotional disorders, in general, and anxiety disorders, in particular. This is a paradigm that, in its formal structural properties, has not really been altered by his followers. Put in its simplest terms, anxiety is about the anticipated danger of experiencing or expressing forbidden ideas, originally of a sexual nature. These ideas therefore must be repressed, and the failure of repression produces anxiety, which leads to other defensive maneuvers. Many of S. Freud's disciples disagreed primarily with his contention regarding the sexual nature of the unconscious forbidden dangers rather than with the basic psychodynamic paradigm. Whereas S. Freud emphasized a basic conflict between impulse gratification and societal restraint, later forms of psychoanalysis highlighted the peremptory significance of relationships in an individual's psychic well-being. Any thought, feeling, or action that might threaten an individual's attachment to the significant people in his or her life may be construed as dangerous.

Regardless of differences in the specific content of the threatening ideas, and of the fantasized catastrophes, many forms of psychoanalysis construe the basic process of an anxiety disorder in terms of the internal psychic dynamics between wishes, fears, and defenses. As Edelson (1985) described the paradigm: "Factors in the external world are positive causal factors with respect to the development of anxiety disorders only insofar as they undercut secondary process thinking and reality testing, intensify impulses relative to defenses, or weaken defenses relative to impulses" (p. 636).

Freud's View of What Maintains an Anxiety Disorder

In S. Freud's view, the key maintaining factors in a neurosis are (a) the lack of insight into the nature of an unconscious conflict and (b) the automatic (and therefore also unconscious) application of specific defense mechanisms that maintain this lack of awareness. Without insight, the individual experiences a continuing need for a solution to his or her basic dilemma: the necessity of honoring both the desire for impulse gratification and his or her moral precepts. If defenses fail to maintain the repression of unacceptable ideas, anxiety symptoms represent a last-ditch attempt to keep these ideas out of consciousness.

Freud's View of Specific Anxiety Disorders

S. Freud originally attempted to differentiate between Aktual neuroses (i.e., anxiety neuroses; neurasthenia) caused by a direct biological sexual etiology and Psychoneuroses (i.e., hysteria, compulsiveness) caused by a psychological, although also sexual, etiology. Thus, anxiety hysteria, his original term for phobias, was differentiated from anxiety neurosis. Anxiety neurosis, an Aktual neurosis, was not based in any kind of psychological process and was therefore presumably based in a constitutional predisposition. S. Freud believed that the Aktual neuroses were caused by sexual practices that interfered with gratification (i.e., discharge of excessive excitations). Such sexual noxiae, as he called them, included coitus interruptus, among others (S. Freud, 1895/1963). Panic was originally viewed by S. Freud as a symptom of an anxiety neurosis that was constitutionally based and therefore unrelated to intrapsychic conflicts. In fact, S. Freud's description of the anxiety attack, an integral part of the diagnosis of anxiety neurosis, contains most of the 13 symptoms listed in the *Diagnostic and Statistical Manual of Mental Disorders* (4th ed.; *DSM–IV*; American Psychiatric Association, 1994) criteria set for a panic attack (S. Freud, 1895/1963). Moreover, despite his distinction between two types of neuroses, it is apparent that as early as 1895, S. Freud had struck another modern note. He had in fact adopted what today would be called a diathesis stress model of the development of an anxiety neurosis. He argued that for an individual to acquire an anxiety neurosis he or she had to be predisposed for such a possibility by heredity and he or she had to experience some problem in his or her sexual life. Thus, hereditary disposition and sexual noxiae were both necessary for the manifestation of an anxiety neurosis.

> The sexual factor is, as a rule, effective only with those persons who are endowed with an hereditary taint; heredity alone is not usually able to produce an anxiety neurosis, but waits for the incidence of a sufficient quantity of the specific sexual noxia. (S. Freud, 1895/1963, p. 134)

Freud on Phobias

S. Freud originally viewed phobias as a variation of hysteria and therefore called them the anxiety hysterias. His view of phobias eventually emphasized the potential threat posed by internal dangers that were threatening to become conscious. Defensive processes automatically kick in but are not completely successful, and the resultant anxiety is partially managed by the formation of a symptom(s). In the case of Little Hans's horse phobia, for example, the internal dangers included forbidden sexual wishes toward his mother and an aggressive wish for his father's demise. The defense mechanisms of displacement and projection operate to keep Little Hans in the dark regarding his real motivations. Thus, horse replaces father and the horse's bite reflects Hans's castration anxiety. His aggressive wish is thereby displaced and projected on the horse and the internal danger becomes an external and presumably more manageable one (S. Freud, 1909/1955a).

Freud on Obsessional Neuroses

S. Freud (1894/1962a) originally defined obsessions as defense hysteria, a splitting off of unacceptable sexual ideas from consciousness. Once he had developed his psychosexual theory of development, S. Freud (1913/1958) came to view obsessions and compulsions as a product of fixations at the anal stage or of a regression to the anal stage as a result of Oedipal anxiety. Obsessions represented the predominance of sexual and aggressive thoughts, a victory of impulse over defense. These obsessions produce anxiety, which, in turn, evoke anal-based compulsions, such as checking behavior or hand washing, in an effort to reduce that anxiety. The regression also undoes the fusion between sexual and aggressive drives, resulting in intense feelings of ambivalence. The symptom of obsessional doubting results from the co-occurrence of feelings of love and hatred and this combination can leave an individual in a state of paralyzing indecision (S. Freud 1909/1955b).

The choice of obsessions and compulsions in this neurosis is governed by the defenses that the individual develops against the offending unconscious impulses. The defenses of isolation, reaction formation, and undoing seem to particularly characterize obsessional neurosis. The isolation of thought from feeling allows the individual to separate the instinctual impulse from its context. Thus an individual might experience a violent fantasy without anger. Reaction formation, in which the individual behaves in ways that are opposite the repressed impulse, deludes the individual into thinking that he or she possesses no such sexual or aggressive thoughts. Thus a person may act in a very gentle manner toward another person to conceal his aggressive intentions. Finally, undoing is an attempt to cancel one unacceptable thought or behavior by a second thought or behavior. This is an attempt, according to S. Freud, to "make the past itself non-existent" (1926/1959, p. 120). Compulsions often attempt to achieve this impossible aim.

Modern Psychoanalytic Perspectives on Anxiety

Space does not permit a comprehensive review of all the various tributaries of psychoanalytic thinking regarding anxiety and its disorders. But certain generalizations can be presented. Most modern versions of psychoanalysis accept a neurobiological diathesis—that some individuals are genetically programmed to be more susceptible to experiencing anxiety and developing an anxiety disorder (Gabbard, 1994). Beyond that, however, the more relational views of psychoanalysis—with some exceptions to be presented below—do not focus on specific anxiety disorders. But they do have a good deal to say about anxiety. Anxiety, from the point of view of object relations theorists, for example, refers to the thoughts and feelings that threaten one's relationships or sense of self in relationship. This anxiety is traceable back to the earliest mother–child dyadic experience. Fairbairn (1952), for example, contended that separation anxiety was the earliest form of anxiety. This anxiety may set the stage for a basic conflict, which arises when the child simultaneously longs for a deeply dependent and a more mature connection to the mother. If the child approaches the maternal object too closely, he or she may feel engulfed, but as the child tries to separate from the maternal object, he or she may experience a traumatic sense of isolation and lack of support. From the object relations vantage point, anxiety has less to do with the gratification of impulses and more to do with the maintenance of affectional ties with significant people in the individual's life. In other words, problems that result in the separation–individuation developmental stage are likely to produce anxiety problems later in life.

Modern Psychoanalytic Perspectives on Specific Anxiety Disorders

Specific Phobias

A modern psychoanalytic view of specific phobias has changed very little from the original Freudian conception. Then as now, it is argued that when forbidden impulses or thoughts that might lead to retaliation threaten to surface into consciousness, signal anxiety appears, which leads in turn to the defenses of displacement, projection, and avoidance. These defenses produce a solution that eliminates anxiety, on the one hand, but produce a phobic neurosis targeting a specific external object, on the other (Nemiah, 1981). Two elements of the psychodynamic model have changed. The first is the recognition that some individuals may be biologically programmed to be more susceptible to the development of a phobia. The second change has to do with the content of the unconscious, forbidden thoughts. Few today accept the Freudian belief that the forbidden thoughts pertain only to sex and aggression. The more relational approaches to psychoanalysis have added conflicts over losing relationships and significant affectional ties as a generative force for the development of a phobia. Arieti (1978, 1979) argued that the phobic object is often not human and its function is to serve as a diversion. By projecting one's anxiety that has as its source a significant human relationship on a nonhuman object, the individual can thereby preserve that relationship. The individual then can live in harmony with the other and the phobic object serves literally as a scapegoat. "By attributing the cause of his trouble to non-human sources, the patient protects the human image" (Arieti, 1979, p. 89).

Social Phobia

Modern psychoanalytic formulations of social phobia include the same acceptance of an interaction between a biological diathesis and environmental stressors. But given the possibility that some people are more predisposed than others toward developing a social phobia, recent psychoanalytic views contend that those with a social phobia have internalized representations of parents and other authority figures who shame, criticize, and humiliate. These early introjects are then projected on people in the contemporary environment (Gabbard, 1994). The symptoms of social phobia represent a solution that compromises between expressing unacceptable wishes and defending against them. Shame experiences in particular play a major role in the generation of a social phobia. An underlying desire to be the center of attention automatically induces feelings of shame and censure from disapproving authorities (e.g., parents). Individuals with a social phobia then avoid situations in which they fear disapproving reactions from others and the unbearable humiliation they imagine such reactions would produce (Gabbard, 1992).

Panic Disorder

In S. Freud's early theory of anxiety, he categorized the phenomena of panic and agoraphobia under the rubric of anxiety neurosis. Anxiety neurosis was viewed as an Aktual neurosis. Later, S. Freud began to view panic attacks and agoraphobia as conceptually distinct phenomena. It is ironic that whereas modern psychoanalytic perspectives on panic disorder reflect many of S. Freud's original psychogenic bases of neuroses, his view of panic was— and continued to be—that it is a constitutionally based neurotic response incapable of being psychoanalyzed (1894/1962b). With respect to agoraphobia, however, S. Freud came to believe that this neurotic disorder clearly possessed a psychogenic basis. In line with his view that psychoneuroses are rooted in unconscious conflicts regarding one's forbidden sexual impulses, S. Freud interpreted agoraphobia as reflecting some forbidden sexual temptation. Agoraphobic avoidance in this view is a defensive maneuver that protects the individual from becoming aware of or acting out the forbidden impulse. Agoraphobic symptoms therefore are viewed as a solution that compromises between the wish and its prohibition.

From an object relations point of view, Frances and Dunn (1975) emphasized a conflict between a wish for attachment to others, on the one hand, and a wish for autonomy, on the other, that seems to underlie and generate agoraphobic symptoms. They assumed that the context of moving through space is the initial arena in which infants develop separation anxiety and self–object differentiation. "The ability to walk away from each other is a paradigmatic symbol and a means of developing and reinforcing psychic differentiation" (Frances & Dunn, 1975, p. 436). The adult with agoraphobia also finds situations outside his or her territory anxiety-provoking and needs a companion to help him or her maintain a sense of safety. The precipitating event of an episode of increased symptomatology is usually something that threatens the patient's real or imagined relationship with the partner.

Bowlby (1973, 1988), in an effort to integrate the then-current findings of ethological psychology with psychoanalysis, argued that there exists in humans an instinctual primary and autonomous attachment system relatively independent of the hunger drive and of sex and aggression. This system comprises such behaviors as smiling, vocalizing, sucking, soothability, and a readiness to respond to objects. Psychopathology for Bowlby related to failures of attachment. In *pseudophobia*, his term for agoraphobia, Bowlby argued that what is feared is the absence of the attachment figure, that is, the lack of a secure base. He believed that agoraphobia was not really a phobia but was better conceptualized as a separation anxiety disorder, resulting from actual experience with unresponsive caretakers. A variation of Bowlby's separation anxiety hypothesis was presented by Weiss and Sampson (1986). They argued that many times people's difficulties in separating are not so much related to anxiety as they are to guilt about leaving their loved ones behind.

A modern psychodynamic conception of panic disorder that addresses both panic attacks and agoraphobic symptoms was presented by Shear, Cooper, Klerman, Busch, and Shapiro (1993). This view reflects the recent emphasis on a biological diathesis for panic disorder. It suggests that an inborn neurophysiological vulnerability predisposes the patient with panic disorder to fearfulness, particularly of unfamiliar situations. This biological diathesis in combination with exposure to parental behaviors that augment fearfulness can produce disturbances in object relations and persistence of conflicts between dependence and independence. These conflicts and disturbances in turn may predispose the patient to fears of being trapped, suffocated, and unable to escape, or feeling alone and unable to get help. Avoidance behavior prevents such patients from developing more mature defenses against internal and external threats, which, in turn, leads to a heightened frequency and intensity of negative affects. If the patient attempts to ignore these negative affects, the somatic aspect of these negative affects becomes the focus of attention and the trigger for conscious and unconscious catastrophic thinking. These negative affects increase the patient's neurophysiological sensitivity, eroding his or her sense of safety and control. The loss of a sense of safety and control may produce a catastrophic fantasy (conscious or unconscious) that, in conjunction with an intrusive negative affect, can trigger a panic attack.

Although conflicts over separation may be the major source of conflict in patients with panic disorder, Shear et al. (1993) described other such patients as *suffocation sensitive* (i.e., a premature tendency to feel like one is suffocating). With respect to this group, it is interesting to note that whereas D. F. Klein (1993), as mentioned before, attributed this sensitivity to a biological defect, Milrod, Busch, Cooper, and Shapiro (1997) suggested that these individuals are conflicted about their unconscious dependence needs, which, because of immature defenses, feel overwhelming.

Milrod et al. (1997) also suggested that conflicts over anger and its expression represent still another content area of unconscious conflicts that motivate patients with panic disorder. They proposed the same biological diathesis but suggested that some patients have experienced a series of traumatic events at the hands of their primary caretakers. The child develops significant anger toward the parents' rejecting or frightening behavior, and that anger gives rise to frightening fantasies that the child fears will destroy the parent on whom he or she utterly depends. As Milrod et al. (1997) put it, "In this vicious cycle, rage threatens the all-important tie to the parent and increases the child's fearful dependence. This process leads to further frustration and rage at the parent, whom the child views as the source of his or her inadequacies" (p. 10). To the immature ego, the threatened and threatening appearance of such anger and rage leads to panic attacks.

One can see that even in the modern psychoanalytic conception of an anxiety disorder, the basic psychoanalytic paradigm remains intact: Unconscious conflicts produce symptoms when defenses are overwhelmed. Unlike other models, this model of panic disorder gives a significant etiological role to traumatic experiences (Milrod et al., 1997; Shear et al., 1993). The model also possesses the virtue of a focus on unconscious phenomena and their significance for the development and maintenance of panic disorder. Given the modern psychoanalytic view on the impact of traumatic experiences on the psyche of the patient with a panic disorder, it is perhaps ironic that S. Freud believed constitutional deficiencies rather than psychogenic issues produced panic attacks.

Obsessive–Compulsive Disorder

Little has changed regarding the classical psychoanalytic formulation that obsessive–compulsive disorder (OCD) represents a defensive regression to the anal stage provoked by anxiety-producing sexual or aggressive thoughts. Because the fusion of feelings of love and hatred has been undone by the regression, the individual with OCD is typically filled with ambivalence. This ambivalence generates chronic doubt regarding the validity of the individual's decisions and courses of action (Gabbard, 1994).

Salzman (1980) argued that the symptoms of obsessive–compulsive neurosis represent an effort to restore a lost sense of control to the individual. Compulsive behaviors reestablish a sense of predictability and order to a chaotic sense of one's life. Salzman, however, thought obsessive–compulsive neurosis exists on a spectrum with obsessional character, which results from the breakdown of adaptive defenses.

Generalized Anxiety Disorders

Because psychoanalysis has not paid much attention to the diagnostic categories of the *DSM–IV*, there is actually very little work involving the psychodynamic perspective on generalized anxiety disorder (GAD). However, as with all psychodynamic theories of psychopathology, GAD is thought to be based in intrapsychic conflicts of varying content (Berzoff, Flanagan, & Hertz, 1996). Crits-Christoph, Crits-Christoph, Wolf-Palacio, Fichter, and Rudick (1995) presented a model of GAD that is based in the more interpersonal forms of psychoanalysis. They hypothesized that one or more traumatic experiences, occurring at any time in a person's life, results in a series of negative basic assumptions about one's self and other people, particularly with respect to the individual's likelihood of successfully meeting one's needs in life and in relationships. Individuals who meet criteria for GAD possess serious doubts about their ability to obtain love, security, stability, and protection from others. These individuals defend against the rising level of fear that these assumptions produce by worrying about certain current events rather than facing painful emotional issues head-on. But these issues continue to influence individuals with GAD and lead them to develop repetitive maladaptive relationship patterns. These patterns are actually vicious cycles in which the individual behaves toward others according to his or her maladaptive basic assumptions, which encourage responses from others that confirm the individual's original beliefs. As Crits-Christoph et al. pointed out, "These self-defeating patterns are cyclical, meaning that they end up re-creating the same sort of perceived circumstances that originally generated the fear (e.g., expectation of losing a loved one)" (p. 51).

These self-fulfilling prophecies keep the individual from developing meaningful, satisfying, or harmonious relationships. These interpersonal and intrapsychic conflicts can be formulated by the therapist by means of the

Core Conflictual Relationship Theme (CCRT) method (Luborsky & Crits-Christoph, 1990), which allows a therapist to detect and analyze the patient's maladaptive relationship patterns. The CCRT focuses on three components: the wishes and needs of the patient, the responses of others (gratifying or frustrating the wishes), and the responses of self that follow. Current and past relationships of the patient and the relationship of the patient with the therapist are analyzed to uncover the relevant CCRTs. Change in patients' CCRTs is effected by helping them to find better ways of coping with painful feelings, expressing their needs, and responding to others.

What Differentiates the Various Anxiety Disorders?

In every variation of psychodynamic models of anxiety disorders, the role of defenses is prominent. Defenses emerge in developmental sequence in line with the prototypical conflicts of a psychosexual stage. For this reason, defenses can be distinguished as being more or less mature. The application of immature defenses in a given situation presents clues for the kind of intrapsychic conflict with which an individual is struggling. The paradigm of a struggle among wishes, fears, and defenses is evident in every version of psychoanalysis regardless of the specific contents. The symptom of anxiety occurs when defense mechanisms fail to provide an adequate solution to these conflicts. The specific anxiety disorder that develops is based on the particular characteristics of the individual's defense mechanisms (Michels et al., 1985). As Anna Freud (1946) put it, neurotic symptoms are a result of the

> unvarying use of a special form of defense when confronted with a particular instinctual demand, and the repetition of exactly the same procedure every time that demand recurs in its stereotyped form. We know that there is a regular connection between particular neuroses and special modes of defense, as, for instance, between hysteria and repression or between obsessional neurosis and the processes of isolation and undoing. (pp. 36–37)

BEHAVIORAL AND COGNITIVE–BEHAVIORAL PERSPECTIVES

The behavioral perspective began as a revolt against the study of consciousness as the basic data of psychology. Its philosophical and methodological commitments spawned a number of learning theories that served as the intellectual scaffolding for the emergence of the various behavior therapies in the 1950s and 1960s. These theories attempted, as much as possible, to focus on publicly observable variables and consequently redefined emotional experiences as behavioral responses. Thus, anxiety was reconceptualized as a conditioned fear response, an observable behavioral response. All of the behavior therapies that subsequently emerged were considered to be applications of modern learning theory to clinical disorders (Eysenck, 1959).

What Is the Nature of Anxiety?

From the behavioral point of view, *anxiety* or *fear* (the terms are typically used interchangeably) is both a basic biological given and a learned response. Behavioral researchers defined two basic learning processes: classical and instrumental conditioning. A classically conditioned fear response is produced by contiguously pairing a neutral stimulus with a stimulus that inherently causes fear or pain. Instrumental conditioning is a process whereby a fear response is learned through the provision of environmental reinforcements for selected, self-initiated behaviors (Mowrer, 1960). The original behavioral account of anxiety, presented by Watson and Morgan (1917), was basically a variation of Pavlovian classical conditioning. The theory was first tested by Watson and Raynor (1920) on Little Albert, an 11-month-old child. The presentation of a white rat contiguous with a loud noise eventually led to the white rat alone producing a fear reaction in Albert.

Although Watson's case of Little Albert is the first demonstration that human fears can be conditioned, it was Mowrer's two-factor theory that explained both the conditioned fear's acquisition and its maintenance. Anxiety in this account is acquired through classical conditioning but then serves as a secondary motivation or drive that produces tension in the organism. Avoiding the fear stimulus then reduces the autonomically mediated tension and this drive reduction reinforces the avoidance behavior (Mowrer, 1939).

These conditioning models were subsequently criticized on numerous grounds, particularly because of their inability to explain individual response differences to similar stimulus conditions (Breger & McGaugh, 1965; Rachman, 1977). The limitations of straightforward conditioning models led to the rise of mediational models. Essentially, mediational models of learning contended that responses to specific stimuli were mediated by variables presumed to be inside the individual, be they internalized stimulus–response (S-R) connections, cognitions, or expectancies. These models represented a compromise: a theoretical formulation that attempted to explain what was going on inside the organism while showing as much fealty as possible to the strictures of academic psychology's guiding scientific philosophy, logical positivism (Mahoney, 1974). The resulting mediational models, which initially postulated limitless numbers of S-R connections inside the head, eventually paved the way for the appearance of cognitive models of learning.

A transition between the behavioral and cognitive perspectives is found in the social learning model of Bandura (1977). His model pointed the behavioral perspective away from a sole focus on environmental contingencies and drive reduction toward symbolic processes, the importance of observational learning, and the development of expectancies. According to Bandura, people do not avoid feared objects and situations to reduce anxiety. Instead, he suggested that aversive experiences create expectations of injury or pain and these in turn produce both anxiety and avoidance behavior. Thus, anxiety and avoidance are coeffects of efficacy expectations rather than being causally linked. As Bandura put it, "Perceived threats activate defensive behavior because of their predictive value rather than their aversive quality" (p. 209). This information-based view of the mediating mechanism suggests a strong relationship between a person's self-efficacy expectations in a specific situation and the amount of anxiety he or she will exhibit.

As the information-processing view of anxiety and other behaviors took hold, the behaviorist paradigm was extended to include a cognitive focus. Influenced by scientific metaphors derived from the paradigmatic operations of the increasingly important computer, information-processing theory allowed the theorist to speak in the language of input, output, storage, and retrieval. Information was retrieved from underlying cognitive schemas that were presumed to powerfully influence an individual's feelings and behavior. Now anxiety was conceived as a product of danger-related cognitive schemas stored in memory. These schemas were developed through painful life experience but, once established, were highly influential in the production of anticipatory anxiety in certain specified situations. Whereas the purely behavioral view of learning considered behavior primarily a function of environmental contingencies, the more cognitive version of behaviorism argued something different—human beings respond more to cognitive representations of the environment rather than directly to the environmental contingencies (Bandura, 1986).

Bandura's social learning model is viewed as transitional because he attempted to explain self-regulatory behaviors without postulating internal entities such as cognitive schemas. A more purely cognitive view of anxiety was presented by A. T. Beck and Emery (1985). Unlike mainstream behaviorists, they viewed anxiety and fear as separate constructs. In their view, anxiety refers to an emotional process that accompanies the perception of danger. Fear, by contrast, is a cognitive process that involves the intellectual appraisal of a threatening stimulus; anxiety is the emotional response to that appraisal. The experience of anxiety consists of a subjectively unpleasant emotional state characterized by unpleasant feelings such as tension or nervousness and by physiological symptoms. Anxiety is considered a normal reaction if it is aroused by a realistic danger and if it dissipates when the danger is no longer present. If the degree of anxiety is greatly disproportionate to the risk and severity of possible danger, and if it continues even though no objective danger exists, then the reaction is considered abnormal.

Barlow (2000), who preferred the phrase *anxious apprehension* to the term *anxiety*, presented a somewhat different cognitive–behavioral model. He viewed anxiety as a coherent cognitive–affective structure at the heart of which is a sense of uncontrollability regarding future threats. Anxiety therefore is a state of helplessness that results because one is unable to predict or control certain salient events and outcomes. A variety of external or internal cues and propositions may be sufficient to stimulate anxious apprehension in the individual, and although Barlow eschewed the language, these cues and propositions are often unconscious. The anxiety state is associated with a shift in attention to a self-evaluative focus, which is prominently characterized by negative evaluations of one's ability to cope with internal or external dangers. This attentional shift inevitably increases the level of anxiety, which, in turn, completes a negative feedback loop.

How Does an Anxiety Disorder Develop?

Behaviorists typically eschewed categorical definitions of behavioral problems. So-called maladaptive behavior is subject to the same laws of learning as are more adaptive responses. What makes a particular learned behavior maladaptive or dysfunctional is that it produces undesirable consequences for someone, either for the individual or for significant others in the individual's life. Early on, Skinnerian behavior modifiers attempted to finesse the value questions involved in any discussion of normal and abnormal behavior by viewing themselves as technicians of behavioral change whose services could honor many different kinds of values and value systems. Later, however, behavior modifiers argued that their efforts were designed to enhance individual autonomy and other humanistic values (Davison, 1976; Thoresen, 1974).

With respect to anxiety disorders, nonmediational models have mostly fallen out of favor. Wolpe, however, has remained a staunch adherent to a noncognitive view of anxiety and panic (Wolpe & Rowan, 1988). Behaviorists have argued that any stimulus can become a learned elicitor of fear but that anxiety problems typically result from three sources: (a) direct experience of painful or traumatic events, (b) vicarious learning, or (c) direct transmission of information (Rachman, 1977). Bouton, Mineka, and Barlow (2001) have more recently presented a modern learning theory perspective on anxiety disorders that I discuss in greater detail later in the chapter.

Bandura (1982) would agree that anxiety disorders may be based in any of these three sources but would argue that this analysis leaves out a crucial mediating factor: the level of self-efficacy expectations. An anxiety disorder, from this point of view, is based in a low level of self-efficacy beliefs about one's ability to cope with specific threat situations.

A. T. Beck's cognitive model suggests that anxiety disorders are rooted in dysfunctional cognitive schemas related to danger and that these schemas represent misperceptions or exaggerations of the amount of danger that exists in particular situations. A. T. Beck made the interesting point that anxiety is not the pathological process in an anxiety disorder. It is the overactive cognitive patterns relevant to the danger that influence the structuring of internal and external experiences as dangerous. It is the inaccurate perception of dangerousness that generates the anxiety. By itself, anxiety is not a problem because it is the proper function of anxiety to signal the appearance of danger (A. T. Beck & Emery, 1985).

Barlow (2000) contended that an anxiety disorder results from an interaction of three kinds of vulnerabilities. First, a generalized biological vulnerability, genetically transmitted, influences the development of a trait of being high-strung, nervous, or emotional. Second, a generalized psychological vulnerability leads individuals to interpret failures and deficiencies as a chronic inability to cope with unpredictable and uncontrollable negative events. Finally, specific psychological vulnerabilities are produced by early learning experiences in which specific objects and events come to be thought of as dangerous. However, Barlow argued that no one set of vulnerabilities alone is sufficient to produce an anxiety disorder.

What Maintains an Anxiety Disorder?

There is virtual unanimity in the view that the central factor in the maintenance of an anxiety disorder is avoidance. Avoidance may involve a specific phobic object, a social interaction or public speaking opportunity, the previous location of a panic attack, or even the experience of an obsessional thought without its usual accompanying ritual. Avoidance does not allow the anxiety to habituate or the association between fear and the feared object or situation to extinguish. In more cognitively oriented behavioral views of anxiety, unmodified fear-based cognitive schemas are also associated with the maintenance of an anxiety disorder (Foa & Kozak, 1986). Or, as Bandura (1977) put it, avoidance prevents a person from learning that real-life conditions have changed. Because the anticipated threat does not occur, the person's belief that avoidance is the best way to prevent this threat is reinforced.

Behavioral and Cognitive–Behavioral Perspectives on Specific Anxiety Disorders

I will now describe behavioral and cognitive–behavioral models of specific anxiety disorders. The reader should note that with respect to some anxiety disorders there may be just one behavioral model, but with respect to other anxiety disorders, there may be more than one.

Specific Phobias

Behavioral Theory. The classical behavioral theory holds that specific phobias are acquired through a process of classical conditioning. The traditional Pavlovian model of classical conditioning assumes that human beings have hard-wired behavior patterns, called unconditioned responses (UCRs), which are activated by specific unconditioned stimuli (UCSs). All learned responses derive from these innate behavior patterns. With respect to anxiety or fear, classical conditioning contends that when a UCS, which uniformly evokes anxiety as a UCR, is contiguously associated with a conditioned stimulus (CS) that does not produce anxiety, the CS will come to evoke anxiety after frequent pairings of the CS with the UCS. The elicited anxiety is referred to as the conditioned response. Through this type of learning, fear patterns can come to be activated by almost any other kind of event.

The original conditioning theory seemed to explain the acquisition of a phobia, but not its maintenance. Mowrer's (1960) two-factor theory of learning attempted to remedy this deficiency of conditioning theory. Whereas the first stage of learning (i.e., the acquisition of the phobia) followed the principles of classical conditioning, the second or maintenance stage is thought to follow the principles of operant conditioning. Accordingly, in this second stage, the individual with a phobia learns that the operant of avoiding the phobic stimulus reduces the fear response.

This model assumes the equipotentiality of any stimulus in becoming a conditioned stimulus. In other words, any object or situation is potentially a fear elicitor (Eysenck & Rachman, 1977). The behavioral perspective on specific phobias has expanded more recently as it has become increasingly clear that phobias can be learned vicariously or through the transmission of information (Bandura, 1969; Rachman, 1977).

Cognitive–Behavioral Theory. Cognitive theories of the acquisition of specific phobias emphasize underlying cognitive schemas that routinely generate phobia-specific automatic thoughts (A. T. Beck & Emery, 1985). Although performance-based methods tend to be more efficacious than purely cognitive ones in reducing phobic fear, changes in specific phobia-related beliefs are clearly related to fear reductions. In addition, the continuing belief in the most central fear-related cognitions was associated with maintenance of the phobia (Rachman, 1993). For example, Shafran, Booth, and Rachman (1992) found that claustrophobia was accompanied by salient cognitions of being trapped, suffocated, or losing control and that removal of these beliefs led to a significant reduction in claustrophobia. These treatment findings support the central role played by specific cognitions in the etiology and maintenance of specific phobias.

Social Phobia

Behavioral Theory. Behavioral theories have typically postulated two separate models for the development of social anxiety. Wolpe (1973) proposed a classical conditioning model of social phobia, which suggests that neutral stimuli associated with social performances or interactions are paired with aversive social consequences. These traumatic social experiences produce anxiety that becomes chronically associated with social performances or interactions. Social anxiety leads to the avoidance of social situations and performances and avoidance behavior is viewed as the major maintaining factor in social anxiety.

A separate behavioral model was originally proposed by Bellack and Hersen (1979). Their skill-deficit model suggests that deficits in the individual's social behavior repertoire lead to anxiety. Poor social skills lead to aversive consequences in social situations, which in turn elicit anxiety in immediate or imagined social situations. Both models have received empirical support from treatment studies that show that both systematic desensitization and social skill training can reduce social anxiety (Bellack & Hersen, 1979; Mitchell & Orr, 1974). These treatments, however, were developed before the official classification in the *DSM–III* (American Psychiatric Association, 1980) of social phobia as a distinct disorder and may not have addressed the full complexity of this disorder.

Cognitive Theory. A more cognitive model of the fear of social evaluation emphasizes underlying negative, self-related cognitive schemas that produce automatic thoughts of failure and humiliation and the drive to be perfect in every performance. As D. M. Clark and Wells (1995) suggested, clients come to believe that they will inevitably behave in an inept or inappropriate manner in social situations, which will lead to such disastrous results as humiliation, loss of status, and, ultimately, rejection. The individual's own behavior or somatic responses become sources of anticipated danger (e.g., one's tremulous voice is interpreted as evidence that one is either incompetent or foolish). This preoccupation with one's thoughts, behavior, and somatic responses interferes with one's ability to focus on actual social cues, leading to an observable deterioration in performance.

In addition, the cognitive model suggests that individuals with a social phobia possess an attentional bias toward threat cues that sensitizes them to notice aspects of their behavior and the behavior of others, which they then interpret "as evidence of actual, or impending, negative social evaluation" (Stopa & Clark, 1993, p. 255). A. T. Beck and Emery (1985) earlier had pointed out this challenging aspect of social phobia, namely that the experience of the fear actually brings about the feared consequences. These in turn reinforce the self-belief that one is inept in a social situation.

To limit their inappropriate behavior, during social events, individuals with a social phobia engage in extensive self-focused attention, which inevitably increases anxiety, exaggerates the negative view the individual believes others have of him or her, and interferes with his or her social behavior or performance. When a person enters a feared situation, for example, his or her attention shifts to self-monitoring to manage the self-impressions he or she wants to convey in a social situation. D. M. Clark and Wells contended that self-focused attention results in the construction of an image of one's self as a social object. A person creates an image of one's self from an observer's perspective. D. M. Clark and Wells pointed out that self-focused attention typically leads to negative images and ideas about the self. The person believes that others see the same distorted self-images, resulting in more anxiety, which now plays a significant role in maintaining the disorder. In addition, self-focused attention distracts the individual from focusing attention on the environment, which thereby eliminates a source of information that might disconfirm his or her fears and negative expectations.

The origins of social phobia are linked to early childhood messages from parents or primary caretakers that social interactions are potentially dangerous (Bruch & Heimberg, 1994). Individuals with social phobia therefore come to think of themselves as unacceptable to other people or believe that people are inherently hypercritical of others.

Panic Disorder With Agoraphobia

Behavioral Models. Wolpe and Rowan (1988) represent the increasingly rare nonmediational view of panic. In their view, panic disorder is brought about by classical conditioning of fear to the physiological effects of hyperventilation. Following the panic attack, the individual develops catastrophic cognitions. In most cognitive views of panic disorder, the misinterpretation of frightening bodily sensations comes first. Through a fear-of-fear process, these misattributions then lead to panic attacks. By construing these sensations as signs of impending physical or mental catastrophe, the patient with panic disorder can generate a full-blown panic attack (D. M. Clark, 1986). Wolpe and Rowan (1988), in contrast, viewed the catastrophic cognitions as a by-product of panic, not as its trigger.

By synthesizing the latest biobehavioral research on conditioning, Bouton et al. (2001) attempted to show that a modified version of classical conditioning theory possesses great explanatory power for understanding the etiology of panic disorder. They proposed that panic disorder develops when the experience of panic attacks leads to the conditioning of anxiety to both external and internal cues. Conditioning-based emotional learning takes place and anticipatory anxiety prepares the individual for the next panic attack, which in turn leads to more anticipatory anxiety regarding future panic attacks. Because of preexisting biological and psychological factors, some people are more susceptible to conditioning than are others.

Agoraphobia is now generally viewed as a secondary consequence of panic attacks. This departs from an earlier behavioral view that considered agoraphobia, panic attacks, and anticipatory anxiety relating to future panic attacks as coequal factors in the behavioral disorder of agoraphobia (Goldstein & Chambless, 1978). Agoraphobia, from this vantage point, represents a behavioral strategy for limiting either the frequency of panic attacks or the location of their occurrence to a place of safety.

Modern conditioning theories of panic disorder have capitalized on the broadening of conditioning theory, on the one hand, and some excellent, well-nuanced human and animal research, on the other. This combination has been able to redress many of the earlier criticisms of conditioning theory, in general, and its application to anxiety disorders, in particular. In the model developed by Bouton et al. (2001), anxiety and panic are seen as distinct aspects of panic disorder, serving different functions. Anxiety prepares the individual for anticipated trauma, whereas panic is a response to a trauma in progress. Conditioned anxiety can be elicited by either interoceptive or exteroceptive cues and this conditioned anxiety becomes a precursor of a future panic attack. Conditioned anxiety potentiates the next panic, beginning the individual's downward spiral into panic disorder.

In the broadest sense, panic disorder is rooted in a biological diathesis, nonspecific psychological vulnerabilities, and some psychological vulnerabilities that are specific to panic disorder. The nonspecific vulnerability factors include early experience with uncontrollable and unpredictable events, whereas the vulnerability factors specific to panic disorder include vicarious learning of anxiety based in certain bodily sensations and the reinforcement of illness behavior during development (Barlow, 2000; Bouton et al., 2001).

Among its virtues, this model highlights the role of unconscious emotional conditioning, a contention typically denied by most other purely behavioral accounts of conditioning, as well as emphasizing a fundamental role for early conditioning episodes in the etiology of panic disorder. Its chief drawback, one that is typical of behavioral accounts, is its ignoring of the significance of the implicit meaning of panic attacks.

Cognitive Model. Cognitive models consider an individual's catastrophic misinterpretations of somatic sensations as the prime causal agent in panic disorder (A. T. Beck & Emery, 1985; D. M. Clark, 1986, 1997). This model suggests that an individual experiences a panic attack when his or her preoccupation with bodily sensations results in catastrophic thoughts about their impending meaning. These thoughts produce anxiety in and of themselves, but they also result in further bodily sensations, which in turn produce more catastrophic thoughts, eventually resulting in a panic attack. This preoccupation with bodily sensations is characterized by an intensely vigilant focus on even otherwise normal bodily sensations.

This model provides a particularly useful explanation of what happens to patients with panic disorder once they have had their initial panic attack. It is not, however, a sufficient explanation as to why the person has the initial panic attack. This attack appears to occur without any conscious cognitive mediation. The learning theory model previously discussed correctly came to the same conclusion, although its explanation for the initial attack requires substantial elaboration.

Obsessive–Compulsive Disorder

Behavioral Models. Behavioral models of OCD are based on Mowrer's (1939) two-stage theory of fear and fear avoidance. According to his model, obsessions are developed through classical conditioning, whereas avoidance behavior is learned through instrumental conditioning. Through higher-order conditioning, many stimuli such as words, thoughts, and images develop the capacity to evoke anxiety. The individual then learns responses (i.e., rituals) that will reduce or eliminate the anxiety associated with the conditioned stimuli. These rituals then are repeated every time an anxiety-inducing word, thought, or image appears and therefore take on the characteristic of a compulsion.

In a later revision of this theory, Mowrer (1960) proposed that a neutral event becomes associated with fear by its contiguous association with a stimulus that naturally provokes anxiety. These stimuli may include objects as well as thoughts and images. In the second stage, avoidance behaviors are developed that successfully reduce the anxiety. In the case of OCD, the avoidance behaviors that appear to have some success in reducing anxiety include mental and behavioral rituals (i.e., compulsions). The unique aspect of OCD is that in order for the patient to reduce the anxiety and discomfort to a tolerable level, he or she must use active avoidance responses (Foa & Tillmanns, 1980).

Cognitive Models. Early cognitive models (A. T. Beck, 1976; Carr, 1974) were based on the idea that individuals with OCD overestimate the likelihood of negative outcomes. McFall and Wollersheim (1979) emphasized irrational perfectionistic beliefs and the corollary that one should be punished for not living up to one's ideals. In this view, individuals with OCD believe that only magical rituals can cope with the threat and anxiety produced by their obsessional beliefs. Salkovskis (1985) has proposed that intrusive obsessional thoughts lead to negative automatic thoughts that typically possess the theme of being responsible for causing harm to others. Behavioral and cognitive compulsions are used to reduce this sense of responsibility and to stave off blame. Salkovskis contended that a significant feature of this disorder is the fusion of thoughts and actions—in other words, that thinking certain thoughts is equivalent to acting them out. According to Salkovskis (1985), five dysfunctional beliefs characterize people with OCD:

> 1) Having a thought about an action is like performing the action; 2) failing to prevent (or failing to try and prevent) harm to self and others is the same as having caused the harm in the first place; 3) responsibility is not attenuated by other factors (e.g., low probability of occurrence); 4) not neutralizing when an intrusion has occurred is similar or equivalent to seeking or wanting the harm involved in that intrusion to actually happen; 5) one should (and can) exercise control over one's thoughts. (p. 579)

Foa and Kozak (1985) contended that individuals with OCD experience both the pathological content of their obsessions and problems in the way they process information. One notable information-processing difficulty is that individuals with OCD often interpret a situation as dangerous because there is no evidence that it is safe. In like fashion, they often fail to conclude that a situation is safe when there is no evidence of danger. As Foa and Franklin (2001) put it, "Consequently, rituals that are performed to reduce the likelihood of harm can never really provide safety and must be repeated" (p. 216).

The Obsessive–Compulsive Cognitions Working Group (1997), a team of international researchers, identified six domains of beliefs that frequently appear in the thinking of patients with OCD: (a) inflated sense of responsibility, (b) overimportance of thoughts, (c) control over one's thoughts, (d) overestimation of threat, (e) intolerance of uncertainty, and (f) perfectionism. Although these schemas generate the obsessional thoughts, all of these cognitive–behavioral models agree on the functional value of rituals, which is to reduce the anxiety generated by the obsessions.

Generalized Anxiety Disorder

Behavioral Model. A purely behavioral model of GAD does not exist. As Borkovec, Alcaine, and Behar (2004) pointed out, two separate trends in behavioral therapy helped produce a conceptual foundation for GAD. Bandura's (1969) social learning theory suggests that human beings might cognitively avoid fear stimuli, which would result in the preservation of anxious meanings despite repeated behavioral exposures. The second trend was the increasing realization that avoidance of internal fear cues maintains anxiety. These two trends led to Foa and Kozak's (1986) theory that the entire fear structure stored in memory must be accessed and modified by corrective information.

Borkovec's work on generalized anxiety dates back to the early 1970s. His early research led him to develop a cognitive–perceptual extension of Mowrer's two-stage theory. Borkovec proposed that cognitive avoidance might (a) help develop anxious responding, (b) maintain existing phobias, and (c) interfere with the positive benefits of repeated behavioral exposures to fear stimuli (Borkovec et al., 2004).

Cognitive Models. Borkovec began to view worry as a cognitive process significantly related to anxiety. Primarily because of Borkovec's extensive and seminal investigations of the process of worrying, most cognitive–behavioral views of GAD have focused on the centrality of the worry process. Individuals with GAD seem doubtful about their ability to cope with life in general. Borkovec and Roemer (1995) have identified six basic reasons for worry: (a) motivation to get tasks done, (b) general problem solving, (c) preparation for the worst, (d) planning ways to avoid negative events, (e) distraction from more emotional thoughts, and (f) superstitious effects on the perceived likelihood of future events. These authors contended that a major function of worrying is to prevent painful effects associated with aversive memories, and it thus serves as a distraction from more emotional issues. Worry therefore is conceived of as an avoidance tactic. Foa and Kozak (1986) also suggested that worry can interfere with the extinction of anxiety because it prevents the activation of the relevant tacit fear structures.

Another cognitive–behavioral model suggests that GAD is characterized by four basic cognitive characteristics: (a) intolerance of uncertainty, (b) belief in the positive value of worry, (c) poor problem orientation, and (d) cognitive avoidance (Dugas et al., 1998). Such patients' intolerance of uncertainty seems to initiate or exacerbate the tendency to ask "what if" questions, and these questions ensure the continuation of the worrying process. Patients with GAD also find a number of reasons to justify worrying (e.g., "worrying protects loved ones"). The third cognitive characteristic, poor problem orientation, refers to their inability to focus clearly on a problem and begin to generate potentially viable solutions. Instead, they may react with alarm to an awareness of a problem and use an insufficient approach to its resolution. The final characteristic, cognitive avoidance, is similar to Borkovec's contention that worrying is a defensive process designed to avoid threatening mental images. Both cognitive–behavioral models of GAD seem to capture the cardinal feature of this disorder: the inability to cope with external demands and internal (i.e., emotional) responses.

What is particularly noteworthy about Borkovec's model is his view that worry is pervasive and uncontrollable because it prevents somatic anxiety without the individual's awareness. Thus, the most sophisticated cognitive–behavioral model of GAD acknowledges the role of unconscious processes in the maintenance and perhaps the development of this disorder.

What Differentiates the Various Anxiety Disorders?

From the behavioral point of view, all anxiety disorders are acquired by the same principles of learning. However, they are differentiated in terms of the differing sets of environmental contingencies and functional reinforcements that characterize each disorder. From the cognitive–behavioral perspective, anxiety disorders can be distinguished on the basis of distinctly different fear structures. Persons with agoraphobia construe fear responses as dangerous. In contrast, persons with an animal phobia are afraid of the specific stimulus situation (e.g., rats). Individuals with panic disorder interpret specific somatic sensations as heralds of either a panic attack or a catastrophic physical or mental event. Those with a social phobia apparently have learned from early experiences that social evaluation is dangerous, whereas many patients with OCD have learned to equate dangerous thoughts with dangerous actions (Barlow, 2000). Barlow, like A. T. Beck, argued that the presentation of the different anxiety disorders varies by the content of the focus of anxiety.

THE BIOMEDICAL PERSPECTIVE

The biomedical perspective on anxiety disorders reflects the basic tenets of the biomedical perspective on mental illness in general. Andreasen (1984) nicely summarized these tenets:

- That major psychiatric illnesses are diseases (i.e., medical illnesses).
- These diseases are caused principally by biological factors, and most of these factors reside in the brain.
- As a scientific discipline, psychiatry seeks to identify the biological factors that cause mental illness. These would include biochemical, neuroendocrine, genetic, and structural brain abnormalities.
- The biological model tends to emphasize the study and management of more serious or severe mental illnesses.
- The treatment of these diseases emphasizes the use of somatic therapies. Because these illnesses are seen as biological in origin, therapy is seen as correcting an underlying biological imbalance.
- Mental illnesses are not due to "bad habits" or weakness of will.
- Bad parenting or bad "spousing" does not cause mental illnesses.
- The somatic therapies are very effective methods for treating many mental illnesses. (pp. 29–32)

What Is the Nature of Anxiety?

The biomedical perspective on anxiety begins with the assumption that human beings have been equipped by evolution to experience anxiety when danger is perceived. Normal anxiety is assumed to prepare the individual for either fight or flight (Cannon, 1929) as well as serve as an alarm that warns the individual of an impending threat. From this perspective, an anxiety disorder represents some malfunction in these basic biologic mechanisms of anxiety. Despite these orienting assumptions, there is currently no overall biological theory of anxiety and the anxiety disorders. There has been, however, a virtual explosion of information about the biological correlates of anxiety, as well as innumerable part-theories of what supposedly has malfunctioned in the human neurobiological system and resulted in one or more anxiety disorders.

During the past two decades, hundreds of studies have been conducted to uncover the mechanisms by which neuropharmacologic, neuroanatomic, and neurophysiologic factors increase or decrease the experience of anxiety (M. R. Johnson & Lydiard, 1995). Much of this work has focused on the investigation of the neurochemical actions of a number of anxiolytic drugs. The demonstration of neural receptors for benzodiazepines and their apparent relationship with the inhibitory neurotransmitter gamma-aminobutyric acid (GABA) have provided a major stimulus to research on antianxiety drugs (Lydiard, Brawman-Mintzer, & Ballenger, 1996).

How Does an Anxiety Disorder Develop?

Preclinical and clinical data suggest that a variety of neurobiological abnormalities are associated with anxiety disorders including abnormalities in several neurotransmitter systems such as norepinephrine, serotonin, dopamine, the GABA receptor complex, and several neuropeptides (M. R. Johnson & Lydiard, 1995). All of these abnormalities are presumed to have a genetic basis.

With an increasing focus on the genetic basis of mental disorders, a commonly accepted view is that some individuals are biologically more prone to develop an anxiety disorder because of a genetically transmitted vulnerability such as a pathologically lowered threshold for the release of anxiety, as in the case of separation anxiety (D. F. Klein, 1981), or a labile overly responsive autonomic nervous system (Eysenck, 1967). In the case of panic, the presumed biological mechanism is a malfunction in the brain's suffocation monitor, which erroneously signals a lack of useful air and maladaptively triggers the suffocation alarm system (D. F. Klein, 1993).

What Maintains an Anxiety Disorder?

Because, according to the biomedical perspective, anxiety disorders are based in a neurobiological malfunction, the disorder continues as long as the hypothesized malfunction(s) continue to operate. The list of neurobiological malfunctions, however, is long, varied, and currently unsubstantiated.

Biomedical View of Specific Anxiety Disorders

There are currently few biomedical models of specific anxiety disorders. The research findings have produced a collection of tantalizing clues that have not as yet been organized into convincing models of specific anxiety disorders.

Specific Phobias

Biological models of specific phobias emphasize the fact that certain structures within the limbic system of the brain mediate emotional responses and emotional memories. The amygdala is an organ of appraisal (Cozolino, 2002) for danger, safety, and familiarity. It associates emotional value to our sensory perceptions. When the amygdala appraises a situation as dangerous, it starts the process of getting the body ready for fight-or-flight responses. Thus, it is particularly involved with implicit learning and memory. The hippocampus is involved in explicit learning and memory. According to several biological models of phobias, the amygdala mediates unconscious fear-conditioning, whereas the hippocampus, in conjunction with the cortex, provides contextually relevant information that signals us whether the rapid fear appraisals are appropriate (Cozolino, 2002; Jacobs & Nadel, 1985; LeDoux, 1996). LeDoux, for example, has suggested that during traumatic situations, conscious memories are organized by the hippocampus and related cortical areas, and unconscious memories are established by fear conditioning mediated by the amygdala. These are parallel memory systems that store different information. Whenever stimuli connected to the original trauma are encountered, each system potentially retrieves its memories. "In the case of the amygdala system, the retrieval results in expression of bodily responses that prepare for danger, and in the case of the hippocampal system, conscious remembrances occur" (p. 239).

With respect to the choice of phobic objects, the major biologically based theory is Seligman's preparedness theory of phobias. The basic premise of the preparedness theory is that humans are biologically prepared (by evolution) to learn to fear objects and situations that threatened the survival of the species throughout its evolutionary history (e.g., snakes, thunderstorms, and the dark). Biological preparedness is responsible for the rapid acquisition, irrationality, belongingness, and high resistance to extinction that are characteristic of phobias (Seligman, 1971).

One other etiological hypothesis should be mentioned: the idea that specific phobias are largely inherited. Although there is significant evidence that anxiety in general may have a significant genetic component (L. A. Clark, Watson, & Mineka, 1994), there is little evidence of a genetic basis for specific phobias. However, Fyer, Mannuzza, Chapman, Martin, and Klein (1995) did find evidence that specific phobias run in families.

Social Phobias

The major contribution of the biomedical model is its suggestion that certain people possess a genetically transmitted predisposition for developing social phobia. This predisposition may be manifested as shyness or as a tendency toward behavioral inhibition (Fyer, Mannuzza, Chapman, Liebowitz, & Klein, 1993; Kagan, Reznick, & Snidman, 1988). Behavioral inhibition is defined as an inherited temperamental trait of withdrawing from unfamiliar settings, objects, or people. The physiologic indicators of increased arousal that behaviorally inhibited children exhibit are closely associated with the hypothesized neurophysiologic mechanisms in anxiety disorders. In fact, a number of studies suggest that behavioral inhibition in a young child may be a risk factor for the development of an anxiety disorder in adulthood, particularly if one of the child's parents has an anxiety disorder (J. F. Rosenbaum, Biederman, Pollock, & Hirshfeld, 1994).

Although no elaborated biological model of social phobia has been offered, one model of specific phobias can be extended to social phobias by assuming that other people become fear stimuli. It may be possible that because of the specifics of the individual's learning history, interpersonal interaction opportunities are first appraised by amygdaloid neural networks as catastrophically dangerous, which overwhelm the inhibiting tendencies of the hippocampal system (Cozolino, 2002).

Panic Disorder With and Without Agoraphobia

Biological hypotheses for the generation of panic attacks and panic disorder have described a number of possible abnormalities in brain neurochemistry, metabolism, genetics, and receptor physiology. D. F. Klein's (1993) malfunctioning suffocation system was previously mentioned . Other hypotheses include a dysregulated locus coeruleus (Charney & Heninger, 1986) and the notion of reciprocal innervation among nuclei in the brain stem, limbic lobe, and prefrontal cortex. According to this latter hypothesis, panic attacks stem from hypersensitive loci in the brain stem, anticipatory anxiety from the limbic system, and phobic avoidance from the prefrontal cortex (Gorman, Liebowitz, Fyer, & Stein, 1989). All of these hypotheses presuppose a biological malfunction that produces anxiety and panic attacks without any influence of psychological variables. Although research provides exciting hypotheses about the underlying neurobiological substrate of panic, at the same time it ignores the accumulating evidence of the role of psychological variables in the generation of panic disorder.

Obsessive–Compulsive Disorder

Biological views of OCD have focused on the genetic transmission of the disorder and on specific neurobiological anomalies. Although concordance rates are higher in monozygotic (identical) than dizygotic (fraternal) twins (Billett, Richter, & Kennedy, 1998), studies of twins reared apart are rare; thus it is difficult to determine the relative significance of genetic and environmental factors to the genesis of OCD. Brain imaging studies have pointed to a number of anomalies in the brain, but the findings are inconsistent; some consistency in the findings has been found for dysfunctions in the frontal lobes or basal ganglia (Rauch & Jenike, 1997). There is also a growing consensus in the biomedical community that abnormal serotonin metabolism is related to the symptoms of OCD. Support for this notion comes from the efficacy of serotonin reuptake inhibitors in reducing the intensity of OCD symptoms (Zohar & Insel, 1987).

Generalized Anxiety Disorder

Compared with the quantity of research on the biology of anxiety, literature on neurobiology of generalized anxiety disorder is relatively sparse (Cowley & Roy-Byrne, 1991). The shifting definition that has characterized this disorder since the publication of the DSM–III has contributed to the limited neurobiological research. No coherent biomedical model of GAD has yet been developed (Connor & Davidson, 1998). Nonetheless, it appears that GAD may involve abnormalities in a number of different neurotransmitter and neuropeptide systems, including GABA, 5-HT, NE, CCK, and CRF. In addition, many studies show blunted activity in the central and peripheral nervous systems. These findings suggest that, in general, patients with GAD are characterized by general nervous system dysregulation, failure of the adaptive stress response, and prolonged hyporesponsiveness (Sinha, Mohlman, & Gorman, 2004).

What Differentiates the Various Anxiety Disorders?

In the absence of a developed etiological theory of anxiety disorders, the biomedical perspective lacks a clear set of hypotheses regarding what neurobiological factors clearly distinguish the different anxiety disorders. What I have been able to glean from the literature is the hypothesis that different anxiety disorders are based in different malfunctioning neurobiological mechanisms.

THE EXPERIENTIAL PERSPECTIVE

Falling under the rubric of experiential psychotherapy are such therapeutic approaches as person-centered therapy, gestalt therapy, and existential psychotherapy, or a combination of them. These psychotherapies traditionally have eschewed diagnostic categories; they have tended instead to diagnose the client's in-session emotional processing (L. S. Greenberg, Rice, & Elliott, 1993). However, partly in response to political and economic pressures, experiential psychotherapies more recently have been applied to *DSM*-defined disorders (e.g., Elliott, Davis, & Slatick, 1998; L. S. Greenberg, Watson, & Goldman, 1998; Wolfe & Sigl, 1998). With respect to the experiential view of anxiety and anxiety disorders, my work represents perhaps the only available example. In fact, my experiential model of anxiety disorders represents an earlier iteration of my current integrated perspective (Wolfe & Sigl, 1998).

What Is the Nature of Anxiety?

My earlier experiential model conceived of anxiety and its disorders as fundamentally a fear of a future catastrophe that will produce unbearably painful feelings about the self (Wolfe, 1992). Anxious feelings are usually accompanied by future-oriented thoughts about possible catastrophes to the self. Anxiety from this vantage point represents a future-oriented emotion that prevents an individual from focusing on his or her present emotional experience of the world. The perceived or imagined danger may be internal or external.

This model is based on the assumption that embedded in each of the several anxiety disorders are a number of emotional-processing difficulties that include the interruption of one's immediate organismic experiencing. Moreover, the various ways in which persons interrupt, deflect, disavow, and avoid their primary emotional experience reflect underlying disturbances in their sense and concept of self. The conscious experience of self-endangerment (i.e., the subjective experience of anxiety and panic) is based in underlying intrapsychic conflicts, negative self-beliefs, and a holistic sense of shame about one's value or lovability. All of these forms of self-pathology produce painful self-awareness. Sometimes this painful and immediate self-awareness is experienced as dangerous, and this dangerous self-experience may evolve into a chronic sense of self-endangerment. Although different anxiety disorders reflect variations in the contents of threatening self-experience, they also represent variations in the experiential processes used to stave off the danger.

How Does an Anxiety Disorder Develop?

A common sequence can be described for the development of an anxiety disorder that reflects the importance of self-experiencing and its vicissitudes. This sequence typically begins with the impact of early traumatic experiences on the individual's capacity for immediate self-experiencing. Most of these traumas occur in an interpersonal context and in each instance leave the individual feeling helpless, trapped, and unable to forestall what is perceived to be certain doom to one's experience of a subjective self (i.e., self-endangerment). Self-endangerment experiences appear to be confined to the psychological realm—to fears associated with separation, rejection, loss of a primary caretaker or loved one, intensely humiliating experiences, disillusioning experiences at the hands of primary caretakers or loved ones, and the experience of self-loss (i.e., the completely subjective sense of the disappearance of self-experience entirely). Self-endangerment experiences can range from a painful self-awareness to extreme trauma. What must be kept in mind, however, is that trauma is a relative term, referring to the amount of pain one experiences relative to one's ability to bear it. People with very different abilities to cope with or bear pain may process the same events quite differently.

The most fundamental impact of traumatic or self-endangerment experiences is that it makes it difficult for individuals to allow themselves to become aware of their immediate, in-the-moment organismic experience. Therefore, anytime an individual finds him- or herself in a situation that resembles the context of a self-endangerment experience, he or she will experience anxiety. Anxiety serves as an alarm or signal that cues the individual that further immediate self-experiencing would be dangerous. The individual typically interprets the anxiety to mean that a potentially catastrophic event is about to take place. This catastrophic interpretation, although incorrect, has a number of other important implications. The feared object, situation, or sensations relate to earlier traumas. Also, catastrophic interpretations indicate that the individual's attention has been shifted from direct or immediate experience of self or world to the reflexive experience of one's self being fearful. In other words, the individual experiences a secondary emotional reaction (L. S. Greenberg et al., 1993) to his or her primary experience of anxiety. When having a secondary reaction to one's primary experience, one's attention shifts from immediate experiencing to thinking about one's immediate experience. In thinking about our experience, we necessarily are one step removed from our immediate experience. The result of this reflexive focusing of attention on one's anxiety is invariably to either increase the intensity of the anxiety or experience other dysphoric emotions and negative evaluations of one's first-order anxiety (e.g., being angry at one's self for being fearful). Goldstein and Chambless (1978) first described this phenomenon as the fear-of-fear response.

A third phase in the development of an anxiety disorder is avoidance behavior. Very often, patients with anxiety associate the various contexts in which they experience anxiety or panic with the pending recurrence of anxiety and panic. Consequently, in an effort to control the anxiety, the individual begins to avoid the contexts of prior self-endangerment experiences. Avoidance then increases the difficulty of reentering the feared situations. Thus, the common anxiety disorder sequence can be summarized as follows: self-endangerment experiences lead to compulsive, reflexive self-experiencing that increases the anxiety, which in turn leads to avoidance behavior in particular contexts as an attempt to control the recurrence or intensification of anxiety.

Experiential Perspectives on Specific Anxiety Disorders

Experiential theories of specific anxiety disorders differ from other theories in two basic ways. First, each anxiety disorder is rooted in an emotional conflict generated by early traumatic events. Second, the specific anxiety disorder appears to be determined by two factors, the nature of the trauma and the cognitive–emotional processes that are erected to interrupt the reexperiencing of the trauma.

Specific Phobias

In the case of specific phobias, some external object or situation serves as a signpost for an underlying catastrophic or self-endangerment experience(s). A symbolic or accidental connection is formed in memory between the phobic object and the catastrophic event(s). The catastrophic memory typically involves some kind of interpersonal trauma that left the patient feeling psychologically endangered, that is, helpless and powerless to prevent abuse, domination, humiliation, or pain.

Social Phobia

Social phobias are rooted in a series of painful interpersonal encounters that convince the individual that he or she is inferior in some manner. Social or public speaking engagements become occasions for humiliation. These encounters compel an automatic shift of attention from a focus on the other person or the audience onto one's self as the potential personification of error and foolishness (Wolfe & Sigl, 1998). Such reflexive focusing makes it difficult to give a smooth social or speaking performance, which leads to a vicious cycle (Wachtel, 1997) in which his or her original fear is realized.

The experiential model of social phobia bears many similarities to the cognitive model. But there are two significant differences. The first is that the underlying negative beliefs of the individual with a social phobia are interwoven with powerful and painful emotions that are themselves difficult to bear. In other words, the individual fears the painful feelings that accompany the negative self-message. These painful, emotion-laden beliefs lead to emotional-processing conflicts and difficulties that are designed to protect the individual from the awareness and experience of the negative self-belief and its accompanying painful emotions (Wolfe & Sigl, 1998).

Panic Disorder and Agoraphobia

For many patients, the initial unexpected panic attack heralds the onset of panic disorder, yet, with the exception of the psychodynamic perspective, none of the perspectives covered here addresses the underlying meaning of this allegedly spontaneous attack. The experiential view suggests that this attack represents the surfacing of an implicit threat to the individual's sense or concept of self. It is a bodily trace of earlier self-endangerment experiences. Patients with panic disorder become so sensitized to these somatic traces of earlier self-endangerment experiences that they become extremely fearful of their occurrence. The specific bodily sensations that they fear bear a significant relationship to the earlier self-endangerment experience. Thus, they become stuck in a pattern of obsessively cogitating about their feared bodily sensations. Agoraphobic avoidance often develops in an effort to minimize the occurrence of panic attacks. This vicious cycle explained by D. M. Clark (1997) adequately describes a patient with panic disorder stuck in cogitating about these sensations.

This view provides an adequate explanation of both the source of the initial panic attack and the process of catastrophic misinterpretations of body sensations that occur subsequent to the initial attack. This model also presents an explanation for the subsequent agoraphobic avoidance behavior, albeit one that is by now generally shared by clinical theorists of all orientations. This avoidance behavior often develops in an effort to minimize the occurrence of panic attacks. This model, however, proposes only one access point to the modification of panic disorder: through one's immediate emotional experience. Individual differences in human personality indicate clearly that many individuals would be uncomfortable, at least initially, with an experientially based treatment.

Obsessive–Compulsive Disorder

Wolfe and Sigl's (1998) experiential model of anxiety disorders suggests that OCD is rooted in a sense of self-endangerment, reflecting specific forms of self-pathology that are directly or symbolically connected to the obsessional thoughts. The primary form of self-pathology in OCD is a sense and concept of self as a bad person. The unbearably painful underlying fear is that the individual may be culpable in causing significant harm to a loved one. The obsessions and accompanying rituals represent emotional-processing difficulties that keep the individual from experiencing these painful feelings. As with the other anxiety disorders, rage, shame, and despair are extremely painful feelings that the individual with OCD attempts to avoid through the manifestation of his or her symptoms.

Generalized Anxiety Disorder

Wolfe and Sigl's (1998) experiential model is similar to Borkovec's cognitive–behavioral model in that it also views worrying as a defensive process designed to shield the individual from unbearable affects. This model suggests that prior self-endangerment experiences prime the individual to protect one's self-concept and self-image from extremely painful shame-based emotions. The failure to emotionally process these shame-laden self-endangerment experiences from the past results in the individual relying on worry as a primary defense against being exposed as inadequate or inferior and the painful humiliation that would accompany that exposure. Worrying in this model, however, is construed as a form of obsessive cogitation that serves the same protective function as Borkovec hypothesized—a defense against painful emotions.

What Differentiates the Various Anxiety Disorders?

Many of the same emotional-processing difficulties are observed in the various anxiety disorders, but two main factors differentiate them. As with the cognitive perspective, the experiential view contends that there are different focal issues in the different disorders. For example, patients with OCD greatly fear the possibility that their mistakes may cause significant harm to loved ones. The feared catastrophe is manifested in terms of obsessional thinking, which is then defended against by means of active ritualizing. Contrast this with individuals with a social phobia who fear that their social performances may lead to their being rejected or losing status in the eyes of others.

The second differentiating feature involves the use of different cognitive–emotional strategies for avoiding in-the-moment experiencing. Patients with panic disorder catastrophize the meaning of frightening bodily sensations. Patients with GAD constantly worry about coping with most of life's demands. And patients with OCD attempt to cancel the frightening implications of their obsessions through mental and behavioral rituals.

Meaning Versus Mechanism in Perspectives on Anxiety Disorders

The theories of anxiety disorders under consideration have attempted to simultaneously address two seemingly incompatible foci. On the one hand, they have attempted to address the idiosyncratic meanings that the symptoms of anxiety possess for the individual; on the other hand, they have attempted to delineate the basic causal mechanisms underlying an anxiety disorder. Contemporary biomedical and behavioral views seem to disregard the question of meaning altogether, focusing single-mindedly on the delineation of the biological and psychological mechanisms of anxiety, respectively. In contrast, the experiential perspective seems to be primarily concerned with the meaning of anxiety. This polarity of views is part of a larger debate on whether anxiety and its disorders are better investigated from a natural science point of view or from a more hermeneutical perspective (Barlow, 2000; Messer, Sass, & Woolfolk, 1988). Some of these perspectives seem to steer a more ambivalent course between anxiety's meanings and its mechanisms.

In S. Freud's first theory, he conceptualized anxiety in biopsychological terms as the result of an automatic transformation or conversion of libidinal energy that had been blocked from being discharged. The repression of libido resulted in a passive reaction of restless tension and in diffuse feelings of anxiety (S. Freud, 1894/1962b). This was a physical process with psychical consequences, rather than a purely psychological phenomenon. By the time S. Freud had formulated his second theory of anxiety in 1926, the balance of his conceptualization had shifted significantly toward the psychological. This second theory was therefore more concerned with the meaning of anxiety.

In keeping with the zeitgeist of 19th-century medicine, S. Freud's handling of the subjective involved linking subjective experience to the biological givens of human nature, namely, the instincts. All subjective experience is then tied to the instincts and their vicissitudes. Experience, both unconscious and conscious, then, is the representations and derivatives of instincts. Although S. Freud considered experience to be epiphenomena (i.e., a side effect of or determined by) of biological processes, he provided a detailed manner in which epiphenomenal experience can be studied scientifically. Despite the fact that his biological premises are out of date, S. Freud's biological account of psychic experience still represents the most detailed effort to link experience to human biological givens.

The more recent relational approaches in psychoanalysis focus even more on the meaning of anxiety symptoms. Although framing their ideas in terms of psychological processes and mechanisms, object relations theorists and self psychologists maintained a single-minded focus on the conscious and unconscious meanings of an individual's interpersonal interactions (Guntrip, 1968; Kohut, 1978).

The biological perspective on anxiety avoids its subjective meaning altogether. It begins with the assumption that human beings have been equipped by evolution to experience anxiety when danger is perceived. Normal anxiety is assumed to prepare the individual for either fight or flight (Cannon, 1929) as well as to serve as an alarm that warns the individual of an impending threat. From this perspective, an anxiety disorder represents some malfunction in these basic biologic mechanisms of anxiety.

In contrast, most humanistic–existential accounts focus primarily on the meaning of anxiety. May (1979), for example, defined anxiety as "the apprehension cued off by a threat to some value that the individual holds essential to his existence as a personality" (p. 180). Fear, in May's view, is an effort to objectify basic anxiety; fearing something specific makes anxiety manageable.

Just as the proponents of the biomedical perspective avoided the subjective meaning of anxiety, the early behaviorists reconceptualized anxiety as an observable behavioral response. As the behaviorist paradigm was extended to include a cognitive focus, an information-processing view of anxiety began to emerge. On the face of it, an information-processing view of anxiety seems to be concerned with meaning. In fact, it is concerned with defining and explicating the mental mechanisms used to manipulate symbolic information, independent of its content. Meaning is now subordinated to cognitive processes or mechanisms.

This turn toward exclusively mechanistic accounts is viewed by some as a wrong turn in the evolution of psychology. Bruner (1990), one of the pioneers of the cognitive revolution in psychology, has argued that cognitive psychology very early on took a wrong turn with the subordination of meaning to mechanism. He contended that what cognitive psychology should be about is the study of "meaning and the processes and transactions involved in the construction of meanings" (p. 33). This statement implies a cultural or folk psychology that investigates the shaping hand of culture in determining human intentional states, desires, beliefs, and actions.

It is my opinion that there is a need for a renewed emphasis on the implicit as well as explicit meaning of anxiety, but at the same time I am reluctant to entirely give up on the quest for the mechanisms of anxiety. A useful theory of human anxiety must address the individual's subjectivity and intentionality, on the one hand, and natural science-based causal processes involved in the generation and maintenance of anxiety, on the other. Thus an understanding of the causes of behavior must be integrated with an interpretive appreciation of the individual's reasons for his or her behavior. As Smith (1978) suggested in the following:

> Both perspectives are required . . . to make sense of such phenomena of selfhood as intentionality and responsibility; both are required for the guidance of interpersonal strategies of applied psychology, which have to be as much concerned with the effects of the causal world as they are with meanings in the personal one. (p. 1060)

The evolving theory of anxiety and its disorders as presented in this book attempts to integrate the exploration of anxiety's meaning with a quest for its mechanisms. In the next chapter I begin the task of teasing out the common useful threads of the various perspectives on anxiety disorders, as well as making a case for the selection of specific ideas from each perspective for the development of an integrative etiological model.

II

AN INTEGRATIVE THEORY
OF ANXIETY DISORDERS

4

TOWARD AN INTEGRATIVE
ETIOLOGICAL MODEL OF
ANXIETY DISORDERS

Like many of my colleagues, I often despair at the size of the gap between our theoretical maps and the experiential territory they are supposed to represent.

—Michael J. Mahoney (1985)

This chapter describes the process by which I selected the specific constructs from each of the therapy orientations to be woven into an integrative etiological model for the anxiety disorders. First, three basic questions must be answered by any etiological model of anxiety disorders:

1. What is an anxiety disorder?
2. How does an anxiety disorder develop or how is it acquired?
3. What are the maintaining factors for an anxiety disorder?

After an in-depth review of the answers offered by each perspective to these three questions, I extract several common etiological factors shared by them all. I view these as factors that have already been integrated; they will therefore form the foundation for a general model of anxiety disorders. However, these perspectives do differ on several key issues, and I make a case for the inclusion (or revision) of some of these factors and the exclusion of others in my integrative model. Therefore, the emerging integrative model is composed of both common and selected factors from all of the reviewed perspectives on anxiety.

COMMON FACTORS IN THE VARIOUS
MODELS OF ANXIETY DISORDERS

All of the considered perspectives agree that anxiety involves both the perception of danger and an apprehensive expectation that danger lurks nearby or in the near future. The perspectives part company, however, with respect to their views on the ultimate sources and sites of anxiety, and the nature of the causal processes responsible for the production and maintenance of anxiety and anxiety disorders.

The Nature of Anxiety Disorders

When one sifts through the differences in theoretical language, the various perspectives yield a number of common factors in the conception of an anxiety disorder. First, all perspectives agree that the human capacity to experience anxiety is hard-wired by evolution. Human beings are equipped by evolution to respond automatically to threats by means of innate biological mechanisms to either flee the threatening object or situation or attempt to fight it off (Cannon, 1929). Every perspective under consideration agrees with this basic fact about anxiety.

Second, all perspectives suggest that an anxiety disorder in some sense represents the misapplication or distortion of a normal anxiety response. Anxiety occurs in situations that by some objective or consensually validated standard should not produce anxiety, or at least not the intensity of the anxiety that is being experienced in these situations. All of these perspectives, with the exception of the experiential, argue that anxiety in an anxiety disorder is out of proportion to the real nature of the threat. Psychodynamic models focus on deviations from their respective models of adult, mature behavior and therefore emphasize infantile unconscious fantasies and conflicts as the underlying determinants of most emotional disorders. The early behaviorists viewed the misapplication of anxiety as based in faulty learning of bad habits or through classically conditioned associations. Later, behaviorally oriented theorists such as Barlow (2000) emphasized the role of false alarms in all of the anxiety disorders. A. T. Beck, too, from a cognitive–behavioral perspective, argued that if anxiety is disproportionate to the severity of the danger and if it continues when no objective danger exists, it is considered abnormal (A. T. Beck & Emery, 1985). These various contentions all suggest that anxiety disorders are based in the irrational or the unrealistic. The experiential therapy perspective, which emphasizes the growth potential in the experience of anxiety, nevertheless presents a theory of dysfunction in anxiety and other disorders that is based in dysfunctional emotion schemes (i.e., emotion-laden beliefs) and blocks or conflicts in the conscious processing of emotional experience (L. S. Greenberg, Rice, & Elliott, 1993; Wolfe & Sigl, 1998).

Third, there is concordance on the proposition that anxiety involves the anticipation of danger, pain, or catastrophe. All perspectives basically accept Darwin's (1872/1965) eloquent characterization of anxiety as the "expectation of suffering" (p. 176). For Barlow (2000), the anticipation of future pain is the defining feature of anxiety. Wolpe's (1958) conditioned fear response encompasses the idea of a conditioned anticipation of harm. Cognitive theorists also emphasize this sense of impending doom in patients with anxiety (A. T. Beck & Emery, 1985). Experiential therapists are also well acquainted with the client's sense of looming disaster (Wolfe & Sigl, 1998). Where perspectives tend to differ is in the location of the anticipated danger. For S. Freud (1926/1959), anxiety was a signal of surfacing internal danger, whereas cognitive and behavioral views tend to emphasize the anticipation of external dangers. Even the biomedical perspective notes the significance of anticipatory anxiety in anxiety disorders, even though most representatives of this point of view would argue that the ultimate cause of an anxiety disorder is a neurobiological malfunction (e.g., D. F. Klein, 1993).

Finally, a consensus seems to be emerging around the proposition that anxiety involves the fear of uncontrollable events. S. Freud (1926/1959) defined trauma as a state of helplessness, in which one is powerless to prevent the impending catastrophe. I suggest that a generally shared idea in psychodynamic circles holds that when internal dangers break through the patient's defenses, he or she experiences this as losing control (e.g., Diamond, 1985). Barlow (2000) postulated that the inability to cope with unpredictable and uncontrollable events is an essential element in the experience of an anxiety disorder. The experiential perspective sees anxiety as involving the fear of uncontrollable emotional experience (L. S. Greenberg et al., 1993; Wolfe & Sigl, 1998).

Common Factors in the Various Etiological Models of Anxiety Disorders

With respect to the etiology of anxiety disorders, there also are some commonly shared factors. Most perspectives, for example, suggest that genetics plays a significant role in biasing certain people toward a greater likelihood of developing an anxiety disorder. No point of view explicitly denies this contention, although some points of view are more explicit in stating this than are other points of view (e.g., the biomedical).

Most perspectives also suggest that painful or traumatic experience plays a significant role in the development of an anxiety disorder, although the perspectives vary in terms of the relative emphasis they place on this factor. Moreover, most assume that the person with anxiety develops a patterned anticipation of future danger through some automatic associative process. S. Freud's original view of neurosis was that it was based on sexual traumas (1894/1962a), whereas the early behavioral therapists viewed trauma-based conditioning as a major source of anxiety reactions (Wolpe, 1958). References to the traumatic origins of negative beliefs can be found in A. T. Beck's work (A. T. Beck & Emery, 1985). From a more experiential frame of reference I have been most impressed by the extent of trauma underlying phobic and other anxiety disorders (Wolfe, 1992).

Most perspectives also imply or explicitly state that a significant role in the etiology of anxiety disorders is played by a patient's self-perception of inefficacy, that is, a perception of one's coping abilities as insufficient to meet the demands of the situation. Again, some points of view treat this factor as more central to the development of an anxiety disorder than do other perspectives. This viewpoint is most directly stated by Bandura (1978), who saw the lack of self-efficacy as the generating force of most anxiety problems. A. T. Beck also defined vulnerability, a core factor in his thinking about anxiety, as a person's self-perception that he or she lacks the skills necessary to cope with a particular threat (A. T. Beck & Emery, 1985). Experiential views focus on the patient's lack of an *agentic self*, that is, the patient does not believe that he or she can take control of his or her life or have an impact on others (Wolfe & Sigl, 1998). These are a few of the apparent common etiological factors shared by the various perspectives on anxiety disorders.

Common Maintenance Factors in Anxiety Disorders

With respect to the maintenance of an anxiety disorder, three major ideas are generally shared. The first is the contention that anxiety typically leads to avoidance of the feared object or situation. Although avoidance brings temporary relief from anxiety, it does not inform the individual that the danger he or she fears is either imaginary or manageable. The short-term relief from anxiety that avoidance brings is purchased at the price of locking in the anxiety disorder. The second factor that maintains an anxiety disorder is the continuation of the root problem, whether this is thought to be an unconscious conflict, a persistent habit or conditioned response, a dysfunctional cognitive schema or emotion scheme, or a neurobiological malfunction.

A third factor that is beginning to appear in both cognitive–behavioral and experiential therapy articles is the notion of self-focused attention. Self-focused attention refers to a person's focusing on "self-referent, internally generated information that stands in contrast to an awareness of externally generated information derived through sensory receptors" (Ingram, 1990, p. 156). This is thought to be an attentional process that both generates and maintains anxiety. Self-focused attention is similar to the concept of objective self-awareness (Duval & Wicklund, 1972) and has been contrasted with the immediate experiencing of the subjective self (Wolfe, 1992). This concept incorporates the earlier fear-of-fear construct (Goldstein & Chambless, 1978) as well as the concept of anxiety sensitivity (Reiss, 1987). The psychodynamic point of view has also focused on the ruminative thinking of patients with obsessive–compulsive disorder (OCD), a phenomenon that is very close to self-focused attention (Salzman, 1980).

Following is a summary of the common factors regarding the nature, etiology, and maintenance of anxiety disorders:

Nature
1. Anxiety is hard-wired by evolution as a response to perceived danger.
2. An anxiety disorder in some sense represents the misapplication of a normal anxiety response.
3. An anxiety disorder is based in the irrational or unrealistic.
4. Anxiety involves the anticipation of danger, pain, or catastrophe.
5. Anxiety involves the fear of uncontrollable events.

Etiology
1. Genetics play a significant role in the development of an anxiety disorder.
2. Painful or traumatic experience plays a significant role in the development of an anxiety disorder.
3. The self-perception of inefficacy plays a significant role in the development of an anxiety disorder.

Maintenance
1. There is avoidance of the feared object, situation, thought, or feeling.
2. There is a continuation of the underlying problems, whether they are unconscious conflicts, a persistent habit, a dysfunctional cognitive schema or emotion scheme, or a neurobiological function.
3. There is obsessive self-focused attention.

In broad outline, then, these are most—if not all—of the common factors that the various perspectives share regarding the nature, etiology, and maintenance of anxiety disorders.

DIFFERENCES IN THE VARIOUS ETIOLOGICAL THEORIES

This apparent consensus on a number of ideas about the nature, etiology, and maintenance of anxiety disorders warrants a word of caution. The fact that theorists of different persuasion agree does not necessarily mean they are correct. But these factors have been frequently observed in clinical situations and, despite some semantic differences, it is reasonable to assume that these theorists are observing very similar phenomena.

Even with this degree of consensus, however, there are significant differences in the various conceptions of these disorders that possess sharp, differential implications for their treatment. I now look at several key issues on which the various perspectives differ and evaluate the relative merits of these differing ideas.

Neurobiological Factors in the Etiology of Anxiety Disorders

In this book, I argue that each perspective has useful things to say about the etiology of anxiety disorders, but none provides a comprehensive perspective on the formation of these disorders. The various perspectives function like the blind men on the proverbial elephant, each reconstructing the entire elephant from the small portion of the animal that it contacts. I wish to reconstruct the elephant by using the most useful insights from each perspective.

I begin with the biological perspective that delineates the physical substrate for the experience of anxiety. Immediately, a dilemma arises: On the one hand, it is very clear that our neurobiological systems are responsible for our subjective experience, thoughts, feelings, and behavior; on the other hand, researchers do not yet know how brain signals are transformed into subjective experience. One intriguing scientific metaphor that has been borrowed from another scientific field and has been proposed in the literature on several occasions is the idea of transduction (Reiser, 1984). *Transduction* refers to the transformation of energy or information from one form to another. Rossi (1986) suggested that all biological life could be viewed as a system of information transduction. Bowers (1977) put forth the contention that

> The entire human body can be viewed as an interlocking network of informational systems—genetic, immunological, hormonal and so on. Each of these systems has its own codes, and the transmission of information between systems requires some sort of transducer that allows the code of one system, genetic, say, to be translated into the code of another system—for example, immunological. . . . If information processing and transmission are common to both psyche and soma, the mind–body problem might be reformulated as follows: How is information, received and processed at a semantic level, transduced into information that can be received and processed at a somatic level, and vice versa? (p. 231)

Rossi (1986) has reviewed several studies that show how mental experience is transduced into the physiological responses characteristic of emotions in a circuit of brain structures that constitutes much of what is now called the limbic–hypothalamic system. He cited, for example, Harris' early work (1948) that showed that certain cells within the hypothalamus could convert the neural impulses that encoded *mind* into the hormonal messenger molecules of the endocrine system that regulated *body*. This work suggests the possible workings of some kind of transduction process, but the transduction code itself has not been delineated as yet.

If the transduction idea has merit, then it becomes a challenge to determine whether the experience of anxiety represents a neurobiological system gone awry or the expression of a learned connection. The debate involves whether people experiencing an anxiety disorder have had their neurobiological functioning modified by learning or whether such individuals possess a genetically transmitted malfunction. As Redmond (1985) put it, "Are anxiety disorders discrete entities with pathophysiological mechanisms or are they continuous variations in the activity of one or more normal neurobiological systems, which are responding or over-responding to internal or external stimuli that would not be threatening to others[?]" (pp. 533–534). In either instance, the individual's neurobiological functioning possesses all of the earmarks of the individual in a state of alarm. It is an open question whether a person's neurobiological functioning in the state of alarm represents a biological malfunction or whether it is a learned alteration of this functioning. Although most biomedical research on anxiety disorders appears to proceed with the assumption that these disorders are based in genetically transmitted malfunctions of neurobiological systems, other research suggests that learning actually sculpts the brain and therefore the observed malfunctions may actually represent changes in the brain's architecture that are induced by experience (see Cozolino, 2002).

Whether an anxiety disorder is based in a purely biological malfunction or is a result of a particular psychological constellation that generates the biological consequences of anxiety is the pivotal question that separates biomedical accounts of anxiety from all other psychologically based accounts. Whereas the biomedical view implies an automaticity with respect to the occurrence of an anxiety disorder as a result of the malfunctioning of one or more neurobiological systems (Andreasen, 1984), the psychological view is rooted in a belief that the present or past intentionality of the individual figures prominently in the development of an anxiety disorder (A. T. Beck & Emery, 1985; S. Freud, 1926/1959; Wolfe & Sigl, 1998).

It is probably the case that some clinical presentations of an anxiety disorder are based solely in a biological malfunction that is innocent of any psychological causal factors, but until the information transduction process is better understood, it will be difficult to distinguish psychological causation from purely biological causation. In the unscientific sample of my private practice, however, virtually none of the patients with an anxiety disorder that I have ever treated can legitimately be said to have had a purely biological causation of their difficulties. As I spell out in much greater detail later, the vast majority of my patients have been involved in an intense struggle with their own subjective experience, intrusive thoughts, and painful emotions and the fears to which these experiences give rise. All of these experiences undoubtedly produce profound biological consequences.

Because of this clinical experience, the approach that I am taking toward the very useful and interesting biological research that has been conducted on the anxiety disorders for the past 30 years is that the regularities uncovered by such research represent the biological consequences of psychological factors (i.e., implicit or explicit subjective constellations of meaning) that, in fact, are governing the acquisition and maintenance of a given anxiety disorder.

One area in which there is a clear and observable interplay of the biological and the psychological is the individual's reactions to his or her bodily sensations or to his or her awareness of an identified biological malfunction. This cogitating about one's bodily sensations (also known as self-focused attention) is often the source of an elaboration of a preexisting psychological constellation guiding an anxiety disorder. Thus, for example, patients with panic disorder often interpret particular body sensations as heralds of pending catastrophic or life-threatening biological events, such as a heart attack or a stroke. Later, when such patients have been reassured regarding their intact biological functioning, they interpret these sensations as heralds of pending panic attacks, which then give rise to increased levels of anxiety. The question that this phenomenon suggests is as follows: What are the differences at the neurobiological level between the immediate experience of fear and the more reflexive fear of fear? To put it somewhat differently, what are the neurobiological mediators of one's immediate experience of anxiety as compared with the neurobiological mediators of the anxiety that is produced by one's cogitating about one's immediate experience of anxiety?

Classical and Operant Conditioning in the Etiology of Anxiety Disorders

Classical conditioning was originally based on the idea that certain innate behavior patterns are regularly elicited by certain stimuli. When a neutral stimulus is contiguous with one of these unconditioned stimuli, it will come to elicit the innate behavior pattern. Classically conditioned responses were thought to be automatic, that is, without conscious effort or apparent cognitive involvement. With respect to anxiety and fear, the conditioning model presumed that the feared object or situation was originally a neutral stimulus paired with a stimulus that regularly produced fear and pain.

Originally proposed as an explanation of the basic process of learning, conditioning theory has been critiqued on numerous grounds. However, the basic research on classical conditioning has undergone significant changes in the past 30 years. Pavlov's basic model of conditioning has been reinterpreted in light of more sophisticated research and more complex conceptualizations. Rescorla (1988) has suggested that what actually takes place in conditioning is very different from the earlier theoretical constructs posed by Pavlov. Rescorla illustrated differences between older and more recent views of conditioning on three issues: (a) the circumstances producing learning, (b) the content of the learning, and (c) the effects of learning on behavior. The sum of his critique is to suggest that conditioning does not involve the association of any two contiguous stimuli. The organism instead perceives relationships between events in the environment and, through these associations, develops representations of the world. Moreover, these associations are much broader and much more complex than the single-association model originally proposed by Pavlov. Thus, modern animal research on conditioning lends more support for an informational view of conditioning than for the contiguity hypothesis.

When considering the adequacy of the conditioning model of fear acquisition, one encounters still other difficulties. Any theory of the development of anxiety disorders must begin with a ubiquitously observed phenomenon—the association of pain with some internal or external stimulus. These associations seem to be rapid and automatic and typically—but not always—take place below the radar screen of a person's conscious awareness. These associations may come about either passively, as suggested in the paradigm of classical conditioning, or through the selective reinforcement of certain actions (i.e., operant conditioning).

Earlier and more recent critiques questioned the validity of conditioning theories of fear acquisition. Early on, Breger and McGaugh (1965), on the one hand, and Weitzman (1967), on the other, found a number of discrepancies between conditioning theory and its application in deconditioning and behavioral treatments and therefore concluded that conditioning theory represents a flimsy and inadequate analogy for what actually takes place in behavioral therapy. Somewhat later, Rachman (1977) argued that although conditioning may be one way in which people learn fear, it is deficient on a number of counts as a comprehensive theory. For example, (a) not all people develop fear reactions in clearly fear-evoking situations; (b) conditioning theory rests on the equipotentiality premise, which assumes that any stimulus has the potential of becoming a fear stimulus through contiguous association; this premise does not comport well with the distribution of fears in normal and neurotic populations; (c) many cases of phobias cannot be accommodated by conditioning theory; and (d) fears can be acquired vicariously and by the transmission of information and instruction.

In the context of treatment, the early behavioral therapists focused only on external stimuli as conditioned stimuli that produced the conditioned autonomic fear response. Thus, for example, it was the snake per se that produced the anxiety. This view led Wolpe (1958) to his well-known principle of reciprocal inhibition, which contends that by associating the snake with responses that are antagonistic to anxiety, the association between snake and anxiety could be diminished or eliminated. Because this view supplied no role for cognition, it paid scant attention to the various idiosyncratic meanings that individuals with a snake phobia associated with the idea, image, or perception of a snake. The irony of course is that Wolpe's behavioral theory and, more specifically, his behavioral therapy relied substantially on the subjective imagery of the patient with anxiety (Weitzman, 1967).

Such idiosyncratic meanings become clearly evident when the clinician explores the entire network of associations a person connects with a particular fear stimulus. In addition, one finds clinically that different meanings are associated to the same fear stimulus by different patients. A few years back, I treated three separate individuals with a driving phobia who had interpreted the act of driving in three idiosyncratic but phobic ways. For one patient, driving meant the strong possibility that she would get lost. The experience of being lost was intolerable, and it resulted consistently in panic attacks. The second patient feared driving because she always felt like she was unprepared or had left some task undone. The third patient with a driving phobia was not entirely clear why he feared driving. He only knew that he would have a panic attack if he drove too far away from home. Through our therapeutic work, it became clear to him that the act of driving was associated with his fear of abandonment. These differences in the idiosyncratic meanings experienced by patients with anxiety have different treatment implications, although exposure therapy is usually a necessary component—necessary, but not sufficient.

An in-depth exploration of a patient's associations reveals not only that he or she connects a number of conscious cognitions with the fear stimuli but also that further work will uncover associated cognitions that are beyond the person's focal awareness. These typically emerge as a result of imagery work or hypnotic approaches, or even during the course of a patient's exploration of his or her immediate experience.

If the purely behavioral account of conditioning is inadequate to explain anxiety disorders, is anything like a conditioned response involved in anxiety disorders? Some aspects of the conditioning paradigm do seem to be very relevant. First of all there seems to be a recurrent association between particular stimuli and fear responses. But keep in mind that this connection actually involves a rich tapestry of catastrophic associations and relationships between the phobic object and the person's fear responses. Second, the fear seems to occur automatically on exposure to the fear stimulus. One question needs to be raised here, however: Does the automaticity of the fear response to exposure involve any cognitive activity at all?

Most important, if conditioning is a relevant process for the formation of a phobia or other anxiety disorder, then what is actually being conditioned? My clinical experience suggests that there is an inordinate amount of trauma in the life histories of those with a phobia and other patients with anxiety. These experiences have the cumulative effect of shaping a sense of catastrophic doom about the future of one's physical or psychological self. In other words, an association develops between a particular situation or object and an overwhelming sense of self-endangerment, which connotes a possible confrontation with unbearable pain. Such a fundamental fear is necessary to explain the extreme panic reaction that some patients with anxiety exhibit when they come face-to-face with their feared situations or objects. Only a fear of such magnitude and gravity can explain the terror that some people feel when they confront a mouse, a hypodermic needle, a public speaking engagement, or, in a more bizarre instance, mayonnaise (Van Dyke & Harris, 1982).

The conditioning paradigm seems to be an incomplete model of how human beings form such anxious connections between certain internal or external stimuli and painful responses. Nonetheless, the model does seem to capture a basic truth about the development of an anxiety disorder: that a rich array of idiosyncratic associations is constructed between the feared object or situation and catastrophic pain.

Underlying Dysfunctional Cognitive Schemas

The conditioning paradigm may provide a useful starting point in the analysis of a developing anxiety disorder, but it needs to be expanded. Although the early models of conditioning suggested that this automatic connection is due to the contiguity of a neutral stimulus to a painful response, this variable could not explain the selective nature of most conditioned associations (Ford & Urban, 1998). As mentioned above, more recent neoconditioning models suggest that some form of associative information processing takes place even in such lower animals as pigeons (Rescorla, 1988). By viewing animal associative behavior in terms of information processing, modern conditioning theories move a step closer to cognitive and social-learning theories. Even the most rapid, automatic process of conditioning is now thought to involve implicit cognitive processes. Rapee (1991), for example, has argued that conditioning is a subset of cognitive processes. He suggested that the dichotomy posed between conditioning and cognitive explanations has more to do with polemics than with science. The latter might be better served, Rapee suggested, if conditioning and cognitive explanations are thought of as falling at different points on the same continuum of used attentional resources. The automaticity of conditioning requires virtually no attentional resources, whereas cognitively mediated processes of fear acquisition require much more.

Most cognitive approaches acknowledge that there may be basic biological variables that predispose some people more than others to developing anxiety disorders (e.g., A. T. Beck & Emery, 1985). Beyond this basic biological diathesis, cognitive approaches depart from more purely behavioral approaches in terms of the following basic assumption—that a person's behavior is determined more by internal cognitive processes than by environmental contingencies.

As is well known, the cognitive perspective emerged because of many of the previously mentioned deficiencies in the behavioral paradigm. Although several tributaries have since veered off from the main cognitive river (Mahoney, 1991), all of the cognitive theories point in a similar direction. They all assume that human experience is internalized and stored in memory in an organized fashion. These psychic structures, by whatever name they assume, are believed to assert a powerful influence on how human beings feel and behave. In particular, these psychic structures influence the kind of anticipations or expectancies that persons develop in specific situations. A core assumption of A. T. Beck's cognitive perspective, for example, is that patients with anxiety have internalized certain cognitive schemas regarding the potential dangerousness of certain situations and the threat they pose, relative to the person's coping abilities. These schemas are presumed to exert a mostly tacit influence on a patient's perspective toward him- or herself, the world, and the future (A. T. Beck & Emery, 1985). The cognitive perspective also argues that the functional relationships that are discovered between certain stimuli and the person's anxiety responses are in large measure shaped by these tacit psychic structures. A. T. Beck did not go so far as to say that cognitions cause anxiety disorders, only that the primary dysfunction is in the cognitive apparatus (A. T. Beck & Emery, 1985).

A related model is Bandura's social-learning model of anxiety. This model suggests that the basic mechanism producing anxiety is the individual's lack of self-efficacy beliefs. The person's expectation of the efficacy of his or her coping maneuvers is that they will be insufficient to deal with the threat. Although this model tries to avoid schemalike concepts, there is a close relationship between danger-based schemas and the belief that one cannot cope with a perceived threat. Although Bandura wanted to avoid postulating such internal entities as cognitive schemas, most cognitive and cognitive–behavioral models have now adopted schema-based models of cognitive functioning. Even the cognitive–behavioral model developed by Foa and Kozak (1986) suggests that anxiety is based in conscious or unconscious fear structures or schemas, which contain stimulus–stimulus associations that do not accurately reflect relationships in the world. Barlow (2000) focused on learned alarms and other psychological vulnerabilities as major contributory factors in the development of anxiety disorders. He did not postulate specific cognitive schemas, but his views are quite compatible with schema-based models of anxiety.

The cognitive model thus expands the conditioning paradigm by suggesting that the initial, automatic association between traumatic experience(s) and a specific object or situation results in the formation of danger-related schemas. These schemas subsequently influence the person's anticipations of catastrophic doom whenever he or she is confronted with the feared object or situation. One individual with a public speaking phobia, for example, had internalized a basic self-schema that suggested that he was an inferior being and a permanent outsider, and therefore others will not respect anything he might have to say. Moreover, he believed that others would ridicule him because of either the content of his communications or how he delivers them. As a result, he vigilantly monitored all aspects of his delivery and was fearful that others would perceive humiliating deficiencies.

One can see in this instance that this automatic association of various aspects of speaking with a network of extremely fearful ideas and images certainly suggests that a conditioning-like process was in operation. Nonetheless, it became clear that the fear and its context were linked by the underlying self-belief of inadequacy and inferiority.

Another aspect of cognitive models of anxiety needs to be considered. To make this point clear, I use as a prototypical example the cognitive model of panic disorder. There are several closely related formulations of cognitively based models of panic (Barlow, 1988; A. T. Beck & Emery, 1985; D. M. Clark, 1986). Most cognitive models of panic disorder postulate that panic attacks are engendered by a misinterpretation of the degree of danger posed by unpleasant internal sensations. The catastrophic interpretations given to these sensations result in spiraling increases of anxiety. Such spiraling anxiety may result in a full-blown panic attack. The increasing panic interferes with the individual's capacity to rationally appraise his or her situation as he or she becomes fixated on the possibility of impending disaster. But typically, the initial panic attack does not come about in this fashion. Instead, it appears to the individual to be a spontaneous emergence of unbearable terror. Subsequently, the person interprets certain bodily sensations associated with the initial panic attack as a signal of impending disaster.

Increasingly, cognitive models have attempted to develop techniques for activating the underlying cognitive schemas (Leahy, 2003; Young, 1990). This strategy is based on the assumption that therapeutic change is predicated on the activation and cognitive restructuring of underlying cognitive schemas (Foa & Kozak, 1986).

Any emerging integrative model of anxiety disorders must accommodate the conditioning-like automatic nature of the association between feared situation and autonomic and emotional distress. At the same time, however, that model needs to account for the cognitive model's emphasis on underlying psychic structures pertaining to danger that appear to greatly influence the formation and maintenance of these associations.

Yet the cognitive view also seems to possess certain limitations. Bohart (1993) noted a number of these limitations. His critique of the cognitive perspective was based in its deficiencies regarding the experientially based process of knowing. "Most modern views of knowing equate it with thought-like processes or structures at some level. These include thinking, conceptualizing, inferring, beliefs, and propositional schemas" (Bohart, 1993, p. 56).

At the conscious phenomenological level, however, the process of thinking differs from both perceiving and experiencing. The apprehension of meaning is directly embedded in the perception or experience itself, and the affect is part of the embodied meaning. In the example Bohart (1993) gave of a jogger's fear of dogs, it is the experience of the dog as dangerous that therapists hope to change, not just the cognitive representation that the dog is dangerous.

Bohart viewed experiential knowing as a more primary form of knowing than thinking. One knows something experientially first and then secondarily one conceptualizes and thinks about the experience. Our conceptual structures are made meaningful by the fact that they arise from our preconceptual bodily experiences. Bohart then raised the following question: If experiential knowing is more primary than thinking, then approaching the task of therapeutic change through a primary focus on changing cognitions is likely to be difficult, or at least less successful than a focus on experiential change would be. Thus, he believed that cognitive therapy, when it is successful, works not by changing conceptions directly but by arranging for the client to have different experiences.

Bohart's critique of the cognitive perspective points us toward yet another deficiency of both conditioning and cognitive models of anxiety. By suggesting the importance of the role of preconceptual, bodily experiences in human knowing, he implied that a focus on unconscious, or at least preconscious, factors is necessary to enhance the explanatory power of theoretical models of human dysfunctions. Bohart's suggestion, as well as several other indirect indications in both the conditioning and cognitive models, lends credence to the idea that unconscious processes may play a significant role in the development of an anxiety disorder. This possibility now needs to be explored.

Unconscious and Preconscious Processes in the Development and Maintenance of Anxiety Disorders

Despite the fact that the early behaviorists interpreted the phenomena of conditioning in a way that avoided any reference to unconscious processes, Pavlov (1928) seemed clear that unconscious processes were at the heart of conditioning. In the evaluation of the purely behavioral view of anxiety disorders, then, a bit of a dilemma arises. Although the phenomena of conditioning clearly implicate unconscious processes, behaviorally oriented clinicians have been loathe to consider such phenomena in their theoretical expositions of anxiety.

The cognitive–behavioral view emphasizes the prepotent influence of cognitive schemas in generating the anticipatory responses of anxiety. Here it is assumed that such underlying beliefs as "I am not good enough" influence the anxiety responses that occur in public speaking situations, for example. These cognitive schemas may or may not be in the person's immediate awareness, but are presumed, nonetheless, to have a powerful influence on a person's behavior, thoughts, and feelings. Whereas early versions of cognitive and cognitive–behavioral therapy focused on conscious cognitions as a major influence on one's behavior and emotional life, more recent versions have emphasized the unconscious nature of cognitive schemas (Foa & Kozak, 1996; Leahy, 2003).

The shift in attitude toward unconscious factors apparent within the cognitive–behavioral therapy literature reflects a corresponding shift that is taking place in the basic science of cognition. There appears to be a growing consensus among basic cognitive researchers that a good deal of preconscious information processing goes on before such information enters consciousness, and that preconscious information can have effects on cognition and behavior without ever entering consciousness (Dixon, 1981; Kihlstrom, 1984). Although cognitive scientists are coming to accept that unconscious cognition has garnered significant empirical support, most believe that such cognition is intellectually fairly primitive compared with its sophisticated functioning as presumed by psychoanalysis (Greenwald, 1992). There is still a yawning gap between psychoanalytic and cognitive science conceptions of unconscious processes, particularly regarding unconscious motivation (Shevrin & Dickman, 1980). However, at least some cognitive researchers suggest that there are data to support a version of the Freudian concept of repression (Erdelyi & Goldberg, 1979). This emphasis on the prepotency of unconscious cognitive schemas moves the cognitive perspective (both its therapy and basic science literatures) a step closer to the psychoanalytic view. However, psychoanalytic and cognitive–behavioral therapies have formulated very different treatment approaches for uncovering or activating these unconscious psychic structures.

The psychodynamic perspective has always emphasized unconscious conflicts and character traits as the driving forces for behavior. More modern versions of psychoanalysis have left behind S. Freud's (1923/1959) original emphasis on the three-way civil war allegedly taking place between a person's instinctual drives, realistic perceptions, and internalized moral beliefs. They have focused instead on the unconscious representations of self and self-with-others as the most influential drivers of conscious thought and expressive behavior. These representations are strikingly similar in many respects to cognitive schemas, although the former always involve the self in relation to others.

Experiential psychotherapy centers its focus on the process of emotional experiencing. Although this perspective accepts the idea of internalized psychic structures, these structures are conceptualized as bathed in emotion. These *emotion schemes*, as L. S. Greenberg called them (L. S. Greenberg et al., 1993), are thought to contain a great deal more information than just representational cognition and are viewed as separate but closely related entities. Emotion schemes are assumed to function below the level of conscious awareness. This point of view suggests that the activation of dormant emotion schemes, which leads to the construction of specific emotions, and their expression to appropriate others are necessary elements in the process of therapeutic change.

The role of unconscious processes in the development of the anxiety disorders is fast becoming a common factor within the psychotherapy literature, although the purely behavioral and the biomedical perspectives still have little use for the idea as a scientific construct. In my clinical experience, it is difficult to account for the observed phenomena of anxiety disorders without some concept of preconscious or unconscious information processing. The imagery and focusing techniques that I use as diagnostic probes consistently reveal numerous catastrophic associations to feared objects and situations that were not in the individual's focal awareness. By focusing on the phobic object in the case of patients with a phobia, on frightening bodily sensations in the case of patients with panic disorder, or on the fear-inducing and ritual-compelling thoughts in the case of patients with OCD, individuals routinely discover the catastrophic life situations that truly terrorize them.

A content analysis of these catastrophic conflicts suggests that in the broadest sense they reflect existential crises. By that, I mean that the feared catastrophes involve confrontations with difficult yet unavoidable human realities. Although these conflicts were most likely developed in the context of historical interpersonal traumas, then and now they relate to several realities that we all must face: the inevitability of loss; the experience of a separate consciousness that is often associated with the fear of being alone; the yoke of personal responsibility; the awareness and acceptance of one's own mortality; the need to equilibrate our actions and our expressiveness in the face of sociocultural demands; and the need to go through a painful process of deciding how much freedom, autonomy, and novelty one needs in one's life as opposed to comfort, security, and safety. All of these issues are involved in the struggle for self-esteem, and this struggle necessarily involves experiencing such self-diminishing emotions as humiliation, guilt, shame, and frightening rage. These are the issues that most frequently appear when patients engage in imaginal probes of the preconscious meanings associated with their feared objects and situations. These issues are illustrated in the specific cases discussed throughout the book.

Experiential–Affective Processes

It is fair to say that most perspectives on anxiety have not ignored affect but, rather, that each perspective conceives of affect differently. Consequently, each perspective assigns a different role to affect in the acquisition and maintenance of anxiety disorders. The behavioral perspective has been mostly concerned with the affect of fear or anxiety. Anxiety then was viewed as a conditioned autonomic response. This perspective had little interest in searching out affects that may underlie the anxiety.

The cognitive perspective initially ignored affect and only more recently has included affect in its theories. A. T. Beck viewed affect as a kind of amplification of cognition (A. T. Beck & Emery, 1985). But cognitive therapists recently have highlighted the necessity of activating fear schemas and all of their associated thoughts and feelings before such schemas can be modified (Foa & Kozak, 1996). This view allows for the possibility that preconscious or unconscious affects may be significantly involved in the development, maintenance, and amelioration of fear schemas.

In contrast, Barlow (2000) has argued that fear and anxiety are fundamentally different emotions. Whereas fear is our emergency defensive reaction, anxiety is a cognitive–affective structure that includes a sense of uncontrollability related to future threats. Barlow, however, has not focused on other emotions that may underlie the observable anxiety. Instead, his focus has been on the cognitive–behavioral modification of conscious anxiety states.

Psychoanalysis has always been concerned with affects—conscious and unconscious—although the theorizing about them tends to be rather fuzzy. Most versions of psychoanalysis, however, acknowledge the necessity of patients experiencing a corrective emotional experience as part of the therapeutic change process (Alexander & French, 1946; Milrod, Busch, Cooper, & Shapiro, 1997; Shear, Cooper, Klerman, Busch, & Shapiro, 1993). The biomedical perspective tends to view affect and emotion as epiphenomena of neurobiological processes. This view therefore is primarily concerned with the neurobiological basis of fear and in developing medications to alter the fear-inducing neurophysiology (D. F. Klein, 1993; Ledoux, 1996).

The experiential perspective has the most to say on the role of emotion in the development and maintenance of emotional disorders in general. This view departs from all of the others in its contention that emotions are a biologically adaptive source of information that individuals ignore at their peril. Problems arise through the learning of faulty ideas about the dangers of emotional expressiveness. L. S. Greenberg et al. (1993), for example, postulated two sources of emotional difficulties in general: (a) dysfunctional emotion schemes and (b) problems in the conscious processing of emotions. Emotion-focused techniques have been developed to facilitate emotional experiencing that will correct the conscious processing difficulties as well as modify the tacit, dysfunctional emotion schemes.

My clinical experience supports Bohart's (1993) contention that the tacit, danger-related beliefs associated with anxiety disorders are not just cognitive representations of experience but, rather, are emotional beliefs that need to be brought into the patient's conscious awareness. When patients focus on the sites and situations of their anxiety, painful emotions typically arise that embed catastrophic beliefs about the self in peril.

SUMMARY OF SELECTED ETIOLOGICAL IDEAS
FROM THE VARIOUS PERSPECTIVES

In this section I review the differing etiological ideas among the five perspectives and choose those that seem to possess either empirical support or clinical validity. Where I deem the research inadequate or nonexistent, I elected to rely on my clinical experience in making certain selections. I am aware that many will view this as a controversial and unacceptable methodology, but it is my considered view that the current state of the empirical literature leaves many questions either insufficiently addressed or not addressed at all.

The following summarizes what I have been able to extract from a review of the etiological differences and commonalities among the various perspectives. In building an understanding of anxiety disorders, it is necessary to include the self (i.e., the sense and concepts of self that each of us lives out) as the core locus of the experience of danger. Negative, emotion-based beliefs about the self seem to be the major drivers of anxiety reactions. These ideas and images—the repositories of one's multifaceted self-experience—appear to generate a wide variety of psychologically based anxieties regarding one's efficacy, worthiness, lovability, and ability to cope with threat. Each of the preexisting models makes a significant contribution to a broader understanding of anxiety disorders.

The biomedical model contributes an increasingly understood neurobiological substrate of anxiety disorders. The conditioning model is accurate in many instances because an anxiety disorder often involves a form of conditioning in which a person perceives a relationship between an object or a situation and what the person believes to be a catastrophic threat to his or her core self. The psychoanalytic and experiential models are correct in their contention that these perceived threats to the core self are believed to entail unbearable pain. The cognitive model usefully contends that this initial, automatic association between traumatic experience(s) and a specific object or situation results in the formation of tacit, danger-related beliefs. These conditioned associations therefore can be thought of as a type of implicit cognition. The experiential model is correct in its contention that these tacit, danger-related beliefs involve more than just cognitive information. These beliefs include emotional, motivational, and relational information as well. Again the psychodynamic and experiential models appear to be correct in their contention that these unconscious emotional beliefs often reflect unconscious, catastrophic conflicts about the individual's relationships with important others or about facing the inevitability of certain human realities such as accepting loss or facing one's own mortality.

All of these models suggest that these danger-related beliefs subsequently influence the person's anticipation of catastrophic doom whenever he or she is confronted with the feared object or situation. Future anticipated encounters with the feared object or situation therefore stimulate anxiety that can vary from moderate levels to the occurrence of a full-blown panic attack. Both cognitive–behavioral and experiential models suggest that a major complicating factor in all anxiety disorders is that the first-order fear reactions compel the person to focus reflexively on him- or herself being afraid, and he or she then misinterprets the meaning of these signs of fear. This reflexive focus or tendency to cogitate about one's self being afraid is closely related to the concept of self-focused attention. This second-order level of fear intensifies the initial fear level, which can often lead to a panic attack. Thus anxiety disorders appear to involve somatic indications of anxiety that possess preconscious or unconscious meaning and another level of anxiety that is basically a reaction by one's self to one's self being fearful (i.e., self-focused attention). A key hypothesis of this book is that various wounds to the self generate both of these levels of anxiety. Self-wounds are unbearably painful ways of experiencing and thinking about one's self.

The next chapter proposes an integrative model of the self. This model serves as a basis for viewing our experience and concepts of the self as the final common pathway of psychopathology and its amelioration. Then I delineate the integrative self-wound model of anxiety disorders.

5

AN INTEGRATIVE MODEL OF THE SELF

The self is a thing perceived and it is also a thing conceived; in both senses it is constantly responded to.

—Gardner Murphy (1947)

The self and the experience of the self are such palpable realities for all human beings that they are next to impossible to deny. At the same time, however, the difficulties presented in the investigation of self phenomena, much less their definition, lead to the periodic conclusion that the construct of the self is scientifically useless. And yet the reality of self-experience cannot be so easily dismissed. As Daniel Stern put it in the following:

> Even though the nature of self may forever elude the behavioral sciences, the sense of self stands as an important subjective reality, a reliable, evident phenomenon that the sciences cannot dismiss. How we experience ourselves in relation to others provides a basic organizing perspective for all interpersonal events. (1985, p. 6)

EARLY PSYCHOLOGICAL THEORIES OF THE SELF

Earlier philosophic views of the self, in an attempt to account for the experienced sense of interiority, defined it as an entity or substance, something akin to a soul (Levin, 1992). But questions regarding the soul or mind gave way to questions about sensation and perception with the advent of experimental psychology in the second half of the 19th century. To avoid the mire of subjectivity and the taint of teleological explanations, the emerging academic departments of psychology consigned the concept of self to at best a partial moratorium from about the 1870s until the 1940s (F. Johnson, 1985). Although the concept of self has reemerged in mainstream psychology, all modern theories of psychology agree that the *substantial self* (i.e., the idea that the self is composed of some physical substance) is a myth and that a clear and convincing definition must be found elsewhere. These theories, however, agree on little else. The self has been variously defined as a knowledge structure (Markus & Wurf, 1987), a process (Crook, 1980; Mahoney, 1991), a narrative (Polkinghorne, 1988), a theory (Epstein, 1973), a superordinate regulatory system (Cooper, 1993), and a collection of our self-interpretations, which themselves are derivatives of language, history, and culture (Broughton, 1986). Some theoreticians have argued that the self is so painfully real that many individuals try to escape it by means of sex, substance abuse, spiritual quests, or even suicide (Baumeister, 1991). Other theorists, on the contrary, have maintained that the self is either so evanescent (R. Rosenbaum & Dyckman, 1995) or diminished by malevolent socioeconomic forces (Cushman, 1990) that, for all intents and purposes, it is empty. James's (1890) distinction between the searching *I* and the discovered *Me*, the self as knower and the self as known (i.e., as the object of knowledge), set the cast for all future theorizing about the self. However, he saw no scientific value in pursuing the *I* and felt it should be banished to the realm of philosophy. The self as an object of knowledge includes all of the characteristics that a person would assent to as belonging to him or her, including his or her body, abilities, and even possessions. Emphasizing the interactional context for its development, James did not see the self as unitary; rather, he believed that a person "has as many social selves as there are individuals who recognize him and carry an image of him in their mind" (p. 294). For James, the self was basically a self-concept developed in terms of the reactions of other people to one's behavior and personal characteristics. To the extent that this is true, it leaves the person somewhat at the mercy of the opinions others have of him or her.

Cooley's (1902) capstone notion of the looking-glass self, which refers to an individual viewing him- or herself the way other people view him or her, was premised on the assumption that self-knowledge depends on the personal other and that interpersonal relationships were both the context and the means by which one develops a concept of self. Mead (1934) expanded on Cooley's looking-glass self, noting that to achieve selfhood, the individual must step outside his or her immediate experience and imagine how others perceive him- or herself. Thus self-awareness involves taking the role of the other and seeing one's self as others see one. For Mead, there was no duality in the self but solely a self-concept that emerges through, and is based in, the perceptions of others. According to Mead, the reflexivity of language allows a person to be able to take the role of the other to obtain knowledge of the self.

The views of James, Cooley, and Mead have been influential in defining several of the necessary elements in any adequate account of the self: (a) accounting for the duality of self (i.e., self as subject; self as object); (b) the importance of the interactional context for the development of self; and (c) the power of the opinions of others in shaping one's view of one's self.

THE SELF IN PSYCHOTHERAPY THEORIES

In the major theoretical traditions in psychotherapy, the self, however it may be constituted, has been a major focus of theorizing. It is increasingly thought of as a core locus of psychopathology and the ultimate site of therapeutic change. One can find within the psychoanalytic, cognitive, cognitive–behavioral, behavioral, and experiential perspectives evidence of the growing importance of some concept of the self in psychopathology and its remediation. Even in the neurobiological perspective, one can find some nascent signs of the self being discussed in various psychopathological contexts (e.g., Damasio, 1994; Melzack, 1989). Psychoanalytic theorists have focused mostly on the unconscious organization of self-representations and their unwitting influence on the individual's interpersonal behavior, whereas cognitive therapists have centered on specific negative self-beliefs as a major contributor to psychopathology. Some cognitive–behavioral theorists have recently adopted the language of self-representations but have embedded this construct in the context of information-processing theory (Segal & Blatt, 1993). Experiential theorists view as central to mental health and psychopathology the characteristics of an individual's self-experiencing and the emotional processing of personally relevant meanings (L. S. Greenberg, Rice, & Elliott, 1993). The model I propose here reflects an attempt to synthesize ideas from all of these perspectives.

There seems to be good reason to believe that the self is a necessary integrative focus of psychopathology and its amelioration. Such a perspective is supported by the clinically observable fact that most psychopathology involves an individual struggling with self-related thoughts, feelings, and actions. This struggle entails the pain of becoming aware of actions and thoughts that diminish one in one's own eyes or in the eyes of others. This common struggle also induces feelings that are painful to contain within one's body and threatening in their implications for the self. The role of the self also figures prominently in any adequate theory of psychopathology because it points to a level of concern beyond surface symptoms that appears to exist in most mental disorders.

Moreover, the self appears to be necessary because this construct points to a number of complex human processes that many existing theories and symptom-focused treatments have tended to ignore. These include the person's subjective awareness, intentions, quest for meaning, ownership (or lack thereof) of one's emotional reactions and the implications of one's behavior, idiosyncratic manner of processing emotions, and preconscious or unconscious influences on one's feelings, thoughts, and action.

Most important, one needs to postulate the self because it is the only means by which a theorist can capture a ubiquitous and uniquely human characteristic: the person's relationship with him- or herself. As Mahoney (1985) pointed out, we have a relationship with ourselves that is similar in many respects to the relationship that we have with any given individual. For example, we do to ourselves what we fear, hope, or believe other people will do to us. We self-spectate, self-doubt, and self-judge. But we also praise, admire, and adulate the self. Through one's relationship with self, one can simultaneously give and receive love, hate, and criticism. Blasi (1988) has referred to this unique relationship that one has with one's self, one's actions, thoughts, and feelings, as a *stance*, that is, the person's affective relationship to his or her statements and acts in the very moment that he or she says or does them. This, for Blasi, is the essence of a person's intentionality: "To say that an action is intentional is to say that the action expresses the subject's stance with regard to the object. The subject's stance—his believing, desiring, controlling, or hoping—is not one component among others, but permeates every aspect of the action and gives unity to it" (p. 232).

AN INTEGRATIVE MODEL OF THE SELF

Before explicating an integrative model of the self, I must clarify my terminology relating to the self. A clear statement of my terminology may help reduce the confusion wrought by the variety of perspectives on the self (Wolfe, 2003).

Organism, Person, and the Self

To begin with, it is important to distinguish between the human organism, person, and self. By *organism*, I refer to all of our neurobiological processes that characterize and sustain us as living entities. By *person*, I refer to several interrelated characteristics that are distinctive of human beings. The first is that human beings are conscious agents of causation. They have conscious intentions that they enact (Baumeister, 1991; DeCharms, 1987). Second, humans possess linguistic abilities that allow them to attribute socially constructed meanings to their organismic experiences. Third, humans are capable of forethought and afterthought which allow them to both plan the future and reflect on the past as unique sources of information (Bandura, 1978; Smith, 1978). Fourth, a person needs a social context in which to become a person. One's experience and concept of the self are continuously defined in one's experience in interaction (Smith, 1978). Personhood seems meaningless without it. Fifth, human personhood is characterized by reflexivity, the ability to represent one's self to one's self. It is this ability that allows a person to develop an awareness of self.

Hence, the term *self* is reserved for one's reflexive awareness of one's own behavior, thoughts, and feelings—that is, one's person. This definition is quite in keeping with the original Anglo-Saxon meaning of the word *self* as same (as in *selfsame*). In evolutionary terms, humans began as organisms, eventually became persons, and, in the process, discovered and created their selves (Crook, 1980). The human organism achieved personhood through his or her symbolizing and self-reflexive capacities. As part of the ongoing process of physical and cultural evolution, human beings learned to symbolize and express their experiences to other human beings, thereby developing intersubjective links among human persons.

It seems linguistically more accurate to describe the self as the awareness of one's own person, that is, the immediate experience as well as the concepts that one holds about one's person. By keeping person and self separate, I hope to avoid such terminological quandaries as the self relating to itself or the self being defined as the collection of self-representations that one holds about the self (Markus & Wurf, 1987). As Westen (1992) has pointed out with respect to the meaning of the term *self-representation*, this definition of self leads to the question of what is being represented. "The only consistent use of the term *self* is to use it . . . to refer to the person" (p. 7). Selfhood, most simply put, refers to one's reflexive awareness of one's personhood.

With self and person clearly distinguished, it then should be apparent that much of what has been attributed to the self, such as what psychodynamic theorists have referred to as ego functions, is more appropriately attributed to the person. Such functions include perception, thought, and memory. Self thus refers to an experiential or conceptual awareness of the person in interaction with the world, which of course would include these functions. This model would therefore eschew any notion of the self as a mental executive. Executive functions reside within the person, but when a person becomes aware of his or her own executive functions in action, through his or her immediate experience or concepts about these functions that have been stored in memory, one can then legitimately speak of the person's self-awareness of these functions (Westen, 1992).

The person is conceived of as an experiencing organism that acquires socially constructed meanings through learning. In terms of this model, human beings are viewed as constant meaning makers, that is, they are involved in a continuous process of acquiring and constructing emotion-laden or emotion-free beliefs about the self, others, and the world. Many of these become deeply held beliefs that are not immediately in the person's focal awareness. The process of acquiring and constructing meanings involves a person experiencing physical and symbolic events in the world and sifting through these experiences for meanings that pertain to one's self. In a humorous vein, Baumeister (1991) captured this unique human characteristic—an organism existing within an inescapable web of socially constructed meaning—by referring to the self as "the beast with a credit card and a social security number" (p. 4).

Mind, Body, and the Self

The mind–body problem continues to pose a problem, despite the fact that many philosophers and psychologists feel that they have provided satisfactory philosophic and scientific solutions to the dilemma (Churchland, 1986; Damasio, 1994; Pribram, 1986; Sperry, 1988). Space does not allow a detailed coverage of this debate, but suffice it to say that although the organismic substrate of experience and particularly self-experience cannot be denied, the precise relationships between subjective experience and biological processes have not as yet been clearly delineated. For example, it is true that there is no independent existence of a conscious mind apart from a functioning brain; but it is equally true that it has been difficult to show the precise relationships between phenomenal experience and patterns of brain function. One cannot begin with brain function and predict subjective experience; without first referring to phenomenal experience, one cannot know to what the empirically derived neurobiological regularities refer. As Arnold (1960) has suggested, "Only on the basis of a phenomenological analysis of the psychological activities from perception to emotion and action will it be possible to work out a theory of brain function that provides a neural correlate for psychological experience" (p. 17). The paramount question, then, is whether subjective experience can be reduced to brain states and, if so, how (Churchland, 1986). I assume that there is a neurobiological foundation for all subjective experience without committing myself to a particular view as to the precise relationships between the patterns of neural firing and specific experiences of self and world.

Those investigators who have been brave enough to speculate about the neurobiological–experiential bridge seem to be heading in the same direction. Both Melzack (1989) and Damasio (1994) grounded mental imagery—and therefore experience in general—in the patterned webs of neural firings. Moreover, both suggested a neurological basis for recognizing one's own body and that one's anatomy as well as body sensations belongs to one's self. Melzack posited a body–self matrix, whereas Damasio suggested that the self is a continuously repeated biological state involving the activation of two kinds of self-representations: (a) autobiographical representations and

(b) primordial representations of the individual body. In addition, Damasio posited a metaself that is aware of one's organism as it is perceiving and acting. Both of these conceptions provide a foundation for what can be called the embodied self, which is formed by biologically mediated information processing. Although the particular contents of self-representations may be mostly, if not completely, socioculturally based mental constructions, they are all felt in the body and therefore based in neurobiological processes. As investigators have increasingly noted, it is now difficult to properly conceptualize such former disembodied mentalisms as *self, mind,* and *subjectivity* without some conception that all of these are embodied.[1] Here is a subjectively experienced self, neurologically explained, that can be the subject of immediate organismic experience that subsequently can be conceptualized, and those conceptualizations can be reflected on by the person.

To reiterate Melzack's (1989) conclusion, "it is evident that the brain processes that underlie the experience of our bodies must include the signal that says: this is *my* body, it belongs to *me*, is part of my *self*" (p. 5). No model of the self, integrative or otherwise, can be complete without an awareness that our experience of the self is based in organismic processes. That self-experience has a biological foundation should be past denying. At the same time, however, I retain some doubt about the extent to which subjective experiences can be reduced to specific neurobiological processes. No one-to-one isomorphism between symbolically constructed experience and organismic process has been—or probably can be—established. Models of self phenomena based on the simplified assumption that experience is merely the epiphenomena of neurological processes are surely in need of some revision. On the other hand, models of self phenomena that ignore their biological underpinnings are also in need of revision. If the code linking biology to experience is ever going to be cracked, technological breakthroughs in the future are needed. For now, it must suffice to argue that subjectively experienced meaning is simultaneously a personal, symbolic construction as well as an organismic reality. This is what is meant by the *embodied self*.

The Significance of Human Reflexivity

I have explained how subjectivity and self-experience might emerge from neurobiological processes. One complication, however, of this understanding of the biological contribution to the self is the fact that human beings not only have a biological basis for their perceptions and reactions to external events but also, because of our reflexive capacities, routinely have second-order reactions to bodily experiences associated with these same per-

---

[1]Several theorists have taken up the theme of the embodied mind or self in recent books. See, for example, G. Edelman (1992), *Bright Air, Brilliant Fire: On the Matter of the Mind*; M. Johnson (1987), *The Body in the Mind: The Bodily Basis of Meaning, Imagination, and Reason*; and F. Varela, E. Thompson, and E. Rosch (1992), *The Embodied Mind: Cognitive Science and Human Experience*.

ceptions and reactions. For example, if a person is experiencing acrophobia, a fear of heights, he or she will react with fear when standing atop a tall building. But the body sensations associated with the fear of heights make him or her even more fearful. These reflexive reactions also have a biological basis. It is, however, not immediately clear how the neurobiological processes associated with the phobic fear articulate with the neurobiological processes correlated with our fear-of-fear. Also unclear are the differences at the level of neurobiology between becoming excited at a football game and noticing ourselves becoming excited at the game. This second-order reflexive capacity, unique to humans, allows us to ponder or cogitate the significance of our first-order perceptions and responses.

Whether human reflexivity is an evolutionary emergent, as Crook (1980) suggested, or a product of language, as Smith (1978) contended, our reflexive capacities are integral to our understanding of what we mean when we refer to specific characteristics of the self. For Crook, human reflexivity, or the individual's ability to represent one's self to one's self, is what turns the human organism into a human person. This self-process

> makes it possible to learn about the relationship between bodily states and emotion and different experiences of identity. It is this connection that in turn allows an individual to express his own emotion to another and, further, eventually to appreciate the intentionality of another through empathy. The complex intersubjectivity of human relationships would be impossible without these abilities. (Crook, 1980, p. 243)

The person's relationship with the self is primary. Because of human reflexivity, everything that a person may think and feel about another, he or she can think and feel about his or her self. One can even deceive one's self, as one can another person (Wachtel, 2001).

Although reflexivity makes self-experience possible, a compulsive form of reflexive self-experiencing (i.e., obsessive cogitation) is typically associated with most anxiety disorders as well as other forms of psychopathology (Barlow, 1988; Ingram, 1990; Wolfe, 1995). In fact, obsessive cogitation is a key indicator of a person's sense of vulnerability, a state that can become so intense that it is next to impossible for the person to contact and understand his or her emotional experience. There is definitely a dark side to human reflexivity.

The Process of Experiencing, Symbolizing, and Construing

In this model, experiencing is one of two basic human processes by which we relate to the world, other people, and ourselves. The results or contents of the experiencing process are experiences, and as such, represent the basic data of human functioning. Experiencing is conceived of as a continuous cycle of feeling-based information processing that involves the reception of internal or external information, the appraisal of the meaning of that information, and the rapid processing of response options. Experiencing involves the symbolization of our perceptions and body sensations. Subjectively, experiencing is the process of becoming aware of *felt meanings*. Initially, experience is preconceptual, but as we focus on our experience we become aware of its personal meaning. By paying attention to the feelings and sensations in his or her body, a person eventually will construe their meaning. "Experiencing is thus implicitly meaningful. It is something present, directly referred to and felt" (Gendlin, 1962, p. 243).

By this means, an individual becomes aware of the *felt meanings* of a given situation. Felt meanings refer to how some situation, concept, or person feels to the individual—the feeling qualities associated with one's thoughts (Gendlin, 1962). Felt meanings, which imply an affective-based appraisal process, can be located on a feeling spectrum that can range from virtually little or no feeling attached to one's thoughts to a full-blown emotional experience.

Self-experiencing, therefore, refers to the person's continuous perception, evaluation, and assimilation (or rejection) of internally generated or externally imposed felt meanings. When we directly experience ourselves, we perceive and symbolize our in-the-moment experiences of our person acting and interacting in the physical and social world. This is Gendlin's (1962) notion of experiencing as a process by which we symbolize our sensory and visceral reactions.

A second basic process by which we relate to the world is cogitation,[2] which means thinking about. When we cogitate, we reflect on the various thoughts and beliefs we have internalized. When we cogitate about ourselves, we reflect on stored or constructed ideas about ourselves. We think about ourselves almost as if we are contemplating the attributes of a separate individual. The cogitating self is akin to the Jamesian *Me*. Cogitating is also the Meadian process of taking ourselves as an object and viewing ourselves as others might see us.

When we cogitate about ourselves, we shift the focus of our attention away from our direct, organismic experience toward the stored emotion-based conceptualizations we possess about ourselves. The positive form of cogitation is reflection, which allows us to take stock to locate ourselves socially and to plan for the near and distant future, on the basis of our conception of our abilities. The negative form of cogitation is perseveration, that is, the spontaneous recurrence in the mind of the same affect-laden idea or mental image. In the extreme, perseveration shades into obsessive cogitation. I want to clarify that cogitation does not involve just thoughts. It also involves feel-

---

[2]In earlier articles (e.g., Wolfe, 1992, 1995), I described *cogitation* as "reflexive self-awareness" and *direct experiencing* as "sentient self-awareness." As it is now clear that the process of symbolizing direct experience is also a reflexive process, I have changed the terminology.

ings (i.e., emotion-based appraisals) and feelings about feelings. As one of my patients put it, "I am afraid of being afraid."

In contrast, focusing one's attention on one's direct, immediate experience enhances the possibility of new learning and of changing old ideas. Whenever an individual attempts to learn a new skill, there may be resistance not only because of a fear of failure but also because one's stored concepts and images of one's self do not include the mastery of that skill. The direct experience of one successfully performing the skill has a good chance of resulting in a positive self-evaluation and a modification of one's self-concept. The impact of direct experience on previously stored representations of the self (if one is open to it)[3] is hypothesized to be the most efficient means to new learning and new living.

Attentional Focus in Self-Knowledge

Our conscious experience and the information we obtain from it depend on how we allocate our attention. We may focus attention on internally and externally generated information. Internally, we pay attention to bodily sensations and their meaning, that is, to felt meanings. We also pay attention to beliefs and constructs about ourselves, that is, who we are or what we can or cannot do. We also pay attention to internalized standards and use these as guides to evaluate our actions and communications as well as to compare ourselves and our behavior to that of others. In addition, we pay attention to memories of our experiences and to self-generated images or ideas of what is believed to be real, what is feared might be real, and what is hoped is real.

In the external environment, we pay attention to the physical events of the world, which take place outside our skin. We also pay attention to interpersonal and sociocultural meanings of external events, particularly to the meaning of what people say and do. Attention is as likely to be paid to internal events (e.g., memories, thoughts, and images) as it is to the external sensory flow. Thus it is possible for individuals to engage in a process of attending to and interpreting the meaning of internal stimuli without aid from any information from the environment.

There are certain kinds of information to which individuals do not wish to pay attention. These include (a) painful emotions such as humiliation and despair (this includes the body sensations that constitute the feelings as well as the meanings associated with the dysphoric feelings) and (b) painful violations of implicit or explicit expectations of what they will perceive in the world (e.g., the world is not a safe place).

---

[3] I will mention momentarily, and consider in greater detail in the next chapter, the numerous ways in which people prevent themselves from being open to their organismic experience.

Human beings have developed numerous ways to avoid paying attention to painful or self-diminishing information. In attempting to cope with painful realities, people learn or develop a variety of ways of interrupting or shifting their focus of attention. These defensive interruptions of one's direct experience are covered in more detail in the next chapter. The point is that different information is obtained from the different foci of attention. When we allow ourselves to be in contact with the world and become aware of the self-relevant felt meanings of that contact, we are directly experiencing the world. Felt meanings register immediately, even though their full implications may not be understood until much later. The information yielded by direct experience involves two classes of felt meanings: (a) the immediate apprehension of various senses of self and (b) the felt meanings of the communications and actions of others toward us. Theorists have identified a number of experienced senses of self, including agency, physical coherence, continuous identity, authenticity, and a sense of being subjectively different than others. This list is not comprehensive but rather includes the senses of self generally thought to be involved in the organization of personal and social experience (Blasi, 1988; G. S. Klein, 1976; Pine, 1990; Stern, 1985). As Stern (1985) has suggested, we directly experience many senses of self:

> There is a sense of self that is a single distinct integrated body; there is the agent of actions, the experiencer of feelings, the maker of intentions, the architect of plans, the transposer of experience into language, the communicator and sharer of personal knowledge. (pp. 5–6)

As a felt experience, the sense of self, in any of the previously mentioned dimensions, can vary from fragile to solid, from vaguely sensed to fully articulated. One's in-the-moment awareness of self is characterized by expansions and contractions in all of the various senses of self. For example, a person's sense of agency may vary from experiencing one's self as a passive victim of events to experiencing one's self as the chief executive of one's life, and the individual may feel different ways in different situations.

In addition to the various in-the-moment senses of self, direct experience provides information regarding the individual's felt meanings that result from communications and actions of others toward him or her. Becoming aware, for example, during an argument with a loved one, that one is both hurt and angered by the loved one's sarcasm illustrates the direct experience of felt meanings. It is important to note that direct experience involves contact with the outer world, openness to the information made available by such contact, and the emotional processing of immediate self-relevant information made possible by such openness.

The information yielded by cogitation includes various beliefs about the self, or self-representations. These representations occur to us in various formats: (a) propositions, (b) images, and (c) somatic traces. For example, we may become aware of the proposition that we are endangered, or we may

TABLE 5.1

Comparison of the Experiential and Rational Systems

Experiential system	Rational system
More holistic	More analytic
More emotional; pleasure- and pain-oriented (what feels good)	More logical; reason-oriented (what is sensible)
More associationistic	More cause-and-effect analysis
Encodes reality in concrete images and metaphors	Encodes reality in abstract symbols (words and numbers)
Orients toward immediate action; rapid processing	Orients toward delayed action; slower processing
Changes with repetitive experience, direct or vicarious; relatively slow to change	Changes relatively rapidly with speed of thought
Experiences passively and preconsciously; seized by emotions	Experiences actively and consciously; in control of thoughts
Self-evidently valid; "Experiencing is believing"	Requires justification via logic and evidence

Note. I have included only those comparisons that easily comport with my theoretical model. There are several comparisons with which I disagree. From "The Relational Self" (p. 123), edited by R. C. Curtis, 1991, New York: Guilford Press. Copyright 1991 by Guilford Press. Adapted with permission.

recall an image or memory of a specific instance in which we were in danger. Or we may have in our conscious awareness only the bodily sensations (i.e., somatic traces) associated with context-specific memories, images, or beliefs about one's self in danger that have not been—or, at that moment, cannot be—articulated.

This conception of two ways of knowing the self is similar in some respects to the cognitive–experiential self theory of Epstein (1991). According to this theory, most behavior is automatically regulated by an experiential conceptual system that operates primarily at the preconscious level of awareness; the rules of operation for this system differ from that of the more rational cognitive conceptual system. Epstein's experiential and cognitive conceptual systems map fairly well on the two processes of self-knowledge described here: direct experiencing and cogitation. Epstein provides a table that compares the features of the two systems (see Table 5.1).

Like Epstein, I argue that each process has advantages and disadvantages. An integration of these two self-knowledge processes will yield better information for action and decision making than would a reliance on either alone. An example may make this clearer. A person is offered two jobs. The first has a better salary and more opportunity for advancement. Relying on one's rational capacities alone would point to the first job opportunity, without question. The second job, however, involves work that the individual loves and finds most personally satisfying. Relying on feelings alone may lead the person to accept a position in which he or she is trapped with no clear path to advancement and no clear indication that the salary will ever improve. Integrating both sources of information, however, might lead to a decision to pursue a third opportunity that has a clear advancement track and a better salary than the second and involves at least some work that the person truly loves to perform. If I were counseling such an individual, I would ask him or her to conceptually review what is important with respect to a job. I would then do some imagery work by having the person imagine what it would be like to go through a workday in each of the positions under consideration. Then it would be up to the individual to integrate the information obtained and to use it as he or she wishes en route to making a decision.

Another example may make clear the kind of difficulty an individual may encounter when he or she relies on just one source of information and totally ignores the other. I once worked with a young man who was in search of the right mate. He was living at the time with a young woman whom he thoroughly enjoyed and even seemed to love. But he also had an extensive list of characteristics that the right mate for him should possess. His current love possessed some but not all of the characteristics on the list. He therefore concluded that she was not appropriate for him for a long-term commitment. When I asked him about his daily experience of the relationship, he described it in rather glowing terms. But she would never be his mate because she lacked several characteristics on the list. One could easily postulate that the list served some unconscious motive of this individual to protect him from having to make a commitment. However, at the level of his conscious experience, he was focusing exclusive attention on only one source of information, the list, which represented his cognitive analysis of the appropriate mate, and totally ignoring another source of information, his day-to-day experience with the woman with whom he lives.

PROCESSES IN DEVELOPING SELF-KNOWLEDGE

In this section I discuss the several different processes by which individuals can develop self-knowledge. First I address the two paths of knowing the self, then the role of emotions in self-knowledge, and finally the place of the unconscious and preconscious in these processes.

Two Ways of Knowing the Self

Self-knowledge is obtained through the dynamic interaction of the two ways of knowing the self: (a) direct experiencing and (b) cogitation. Guidano (1991) conceptualized the interaction as follows: the *Experiencing I* is always a step ahead of the *Explaining Me*. He viewed the process of self-understanding or the acquisition of self-knowledge as entailing an endless circularity between the immediate experience of one's self (the acting and experiencing *I*) and the sense of self that emerges as a result of abstractly self-referring the ongoing experience (the observing and evaluating *Me*).

The self as subject and the self as object, Guidano argued, emerge as irreducible dimensions of a selfhood dynamic. The acting and experiencing *I* is always one step ahead of the current appraisal of the situation, and the evaluating *Me* becomes a continuous process of reordering and reconstructing one's conscious sense of self.

Bypassing One's Organismic Experience

But Guidano captured only part of the process by envisioning the cycle running always from organismically based direct experience to conceptualization. People very often bypass their organismic responses entirely, moving instead from conception to conception, from idea to idea, about one's self. In fact, frequently, one of the negative consequences of the Western bias that demeans emotion in favor of reason is that it encourages this organismic bypass. The result is that a very important source of self-related information is frequently ignored or suppressed. For example, the individual who fails to pay attention to the accumulating bodily felt disenchantments with a romantic partner (because conceptually, he or she appears to fit the bill) may soon be in for a rude awakening.

In fact, there seems to be some reciprocal relationships between the two sources of self-information. Negative self-concepts narrow the range, intensity, and expressiveness of organismic experiencing. But truncated senses of self reinforce negative self-concepts.

The Dialectic Between Experiencing and Conceptualizing

L. S. Greenberg et al. (1993), I believe, were closer to the mark in their description of a personal meaning construction process that involves a dialectic between reflexive and acquired conceptions of the self (what we have been calling the *Me*) and one's immediate experience of how things actually are (the *I*). They envisioned two sources of information dialectically interacting in the creation of personal meaning and self-experience. The first source is what they called a set of processors that automatically generate emotional experience. The second source of self-experience and meaning is our conscious synthesizing construction process. This process, which is involved in problem solving and adaptation, is highly dependent on our attentional focus and conceptual capacities. Conscious self-experience can be based on our organismic experience, social learning, learned conditions of worth, or introjects obtained from others or inferred from past experience.

L. S. Greenberg et al. (1993) seemed to be arguing that individuals have a choice regarding which source of information to focus on reflexively: their conceptual and emotional information stored in memory or their in-the-moment experience. In their words, "Consciousness is thus the arena for the dialectical synthesis of the different sources of information about the self as the person encounters and resolves felt contradictions between aspects of self and between self and the world" (1993, p. 60).

The Optimal Relationship Between the Two Forms of Self-Knowledge

Whereas Guidano's description seems to capture only the optimal use of organismic experience, L. S. Greenberg et al.'s (1993) view provides for several more options regarding the possible interactions between the two sources of self-related information. Both models do, however—as does mine—tilt in favor of the role that direct experience of contact with the world plays in providing the optimal information for the construction of healthy self-schemas or, in my lexicon, self-images and self-beliefs. In other words, the basic hypothesis underlying my model is that the most reliable source of information for a particular self-belief is one's own bodily felt experience that occurs while one is in action and interaction. At the same time, however, what all three models suggest is that the optimal *I* and *Me* dynamics would entail a healthy balance between immediate and conceptual experience, that is, between experiencing and cogitation.

Emotional Processing and Self-Knowledge

A large proportion of self-knowledge involves emotional processing of self-relevant meanings, ideas, and images. In this model, emotions involve immediate, intuitive appraisals of the personal significance of interactions and events (Arnold, 1960). Emotions are often accompanied by certain action tendencies (L. S. Greenberg & Safran, 1987) and there is often a degree of specificity between the emotion that is experienced and the type of situation that typically elicits it. For example, persons typically experience sadness when they lose a loved one by either death or a broken relationship, and anger when an expectation has been violated or when someone transgresses against them. In the process of interacting with other people, persons experience in-the-moment, emotion-based, self-relevant meanings of these interactions. These perceptions may or may not be conscious in the moment. Often the emotional significance of an interaction becomes clear later, when a person replays the imagery of the interaction and pays closer attention to the emotional meanings that were attributed to these interactions. Because emotional experience possesses hefty somatic and imagery components, emotional meanings can be discovered through a replay of the imagery of an interaction or by an attentional focus on the accompanying somatic sensations. Later in the book, I describe a focusing technique that facilitates the process of articulating emotional meanings implied by one's sensory or visceral reactions. The complete processing of an emotional experience leads to a shift in the nature of the emotional experience. Fully experienced and processed anger, for example, often shifts into a sense of greater acceptance of the person who initially was the target of the anger (Gendlin, 1978; L. S. Greenberg et al., 1993).

The product of emotional processing of self-relevant information is specific ideas, beliefs, and images about the self (i.e., self-concept) and others. Repeated or intense experiences tend to increase the stability of a particular belief about the self. These beliefs are probably organized hierarchically (Mahoney, 1991), varying from easy-to-change surface-level self-beliefs to extremely difficult-to-change core self-beliefs. Self-beliefs stored in memory appear to be quite influential in terms of priming persons to choose certain people with whom to interact (Swann, 1990) and certain environments in which to interact (Goldfried & Robins, 1983).

Emotional Adaptation Level

The somatic sensations associated with the processing of emotional meanings can vary from mild to extremely intense, from manageable to overwhelming. At some point, and for a variety of motivations, persons automatically block out very intense emotional experience or at least attempt to reduce or control the intensity. Persons seem to vary in terms of an emotional adaptation level, which refers to the amount and intensity of body-based feelings that they can tolerate. Emotionally overcontrolled individuals possess a very low adaptational level; for them, the experience of minute body sensations associated with emotions can cause anxiety. At the other extreme, individuals with a very high adaptational level seem to be comfortable with intensely felt emotions and energetically expressed feelings. The experience of feeling beyond one's emotional adaptation level is often perceived as losing control.

Imagery and Metaphors in Emotional Processing

Emotional meanings are frequently represented in the mind as images or metaphors. The extent to which our mental life is governed by metaphors may be the single most underestimated aspect of our subjectivity. Lakoff and Johnson (1981) contended that virtually all of our conceptual categories are metaphorical in nature, grounded in our everyday experience. And these metaphors structure "how we perceive, how we think, and what we do" (p. 4).

The close connection between emotional processing and the experience of personally relevant meanings is nicely summarized by L. S. Greenberg et al.:

> Personal meaning . . . essentially depends on affect. . . . In a sense, feelings are ultimately the meeting place of mind, body, environment, culture, and behavior. They can bring together in conscious experience various physiological and hormonal changes, appraisals of the self and situation, memories, cultural rules, and characteristic expressions and behaviors." (1993, pp. 53–54)

Preconscious and Unconscious Information Processing in the
Development of Self-Knowledge

Unconscious processes traditionally have been the dividing line between behavioral and psychodynamic conceptions of human behavior. Behavioral psychologists have always demanded a level of empirical proof of unconscious phenomena that psychoanalysts were either unable or disinclined to provide. As mentioned before, evidence has mounted from several diverse fields of psychological research supporting a concept of a psychological unconscious (Greenwald, 1992; Shevrin & Dickman, 1980). This research supports the idea of information processing taking place outside an individual's focal awareness, but it does not come close, either in conception of the research aims or in its findings, to the psychoanalytic notion of the dynamic unconscious or even its simplified stand-in, unconsciously motivated forgetting.

Clinically, however, a number of observable phenomena make the inference of unconscious motivation compelling: (a) the inconsistencies between verbalization and behavior and between observable signs of emotions and a quality of vocal expression that belies them; (b) the phenomena of phobias that often involve intense morbid fear of objects that even the individual with the phobia knows cannot bring him or her any harm; (c) the repetitive choice of a toxic individual for a primary relationship; and (d) the phenomena of transference, which often involve puzzling (to the patient as well as to the therapist) reactions by the patient to the behavior or verbalizations of the therapist. These are just a few of the myriad situations that have been frequently observed in the therapy context and that are difficult to explain without inferring an unconscious reason behind them.

Our self-views (i.e., self-concepts, beliefs, and images) not only lie outside our focal awareness for much of our waking life but also are enormously influential in the everyday decisions we make about (a) which people we will have in our lives, (b) which vocational and avocational possibilities we will pursue, (c) what will become our supreme passion, and (d) what our boundaries of self are to be. Sometimes these self-views are conscious, but more often they are not. I remember a young college freshman I once saw in therapy who came to a session one fateful day after having just been told that he did not have the potential for a career as a concert pianist. He sat and violently shook, trembled, and cried for just about the entire therapy hour. It took the better part of that session and the next for him to realize that his belief that he was destined to become a concert pianist was the linchpin of his current identity or self-concept—and he would have to give up both his dream and his self-concept as a potential concert musician.

It also seems clear that although many of these beliefs and images are accessible to our conscious awareness, their influence may be felt even when we are not consciously aware of any particular self-belief. A person who typically sees him- or herself as reserved and not one who likes to be the center of attention might have difficulty responding to a request to spontaneously entertain at a cocktail party.

The process of acquiring self-knowledge, then, includes unconscious and preconscious phenomena, often the source of internally generated information. This information, in conjunction with external information determined by one's attentional focus, produces a conscious experience of self. When all is working well, the integration or dialectical synthesis of information obtained from both experiencing and cogitation leads to positive and comfortable ideas, beliefs, and images of the self.

THE CONTENTS OF OUR SELF-KNOWLEDGE

Thus far, I have focused on the dynamic interaction of our self-relevant direct experiencing and cogitating as the process by which we obtain self-knowledge. But what is it that we obtain? Although a precise understanding of the internalized structures of self-knowledge is lacking, it is clear from both research and clinical evidence that our self-related experiences become organized into concepts and images[4] that implicitly or explicitly describe our interpretation of self-related events. The development of one's self-concept is a very social phenomenon. Not only does it occur primarily in an interpersonal context, but the terms of self-conception are also socially generated. As Neisser (1976) suggested, "A child eventually comes to . . . think of himself [sic] as a particular kind of person, but only with the aid of socially developed conceptions of what a person might be" (p. 192). For this reason, the contents of one's self-concept may vary with culture and historical epoch.

The Construction of Our Self-Beliefs

On the basis of her extensive research on the development of self-concepts in childhood and adolescence, Harter (1999) suggested that the individual's construction of a self-concept is both a cognitive and a social phenomenon. She traced out normative-developmental changes in self-concept as individuals move through early, middle, and late childhood and early, middle, and late adolescence. Cognitive development throughout these stages produces an increasingly differentiated set of self-representations across various domains of experience. The older child eventually is able to distinguish between real and ideal self-concepts which can be subjected to comparison and which may result in discrepancies that often are problematic.

---

[4]Space does not allow me to describe in any detail the very interesting debate in the cognitive psychology literature over whether images, propositions, or a third option in between represents the basic irreducible element of mental representation (see M. Johnson, 1987; Kosslyn, 1980; Pylyshyn, 1984).

With their newly developed cognitive capabilities, adolescents can construct multiple self-concepts in different relational contexts.

In addition, cognitive abilities that develop over time allow the creation of a more integrated set of self-representations. This becomes possible because the individual eventually is able to construct higher-order generalizations about the self. In middle childhood, an individual begins to construct a concept of self-worth (i.e., global self-esteem). In adolescence, the further development of cognitive abilities allows the individual to synthesize seemingly contradictory self-representations (e.g., How can I be both happy and sad?) into meaningful beliefs about the self (e.g., I'm a complex person).

Our self-concept is also a social construction. Harter (1999) detailed the various socialization experiences with caregivers, peers, and teachers that produce the particular content and valence of an individual's self-representations. That the self-concept is both a cognitive and a social construction highlights the fact that children are both active agents in the construction of their self-concept and passive recipients of attributions and evaluations of their particular caregivers.

The Content of Our Identity

Many of these self-beliefs are organized as part of a larger entity: our identity. Identity, as Westen (1991) noted, includes several senses of self, including a sense of continuity in our lived experience and a sense of stability in how we see ourselves (i.e., our self-representations). Moreover, it includes a sense that we are recognized by others as identical to who we say we are. In addition, our identity includes a number of self-conceptions that express our cultural and ideological commitments (e.g., I am a Reformed Jew or a charismatic Christian). These self-beliefs and commitments are emotionally weighted, revealing the importance of seeing ourselves in these particular ways.

The contents of our identity influence the choices we make and the actions we take, which are often in the service of influencing others to validate our beliefs about ourselves. Sometimes, we seek validation from others of negative beliefs that we hold about ourselves, and we may reject those individuals who invalidate these beliefs with excessive praise (Swann, 1990).

Westen summed up his view of identity in the following manner:

> Identity thus includes a coherent self-concept, an investment in goals and standards that make life meaningful and worthwhile, a weighting of the importance of various aspects of the self, and meaningful attempts to actualize one's ideal self-schemas. It also includes two other elements. The first is a commitment to a set of cognitive principles that orient one to the world; these may be largely unconscious but include ideological commitments typically related to values. In anthropological terms, this refers to a commitment to both an "ethos" and a "world view" . . . that is to both a set of moral, esthetic, and evaluative principles that govern

one's actions, and a "picture of the way things in sheer actuality are," including fundamental assumptions about the world, society, and the self. (1991, p. 190)

Values and Identity

Our ideological commitments and our moral and ethical values contain a number of standards by which we evaluate our behavior. As Bandura (1978) suggested, these standards are acquired through "precept, evaluative consequences accompanying different performances, and exposure to the self-evaluative standards of others" (p. 353). The healthy functioning person does not passively absorb standards from the environment (one hallmark of neurotic living is that one does just this). Instead, the healthy individual selects generic standards from the many evaluations supplied by others regarding different activities in different settings. He or she synthesizes the divergent information to arrive at personal standards against which to compare his or her behavior. The importance of self-standards lies in the rather trite truism that people feel good about themselves when they behave according to their standards and feel bad when they do not. Much self-related misery observed in psychotherapy patients stems not only from transgression of their own standards but also from internal conflicts between different self-standards or between standards and wishes. The work of Strauman and Higgins suggests that different emotional consequences correspond to discrepancies among different types of self-standards (Higgins, 1987; Strauman & Higgins, 1988).

The Cultural Patterning of Our Identity

Another aspect is the cultural patterning of our identity and its constituent self-conceptions and to some extent the process of self-experiencing. For example, the Western emphasis on individualism shapes a very different view of the self than does a collectivist orientation that characterizes many present and past traditional societies (Westen, 1991). The historical era also makes a significant difference with respect to how the self is viewed and experienced. Westen (1991) suggested:

> . . . that selfhood has changed dramatically since the rise of agriculture and again since the Industrial Revolution in the West, and that this appears ultimately to occur everywhere similar social transformations occur. Indeed, available evidence suggests that technological development is associated with changes in self-structure and value orientations related to individualism in people maximally exposed to modernizing forces even in traditionally collectivistic cultures. (p. 204)

The growing importance of the self-concept in Western society is now thought to be, by many investigators, itself a product of cultural evolution (Baumeister, 1991; Broughton, 1986; F. Johnson, 1985; Westen, 1991). As Westen (1991) has noted, however, cultural differences need to be carefully distinguished from the impact of more universal forces. It is not yet entirely clear what self phenomena, if any, are universal. Contents of self-knowledge, then, are bounded by culture, history, language, social location within a particular society, and the idiosyncratic personal experiences within an individual's family or peer group.

Self-With-Other Representations

Not only do we form mental representations pertaining to specific characteristics, traits, and feelings related to the self, but we also form summary beliefs and images of our interactions with others (i.e., how we act and feel with specific other people). Theorists from both psychodynamic and cognitive therapy traditions have suggested that human beings store many representations that involve how the self generally behaves with specific others. Kernberg (1976), from the psychodynamic perspective, spoke of self and object representations linked by a particular affect disposition. Kohut (1977) described a process of internalizing *selfobjects*, which are people or things outside of the self that become vitally necessary to the individual. Horowitz (1988) spoke of role–relationship models, which are mental schemas that allow the person to interpret what another person is intending, whereas Stern (1985) suggested that even an infant develops summary generalizations of interactions with his or her mother that he called *RIGS* (i.e., representations of interactions that have become generalized).

Safran and Segal (1991), from a more cognitive perspective, referred to similar phenomena as interpersonal schemas, which pertain to beliefs and expectations about specific others as well as assumptions regarding how the individual must act to maintain safety in the relationship. These *self-with-other representations*, as Ogilvie and Ashmore (1991) have labeled them, refer to images that we form of "what we are like and how we feel when we are with specific other people in our lives" (p. 286).

Although mostly unconscious, self-with-other representations appear to be very influential in terms of defining the boundaries of permissible behavior and feelings with specific individuals: "I can allow myself to be angry with Mom, but I don't dare show any sign of anger to my father." In the optimum case, self-with-other representations are capable of growth and change, which involves the revision of earlier representations to make them more congruent with interactive experiences in the present. Rigid and unchanging self-with-other representations characterize the internal life of people experiencing very different forms of psychopathology.

Sources of Beliefs and Images About the Self, or Self-Representations

If self-representations vary by class, historical era, and culture, what are their specific sources? Some self-representations result from inferences that people make about their attitudes and dispositions while watching their own actions; some make inferences on the basis of their physiological reactions—their cognitions, emotions, and motivations. Representations also derive from direct attempts at self-assessment. People also learn about themselves from others, through both social comparison and direct interactions. Some self-representations come from a wholesale internalization of the opinions of others. Some self-representations may be characterized as aspirations, ideal views of the self that a person hopes someday to merit (Markus & Nurius, 1986). These aspired-to self-representations may underlie a person's commitment and motivation to achieve in a certain sphere of activity (e.g., "I will become a concert pianist. That is all I ever wanted to do."). Individual role models, celebrities, or people who have been influential in the individual's life often serve as major sources of ideal self-aspirations.

POSITIVE SELF-KNOWLEDGE

Now I take a closer look at what positive self-knowledge looks like. In this model, healthy self-knowledge is based on an integration of information acquired from several sources, most particularly from one's organismic experience and one's increasingly complex, accurate, and sophisticated conceptualizations of how the physical and social worlds operate. Self-knowledge becomes increasingly trustworthy to the extent that it is based on an ability to listen to one's organismic experience and acquire accurate information regarding the social and physical environments. This view is similar to the Rogerian idea of openness to experience, which Rogers (1961) believed encompassed both of the previously mentioned processes:

> To the extent that this person is open to all of his experience, he has access to all of the available data in the situation, on which to base his behavior. He has knowledge of his own feelings and impulses, which are often complex and contradictory. He is freely able to sense social demands, from the relatively rigid social "laws" to the desires of family and friends. He has access to his memories of similar situations, and the consequences of different behaviors in those situations. He has a relatively accurate perception of this external situation in all of its complexity. . . . Out of this complex weighing and balancing he is able to discover that course of action which seems to come closest to satisfying all of his needs in the situation, long-range as well as immediate needs. (p. 118)

Through the integration of these various sources of self-knowledge, the person not only retains a positive view of him- or herself but also is more likely to make beneficial life decisions.

The Nature of Self-Esteem

There are many facets of positive self-knowledge for which there are different but corresponding terms, such as self-confidence, self-esteem, self-efficacy, self-control, self-mastery, and resilience. Each of these achievements is presumed to result from a proactive stance toward the world and other people in which one actively confronts whatever situation one faces and, more often than not, achieves mastery or success. Each success is felt bodily and therefore becomes part of our organismic experience, which in turn modifies the preexisting ideas people have about themselves. When people learn a new skill, for example, they may have had doubts that they could master this skill (e.g., using a personal computer). Once they master the skill, however, their ideas about themselves expand to now include a realization that they can confidently use a computer. Here I am merely suggesting that when all goes well and the connection between direct experience and stored self-idea is not interrupted, experience does eventually lead to the modification of one's self-concept. But there are other positives, less often discussed, associated with an increasing awareness of one's emotional experience.

Facing Reality and Self-Esteem

Self-esteem is the term that is usually used to describe a general characteristic of positive self-regard. Bednar and Peterson (1995) defined self-esteem as "an enduring and affective sense of personal value based on accurate self-perceptions" (p. 4). In an interesting departure from mainstream wisdom, Bednar and Peterson argued that self-esteem relates more to how individuals deal with feedback than to the nature of the feedback itself. They did not view rejection as a major cause of low self-esteem. Instead, they suggested that individual response styles to rejection involve varying degrees and mixtures of coping and defense. To the degree that a response style favors coping, it increases the development of a realistic sense of personal identity. To the degree that a response style favors avoidance, it increases one's tendency to try to gain the approval of others by *impression management*, that is, pretending to be what one believes is most acceptable to others. When people respond to rejection with impression management, they unwittingly create the conditions that will make it impossible for them to believe most favorable feedback because of their awareness of their own facade.

Global self-esteem, then, may be a generalized view and evaluation that one holds of one's self, reflecting one's perceptions of one's successes and achievements, of one's ability to live according to one's values, and of one's confident awareness that at least some people in one's life value and approve of one's self. Self-esteem is also based on self-acceptance, or at least some social connections, mastery experiences, and experiences of agency (i.e., that one can lead one's own life and that one's actions make a difference). It also implies a tolerance for painful feelings that develops over time, as well as a willingness to confront fears, take responsibility for feelings, decisions, and actions, and push on despite obstacles and adversity. All this is implied by the colloquial phrase *facing reality*.

Emotional Intelligence

When the process of self-experiencing is working well, it is hypothesized that persons are in a prime position to develop what Salovey and Mayer (1990) have called *emotional intelligence* (see also Goleman, 1997). They defined emotional intelligence as

> a set of skills hypothesized to contribute to the accurate appraisal and expression of emotion in one's self and in others, the effective regulation of emotion in self and others, and the use of feelings to motivate, plan, and achieve in one's life. (p. 185)

Even more specifically, they defined emotional intelligence as a subset of social intelligence that involves the capacity to perceive and differentiate one's own and others' feelings and to use this information in one's interpersonal behavior and relationships. This form of intelligent behavior involves (a) knowing one's emotions, (b) managing emotions, (c) marshaling emotions in the service of a goal, (d) recognizing emotions in others, and (e) handling relationships.

SUMMARY

This model of the self privileges both our immediate, organismic experience and our thoughts about ourselves having experience. The kind of information we obtain about our person depends on how we focus our attention. The dynamic interaction of these two forms of self-knowledge produces our immediate senses of self as well as our core self-beliefs. When all goes well, people develop a positive sense and concept of self that envisions a proactive, self-initiating individual who is willing to engage with the world and other people, face the rigors of such engagement, and learn from the resulting direct experience of that engagement (Bednar & Peterson, 1995). The model's inclusion of the characteristics of the healthy self serves as a reference point against which I describe in the next chapter the problems and dysfunctions that can occur during the development of one's sense and concept of self. I refer to these problems collectively as representing various wounds to the self.

6

THE WOUNDED SELF:
AN INTEGRATIVE ETIOLOGICAL
MODEL OF ANXIETY DISORDERS

Only man clogs his happiness with care, destroying what is, with thoughts
of what may be.

—John Dryden (1670)

In the previous chapter, I presented an integrated model of the self,
which drew from ideas based in the five separate perspectives. The integrative etiological model that I present in this chapter represents a synthesis of
the shared and differentiating ideas about anxiety and its disorders that were
abstracted from the several perspectives in chapter 3.

THE NATURE OF AN ANXIETY DISORDER

An anxiety disorder can be viewed from two very different perspectives: as it is observed (e.g., by a research scientist) and as it is experienced.
An anxiety disorder is observed when individuals perceive extensive danger
in situations that the observer deems to be unwarranted. The definition of an
anxiety disorder necessarily includes the idea of excessive anxiety relative to
some commonsense notion of the predictable harm that a feared object or
situation is likely to produce. From the point of view of the observer, in other
words, an anxiety disorder incorporates excessive harm estimates for specific

objects and situations. As Barlow (2000), for example, suggested, an anxiety disorder involves false alarms.

In a person with an anxiety disorder, however, anxiety is experienced as a fundamental threat to one's core self-beliefs. Phenomenologically, this is a quantum leap from anxiety experienced by someone without an anxiety disorder. People with severe anxiety feel as if they are in catastrophic jeopardy. There is an apprehension of physical or psychological catastrophe that is elicited by specific external objects and situations or by specific internal stimuli. The feeling that one is in immediate, catastrophic danger is the common thread in all anxiety disorders. This feeling of severe anxiety I refer to as an experience of self-endangerment. The construct of self-endangerment is similar to A. T. Beck and Emery's (1985) notion of vulnerability, which they defined as "a person's perception of himself as subject to internal and external dangers over which his control is lacking or is insufficient to afford him a sense of safety" (p. 67). The term *self-endangerment* is used, however, to emphasize the fact that the conscious meaning of severe states of anxiety and panic attacks goes beyond a sense of vulnerability. Rather, it reflects a feeling of catastrophic danger to the person (Wolfe, 1992, 1995; Wolfe & Sigl, 1998).

Self-endangerment is characterized by a variety of phenomenal states, including a sense of losing control, of lacking safety, or of feeling powerless. These phenomenal states compel people to believe that they are unable to prevent a traumatic or extremely painful or humiliating experience. When individuals with anxiety experience any situation that is directly or symbolically connected to one or more of these catastrophes, they experience a profound sense of self-endangerment (Wolfe, 2005).

Thus far, I have discussed the meanings of anxiety of which people are consciously aware. When people are in the middle of a self-endangerment experience, they typically do not allow themselves to experience the anxiety fully to explore its implicit or preconscious meaning. Instead, they automatically shift their attention from the direct experience of anxiety to cogitating about being anxious. In other words, they assume an observer's stance to their own experience of anxiety and begin to speculate about its possible catastrophic meanings. This automatic shift of attention from directly experiencing anxiety to thinking about one's self as anxious invariably increases the level of anxiety. But suppose people could suppress this tendency to shift attention and remain within the immediate experience of anxiety—what would they learn? They would apprehend that self-endangerment represents a feared confrontation with an excruciatingly painful view of the self. Moreover, they would clearly experience the specific painful self-view that is felt to be so threatening. It is only with the exploration of the implicit meaning of the anxiety that the underlying issues become clear (Wolfe, 2005).

These self-views may be specific memories of traumatic, painful, or humiliating encounters a person has experienced with a significant other or they may represent a generalized view of self that has been constructed out of a series of such painful experiences. In either case, these specific representations of the self are virtually unbearable for a person with an anxiety disorder to experience. The person implicitly fears the medium—the powerful emotions that typically accompany the painful self-view—and the message—the personal meaning that the self-view has for the individual. For example, I once treated a patient who could not bear the self-view that she was worth so little that her father actually abused her repeatedly. Moreover, the powerful feelings of shame and rage that accompanied the images of her ordeal were also virtually unbearable. Thus any situation that resembled the context of abuse evoked severe anxiety.

These painful self-views I call *self-wounds*. Wounds to the self are basically organized structures of painful self-related experience—or generalizations of such painful experience—that are stored in memory. These wounds may be known directly in one's immediate experience of a damaged sense of self (i.e., the extremely painful feeling or image of the self that arises in the moment) or conceptually in terms of the ideas, beliefs, and propositions one holds about the self. Self-wounds are mainly outside the person's immediate awareness but are often very close to the surface (i.e., preconscious). They nevertheless influence one's decisions, choices, feelings, and actions. Self-wounds not only limit one's emotional life but also profoundly affect one's behavior. They largely determine the people we choose to have in our life, the environments in which we choose to interact, the emotional experiences we deem acceptable to experience, and the risks in life we are willing to take (Wolfe, 2005).

For most patients with an anxiety disorder, the direct experience of any of these self-wounds is so painful that they try to avoid them at all costs. Such experiences are viewed as self-endangering or as catastrophes for the person. Any internal or external stimulus connected to these self-views can provoke severe anxiety. This anxiety, in turn, can become so great as to reach the level of a panic attack. Bodily sensations, thoughts, and images (i.e., internal stimuli), on the one hand, and specific fear-inducing external events and situations (i.e., external stimuli), on the other, can provoke an experience of self-endangerment because they signal a pending confrontation with an unbearably painful view of the self. The patient's attention is vigilantly focused externally, on the one hand, to sniff out any dangers to the self that may be lurking in the environment, and internally, on the other, as one's own thoughts and feelings come to be viewed as the prescient heralds of impending doom.

The relationship between self-endangerment experiences and self-wounds, therefore, is as follows: The experience of self-endangerment signals the potential exposure (to one's self or others) of a painful self-wound. Self-wounds activate self-endangerment experiences in selected situations. Thus, self-endangerment experiences are mediated by the interaction of selected fear-inducing situations and the self-wounds they activate. Examples of such self-endangerment experiences and the self-wounds they activate include

(a) the individual with a public speaking phobia who is terrified that if he has a panic attack while speaking, he will be viewed as pathetic and lose status among his academic peers; (b) the patient with panic disorder whose sensation of rubbery legs evokes the terrifying memory of nursing home residents with whom she once worked who were unable to control either their body or bowel movements; thus rubbery legs invoke the specter of invalidism and permanent dependency; and (c) the patient with obsessive–compulsive disorder (OCD) who construes his intrusive thought of hitting his girlfriend as conclusive evidence that he is a violent person destined to be alone for the rest of his life. In each instance, these self-views are unbearably painful.

Types of Self-Wounds

The feared catastrophes that are signaled by the sense of self-endangerment relate to physical and psychological survival or well-being. Physical fears include the fear of death, paralysis, or physical breakdown. Fears associated with psychological survival or well-being include the fear of being unlovable, unworthy, unacceptable, inadequate, abandoned, isolated, rejected, weak, pathetic, humiliated, dominated, or controlled. In addition, dread is associated with the pending loss or destruction of one's meaning in life. All of these catastrophic fears may be grouped into five types of painful self-views that generate intensive anxiety: (a) the biologically vulnerable self; (b) the inadequate or incompetent self; (c) the shamed, defective, or humiliated self; (d) the disaffected or isolated self; and (e) the conflicted or confused self (Wolfe, 2005).

The Biologically Vulnerable Self

Many people with anxiety disorders that I have treated carry around an incessant fear that they are extremely vulnerable to physical illness or limitations. They fear that their bodies will let them down, that they will lose control of their bodily functions and capacities. Although this fear is often a variant of the fear of losing control, which is prominent in patients with an anxiety disorder, an exploration of the meaning of this fear usually leads to the patient's fear of death. Typically some life transition (such as the death of a loved one) brings one's mortality into sharp focus. Such patients walk around with a profound sense of physical vulnerability, fearing even to make appointments with their physicians because they do not want to discover that they have some life-threatening illness.

The Inadequate or Incompetent Self

For many patients, the feared self-related catastrophe is that they will be exposed as inadequate or incompetent. The pain of having to face this self-belief is so great that patients with anxiety become fearful whenever they are in a situation that resembles a past performance failure. In fact, it is often not the whole situation but some element of the situation that be-comes associated with this painful self-view. This element functions as a kind of psychological shorthand of the possible exposure of this self-diminishing view. An individual with a public speaking phobia came to learn through a focus on the implicit meaning of a panic attack that he was terrified of being viewed by his academic colleagues as pathetic and incompetent if he were to have a panic attack while delivering a paper.

The Shamed, Defective, or Humiliated Self

For many individuals who meet criteria for a variety of anxiety disor-ders, the unbearable self-image is the picture of one's self as shamed, humili-ated, or defective. For example, one patient became extremely anxious at the mention of Puerto Rico. A complex associative network was uncovered whereby the mention of Puerto Rico or virtually any stimulus relating to Puerto Rico was connected to a sense of humiliating inadequacy as a man. One image involved his being impotent in both a literal and a figurative sense. The image of Puerto Rico would segue into an image of a pregnant blond woman, which would then change into an image of his blond, reject-ing mother. This rejection would leave him feeling humiliated and convinced that he was a defective human being.

The Disaffected and Isolated Self

The terrifying image of the self as alone and isolated characterizes the implicit meaning of panic for many patients. One patient with a social phobia believed that if others discovered that he sometimes felt weak, he would be treated as an outcast. The metaphor for his fear was captured in a haunting image that he frequently experienced of himself following 20 steps behind the rest of the tribe. The thought of his growing old alone was unbearable.

The Confused or Conflicted Self

One of the most painful experiences of self that patients with anxiety have is the experience of confusion or conflict about their identity. Such confusion and conflict renders them chronically vulnerable to anxiety at-tacks. Often one's problems and anxiety symptoms become embedded within one's identity so that it becomes difficult to distinguish self from one's prob-lems (Mahoney, 1991). As one patient with agoraphobia put it, "I don't know who I am without my phobias."

Many individuals have internalized conflicts around the self. These are typically characterized as simultaneously experiencing self in two incompat-ible ways. L. S. Greenberg, Rice, and Elliott (1993) labeled these as *self-splits*, in which two different aspects of the self are in direct opposition. One type of self-split involves a conflict between the basic needs of an individual and his or her standards. As L. S. Greenberg et al. put it in the following:

Failure to recognize needs and wants leaves the person unclear and confused, whereas failure to meet the standards and values produces negative self-evaluation and loss of self-worth. (p. 187)

These self-splits are very painful when the individual is aware of them. When they are out of the individual's focal awareness, they generate intense anxiety.

A Word About Terminology

The medical metaphor of wounds, I believe, has certain advantages over other possible terminology (e.g., self-pathology or dysfunction or self-related schemas). It analogizes several aspects of wound formation that are particularly relevant to the problems people confront in their experience of living in the world. One's view of self is damaged by certain kinds of life experiences and the interpretations that one gives them. A number of conceptual and emotional processes, which are designed to protect the wounded self, are immediately set in motion. During the healing process, a person's capacities are in some respects reduced, limited, or constrained. Considering the many treatment-relevant implications that can be drawn from this metaphor, the term *self-wound*, I believe, gains more in communicative value than it loses in precision.

The self-wound hypothesis integrates a growing consensus among psychodynamic, behavioral, cognitive–behavioral, and experiential–humanistic perspectives, which increasingly emphasize a below-the-surface dimension of human functioning that is responsible for the surface manifestations of particular disorders. Psychodynamic theorists have always identified unconscious conflicts usually centering on interpersonal relationships as the core locus of psychopathology (Eagle, 1987; S. Freud, 1926/1959). Although behavioral theorists endeavor to eschew any construct suggesting the existence of mentalisms or other internal dispositions, recent accounts of borderline personality disorder describe a damaged or deficient self, operating under many tacit rules (Linehan, 1993). Cognitive–behavioral theorists increasingly have emphasized deep-structure schemas (A. T. Beck, Freeman, & Associates, 1990), particularly those that relate to interpersonal issues (Safran & Segal, 1991), as etiologically primary in the manifestation of specific emotional disorders. Although experiential therapists work clinically with conscious experience, it is also increasingly clear that experiential theories emphasize preconscious, preconceptual experiencing as critically important in the generation of emotional-processing difficulties (L. S. Greenberg et al., 1993). From the vantage point of each of these four theoretical perspectives, this below-the-surface dimension indicates a self in jeopardy. All explicate or imply a construct or *felt sense* (i.e., one's in-the-moment or feeling-based perception) of a self that is damaged, deficient, dysfunctional, or disturbed.

The Three Nodes of an Anxiety Disorder

As previously mentioned, anxiety disorders typically include an immediate experience of anxiety and the subsequent automatic shift of attention to one's self being anxious. This latter, more reflective kind of focus on the self is similar to the idea of *self-focused attention* that is now prominent in the literature. Self-focused attention incorporates the idea of a distanced perception of one's self as anxious (Ingram, 1990). Another related idea is referred to as anxiety sensitivity (Reiss, 1987), which denotes individuals who become fearful of their first-order anxiety.

According to the integrative perspective under consideration, there are typically three nodes in an anxiety disorder: (a) the immediate experience of anxiety; (b) a more perceptually distanced focus on the self as anxious (i.e., cogitating); and (c) the tacit but painful self-view. These three nodes are most easily seen in patients with panic disorder whose immediate experience of anxiety involves a number of frightening bodily sensations to which they automatically respond by taking the observer's perspective with respect to their own experience and speculating on—or cogitating about—the catastrophic meaning of these frightening bodily sensations. This is the basic idea in D. M. Clark's (1986) cognitive model of panic disorder: that patients misinterpret the meaning of frightening bodily sensations. But this perspective does not sufficiently address the source of those frightening sensations, particularly their preconscious meanings to the patient.

This second-order awareness of one's self as anxious can also be seen in patients with social anxiety disorder. Instead of smoothly and easily engaging in conversation with others, they are caught in an incessant litany of self-derogatory thoughts about themselves as socially inept and about their expectations that their anxiety will lead them to do or say something that will evoke ridicule. Such ridicule, they imagine, will lead to unbearable feelings of humiliation and will result in their viewing themselves as pathetically inadequate. This anticipatory anxiety makes it more likely that they will in fact perform badly and thus a *vicious circle* comes to characterize their social interactions (see Figure 6.1; Wachtel, 1997). A similar idea was put forth from a cognitive perspective by Safran and Segal (1991). They referred to these vicious *cycles* as maladaptive cognitive–interpersonal cycles. The fact that anxiety disorders appear to possess three nodes has significant treatment implications. As I suggest later in the book, my integrative treatment approach focuses initially on the anxiety symptoms and the attentional shift to cogitation, that is, the second-order anxiety that results when one realizes that he or she is very anxious. Only after some progress is made on this layer of anxiety does treatment proceed toward the exploration, identification, and amelioration of the underlying layer, the implicit meaning of the anxiety or panic. It is my contention that the existing treatments, particularly those that have received empirical support, have been quite effective in dealing

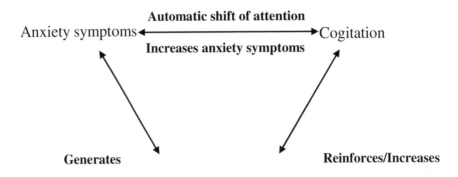

Implicit meaning of anxiety symptoms

Figure 6.1. Schematic model of an anxiety disorder.

with this second-order anxiety but less so in uncovering and treating the implicit meaning of anxiety or panic and its preconscious sources.

THE DEVELOPMENT OF AN ANXIETY DISORDER

Research increasingly points toward a number of possible etiological factors in the generation of an anxiety disorder. Biomedical research increasingly indicates that, for some people, a genetically transmitted predisposition plays a significant role in the development of an anxiety disorder (L. A. Clark, Watson, & Mineka, 1994). It is difficult, however, to tease out pure genetic or biological factors from the extensive experience of trauma or from the developmental deficits that are characteristic of patients with an anxiety disorder. It is clinically observable, however, that an individual's struggle with the pain and fear of his or her own subjective experience produces profound and measurable biological consequences. From this point of view, the biological regularities uncovered by research are most often the bodily substrate of danger perceptions. For example, when individuals experience themselves in danger, the firing rate of the locus coeruleus increases (Redmond, 1985).

Cognitive–behavioral researchers are accumulating data that support an emotional/information-processing perspective in the generation of an anxiety disorder. Older conditioning theories have been replaced by ideas from both neoconditioning and cognitive theories that suggest that the perception of relationships between one's fear and internal and external stimuli is at the heart of fear learning (Rapee, 1991; Rescorla, 1988). These relationships are heavily influenced by underlying cognitive schemas (A. T. Beck & Emery, 1985). Foa and Kozak (1986), for example, contended that anxiety disorders are based in implicit fear structures that need to be activated (i.e., brought into conscious awareness) before they can be modified by the processing of more realistic information.

It has been clinically observed that a large network of emotion-laden thoughts and images is associated with an individual's fear situations and objects. This associative network involves a rich tapestry of idiosyncratic associations and relationships between the fear situations and catastrophic pain. The selectivity of the association between specific objects and situations and the person's anxiety and panic is determined by what the individual believes to be a catastrophic threat to his or her self-related issues. These perceived threats to the core self are believed to entail unbearable pain.

Sources of Self-Wounds

There are many sources of self-wounds, and most of these are interrelated. This is particularly clear with the five sources that I consider: (a) traumatic experiences, (b) shaming or toxic ideas, (c) betrayals by critically important significant others, (d) emotional miseducation, and (e) ineffective responses to the existential givens of life. I look at each in turn.

Traumatic Experiences

The *Diagnostic and Statistical Manual of Mental Disorders* (4th ed.; American Psychiatric Association, 1994) defined a traumatic experience as one that is either life-threatening or one that leaves the person feeling helpless or horrified. This definition, however, insufficiently emphasizes the relative nature of the concept of trauma. In the broadest sense, a trauma is any experience that overwhelms an individual and leaves him or her feeling helpless and powerless. S. Freud (1926/1959) was the first one to describe trauma in terms of an experience that leaves the individual helpless and powerless. Trauma represents the intensity of the painful or threatening experience relative to the person's ability to cope with such experiences. Accordingly, there are significant individual differences in the kinds of experiences that a person may find traumatic.

Trauma leads to several types of distortions of the process by which a person obtains self-esteem and self-confidence. First and foremost, it creates the unexpected impression that one is unsafe in a dangerous world. As Herman (1993) put it, "Trauma robs the victim of a sense of power and control" (p. 159). Herman then pointed out that "Survivors feel unsafe in their bodies. Their emotions and their thinking feel out of control. They also feel unsafe in relation to other people" (p. 160). Traumatic experiences distort one's sense of self-efficacy, safety, and self-worth.

As a result of traumatic experiences, patients with an anxiety disorder develop associations between traumatic situations of the past and present external objects or situations or internal sensations. A man with a commitment phobia whom I recently treated had a repetitive pattern of getting close to a woman and then, when he met her friends, he experienced panic attacks and decided she was not the one. These panic attacks were traced back to a youthful love affair when his beloved unceremoniously dumped him when her friends convinced her that he was not good enough for her. By the time he entered therapy, he had followed the same pattern in several subsequent relationships.

Betrayals by Significant Others

What has been particularly traumatic for my patients with an anxiety disorder are the betrayals they experienced in childhood. As a human experience, betrayal is one of the most difficult with which to cope. It corrodes trust in others as it simultaneously undermines one's sense of personal worth. My clinical work with patients who have anxiety disorders has uncovered an astonishing amount of betrayal experiences. Most often, my patients experienced these betrayals in childhood, which increased their difficulty in making sense of—as well as coping with—these experiences. Moreover, these betrayal experiences were found to possess a direct connection to my patients' anxiety disorders. One patient with agoraphobia, for example, experienced his first panic attack at 9 years of age when he was left to care for two younger siblings while his alcoholic parents went barhopping. Another patient who was terrified of getting lost when she drove in unknown areas discovered that her fear was related to being kidnapped as a young child by her own father and placed in a house of strangers. In every instance, such experiences compromised my patients' trust in others and belief in their self-worth.

Shaming Opinions and Toxic Ideas From Significant Others

Many authors have described the experience of shame as a sense of one's self as defective, inferior, or unlovable and unworthy of membership in the human community (Karen, 1992; Kaufman, 1985; Nathanson, 1987). This totalistic sense of shame derives from the toxic opinions of and treatment by significant others, particularly parents and other caretakers. One comes by such corrosive views of the self initially through the shaming attitudes and responses of others and later through one's own appraisals of one's behavior and person. As Kaufman (1985) put it, "Shame originates interpersonally, primarily in significant relationships, but later can become internalized so that the self is able to activate shame without an interpersonal event" (p. 7). In my view, shame and its accompanying view of one as deficient are a core element of the wounded self. Whenever individuals are in danger of encountering a shameful view of themselves, anxiety usually results.

This sense of shame leads to the emergence of a number of defensive processes designed to protect the individual from confronting these painful self-views. A great deal of anxiety relates to the fear of experiencing these derogatory self-views and thus has been labeled *shame anxiety* (Wurmser,

1981). Shame anxiety figures prominently in virtually all anxiety disorders, but it is particularly prevalent in social phobias, generalized anxiety disorder, panic disorder, and OCD. Often these shaming ideas lead to irrational ideas about the self whose credibility inheres in the weight the individual gives to the opinions of selected people in his or her life.

Emotional Miseducation

Evidence is increasing regarding the adaptive value of experiencing and expressing one's emotions. Emotions increasingly are viewed as a necessary source of information that aid in biopsychosocial adaptation (L. S. Greenberg, 2002). Patients with anxiety disorders, however, often learn dysfunctional attitudes with respect to experiencing and expressing their emotions. Many have learned that it is actually dangerous to express one's feelings. As a result of these toxic messages, such individuals become frightened of emotions of any intensity. The interpersonal consequences of such messages are variable. Some may develop an unassertive, timid stance toward other people. Others may behave maladaptively because they have no awareness of the underlying emotions that are generating the maladaptive behavior. As L. S. Greenberg (2002) put it, "For example, clients who do not attend to the information provided by their emotions become passive when abused or depressed when angry, and those who are overly inhibited when they are either happy or sad lack vigor" (p. 42).

An implicit rule that emotion must be suppressed often results in the experience of panicky sensations when forbidden or disavowed emotions are surfacing into awareness. In this context, the connection between emotional miseducation and anxiety is quite direct: It is dangerous to feel and to express what one is feeling.

Ineffective Responses to the Existential Givens of Life

A final source of self-wounds concerns the unavoidable realities of human existence. These include failure, loss of loved ones and valued relationships; life transitions; the recognition of one's mortality and of one's existential aloneness; the constant challenge of living a meaningful life; and the struggle involved in resolving the search for maximum freedom, on the one hand, and maximum security, on the other. Accompanying each of these realities is the experience of severely painful affects such as humiliation, shame, rage, and despair. These are universals of human living. Every human being is faced with each of these ontological realities, but one's self-esteem is critically affected by whether one confronts them directly or avoids, ignores, buries, or otherwise denies them. Very often in my clinical work with patients with anxiety or panic disorder, I have found that the underlying meaning of their anxiety symptoms and panic attacks relates to an internal struggle with the acceptance of these realities and their accompanying emotions. For example, consider the inevitability of failure and rejection. Failures and rejections can lead to self-diminishing views with concomitant feelings of humiliation and shame. If these failures and rejections are frequent and continuous, one may begin to experience frequent feelings of helplessness, hopelessness, and despair, or even self-hatred. Failures, faced forthrightly, however, need not devastate self-esteem. Bednar and Peterson (1995) suggested that each failure or rejection prompts a choice point where one may either avoid facing the failure or cope with it. By coping I mean three things: (a) an ability to tolerate the emotions that arise because of the failure, (b) a willingness to conduct an analysis of the reasons for failure or rejection, and (c) a commitment to remedy the identified deficiencies. If the information that is available in one's failures is avoided, one inevitably descends into self-deception and avoidance behavior. By contrast, facing reality refers to a capacity to confront and assimilate information that is difficult to hear, as well as to an ability to tolerate the painful emotions and feelings that accompany these self-diminishing messages.

Another example is the fear of dying, which is prominent among patients with anxiety disorders. Much of the time, people walk around with an implicit feeling of invincibility. They know death exists and that people die but they rarely possess any emotional awareness that death will find them in the near future. But certain experiences (e.g., the loss of a loved one) may shred that veil of invincibility and leave them quaking in fear of their own demise (Yalom, 1980). I treated one patient who experienced an episode of OCD that seemed to be triggered by the death of his mother. He was chronically fearful that certain substances entered his body (or those of his family) through his own neglect and therefore he or they were doomed by his mistake. To assuage his fear, this man immediately went online and rapidly acquired all information available regarding the probabilities of these substances (e.g., asbestos) causing a life-threatening illness. The infinitesimally small probabilities that he usually found for such events reassured him for only a short period before the cycle reoccurred.

Interrelationships Among the Various Sources of Self-Wounds

The interrelationships of these various sources of self-wounds are fairly easy to observe. Traumatic experiences such as physical or sexual abuse, for example, represent betrayals by important people in the victim's life. Such experiences can easily lead to the victim internalizing toxic or shaming ideas about him- or herself (e.g., "I must really be worthless for my father to do this to me"). If, in addition, the victim is threatened with reprisals from the perpetrator of the abuse, such threats may suppress the victim's willingness or ability to emotionally process, and most certainly to express, these experiences. In fact, the victim may learn to associate danger with his or her emotional life in general.

The self-wounds that generate anxiety disorders are mostly the product of damaging life experiences. They produce measurable biological consequences; influence maladaptive interpersonal behavior; result in dysfunctional beliefs about the self, others, and the world at large; and cripple one's ability to experience and express one's emotions. In addition, they interfere with a person's ability to directly take in actual information from the world. In other words, self-wounds make it difficult for an individual to trust his or her immediate experience of the world.

THE MAINTENANCE OF AN ANXIETY DISORDER

Anxiety disorders are maintained by several different factors, which mostly have to do with protecting one's self from an excruciatingly painful view of the self. As mentioned before, a series of cognitive and emotional processes automatically spring into action to protect the wound to the self. Here the analogy with a real physical wound breaks down, however. Instead of these protective processes making it possible for the wound to heal on its own, they in fact guarantee that the wound will not heal. Unhealed self-wounds are the primary reason for the maintenance of an anxiety disorder. For a self-wound to heal, there must be a fundamental change in perspective toward the self. The patient must come to perceive and conceive of the self in a more positive and accepting light. Such a fundamental change in perspective can be brought about by insight, emotional processing of painful material, and behavioral change.

Instead of confronting the self-wound head-on, patients with anxiety typically engage in strategies designed to keep them hidden from one's self and others. These patients typically use three types of strategies: (a) cogitation, (b) avoidance, and (c) negative cycles of interpersonal behavior.

Cogitation

When patients experience anxiety, their attention automatically shifts from the direct experience of the anxiety to a focus on the self as anxious. Rather than exploring the implicit meaning of the anxiety, patients observe themselves being anxious and begin to cogitate about the potential catastrophe that they expect to occur. Such cogitation, however, tends to increase the level of anxiety, which in turn increases the amount of cogitation. This vicious cycle can spiral upward to the level of sheer panic. For example, a major criterion of panic disorder is the tendency for such patients to experience body sensations that frighten them. Once patients with panic disorder begin to experience these sensations, they shift to cogitating about the potentially catastrophic meanings of those body sensations, such as "I am losing my mind" or "I am going to have a heart attack." Such cogitation increases their anxiety and their cogitation about their anxiety until they experience a panic attack.

Avoidance

Patients with anxiety disorders develop a variety of defensive processes designed to protect their self-wounds from dangerous exposure. These processes involve responses across all three spheres of human functioning: behavior, cognition, and emotion. Chief among these defensive processes is avoidance. Anxiety frequently leads to avoidance behaviors. Thus the individual with a height phobia avoids the higher floors of tall buildings, the person with a social phobia avoids people or performance opportunities, and the patient with panic disorder avoids places where he or she has experienced panic attacks. Out of an intense fear of making a mistake or being the source of harm to loved ones, patients with OCD engage in active behavioral efforts to cancel the error or the reason for blame. These active efforts or rituals are attempts to rewrite a feared scenario so as to leave the individual blameless or to convince the person that the feared catastrophe will not take place (Salkovskis, 1985). Such behavioral avoidance possesses three problematic results: (a) it ensures that anxiety will recur in similar situations (i.e., it reinforces the anxiety response); (b) it does not allow the individual to learn that the anticipated danger is manageable; and (c) it does not allow the person the opportunity to explore the implicit meaning of his or her anxiety. Moreover, these behavioral avoidance strategies may have unwanted interpersonal consequences.

Behavioral Avoidance

Persons who experience significant interpersonal anxiety often have used one of the most interesting behavioral strategies of avoidance. In an effort to feel interpersonally safe with others, individuals with social anxiety may attempt to manage the impressions that others have of them. This impression management strategy is designed to convince others (and therefore him- or herself) that the individual possesses certain laudable characteristics. Feedback from others that the person with social anxiety seems to possess such characteristics reduces his or her anxiety—but only temporarily. At some point, the individual experiences the gap between self-beliefs and self-presentation. The experience of this gap produces anxiety associated with the knowledge that one does not actually fit the self-created impression (Wolfe & Sigl, 1998). When a person responds with impression management, he or she unwittingly creates the conditions that will render most of the favorable feedback received untrustworthy, unbelievable, and psychologically impotent because of one's internal awareness of the discrepancy between the way one is behaving and one's authentic self-evaluation. Impression management is considered a form of behavioral avoidance because it allows the individual to avoid awareness of his or her authentic organismic experience of the social interaction.

Cognitive Avoidance

Cognitive avoidance strategies refer to those conceptual processes people use to avoid facing their derogatory self-beliefs head-on. Many of the defensive processes first discussed by the early psychoanalysts, such as denial, rationalization, and projection, would fall in this category (A. Freud, 1946). Individuals with social phobia, for example, cognitively avoid their shame-based self-beliefs by projecting these negative attitudes on their audiences. Patients with OCD engage in a variety of mental rituals in an effort to reduce anxiety generated by their obsessional thoughts (Foa & Franklin, 2001).

Emotional Avoidance

The avoidance of emotional experience is particularly characteristic of individuals with anxiety disorders. The process of experiencing one's feelings can be conceptualized as a spectrum that begins with awareness, proceeds to expression, and culminates in action. Avoidance also takes place in one other area—the processing of the meaning of another person's response to one's expressions and actions. Patients with anxiety disorders, therefore, may interrupt their (a) awareness of emerging emotions, (b) expression of these feelings or the associated actions, and (c) assimilation of the impact of their actions on others and vice versa. People learn nothing from avoidance, and increased avoidance increases the difficulty of directly engaging the world. The inability to engage the world directly does nothing to enhance a person's level of self-confidence, efficacy, or esteem. Thus the short-term gain of anxiety reduction makes it impossible for a person to fundamentally shift his or her self-perspective. Without such a shift in perspective, the self-wounds cannot heal.

Negative Cycles of Interpersonal Behavior

Because of a wound-driven sense of vulnerability, people with anxiety disorders are frightened of being open with other people. Being authentic with others becomes very difficult because it is encumbered by fear that others will find them unworthy or unlovable. Instead, such individuals engage in a variety of interpersonal strategies that are designed to protect their self-wounds from exposure and therefore from being truly known by others. I have already mentioned the difficulties experienced with two of those strategies, impression management and avoiding contact with other people. A third pattern emerges when one observes the interpersonal consequences of anxiety, although it is not specific to just people with anxiety. This pattern involves a self-fulfilling negative interpersonal cycle. Self-wounds are particularly characterized by negative beliefs about the self. These beliefs often shape a more general negativistic perspective toward other people, resulting in diminished expectations regarding other people's kindness, caring, or good will. To protect themselves from the expected negative responses, patients often behave in ways that influence others to respond in ways that reinforce the patients' original expectations. Thus a man with a social phobia, for example, may gather up his nerve and attend a party but, once there, assumes that other people are not interested in him. He takes no initiative in introducing himself to others, fearing that they will ignore him or in some other fashion respond negatively. Instead, he waits for someone to initiate a conversation with him. When this does not happen, he leaves the party feeling very foolish and convinced that his original presupposition was correct. This is a self-fulfilling negative interpersonal cycle, a *vicious cycle* in Wachtel's (1997) terms.

Defenses as Self-Image Protective Processes

In the original Freudian paradigm, the concept of psychological defense pertained to the mostly automatic, unconscious processes that spring into action to prevent a person from becoming aware of threatening instinctual impulses. Consequently, defenses refer to drives and the pressure they place on the executive ego which must mediate the emerging conflict between impulse gratification, internalized moral stricture, and reality. Both Horney (1945) and Sullivan (1953), from a more interpersonally based approach to psychoanalysis, conceptualized psychological defenses in terms of self-image maintenance processes. Horney (1945) discussed the concept of the *idealized image*, which is an unconscious self-image that an individual with a neuroses creates to maintain his or her self-esteem. Sullivan (1953) described the *self-system* as a collection of self-protective mechanisms designed to regulate interpersonal anxiety. These notions of defense are very close to my general conception of psychological defenses.

In my model, defenses serve the purpose of interrupting the immediate experience of painful feelings and their associated meanings to preserve the viability of the experience of acceptable representations of the self. Despite the fact that my notion of defense is more about meaning than about drive reduction, most of the defenses described in the psychoanalytic literature are clinically observable and therefore relevant for this integrative model.

The defense of projection represents the interruption of an immediate experience and attributing the experience to another individual. For example, people who find the emotion of intense anger threatening are likely to be unable to acknowledge its experience but instead conclude that the anger they sense belongs to their interlocutor. The projection of their anger on another person protects them from the painful experience of anger and its profound implications for their self-representations. The defense of intellectualization also protects people from the heat of the immediate experience of an intense feeling and the potential pain or shame that the meaning of that intense feeling might have for their vulnerable self-image.

The entire catalog of psychoanalytic defenses seems to be concerned with the protection of the person from painful or shameful self-evaluations. Sometimes even positive feelings may be construed as threatening to a particular self-belief, as in the case of people who become fearful of the possible implications of an extraordinarily positive evaluation of their work from their boss. Such an evaluation may evoke positive feelings of pride mixed with fearful anticipation of the increased expectations they imagine will be placed on them—expectations that significantly exceed their own estimate of their abilities. Such people seem to fear the old adage, "If you do more than what is expected, the more they expect you to do."

Although the defensive interruption of one's in-the-moment experience is more or less successful as a blockade for psychological pain, this aim is achieved at a price. The avoidance and deflection of painful meaning lead to distortions in one's sense and concept of self. Moreover, avoidance does not allow the individual to learn how to cope with the processing of painful emotions that life's demands and dilemmas inevitably bring. In addition, these distortions in people's self-concepts result in unsatisfying or painful interactions with others and in negative interpretations of one's own interpersonal behavior.

SUMMARY

A basic premise of this integrative model is that anxiety disorders are based in troubled self-perception and experiencing. For patients with anxiety disorders, wounds to the self generate a chronic struggle with their own subjective experience. This struggle with painful subjective experience around the self is the key integrative locus for emotional difficulties for most people, but particularly for people with anxiety disorders. The experience of severe anxiety in selected situations gives rise to conscious anticipations of impending catastrophe, which, at an implicit level, reflect a fear of exposing unbearably painful views of the self. The exposure of these self-wounds is accompanied by overwhelming affects such as humiliation, rage, and despair. Thus anxiety disorders seem to possess a conscious layer and an implicit layer in terms of what the anxiety symptoms mean to the individual.

The external and internal cues that provoke anxiety are developed through the perception of relationships between certain life experiences and intense fear—that is, certain experiences are perceived as self-endangering. The cues themselves often function as a kind of abbreviated shorthand for the painful memory that exists beyond the individual's conscious awareness. Thus, for example, in a female patient with agoraphobia, fear of losing control is signaled by a feeling of lightheadedness, which was the same feeling she had when she panicked at the sight of people with physical disabilities years before. Moreover, the panic that a female patient with a driving phobia experiences when she is lost is a shorthand signal of the terrorizing memory of being kidnapped by her own father when she was 4 years old and placed in the home of strangers.

The unbearably painful views of the self that constitute the various self-wounds can be grouped into five basic patterns: the biologically vulnerable, inadequate, defective, disaffected, and confused self. All of these views suggest a perception of self as one who cannot cope with—and therefore needs protection from—the rigors and realities of everyday living. Because these realities are unavoidable, the individual with anxiety must create indirect strategies for coping with them that protect her from intolerable affective states while at the same time keep her from facing these realities head-on. Such strategies range from behavioral avoidance to cognitive ritual and emotional constriction, and they usually produce unintended interpersonal consequences that have the paradoxical effect of reinforcing the patient's painful core beliefs about the self.

Although this model acknowledges the possibility that certain patients may have a genetically transmitted predisposition for developing an anxiety disorder, the bulk of the causative weight is placed on the damaging life experiences that such patients have had, the self-wounds that those experiences generate, and the ineffective protective strategies that are used to prevent the exposure of those wounds. These damaging experiences stem from a variety of sources, including traumatic experiences, shaming or toxic ideas, betrayals by significant others, emotional miseducation, and ineffectual responses to the realities of ordinary living. In a drift toward a more biomedical view of mental illness, the field of mental health has seriously underestimated the extent of damaging life experiences and their role in the generation of emotional disorders.

Damaging life experiences, however, are not the only factors involved in the protracted nature of many cases of anxiety disorder. Patients with an anxiety disorder create a number of cognitive and emotional strategies to protect them from their feared catastrophes. These strategies, however, keep the person from facing his or her fears and self wounds head-on. In response to the initial anxiety, patients typically cogitate about being anxious (i.e., self-preoccupation), avoid the fear-inducing objects and situations, or engage in negative interpersonal cycles. These strategies result in the temporary reduction of anxiety and the reinforcement of the patient's underlying maladaptive self-beliefs. Psychological defenses in this model serve as self-defeating efforts to protect one's image of the self.

I hope that it is apparent to the reader that all of the traditional orientations of anxiety disorders contribute to this model. The psychodynamic framework is honored in the consideration of the implicit meaning of anxiety. Moreover, I believe the model gives a more significant etiological role to traumatic experiences than do most other orientations. The cognitive perspective is acknowledged in its basically accurate portrayal of the dynamic process involved in the person's second-order reactions to first-order anxiety experiences, whether these are somatic or cognitive. This process is most easily seen in panic disorder in which the patient generates catastrophic cognitions when he or she misinterprets the implications of feared bodily sensations. The experiential orientation is recognized in its critical distinction between immediate experiencing and a more distant conceptual focus of attention on the phenomena of anxiety. The behavioral orientation is recognized in its conception of multiple conditioning and associative processes involved in the development and maintenance of the various anxiety disorders. The next chapter addresses the application of this model to a number of the specific anxiety disorders.

7

THE APPLICATION OF THE INTEGRATIVE MODEL TO SPECIFIC ANXIETY DISORDERS

There is nothing so practical as a good theory.

—Kurt Lewin (1935)

The general etiological model presented in the previous chapter pertains to each of the specific anxiety disorders under consideration. Although many similarities exist in terms of the parameters of each anxiety disorder, there are differences that are characteristic of each specific disorder. These differences sometimes involve the hypothesized precipitating events or the type of self-wound that is involved. But another major factor that differentiates the various anxiety disorders is the choice of cognitive and affective strategies that individuals develop to protect themselves from exposure to the self-wounds in question and their accompanying painful affects. These strategies result in short-term protection against anxiety, but at the same time, help maintain the disorder. In addition, they often result in problematic interpersonal consequences.

SPECIFIC PHOBIAS

It is likely that multiple processes lead to the formation of a specific phobia. But I have been much impressed with the frequency of occurrence of a certain process in the patients I have treated. The typical sequence appears to be childhood trauma or disillusionment experienced by the patient at the hands of primary caretakers that was associated directly, adventitiously, or symbolically with a phobic object and that represented a severe danger to one's physical or psychological survival or well-being. A catastrophic association between a vital aspect of the person's sense of well-being and an external object was made and stored in memory. This connection is not just painful but is catastrophic as viewed by the individual. Most often the phobic connection is unconscious, and the person typically does not become aware of it except through a depth-oriented diagnostic probe such as the imagery techniques mentioned in previous chapters and described in detail later in the book.

When commenting on the objectivity of the fear, one has to keep in mind when in the person's life the phobia began, and his or her developmental level at that time. Although most specific phobias develop in childhood, these children may well be at different developmental stages. I have already mentioned the traumatic event that a woman named Virginia experienced when she was 4 years old that led to her fear of being lost. Her older sister, Dorothy, also developed a driving phobia whose self-endangerment issue centered on the theme of not being adequately prepared. She was 9 years old when the family was disrupted, and she therefore had a very different perspective on her father's kidnapping of his children. She understood much more than did 4-year-old Virginia what was happening and why. As the oldest sibling, Dorothy functioned as a surrogate mother. The kidnapping placed her in mortal fear that she would be unable to take care of her siblings because she was being driven away from them. It is fascinating that both sisters ended up with the same nominal phobia, but with dramatically different self-endangerment issues, reflecting different types of self-wounds, and these in turn reflected their different developmental level.

The Phobia Formation Process

The reader may be able to discern in the previous description elements of both the psychodynamic and behavioral models of phobias. These two models can achieve some reconciliation and integration, however, if it is acknowledged at the outset that, without necessarily stating it, both psychodynamic and behavioral theorists have emphasized an automatic unconscious association that is established between the phobic stimulus and the patient's fear. The models differ in terms of what is being conditioned and in terms of the hypothesized nature of the association process. The original conditioning model proposed an automatic and immediate association between a heretofore-neutral stimulus and a simple painful response when the neutral stimulus is contiguously paired with a stimulus that consistently induces the painful response.

In terms of the present model, something akin to a conditioning process takes place, if *conditioning* refers to a process of rapid, automatic, and unconscious association. Moreover, because of the complexity of human emotional and cognitive processes, neither the painful stimulus nor the heretofore-neutral stimulus is simple, nor is contiguity the only or primary variable involved in the formation of the association. In the case of specific phobia, what is being associated with a specific external object is the experience of one's self in catastrophic danger (i.e., self-endangerment). The external object is chosen because of its accidental (i.e., contiguous), signal, or symbolic relationship to the experience of self-endangerment. The experience of self-endangerment threatens some vital aspect or value of the individual, and he or she is helpless and powerless to prevent the impending catastrophe. When an individual is in the middle of a self-endangerment experience, he or she usually experiences strong and painful emotions that typically include one or more of the following: humiliation and shame, anger and rage, or despair.

As previously mentioned, the connection between the phobic object and the endangerment experience may be straightforward, symbolic, or adventitious. For example, Virginia's fear of driving actually was a fear of becoming lost. Her being lost represented a symbolic connection between the trauma of her kidnapping and the fear of driving into unknown territory. Trent's fear of bridges is a bit more straightforward. The catastrophe, of course, is death—not merely a fear of dying, but of dying before he lived, before he achieved his most sought after and valued goals. For most of my patients, the connection is symbolic. Virtually none of my patients revealed an adventitious connection between primal fear and phobic object. But the literature does. There is the case of mayonnaise phobia in which the phobic object was in fact an incidental and accidental element in a horrific family quarrel between the patient's parents that took place when he was 6 years old. This quarrel eventually led to a divorce and therefore the destruction of the patient's family and with it his sense of psychological well-being (Van Dyke & Harris, 1982).

A complex form of emotional conditioning appears to take place in the formation of many phobias. A heretofore-neutral external stimulus is paired with a self-endangerment experience, and this neutral stimulus eventually comes to elicit the same morbid dread as does the pending self-endangerment experience. A child would undoubtedly find it easier to focus on an external object rather than on the unbearable chaos that is felt within, which seems to lend some support to the psychodynamic model of the displacement and projection of an internal danger on the environment. But this is a mental mechanism that is difficult to verify except indirectly. What is clearer, however, is that the psychodynamic model seems to be on target in its hypothesis of a connection between an internal danger and an external object in the case of many specific phobias. The internal danger may involve what a patient construes to be a forbidden impulse that leads to some catastrophic reaction from others or from him- or herself, but the range of self-endangerment experiences is much broader and much more idiosyncratic than the psychodynamic model captures.

The nature of the connection between the phobic object and the internal danger presents a fascinating if thorny theoretical issue. As previously mentioned, at least three kinds of connections have been observed: accidental, straightforward, and symbolic. The straightforward connection is the easiest to understand and is often the easiest to verify. A person gets into an automobile accident and then becomes fearful of driving. The connection between the traumatic event and the fear of driving is direct. The available data, however, suggest that this kind of phobic connection occurs infrequently (W. A. Howard, Murphy, & Clarke, 1983). The symbolic connection between phobic object and self-endangerment issue achieves its plausibility through a recognition of the complex, symbolic cognitive–affective processes characteristic of human beings. The extensive role that metaphor plays in our concepts—to say nothing of our figures of speech—has been explicated by Lakoff and Johnson (1981). But these connections are most frequently idiosyncratic and therefore require an in-depth understanding of the individual case. A glossary of such connections for human beings in general is lacking, although this is precisely what Sigmund Freud tried to present in his various theories. S. Freud may have conceded the virtual impossibility of establishing a universal glossary of symbolic themes with his famous reply to a disciple's attempt to analyze S. Freud's fondness for cigars in terms of phallic imagery. S. Freud reportedly responded, "Sometimes a cigar is just a cigar."

The range of self-endangerment issues is as broad as a person's ability to construct catastrophic scenarios. Individual differences in self-endangerment issues reflect differences in life experiences, which in turn may reflect differences in gender, ethnic, or sociocultural identities. Given the state of knowledge in the field, any biological model of specific phobias is necessarily rudimentary. Specific phobias appear to be based in amygdala-driven initial appraisals of potentially catastrophic or traumatic situations. Specific internal and external stimuli come to serve as triggers or signposts of a potential catastrophe to the person's fundamental sense of well-being. Neural networks then develop around the theme of catastrophe and become focused on particular internal and external trigger stimuli (LeDoux, 1996).

Phobia Maintenance Processes

There are two primary maintenance factors in specific phobias. The chief maintaining factor is avoidance. Individuals with specific phobias experience a strong desire to avoid their feared objects or situations. Avoidance results in the short-term gain of reduction or elimination of anxiety.

But avoidance also prevents individuals from learning that the feared object or situation is basically harmless. Instead it reinforces the phobia. The second maintaining factor is more controversial. It is my conviction that specific phobias are never completely eliminated until the catastrophic associations are activated and modified. In other words, the self-wound that is implicit and complicit in the formation of the phobia must be repaired.

Typical Self-Wounds

The self-wounds associated with specific phobias run the gamut. Any of the self-wounds that have been mentioned can be rapidly and tacitly associated with a phobic object or situation. These connections are typically made in childhood and are based on a child's understanding of what feels catastrophic to his or her developing sense or concept of self. Fears of death, humiliation, rejection, abandonment, and loss of status, among others, have all been associated with specific phobic objects and situations.

Typically, different catastrophes and self-wounds have been connected to the same nominal phobia. For example, three of my patients with a driving phobia had different self-wounds underlying their disorder. One patient became phobic after he had a panic attack when his wife informed him during a drive that their marriage was over. He was unable to drive after that. In therapy, his abandonment fears emerged as his most prominent concerns. A second patient feared that if she drove away from home, she would never come back. She was conflicted between staying in an unhappy marriage in which she could remain dependent on her husband or leaving and facing her fears of living autonomously. Finally, a third patient's driving phobia was rooted in a fear of seeing herself as a failed mother if she drove off and left some child-caring task uncompleted. This fear persisted as she drove even though she was typically scrupulous in completing her tasks before leaving her house.

Interpersonal Consequences of Specific Phobias

The most typical interpersonal consequence is that people who are important participants in the patient's life will have to adapt to the patient's phobic tendencies. If a person is afraid of driving, for example, but does not mind being a passenger, then his or her significant other may have to do all of the driving. A loved one may have to walk up many flights of steps in a building if the patient has an elevator phobia. But another consequence will be the appearance of the underlying phobogenic self-wound in other contexts. For example, in the following case, Jim's fear of being trapped in an elevator is symbolically connected to his fear of being trapped in a committed relationship with a woman. He in fact experiences identical body sensations in both contexts.

Jim: A Case of Multiple Specific Phobias—Fear of Flying, Subways, Elevators, and Commitment

Jim is a 35-year-old computer programmer with an internationally known computer company who presented with multiple specific phobias, including fears of flying, traveling on the subway, and commitment to a life partner. He has had these problems for years but has never sought treatment for them until now. In the past, Jim's fear of flying restricted his vacation travel, in particular, but only recently has his fear begun to have profound consequences for advancement in his career. He is up for promotion to a middle management position with a substantial pay raise, but the new position will require frequent air travel. It is not surprising that he views this new opportunity with great excitement and great terror. The year before, he had refused to be considered for another promotion because of his fear of flying. He now realizes that more than his promotion is at stake because his supervisor told him that he takes a dim view of Jim's "self-imposed limitation" and that Jim may have to rethink his career goals with the company. Consequently, Jim arrived at my office in a state of agitation, feeling desperate about the need to alleviate or cure this problem, doubtful that it was possible, and fearful of what he might have to go through to be able to fly.

The fear of flying can be based in several different fears such as fear of dying, fear of heights, fear of having a panic attack, or fear of feeling trapped (W. A. Howard et al., 1983). For Jim, it was the last fear. When the doors to the plane shut, he invariably was seized by a severe claustrophobic reaction. It would begin with a severe tightening in his chest and progress to a feeling that he could not catch his breath; then, he would hyperventilate and become light-headed and eventually reach a state of panic. His fear was most prominent on airplanes, but he frequently had the same reaction on elevators and on the subway. Although these claustrophobic feelings had their origin many years before, the mere awareness of his chest tightening or his becoming light-headed was now enough to trigger a panic attack.

Through a guided-imagery exercise, Jim was able to remember an early—if not the first—panic attack. I asked him to imagine that he was on an airplane that was about to take off. I asked him to imagine further the door to the plane being shut and to notice what feelings or thoughts automatically occurred. At this point, he began to remember flying to California with his mother and older sister. They were going to visit his grandparents in San Francisco, and he did not want to go. In fact, his mother had lied to him about their eventual destination. She had told him they were going to Disneyland. But when they arrived at the gate, he noticed that the posted information designated a flight to San Francisco, not Los Angeles. He was shocked and livid but was unable to express these feelings to his mother. When they got on the plane and the door was shut, Jim began to feel trapped and to experience the aforementioned sequence of bodily reactions, culminating in a panic attack. His mother interpreted Jim's panic attack as a manipulative strategy to prevent the trip, and she would not cancel their plans. He had a miserable flight. He felt helpless, hopeless, and humiliated. The return flight was no better, particularly when the doors shut in preparation for take-off. The same sequence of bodily perturbations occurred, again culminating in a panic attack. Jim was 8 years old then. Since that time, he has been unable to fly. Years later, he experienced another panic attack on a subway, which was stuck for over half an hour during an ice storm. He also had experienced panic attacks in crowded elevators after he was once trapped in one that had become dysfunctional between floors.

There was one more context in which he occasionally experiences panic attacks: when his intimate relationship with a woman begins to get too intimate. Jim would feel the same sense of being trapped, accompanied by the same sequence of bodily reactions. Jim has never been married but has been involved with several women. He even had experimented with living with one woman for 6 months. He tends to be attracted to strong women, and then he becomes afraid that they will steamroll him because he cannot stand confrontations. The prototypical struggle that he inevitably has with his intimate other resembles the struggle that he experienced throughout his childhood with his strong and domineering mother. His father was a successful lawyer, but Jim describes him as little more than a houseboy in his relationship with his wife. Jim has repeated on a number of occasions this pattern of seeking and fearing strong, assertive women.

The panic attack that Jim experienced on the subway occurred while he was on his way to his girlfriend's house. This relationship had grown increasingly intimate and, consequently, he was beginning to experience an increasing sense of being trapped. Although the clarity of the links between the various phobic situations is not always this evident, in Jim's case a fairly obvious thread connected the situations in which he routinely experienced a panic attack. The panic contexts all involved situations in which Jim felt trapped, helpless, and lacking any control or ability to extricate himself. He had remembered (or reconstructed) several instances in which his sense of being trapped in one of his transportation-based phobic contexts appeared to echo the sense of entrapment that he felt in his intimate romantic relationships.

During the imagery exercise, as he allowed himself to experience fully his anxiety about being on the plane and as the panic scene occurred again for him, he eventually became aware of his hurt and his rage, his humiliation, and his despair. He was powerless, trapped, and painfully aware of how much his well-being seemed to depend on the very person whom he felt had betrayed him. He also became aware of a basic contingency that he had allowed to rule his relationship with his mother and later his older sister: that it was necessary to prevent himself from expressing hurt or rage lest these women retaliate by either humiliating him or rejecting him.

The Panic Process

Through imagery work, we were able to see how Jim's phobias related to his way of experiencing himself participating in the world. I asked him to imagine a recent scene with his current girlfriend, Nina. During lunch with Nina, Jim made a faux pas by using sexist language. Nina reamed him out, which he experienced with severe anxiety. He began to experience the usual tightness in his chest, the gasping for breath, the light-headedness, and eventually the panic attack. By slowing the image down, we noticed that his awareness of the chest tightening made him fearful that another panic attack was coming. His tightening chest suggested to him that he was not going to be able to breathe in enough air. In response, he tried to breathe more rapidly in an effort to get more air and, in so doing, began to feel light-headed. The light-headed feeling triggered even more anxiety, which escalated to the level of a panic attack. In another image of an argument with Nina, Jim experienced the light-headedness right away, in effect bypassing the chest-tightening and gasping-for-air sensations. The feeling of light-headedness automatically was interpreted as a sign of an impending panic attack, which made Jim even more anxious. He came away from such confrontations feeling hopeless and trapped. He felt that he needed this woman to make his life meaningful but also felt trapped with a woman who would control his life.

These examples illustrate the two-stage process of panic: anxiety symptoms and cogitating about the symptoms. First, the bodily reactions of fear are implicitly generated by his interactions with his girlfriend or by planes, trains, and subways. These reactions are followed by a shift in the focus of his attention to the bodily reactions themselves, and he interprets them as harbingers of a dreaded panic attack. Jim's fear-of-fear reaction eventually escalates to the level of a panic attack. It is important to note that the shift in Jim's attentional focus from his interaction in the world to his bodily reactions is rapid and automatic. Such an attentional shift is a key marker of the *endangered self*, which is an apprehension of an as yet unclear catastrophe.

The two-stage panic process in this form of specific phobia distinguishes this subtype from the more typical specific phobia. For example, an individual with a typical animal phobia begins to experience extreme anxiety when faced with his or her phobic object, but instead of worrying about having a panic attack, he or she experiences only the presentiment of doom. The individual with a rat phobia does not typically worry about having a panic attack. Instead, he or she just wants to break off contact with the rat (or the picture or image of the rat).

Characteristics of Self-Experiencing

Earlier, I traced a common sequence in the development of anxiety disorders that begins with the impact of early self-endangering experiences on the individual's capacity for immediate self-experiencing. Then the contexts of self-endangerment experiences become triggers for anxiety, which serves as an alarm that further immediate self-experiencing would be dangerous. This anxiety leads to a shift of the individual's attention to cogitation; while cogitating about the possible catastrophes portended by these fearful sensations, the individual inevitably experiences dysphoric emotions and negative evaluations of his or her first-order anxiety. Finally, in an effort to control the anxiety, the individual begins to avoid the contexts of prior self-endangerment experiences. Avoidance then increases the difficulty of reentering the feared situations.

In terms of this model of specific phobias, it is clear that Jim exhibits a number of difficulties in the way he experiences self-related information. First, he interrupts the complete experiencing of anxious feelings. Instead of allowing himself to more fully and completely experience the various bodily manifestations of his fear, Jim notices these manifestations and becomes anxious about them. In other words, instead of trying to explore, understand, and symbolize his immediate experience, he steps out of that experience and cogitates about being fearful. He thereby becomes afraid of his own fear, which increases the severity of his total fear response. The fear of panic leads Jim to avoid those contexts that will produce the sensations that he fears, that is, those situations in which he feels trapped. The presumption is that there are some very painful feelings that Jim cannot allow himself to experience, and the anxiety process protects him from having to experience these feelings. In effect, Jim has interrupted the process of becoming aware of his emotional reactions to his living in the world. Moreover, because he is not aware of these feelings, he therefore cannot take potentially risky actions in response to them that may well place him in a catastrophic position. Although the transformations of meaning eventually become clear when Jim self-interrupts, the mechanism by which this interruption process takes place is not yet clear at either a cognitive or neurological level.

Self-Wounds

For Jim, the experience of being trapped reveals a significant problem with his ability to take decisive action on his own behalf, what other commentators have labeled a problem with agency. Stern (1985), for example, has described *agency* as one of several critically important senses of self that human beings acquire and has suggested that an impairment in one's sense of agency can lead "to paralysis, the sense of non-ownership of self-action, and the experience of loss of control to external agents" (pp. 7–8). In Jim's relationships, this difficulty reveals itself most significantly when he is in conflict with a woman whom he cares about or when the relationship appears to be getting serious. But the fear of being trapped is also the thread that knits together the contexts of his various phobias. The primary self-wound Jim experiences is severe doubts about his agentic capacity. At the behavioral level, this is expressed as a lack of assertiveness. But deficits in one's sense of agency go deeper than this. An individual with a damaged sense of agency views him- or herself as small, insignificant, and powerless to affect the world and other people. Such individuals experience themselves to be totally at the mercy of the actions of others.

Interpersonal Consequences

As previously mentioned, Jim's core vulnerability is the sense of being trapped. He therefore is constantly vigilant regarding any situation, interpersonal or otherwise, that may leave him feeling trapped. Jim functions well interpersonally as long as he is living out his occupational role. He is an excellent speaker and is very successful in his career. But in his relationships, his fear of being trapped and without acceptable options leads him to set severe limits on how intimate he will allow a relationship to become. As he feels himself becoming increasingly attached to a woman, he knows that means he will soon become her slave because he will be unable to confront her. He endeavors to avoid this state of entrapment at all costs. Once he has pushed his romantic partner away, however, he is afflicted with remorse and loneliness that, in turn, leads him to either retrieve his current partner or seek out a new one. Incidentally, the latter example also illustrates the vicious cycles described by Wachtel (1993). This interpersonal pattern, however, flows directly from his core fear of being trapped, which is the same fear that drives his various phobias.

SOCIAL PHOBIAS

The integrative model under consideration argues that specific self-wounds relating to the person's experience of self as socially inadequate, unlovable, or unworthy are the source of social phobia. These wounds typically derive from frequent shaming messages received from the person's original family or his or her expanded social environment. The individual internalizes these toxic opinions, which result in a generalized view of self as defective or inferior. Social situations and public speaking opportunities produce the experience of self-endangerment. The self-endangerment experience is the intense anxiety or panic that protects the individual from having to experience the excruciatingly painful feeling of inadequacy. The extreme humiliation that a person feels when faced with his or her own sense of inadequacy is unbearable and is thus avoided by experiencing instead the often more painful panic attack.

Phobia Maintenance Processes

Self-endangerment leads to a shift of attention to a preoccupation with one's social limitations and with the imagined rejecting reactions of a hostile or disdaining audience. Thus this model recognizes the importance of self-focused attention as a maintaining factor in social phobias, although I prefer to call it *self-preoccupation* (i.e., repetitive or obsessive cogitation). Self-preoccupation reflects a specific attentional stance that the individual takes in relation to his or her experience. Instead of being in touch with his or her in-the-moment experience, a person views him- or herself from an observer's perspective. Self-preoccupation typically results in making the person feel either bad or more anxious. Duval and Wicklund (1972) maintained that focusing attention on the self necessarily leads to self-evaluation, whereby the individual compares his or her current status on the salient dimension of self with some idealized standard. This comparison typically results in the awareness of a discrepancy between the experience of the way one is and the way one ought to be. The experienced gap between the actual self and the idealized standard produces anxiety or pain (Higgins, 1987).

What is sadly ironic about this clinically observable phenomenon is that the ability to take an external perspective toward the self is a critical developmental skill. Piaget (1924/1966) originally conceptualized the ability of perspective taking as a necessary skill for the reduction of egocentrism in the developing individual. The symbolic interactionists such as Cooley (1902), Mead (1934), and Dewey (1929) believed that external perspective taking played a central role in the development of the sense of self. But there are two difficulties with the traditional view. First, this perspective taking has a downside when it shades into self-preoccupation. Second, self-focused attention or self-preoccupation represents only one form of self-awareness. This process is quite different than the immediate awareness of one's feelings and one's reactions to what is happening to him or her in the world. Self-preoccupation occurs when one is feeling vulnerable, that is, when one is in danger of contacting a self-wound. Thus when Bob enters a social situation, he does not stay in touch with his reactions to the people or the surroundings but, rather, focuses on his imaginings that people will not be interested in him. He is preoccupied with signs of rejection from others. Because his primary concern is how others view him, he makes no effort to initiate a conversation. When no one speaks to him, he concludes that he was right all along. No one thinks he is interesting enough to meet. Self-preoccupation leads him into a vicious cycle in which his negative presupposition is reinforced. The chief interpersonal consequence of Bob's social phobia is that he constantly reenacts this self-fulfilling prophecy.

A second major maintenance process is avoidance. Individuals with a social phobia avoid speaking opportunities and social engagements. Avoidance leads to a short-term reduction of anxiety but it reinforces the underlying self-wounds and therefore the social phobia.

A third maintaining factor is the interpersonal strategy of impression management. As mentioned in chapter 5, impression management is an interpersonal strategy used by people who are interpersonally anxious in an effort to create a positive impression on others. When a positive impression is communicated to the individual with anxiety, he or she experiences a temporary reduction of anxiety because he or she does not have to face the feared negative self-belief or self-image. This reassurance is only temporary, however, because the individual knows at some level that he or she is fooling the other person(s). Because the other person has been fooled, his or her credibility as an accurate judge of character has been undermined. People with anxiety, therefore, have great difficulty in believing positive feedback proffered by others. The final factor is that, because of these previously mentioned strategies, the self-wounds remain unhealed, resulting in the continuation of the social phobia.

Glen: A Case of Social Phobia—Public Speaking Type

Glen is a 45-year-old college professor with a moderately severe case of social phobia, which primarily involves public speaking. Glen is afraid of revealing any signs of anxiety, including panicking. He construes the symptoms of anxiety in this context as incontrovertible proof of his incompetence. He is fearful of his voice cracking or tremors in his extremities. But he is most fearful of panicking. To panic in such a situation is extremely humiliating and feels to him like an annihilation of self. His major problem is anticipatory anxiety, which can begin as long as a month or more before he has to give a talk. If he can get into his talk, within a few minutes the anxiety subsides and he is able to perform.

The Panic Process

Glen usually experiences significant anticipatory anxiety well before he is scheduled to speak. This anxiety can build to a significant level and, on occasion, can prevent him from speaking altogether. The anticipatory anxiety is almost exclusively focused on his fear of having a panic attack while he is speaking. Glen construes his experience of anticipatory anxiety to be a cue that a panic attack is very likely. If a panic attack occurs, he fears that many— if not most—members of the audience may change their opinion of his intellectual capabilities. For Glen, having a panic attack is the ultimate emasculating experience.

Characteristics of Self-Experiencing

As is typical with individuals experiencing a public speaking phobia, Glen's attention automatically shifts out of the immediate experience of his task (i.e., what he is trying to communicate) to worrying about the significance of his anxiety. As his talk approaches, his attention automatically switches to cogitating about the potentially catastrophic meaning of having a panic attack. As he cogitates, he is so concerned about how he is seen by others that he cannot focus on the task at hand. More specifically, he is focused on whether his anxiety symptoms mean that he is about to panic and that, if he panics, the audience will think that he is intellectually incapable. Such an attentional focus of course interferes with his being able to smoothly carry out his talk.

Underlying Feared Catastrophes

Imagery work uncovered two closely interconnected catastrophes that appeared to drive Glen's public speaking phobia: that people would view him as intellectually incompetent and insufficiently masculine. The basis for this interconnection lies in Glen's family background. Glen's family has roots in Sicily. During his development, he had learned from many different family members that shame is a major catastrophe and that the most shameful behavior is to act unmanly or unmasculine. Hypermasculinity was prized above all. Therefore, for Glen to reveal any sign of weakness was despicable. Glen was the first member of his family to receive a college degree, much less a PhD. Thus, he expresses his masculinity through intellectual achievement. In doing so, he created for himself within the context of his family a novel pathway to masculine achievement. It became clear during our work that any challenge to his intellectual competence was also a challenge to his sense of masculinity. It also became clear that despite his secure reputation in his field as a respected and productive scholar, Glen harbored significant doubts about his intellectual capabilities. Before certain groups of scholars, he often had the feeling that he was an imposter. To be discovered as a fraud is yet one more feared catastrophe.

Glen has one major hobby. He races cars. Often, he is invited to speak before groups of automobile enthusiasts. He is as fearful of panicking in this context as he is when he must give a major academic address. In both contexts, panic has the same meaning: that he is a weak and pathetic man who has no right to lecture, much less belong to, this masculine group.

Self-Wounds

When I asked Glen to imagine the scene in which he is about to give a talk and he has a panic attack, he became aware that his carefully nurtured illusion of intellectual superiority would come tumbling down. The imagery work also revealed that Glen has substantial doubts about his intellectual capacities, despite the fact that he has published often and that his colleagues value his work. He often feels like an imposter whenever he is invited to give a talk. He believes he is intellectually inferior to all of his colleagues and that he has no right to speak at all because his thoughts are so unintelligent or commonplace. Moreover, his fear of being found out as weak and incompetent is tied up with his views regarding his masculinity so that deficiencies in his work possess implications for his experience of gender identity.

In addition, he became aware of his terror that his colleagues will come to view him as an "intellectual lightweight" and of the various stratagems he uses for presenting himself as intellectually superior. Thus his continual need to perform perfectly conflicts with his self-belief that he is far from perfect, and this conflict produces a wide gap between the view he actually holds of himself and the way in which he presents himself to others, that is, between his self-belief and his self-presentation. Glen became aware of the fact that he works very hard to present himself as intellectually superior. At the same time, however, he often feels like an imposter and is acutely aware that he believes he is not enough of a man, a scholar, or a lover. In fact, he believes he is not enough in any field of endeavor that is important to him. As mentioned before, the interconnection of the ideas of intellectual competence and successful masculinity is traceable to his family history. During his development, his father and uncles harshly criticized him if he did not display appropriate masculine behavior and achievements. Glen has internalized this harshly critical attitude and consequently is now extremely critical of himself and his loved ones, in particular.

Interpersonal Consequences

Glen's harshly critical behavior has produced a severe strain in his 15-year marriage. His wife, who is a practicing social worker, has often felt intimidated by Glen's criticisms of her and now finds it difficult to relate to him in a loving manner. Glen attributes malevolent motives to her growing indifference and becomes enraged at her manipulativeness. In fact, she has emotionally withdrawn to protect herself from Glen's critical outbursts. If, however, she tries to express her concerns to him, he typically disagrees. He fears that to agree with her criticisms and to alter his behavior in response to her concerns would represent a shameful lack of masculine assertiveness. Glen construes such self-imposed behavior modification as capitulation and therefore as a pitiable sign of weakness. He therefore must present to her an image of himself as a man who can take charge, one who is in control of the situation. However, the attrition of his wife's displays of love and passion toward Glen has raised doubts in his mind concerning whether he is enough of a man, lover, or husband for her.

Glen displays the same dynamic in his intimate relationship that characterizes his professional behavior. In the context of his marriage, Glen appears to be implicitly guided by a core self-belief that he does not measure up to his internalized standards of a sufficiently masculine husband. Through the years, he has tried to cope with this painful belief by implementing an interpersonal strategy of impression management, which involves presenting himself as the opposite, as a very assertive, dominant individual who can take charge. In this intimate context as well, Glen is experiencing the hiatus between the way he presents himself to his wife and a core element of his self-concept.

PANIC DISORDER WITH AGORAPHOBIA

As with the other anxiety disorders, the primary generating source of panic disorder is the underlying unconscious self-wounds. In the case of patients with panic disorder, however, these self-wounds were initially established by prior panic attacks, which occurred in the context of the various aforementioned sources of self-wounds (i.e., traumatic experiences, shaming or toxic opinions of significant others, betrayals by critically important significant others, prohibitions against experiencing one's feelings, or ineffective responses to the existential givens of living). Panic attacks occurring in these contexts are experienced as self-endangering. These past self-endangerment experiences have been zipped and are now unconscious except for a somatic trace of the original experience. These somatic traces are the bodily sensations that patients with panic disorder fear will lead to a mental or physical catastrophe.

In a patient with panic disorder, immediate experience of the fearful bodily sensation leads to an automatic shift of attention to cogitating about the implications of these sensations, which, in turn, produces more anxiety. These are two key elements in the *Diagnostic and Statistical Manual of Mental Disorders* (4th ed.; *DSM–IV*; American Psychiatric Association, 1994, p. 402) definition of panic disorder: (a) the presence of recurring unexpected panic attacks that seem to the individual to appear out of the blue, as spontaneous bursts of terror, and (b) individuals begin to worry about the recurrence of these attacks and about the implications of a panic attack or its consequences (e.g., losing control, having a heart attack, going crazy). In terms of the self-wound model, these two key elements represent the initial panic attack and the attentional shift to cogitating about its implications.

The patient with panic disorder, however, feels besieged externally as well as internally. The patient begins to implicitly associate the location of a panic attack with its cause. Therefore, in an effort to regulate the occurrence of panic attacks, the individual begins to avoid panic locations. This is the beginning of agoraphobic avoidance behavior. This process can become so extensive that the person may become housebound. This fact, however, does not preclude the fact that many patients experiencing agoraphobia possess an intrapsychic conflict between dependent and autonomous functioning that often predates their first panic attack (Frances & Dunn, 1975).

Panic Disorder Maintenance Processes

Three interrelated processes maintain panic disorder with agoraphobia: (a) the agoraphobic avoidance behavior; (b) the inability to experience the implicit meaning of the panic anxiety (i.e., obsessive cogitating); and (c) the continuing unhealed nature of the self-wound(s). By associating panic attacks with the venues in which they occur, patients with panic disorder actually mislead themselves into thinking that they understand the panic attack's source and that they have a means for regulating their occurrence. Although patients with panic disorder do experience some decrease in the frequency of panic attacks by avoiding panic locations, they nevertheless continue to have panic attacks even in the alleged safety of their own homes. Agoraphobic avoidance also possesses the additional disadvantage of diminishing the range of locations in which individuals with agoraphobia feel safe. This process may continue until the individual is completely housebound.

As mentioned before, when the bodily sensations occur, patients with panic disorder experience the automatic shift in their attentional focus to cogitating about their implications. This shift of attention prevents them from understanding the implicit meaning of panic anxiety. As I demonstrate later in the book, if the individual can stay focused on the panic anxiety, he or she will be able to experience the underlying self-wound and the feelings that accompany it. The accompanying feelings are very painful, and the patient is often as frightened of these feelings as he or she is of the messages embedded in these feelings. Typically, the feared feelings include anger and rage, humiliation and shame, or defeat and despair. Once the underlying self-wound and its associated feelings are experienced in consciousness, therapy can then focus on the healing of the self-wound. The healing work can then be carried out at behavioral, cognitive, and affective levels. As I argue in detail later, a comprehensive treatment for panic disorder must address all three levels.

Self-Wounds

The prototypical self-wounds associated with panic disorder with agoraphobia include seeing one's self as a humiliated loser, inadequate, unlovable, and unworthy. In addition, fears of death, loss, and being alone and isolated also figure prominently in the underlying concerns of patients with panic disorder. Finally, when a patient's life is in transition, he or she may experience a sense of confusion about the future that also can lead to an initial panic attack. Thus patients have reported initial panic attacks when they leave home for the first time, go away to school, become pregnant, change careers, or lose a spouse or parent.

Interpersonal Consequences

The chief interpersonal consequence of panic disorder with agoraphobia is that the patient enlists the aid and cooperation of a particular loved one (e.g., parent, spouse, or friend) to help maintain his or her avoidant tendencies. For example, if a patient is afraid to go to the grocery store for fear she may panic, then her husband ends up doing all of the grocery shopping. If she will travel by car only as a passenger, her spouse will do all of the driving. Spouses then feel in a bind because they want to be supportive and helpful, but as more and more of the load falls on their shoulders, they eventually become resentful.

Joan: A Case of Panic Disorder With Agoraphobia

Joan is a 30-year-old homemaker with two young children who developed the symptoms of panic disorder with agoraphobia 3 years before coming to see me. Her symptoms became incapacitating after a miscarriage 2 years prior to presenting for treatment. She had moved from one Maryland suburb of Washington, DC, to another and at the same time found out she was pregnant with her third child. She came into therapy after she had had an unexpected panic attack while driving her children to an after-school activity. She had become so frightened that she had to pull the car off the road. Her panic symptoms included light-headedness, hyperventilation, shakiness, rubbery legs, and feeling like she was going to faint. The bodily sensation that she particularly feared was light-headedness. Her husband had to come pick them up. After this panic attack, Joan was unable to drive. Several interconnected fears inhibited her ability to get back into the car: fear of having another panic attack, fear of losing control and wrecking the car, and fear of seriously injuring herself or the children. She began to be fearful of having additional panic attacks and began to restrict her activities in an effort to control the venues in which she might have a panic attack. She is also claustrophobic, particularly in elevators. After some time, it became difficult for her to go into public restaurants that were too great a distance from home. Joan also fears being trapped; thus another panic context is any situation that she is unable to leave for any reason.

The Panic Process

The various bodily sensations that Joan found to be particularly frightening all suggested to her that she was losing control. Although most patients with panic disorder fear the loss of control, they construe the meaning of control in idiosyncratic ways. Whereas Jim had construed loss of control as giving up his agentic powers to another person, Joan viewed loss of control as the loss of appropriate body functions (e.g., incontinence). Joan would experience one of the feared body sensations, most particularly the light-headedness, when she was driving or when she was very far from home. She would interpret these sensations as heralds of an oncoming panic attack and become very fearful of these sensations. As the sensation came upon her, she would begin to ask herself, "What if these sensations lead to a panic attack or worse?" The phenomenon of "what-ifing" is a clear marker that her attention has shifted from the immediate experience of the body sensation to speculating and cogitating about its potentially catastrophic meaning. Inevitably, these fearful sensations would lead her to avoid the contexts in which she experienced them and with which she now associated the occurrence of a panic attack. Joan's panic process followed the same sequence as Jim's: the experience of frightening bodily sensations; the shift of attention to cogitating about the catastrophic meaning of these sensations; the enhancement of fear; and finally, the avoidance of the context(s) associated with panic.

Underlying Feared Catastrophes

When Joan was able to carry out the imagery exercise, we learned that her feared catastrophes are fainting and going crazy: fainting because it brought on unbearable humiliation and because she believed no one would come to her aid, and going crazy because this meant a complete loss of control of her body and her person. The latter catastrophe was by far more frightening. The origins of this fear became clear during our early imagery work. When I had her imagine going crazy, she remembered her first panic attack, which had occurred during her sophomore year in high school while she was visiting an elderly relative in a nursing home. She had been appalled and frightened by their "weird, out-of-control" behavior she observed in some of the other residents in the nursing home. She also remembered having a panic attack when she had visited her sister who had been committed to a mental hospital because of a psychotic reaction to cocaine. Seeing her sister under the influence of a powerful neuroleptic drug and barely able to control her locomotion had traumatized Joan, who had implicitly construed this scene as the worst possible catastrophe. She implicitly equated being crazy and being out of control. She now interprets certain bodily sensations (i.e., light-headedness) to mean that she is about to lose control and therefore go crazy.

Joan has been married for almost 10 years to a self-described entrepreneur who is just beginning to become very successful. They had recently moved into my area from another Washington-area suburb. In her old neighborhood, she had made many friends and was very active in the neighborhood, performing a variety of community services and volunteer activities. In her new neighborhood, she was having difficulty making friends and had not as yet become very active. The move represented a tangible sign of her husband's success as the new house was much larger and much more expensive than their previous one. For her, the rise in socioeconomic level represented by the move meant a change in the kind of people whom she would now encounter, people with whom she felt much less comfortable and to whom she felt inferior. Although Joan clearly meets the DSM–IV criteria for panic disorder with agoraphobia, many pieces of evidence suggest that she also possesses some symptoms of social phobia. Traditionally, this diagnostic distinction has been difficult to make (Marshall, 1996).

PANIC DISORDER WITHOUT AGORAPHOBIA

Some individuals develop panic disorder without the accompanying agoraphobic avoidance behavior. The central question regarding the two major presentations of panic disorder is why some people do not develop the agoraphobic avoidance behavior. Most perspectives have argued that agoraphobic avoidance behavior develops as a secondary consequence of panic disorder and may represent an effort to regulate the frequency of panic attacks (e.g., Barlow, 1988; D. F. Klein, 1981). Although earlier studies had suggested that the severity and frequency of panic attacks were associated with the development of agoraphobic avoidance (Beitman, Basha, DeRosear, Flaker, & Mukerji, 1987; Noyes, Clancy, Garvey, & Anderson, 1987), a review of later studies suggests that this is not the case (Clum & Knowles, 1991). Clum and Knowles concluded that patients with panic disorder who end up becoming avoidant tend to (a) anticipate future panic attacks that will have negative consequences, especially social consequences, or (b) feel depressed in addition to having panic disorder.

Craske and Barlow (1988) argued some years ago that in general, there are two areas of origin of the avoidance behavior pattern: (a) anticipatory anxiety about the occurrence of panic and (b) the prior history of the patient's tendency to avoid difficult situations. The former is considered necessary but not sufficient to establish a pattern of avoidance. In addition to the anticipation of a panic attack, several variables influence the emergence of avoidance as a response style. Craske and Barlow (1988) argued that avoidance behavior is based on the individual's prior history of mastery experiences particularly when responding to stress and the experiences of secondary gain that the individual has obtained or expects to obtain from agoraphobic avoidance. Once avoidance is established as a style of responding, it is maintained by the "(a) disruptive effects of unexpected panic attacks within the context of attempted and often achieved predictability of panics; (b) over-estimations in the judged likelihood of experiencing fear and panic, (c) secondary reinforcement, [and] (d) instrumental effects of fear reduction, and safety signals" (p. 680).

In my clinical experience, patients with panic disorder who were not agoraphobic did appear to have milder symptoms and, in general, seemed to be less disturbed than did patients experiencing panic disorder with agoraphobia. There were also differences in the content of their cogitations. For example, the patient described in the following case was concerned that his panic symptoms meant that he was gravely ill. It was therefore unlikely that he would associate any particular panic location with its future occurrence.

Peter: A Case of Panic Disorder Without Agoraphobia

Peter is a 43-year-old physician who came to see me after experiencing for the past 2 years what he described as "terrorizing panic attacks." He experienced a major panic attack the year before when his eldest son left for college and another when the family was on a vacation in California, a few months before he came to see me. Throughout one night during this vacation, he had a continuous series of panic attacks. Although he had not had a panic attack for several months before coming to see me, he was very anxious and fearful of having another one.

The Panic Process

Peter's panic symptoms primarily involved heart palpitations, breaking out into a cold sweat, and a feeling of impending doom. As a result of his intermittent panic attacks, however, Peter became very fearful of his heart palpitations. As a result, he developed a number of illness fears and tended to interpret any unusual body sensation as a sign that he had a life-threatening illness. His fear of bodily sensations could become so great that Peter would be in a state of panic. Once Peter became aware of his particular frightening body sensations, he experienced the prototypical attentional shift from his immediate experience of his body sensations to cogitation. Peter's construal of these sensations as signs of a life-threatening disease only created more anxiety. It is apparent that there were one or more underlying feared catastrophes of which he was only dimly aware.

Underlying Feared Catastrophes

Peter was aware that the conscious trigger for his last two major panic attacks was his eldest son's pending move to a university far from home. Peter had interpreted his attacks as separation anxiety, a problem with which he has been well acquainted since childhood. But this was far from the whole story. Through our imagery work, we learned that Peter was experiencing the destruction of the life he had endeavored so assiduously to create. He was a successful physician with a loving wife and two growing sons on whom he doted. Three years before, they had moved into a more expensive and expansive house and Peter felt that he had just about everything in life that he ever wanted. As Peter focused intensively on the bodily expressions of his anxiety, he became aware of the rage he felt toward his older son for leaving home. Peter had implicitly blamed his son for triggering the unacceptable changes in Peter's idyllic life, just as his own father had blamed Peter for altering his life by leaving home and going to college. His son's pending departure meant not only change in Peter's life but also a totally unacceptable kind of change. He was growing older.

Peter was an avid tennis player, and his illusion of perpetual youth was maintained as long as he could play. In recent years, however, Peter experienced a number of injuries to his back, knees, and wrists that intermittently prevented him from playing. He construed these injuries as ineluctable signs that he was growing older. The direct awareness of aging evoked sadness in Peter that eventually transformed into despair. When I asked him to imagine life after tennis and after his younger son leaves home, all he became aware of was a void. Peter had developed no life plan or goals after his children left home and after he could no longer play tennis as actively as before. Peter seemed completely identified with his older son and implicitly had assumed that his son would never leave him. In an imagery dialogue with his son, Peter told his son, "You're killing me by leaving!" Peter was quite surprised by the degree of rage and bitterness he felt toward his son for leaving.

The imagery also revealed that Peter had construed life as a contest and that now he was losing. In life, according to Peter, there were only winners and losers and the latter were steeped in shame. Thus the experience of shame came to mean to Peter that he was a loser. Consequently, he became very frightened of the experience of shame because of its catastrophic connotations.

One of his responses to his self-perception that he was losing in the game of life was that he no longer wanted to play. At this point, his anxiety began to transform into depressive despair.

Finally, the imagery work revealed that Peter was terrified of being alone. His anxiety was palpable even when I had him just imagine the possibility that he is in fact a separate being, a separate consciousness. He found this ontological given terrifying. Peter construed his son's leaving him to mean that he would have to face his essential aloneness and this was also catastrophic.

Characteristics of Self-Experiencing

Peter was unable to experience his feared body sensations for very long before he shifted to cogitating about their possible significance. Once his attention was focused on himself being anxious, a variety of negative thoughts and feelings would spontaneously occur. Most often he was aware of his fear of these sensations, but at other times he was ashamed, angry, and despondent about his awareness that he was once again having these portentous body sensations. A typical experiential sequence for Peter was the immediate experience of heart palpitations, which meant that he was ill, which meant in turn that he was a loser in life, which left him with extremely painful feelings of shame. This sequence reveals the complexity of the associative network of thoughts and feelings that constitutes the implicit meaning of anxiety.

Self-Wounds

Peter's primary self-wounds included a painful self-view that he was a humiliated loser who was inferior and who lacked the inner resources to tolerate being alone. He also saw himself as a spent old man whose life was essentially over.

Interpersonal Consequences

As mentioned before, one of Peter's core basic assumptions was that there are winners and losers in life and that it was shameful to be a loser. Thus he was always comparing himself with other people and the lives they led. Because of this competitive schema, Peter approached his relationships, both personal and professional, with an anxious vigilance to make sure that he was not losing (i.e., inferior) in any of his major life endeavors. Was he bright enough? Was he in a career of sufficient status? Was his wife pretty enough, intelligent enough? Did he make enough money? Had he accomplished as much thus far in his life, if not more, than his friends and peers? Were his children as smart or as accomplished as those of his age-related peers? If he were to become aware that he was deficient relative to another person on any of these dimensions, he would become extremely anxious. If he were able to fully experience the reality that he was not doing as well in his life as someone else, he would experience intense shame.

GENERALIZED ANXIETY DISORDER

Theorists from different perspectives have proposed that generalized anxiety disorder (GAD) is the basic anxiety disorder out of which other disorders develop (Brown, Barlow, & Liebowitz, 1994; May, 1979). Individuals who meet criteria for GAD have a generalized difficulty in coping with both external and internal threats. They fear intense emotions as much as they fear their inability to respond to life's challenges. Individuals with GAD tend to view themselves as inadequate, defective, or inferior, and they are very frightened about exposing their inadequacies to anyone. They may be said to be wounded in their image, concept, and sense of self, particularly regarding their abilities and basic worth. Any action that is thought to reveal to themselves or others that they are defective produces enormously painful feelings of shame. They fear both the feelings of shame and the messages embedded in these feelings.

Disorder Formation Processes

My clinical experience suggests that at least three major processes are often involved in the acquisition of GAD. The first is the failure to learn specific social and life-care skills. These are real deficits that leave individuals with GAD vulnerable to anxiety whenever they encounter a specific situation that requires a skill that they do not as yet possess. One patient who worried about most things was particularly worried about buying a house. She had never done this before, knew little about the process, and was fearful that she was going to make a catastrophic mistake. Such a mistake would not only be unbearably painful to cope with, but it would also validate her self-view as inadequate. She also feared that other people would begin to view her differently (i.e., loss of status) if they knew of her inadequacy.

A second process that can lead to the self-wounds that appear to drive GAD is the internalization of toxic opinions of significant others regarding one's basic worth. One may initially get the idea that one is inadequate not only from one's own failures but also from the reactions of parents, siblings, and friends. The frequently encountered negative opinion eventually becomes an internalized truth: "I am inadequate." "I am inferior." Under the weight of such opinions, individuals with GAD lose their confidence and become tentative in their efforts (when they are not avoiding situations outright). Such tentativeness erodes performance, which in turn may lead to the inadequate behavior that the individual had feared and anticipated in the first place. Such a circular process of apprehension eroding performance, which then exposes and validates one's self-wound, happens over and over again, making it difficult or impossible for the individual to escape this vicious cycle.

A third process underlying GAD is the development of unconscious conflicts centering on the expression of one's feelings. Although this issue has not been dealt with explicitly in the research literature, recent efforts to apply a brief psychodynamic therapy to GAD may bring these issues into general consideration (Crits-Christoph, Connolly, Azarian, Crits-Christoph, & Shappell, 1996). I therefore must appeal to my clinical experience. The patients with GAD whom I have treated have often been extremely fearful of their own emotional reactions. The most feared emotion is typically anger or rage, but sometimes even the positive emotions may become sources of conflict. Often these patients are not aware that they are conflicted about their feelings and may view themselves as unemotional people. Exploratory work in therapy, however, often uncovers family taboos against the expression of intense emotions. The expression of such emotions would bring severe punishment, ridicule, or the toxic label that one was mentally ill. Thus, such individuals become severely anxious whenever they are about to experience any intense emotion. The experience of emotion would be interpreted as prima facie evidence that they are unlovable, unworthy, or defective. Such individuals give the impression in therapy of being eternally vigilant and on guard lest they reveal something to the therapist that will validate their self-wound.

Disorder Maintenance Processes

In my experience, four major processes influence the maintenance of GAD: (a) worrying, (b) impression management, (c) avoiding the expression of appropriate feelings, and (d) the perseverance of the underlying conflicts.

Worrying

The seminal work of Borkovec and his colleagues (Borkovec & Roemer, 1995) has highlighted the defensive function of worrying. Worrying is a cognitive event that protects the individual from experiencing painful emotions. In terms of this model, worrying represents another form of cogitation, a flight from one's direct, in-the-moment experiencing. The surfacing of painful emotions leads to an automatic shift of attention to worrying; as long as individuals engage in worrying, they are able to avoid the immediate experience of the dreaded emotions and their catastrophic meanings.

Impression Management

Patients with GAD, like those with a social phobia, use the interpersonal strategy of impression management to create a positive impression on others. The fruits of this strategy are identical with these patients: It leads to a temporary reduction of anxiety followed by an awareness that he or she is fooling the other person(s). Patients with GAD then become distrustful of any positive opinion offered by another individual.

Avoiding the Expression of Appropriate Feelings

Many of the patients whom I treated for GAD were reared either in families in which the expression of feelings was severely punished or in families that were so expressive of hostile angry feelings that my patients differentiated themselves from this appalling model by developing a repressive emotional style. Avoidance, however, prevents the individual from directly confronting and healing his or her self-wounds and negative self-beliefs. Instead, individuals with GAD respond to surfacing feelings by worrying, particularly about what others think of them.

The Perseverance of the Underlying Self-Wound

A basic thesis underlying this book is that unless the self-wound is healed, there is a very high probability that the symptoms of GAD will be chronic and intermittent even after successful symptom-focused treatment. Worry cognitions can be modified; the somatic indicators of anxiety can be relaxed away or meditated into quiescence; and intolerance for uncertainty can be improved. But unless the underlying self-wound begins to heal, GAD is liable to remain a chronic, recurring disorder.

Self-Wounds

The patients with GAD whom I have treated have all had one characteristic in common: They felt deep shame about who they were as persons. They believed themselves to be defective, inferior, or unworthy of anyone's love. They tended to experience enormous pain and humiliation whenever they came into contact with any of their shame-based self-images or beliefs.

Interpersonal Consequences

Patients with GAD adopt a defensive and inauthentic style of relating to others in an effort to feel interpersonally safe. This style of relating inevitably generates vicious interpersonal cycles, which tend to leave others confused about their real motives. In their confusion, other people inevitably behave or communicate in ways that reinforce the negative or distrustful assumptions held by these patients. This in turn reinforces their defensive and inauthentic style of relating.

Don: A Case of Generalized Anxiety Disorder

Don is a 25-year-old single man who presents with more or less constant feelings of anxiety, restlessness, and muscle tension. He has insomnia periodically and lapses into irritability and depressed mood states from time to time. He has difficulty extricating himself from a state of constant worrying. Much of his worry is focused on relationships. He is obsessively concerned with what others think of him, and he experiences extreme pain if he learns that someone—anyone—dislikes him, or is critical of him. It is as if he has a monitor always watching how he is coming across, lest he offend someone. If he receives any indication that he is being criticized, he criticizes himself harshly, which results in extremely painful depressive affect. Yet, at the same time, he becomes frightened if people try to get too close to him. He realizes that he is frightened of his feelings and becomes very angry with himself because of this characteristic. But he finds it difficult to experience anger toward anyone else.

Don finds it very difficult to experience any painful feelings, and he attempts to actively avoid confronting any topic or individual who is likely to generate painful feelings in him. If he hears, for example, that another person has a problem similar to his, he becomes very upset because it makes his problem all the more real. If he is fearful that he may possess a particular problem or deficiency, he does not want to hear about someone else who has this problem or deficiency—again because it makes it all the more likely that he does have the problem.

Underlying Feared Catastrophes

A major focus of Don's generalized anxiety involves his relationships. He is very fearful of close and intimate relationships and constantly monitors and equilibrates his behavior so that he can preserve a comfortable interpersonal environment. He is very concerned with what people think of him and is equally frightened of hurting other people's feelings and of other people hurting his. He fears causing pain but he is also afraid of being ridiculed and rejected. He is vigilant not only about what he says but also about how he says something and how he looks when he says it. He tends to avoid people to protect himself from having uncomfortable interpersonal exchanges, but he then begins to harshly criticize himself for being so frightened of people and relationships. Through our work, Don became aware that humiliation was probably the most painful experience that he has encountered. The catch-

22 (as he labeled it) is that both relating to people and avoiding them lead to intense feelings of shame and humiliation.

When we explored his romantic relationships, it became clear that he could not commit himself to any woman of whom his parents disapproved, so great is his need for their approval. However, he also felt that he was not good enough for any woman who met with his parents' approval. The anxiety that resulted from this construal of his relationships led him to avoid all emotional entanglements. Shame seemed to be his constant companion.

Self-Wounds

Don's primary self-wound is that he believes he is inferior and therefore not deserving of anyone's love. At the same time, there appeared to be a self-view that he was a malevolent presence in other people's lives. He feared not only being rejected but also his propensity to reject others. Whenever he allowed himself to feel angry with another person, he was always afraid that it would seriously hurt or even destroy the other person. That sense of malevolence was directly tied to his discomfort with his own anger, a discomfort that was nurtured by family norms that discouraged its expression.

OBSESSIVE–COMPULSIVE DISORDER

People who develop obsessive–compulsive disorder (OCD) have been subjected to child-rearing practices that emphasize the potential for shame that accompanies even little mistakes. These practices lead to the internalization of opinions from caregivers that one is basically bad, dangerous, or mistake-prone. Self-wounds emerge around these sensed defects of character that, under conditions of stress, produce obsessional thoughts. Another characteristic of the child-rearing discipline is that individuals with OCD learn that thinking a thought is equivalent to acting it out. This fusion of thoughts and acts (Salkovskis, 1985) lends a special power to obsessional thoughts to significantly increase the level of anxiety that the person experiences. The particular mental and behavioral rituals that the individual develops are acts that have had some success in the past in reducing the person's anxiety. These rituals are often developed in childhood when magical thinking frequently characterizes an individual's efforts to control the chaos that is experienced internally or externally.

Disorder Maintenance Processes

In my clinical experience, I have noticed three major processes used by persons with OCD that appear to maintain the disorder: (a) avoidance of the anxiety-producing thoughts, (b) continuation of the compulsive rituals that reduce anxiety, and (c) continuation of the unconscious self-wounds.

Avoidance of Anxiety-Provoking Thoughts

Patients with OCD attempt by any means possible to avoid, disavow, or distract themselves from obsessional thoughts. Because these thoughts are often unbidden, intrusive thoughts, this strategy often fails. Even if it were successful, this strategy would leave the basic self-wounds unaddressed and their protective structures intact.

Compulsive Rituals to Reduce Anxiety

The cardinal strategy that patients with OCD automatically use to minimize the havoc produced by obsessional thoughts is the *ritual*, a compulsive mental or behavioral act that is designed to undo the thought, reassure the patient, and thereby reduce the anxiety. The functional significance of compulsions has been clear to therapists going back to S. Freud (1894/1962a). The dilemma for the individual with OCD is that the reassurance and therefore the reduction in anxiety are only temporary. Soon the terrifying thought returns, which triggers the compulsions and the cycle begins again.

[handwritten margin note: Compulsive ritual to reduce anxiety]

Continuation of Unconscious Self-Wounds

The final reason OCD continues is that the underlying self-wounds have not been addressed. The fearsome self-view as one who is responsible for the most heinous acts is unbearably painful to the individual with OCD and must be avoided at all costs. The fact that such a self-view can exist reflects the person's inability to accept that one can make mistakes without coming to the conclusion that one is incorrigibly bad or morally defective. Because there is a negative core self-view that one is bad and beyond redemption, the individual with OCD must go to great lengths not to see this in him- or herself or show it to others. To hide this devastating self-view from him- or herself and others, the individual constructs an ideal of perfection with regard to his or her behavior and performance. The assumption is that a perfect performance provides perfect protection against this devastating self-view. The problem is, however, that any deviation in one's performance from the ideal produces great anxiety and dread regarding an imagined pending catastrophe. The catastrophic consequences are thought to occur in two separate spheres: The individual would have to face the fact that he or she is deficient, defective, or degenerate (i.e., the internal consequences include facing the devastating self-view), and that he or she will be rejected, abandoned, and isolated (i.e., the external consequences of others seeing the patient with OCD for what he or she really is). As one of my patients put it, "I am afraid that I am actually a loser and will be alone for the rest of my life."

Finally, OCD, like the other anxiety disorders, seems to include some very intense negative affects that the individual does not want to experience. The feelings that are most frequently associated with OCD are anger and rage and humiliation and shame. Rage, for example, is often behind the violent obsessional thoughts that can cause extreme anxiety in a patient with

OCD. One patient, for example, had the recurring obsessional thought of smashing his girlfriend's face to a pulp. This thought was so terrifying to him that he would engage in several compulsive acts, such as looking up or turning his head from side to side, in an effort to undo the violent thought. This patient had no idea that he was angry at his girlfriend because she had shamed him in front of some friends.

Interpersonal Consequences

Patients with OCD experience intense shame over having this disorder. They go to great lengths to keep their problem secret from others and are very fearful of being seen doing crazy things. In addition, patients with OCD typically enlist the aid of spouses, lovers, or friends in reassuring them that they are not morally defective. The constant need for reassurance puts a severe strain on their relationships.

Spencer: A Case of Obsessive–Compulsive Disorder

Spencer is a 25-year-old man who presents with classic symptoms of OCD. He has been plagued and terrified by unwanted thoughts since 6 years of age. Currently, he is particularly fearful of his violent thoughts, which frequently relate to smashing his girlfriend in the face. Initially, he had no idea that his violent thoughts had anything to do with his being angry with his girlfriend. In fact, he carries within him a great deal of anger at his father for his temper and criticism; at his mother for her many emotional problems and suicide attempts; at his grandfather who allegedly had sexually abused his daughter (Spencer's mother) for years when she was a child; and at his grandmother for not knowing about the abuse, or if she did know, for not protecting her daughter.

Spencer can be harshly self-critical and has great difficulty in forgiving himself for earlier mistakes in judgment (e.g., substance abuse; cheating on a previous girlfriend whom he now believes he truly loved). He engages in a variety of rituals to reduce the anxiety generated by these thoughts, and these include clicking a light switch up and down and looking up if he has a negative thought in an effort to cancel it.

Spencer grew up in a Washington, DC, suburb. He is the middle child in an upper-middle-class family. He is close to and protective of his younger brother but not so close to his older sister. His father is a successful lawyer, but his mother has experienced, for most of her life, serious mental problems that have resulted in frequent hospitalizations and suicide attempts. He describes his father as a good man who has taken care of his wife. His father, however, possesses a violent temper and can be hostile and critical.

Disorder Formation Processes

Spencer grew up in a family in which there was a great deal of paternal criticism, parental fighting, and maternal emotional disturbance. The hyperbolic emotional atmosphere of his family induced chaotic feelings in Spencer. When he was 6 years old, he first developed the compulsive ritual of turning a light switch on and off whenever he experienced these chaotic feelings. He has been troubled by this disorder ever since. This ritual provided him with temporary relief from his anxiety and discomfort. In addition, as is typical of persons with OCD, Spencer learned that thinking a thought is equivalent to acting it out. When he has these symptoms, he cogitates about their meaning and concludes that he must be crazy. This is extremely painful.

Disorder Maintenance Processes

Because his rituals do provide him with temporary relief, they serve as a major factor in the maintenance of this disorder. If people were to discover his problem, he believes that they would view him as crazy. He cannot tolerate the anxiety that his obsessional thoughts generate. Consequently, in addition to performing his rituals, Spencer becomes self-preoccupied with thoughts of being crazy and a loser because of this disorder.

Self-Wounds

The implicit catastrophic meaning of his anxiety is that he will be rejected and abandoned if he acts on his thoughts. He will be left alone and will be considered—and see himself as—a loser. His disorder appears to be rooted in a core negative self-view as one who is a loser and therefore alone. This is unbearably painful. Spencer goes to great lengths to hide his disorder from others and the fact that he is seeking therapy for it.

SUMMARY

Thus far I have presented the general, integrative etiological model of anxiety disorders and have shown how it applies to several specific anxiety disorders. The model is sufficiently flexible to characterize the similarities across different anxiety disorders as well as to describe the reasons and causes for the differences that obtain among them. The second half of the book describes a general integrative psychotherapy for anxiety disorders, the process by which I arrived at this model, and its usefulness in delineating the similarities and differences in intervention strategies across the same group of anxiety disorders. On occasion I return to each of the specific cases described in the etiological portion of the book to show how I applied the integrative psychotherapy. I begin with a description of the development of the integrative psychotherapy.

III

AN INTEGRATIVE THERAPY
FOR ANXIETY DISORDERS

8

TOWARD AN INTEGRATIVE PSYCHOTHERAPY FOR ANXIETY DISORDERS

I regret that the various disciplines, particularly psychology and psychiatry, appear to be headed for a cyclic renewal of their periodic internecine struggles. We seem destined to pursue, for yet a while longer, our all too familiar dogma-eat-dogma existence.

—Morris Parloff (1979)

Some years ago, when I conducted a research workshop on psychotherapy integration for the National Institute of Mental Health, H. Arkowitz (personal communication, March 10, 1986) made the perspicacious point that an integrative theory of psychotherapy explains how to bring about change, but does not explain what needs to be changed. The latter is what a theory of psychopathology explains. To identify the targets of change in the anxiety disorders, I have provided an integrative theory. In this chapter I describe the process by which I arrived at an integrative model of psychotherapy, that is, a theory of how to bring about change in the identified targets.

The self-wound model suggests that there are in fact a number of different targets of change. They can be schematically represented as follows: (a) symptoms; (b) cognitive, affective, and behavioral defenses; and (c) underlying self-wounds. The symptoms of an anxiety disorder cut across four dimensions of concern: behavior, cognition, emotions, and interpersonal relationships. For example, panic disorder is characterized by somatic symptoms, their cognitive misinterpretation, behavioral avoidance strategies, and self-based unconscious conflicts that mediate the panic attacks. The defenses that patients with panic disorder typically use include agoraphobic avoidance (i.e., behavioral); disavowed emotions and emotional suppression or repression (i.e., emotional); worrying and catastrophizing (i.e., cognitive); and overly dependent relationships and distrusting others (i.e., interpersonal). Finally, panic-disorder-related self-wounds typically include such searing self-views as seeing one's self as inadequate, unlovable, or inferior.

The range of targets for anxiety disorder change suggests that no single traditional therapeutic orientation will be sufficient to effect change in all of them. But a number of other considerations also suggest the need for an integrative psychotherapy. These include theoretical issues, research findings, and clinical experience.

THEORETICAL CONSIDERATIONS

Different psychotherapies focus on different aspects of anxiety disorders. Psychodynamic therapies, for example, tend to ignore the symptoms of an anxiety disorder on the basis of the assumption that in the heat and light of a successful analysis of the disorder's genetic (i.e., developmental) roots, the symptoms will melt away (Gabbard, 1994). The early behavioral therapists made the opposite error of focusing on only the surface-level symptoms of an anxiety disorder. These practitioners and theorists assumed that the achievement of relief from symptoms constituted the entire scope of an effective therapy (Eysenck, 1960). Cognitive–behavioral (CB) therapists began with the assumption that modifying conscious cognitions would be sufficient, but they have since extended the focus of therapy to unconscious cognitive schemas that are presumed to drive the observable symptoms of an anxiety disorder (A. T. Beck & Emery, 1985; J. S. Beck, 1995; Meichenbaum, 1977). Experiential therapists focus on the conscious emotional-processing difficulties associated with a number of disorders including anxiety disorders as well as on underlying maladaptive emotion schemes that, like cognitive schemas, drive the observable symptoms (L. S. Greenberg, Rice, & Elliott, 1993; Wolfe & Sigl, 1998). Finally, the biomedical perspective has consistently focused on a variety of hypotheses that attempt to relate neurobiological malfunctions to anxiety symptoms (e.g., D. F. Klein, 1993).

In the midst of these differences, however, a number of common factors embedded in these various therapies contribute to the fact that benefits may be achieved with virtually any of these therapies. The common factors may include (a) the developing significance of the therapeutic alliance, (b) the increasing importance of treating more than just the surface-level symptoms of an anxiety disorder, and (c) the role of exposure as a necessary—if not sufficient—ingredient of an effective therapy.

These factors, by virtue of the fact that they are common to most psychotherapies, can be viewed as the foundation of an integrative psychotherapy for anxiety disorders. But the extant therapeutic orientations also differ in significant ways. Some factors persuade me more than others, and I provide a rationale for those factors that I believe are necessary ingredients of an effective integrative psychotherapy.

RESEARCH FINDINGS

Investigations of efficacious treatments for anxiety disorders have focused mostly on behavioral and cognitive–behavioral therapies (CBTs) and various pharmacological agents. Whereas research on psychodynamic therapies is sparse, research on experiential therapies with this population is virtually nonexistent. By and large, the therapies that have been studied have focused on the symptom layer of the disorder. Excellent progress has been made by these symptom-focused treatments with a majority of treatment completers in most studies achieving clinically significant reduction of their anxiety symptoms (Barlow, Gorman, Shear, & Woods, 2000; Borkovec & Ruscio, 2000; Foa & Kozak, 1996; Heimberg & Becker, 2001). However, these treatments are no panacea, and much therapeutic work is typically required after the frequency and intensity of anxiety symptoms have been reduced. In my view, one of the major limitations of these treatments is the narrowing of their focus. Although they are quite useful for symptom reduction, they do not address a range of issues associated with anxiety disorders that are addressed by other psychotherapies for which little research evidence has yet to be aggregated.

CLINICAL EXPERIENCE

My own clinical work has taught me a number of important lessons that have motivated me to develop the integrative models under consideration in this book. First, symptom reduction is not sufficient for a comprehensive or durable treatment effect. Many of my patients make significant progress with exposure-based therapies, for example, but then plateau as they reach the limit of their ability to carry out the often-harrowing treatment. For example, a patient with a driving phobia I once treated was able to drive eight miles from his home after several months of exposure therapy but was unable to go past this self-imposed limit. At this point, issues around his ability to function autonomously without the support and succor of his parents emerged as significant impediments to further exposure therapy. At this point, we had to switch gears and engage in a more psychodynamic–experiential psychotherapy to resolve his dependency issues before he was able to achieve any greater progress with the exposure therapy.

A second lesson I learned from my clinical experience with patients with anxiety is the critical importance of the therapeutic relationship for creating the supportive environment that will catalyze the specific tasks and techniques of therapy. Often the specific tasks of therapy are either precluded or jettisoned by implicit transference-related issues. These need to be addressed before the specific tasks of therapy can be undertaken. These interpersonal issues may be issues that the patient brings into therapy that interfere with its progress, or they may relate to undetected ruptures in the therapeutic alliance (Safran, 1993). For example, I once treated an individual with obsessive–compulsive disorder (OCD). Because of the outpatient nature of the treatment setting, I had suggested and delineated a self-initiated program in exposure and response prevention. The first time I reviewed his homework, he informed me that he had not yet attempted the program. After getting the same answer from him in two successive therapy sessions, I inquired as to what the difficulty (beyond the rationalizations he had already given me) might be. He finally confessed the following: "I hate to do what a male authority figure tells me to do." This led to a diversion in our therapeutic focus as we uncovered and explored his painful and humiliating relationship with his demanding and hypercritical father.

A third lesson obtained from my clinical experience is that an anxiety disorder is about much more than just its symptoms. Although the *Diagnostic and Statistical Manual of Mental Disorders* (4th ed., text revision; DSM–IV–TR; American Psychiatric Association, 2000) may define an anxiety disorder in terms of a specific cluster of observable symptoms, the therapy context reveals that much more is involved. I discovered this in a variety of ways. First, as I have mentioned before, the application of imaginal exposure often guided me to a host of painful issues and emotions that seem to drive the anxiety symptoms. Images of physical and psychological catastrophe would arise during imaginal exposure. These catastrophes reflected wounds to the self that had never healed. When I would explore the implicit meaning of his or her anxiety with a patient, we would frequently discover the patient's interpersonal fears and the maladaptive interpersonal strategies that he or she would use to reduce anxiety. These fears and strategies are based in internalized models of the self, others, and the world and they reflect painful and disillusioning encounters with—as well as problems with attachment to—the client's early caregivers (Bowlby, 1973). And these strategies often continue to be active even after the symptoms of anxiety have been reduced.

Finally, I learned from clinical experience that the symptoms of an anxiety disorder cannot be ignored in favor of an analysis of underlying unconscious conflicts. I learned early on that using a psychodynamic approach alone in the treatment of anxiety has severe limitations. Insights into the implicit meaning of the anxiety symptoms may be obtained, but the anxiety symptoms tend to persist (Wolfe, 2001a). The optimistic assumption from which psychoanalysts have typically proceeded—namely, that the symptoms will disappear once the genetic roots of the anxiety have been successfully analyzed—has rarely been borne out.

SEARCHING THE MODELS

Theoretical considerations, research evidence, and clinical experience have all convinced me of the need for an integrative psychotherapy for the anxiety disorders. It should be clear, however, that there is no need to develop a new therapy. The elements of an effective integrative psychotherapy exist within the various extant therapeutic orientations and it is worth sifting through their respective models of treatment for the basic elements of such a therapy. I now briefly review psychodynamic, behavioral, CB, experiential, and biomedical models of treatment for the anxiety disorders.

Psychodynamic Treatment Models

As I suggested earlier, psychodynamic models contend that anxiety disorders are rooted in interpersonally based unconscious conflicts that bear a symbolic relationship to the fear stimuli. Treatment is therefore focused on the analysis of the genetic roots of the anxiety and in uncovering the unconscious conflicts that seem to maintain the disorder. The means of change is the therapeutic relationship itself. The analytic or psychodynamic therapy conversation will eventually result in the appearance of the transferential roots of the patient's anxiety and it is the analysis of the patient's transferential feelings toward the therapist that will lead to the uncovering of the unconscious conflicts that maintain the patient's anxiety. Before the analysis of transference, however, the psychodynamic therapist analyzes the psychological defenses that the patient uses to both reduce the anxiety and protect him or her from exposing (to him- or herself and others) the conflicts that exist outside of his or her awareness (Michels, Frances, & Shear, 1985).

Therapeutic Relationship and Stance

The basic therapeutic stance of the psychoanalytic therapist involves the assumption of the role of passive listener who occasionally interprets the symbolic meaning of the patient's communications. The focus of intervention has moved away from the classical analytic interest in free association toward an intense focus on the face-to-face communications between the therapist and the patient. These communications are assumed to be multilayered, reflecting aspects of the real relationship as well as the transferential relationship between therapist and patient (Gill, 1984). The therapist makes interpretive links between the patient's present mode of interpersonal functioning and previously adopted interpersonal scenarios, including the thoughts and feelings that accompanied these behavioral patterns. As insights emerge in the therapy session and are thoroughly worked through, the patient gradually experiences a stronger sense of self, a greater sense of control over his or her life, and increased energy with which to live it.

The therapeutic relationship, therefore, is viewed not only as the catalyst to change but also as the means of therapeutic change. The therapeutic work comes through the interactions between therapist and client. The in-session change process provides the client with new information about his or her interpersonal patterns of behavior. As a result of successful therapy, the client now has the choice of whether to use this new information to change his or her behavior outside of therapy. For this reason, behavioral change per se has been of less interest to psychodynamic therapies than it has been to the behavioral and cognitive–behavioral therapies.

Major Techniques

The major techniques of psychodynamic therapy include empathy, clarification, interpretation, and the analysis of transference. Establishing an empathic connection is a critically important component of psychodynamic therapy. From the dynamic perspective, empathy has functioned primarily as a method of observation and data gathering and as an enabling condition for the major processes of change (Wolitzky & Eagle, 1997).

Interpretation has been the primary technique of most forms of psychodynamic therapy. It involves tactful phrasing of the subliminal meanings of the patient's current mode of relating. Interpretation is the primary means by which the psychodynamic therapist analyzes the patient's defenses and transferential reactions. Initially, the therapist attempts to elucidate the defensive patterns the patient uses in the therapeutic relationship and presumably in other relationships outside of therapy. Only after the patient's defensive patterns are thoroughly experienced and understood by the patient does the therapist attempt to interpret the instinctual impulses or unconscious conflictual patterns of relating that are being defended against.

Mechanisms of Change

Originally, the basic process of change in psychoanalytic therapy has been the acquisition of insight. Insight involves both intellectual understanding and emotional experiencing. The emergence of an insight, however, is not sufficient to resolve an infantile neurosis. Insights must be worked through, which means that interpretations in many different contexts must be repeated so that the widely dispersed elements of the patient's maladaptive interpersonal scenario can be integrated into a coherent whole (Greenson, 1967). Thus, the change process, as conceived by the psychodynamic perspective, is construed to be a slow but steady accretion of new thoughts, feelings, and experiences and their integration (Wachtel, 1997).

The relational approaches of psychoanalysis (i.e., object relations and self psychology) have more recently placed a greater focus on the support and empathy provided by the therapist. The basic theoretical assumption is that by offering something different and more benign by way of a relationship, the therapist provides a positive model to be internalized by the client, which in turn will bring about positive changes in his or her view of self and others (J. Greenberg & Mitchell, 1983; Kohut, 1979).

Psychodynamic Therapy Applied to Specific Anxiety Disorders

Although anxiety has always been a focal point of psychodynamic treatment, the psychoanalytic perspective has generally eschewed the idea of specific anxiety disorders, at least as the *DSM* defines them. However, some psychodynamic clinicians have begun to develop dynamically oriented psychotherapies for specific disorders diagnosed according to the *DSM–IV* (American Psychiatric Association, 1994), including generalized anxiety disorder (GAD). Crits-Christoph and colleagues (1995), for example, have developed a short form of Luborsky's (1984) supportive–expressive (SE) treatment for GAD. They hypothesized that one or more traumatic experiences contribute to the formation of basic cognitive schemas about one's self and others, particularly regarding one's ability to meet one's needs. These schemas focus primarily on uncertainty about obtaining love, security, stability, or protection from others. These concerns are so laden with fear that patients with GAD avoid such emotional issues by defensively worrying about current life events. The unconscious emotional issues, however, influence the worrying and the development of maladaptive interpersonal scenarios with others. The therapy attempts to analyze the anxiety symptoms in terms of unconscious interpersonal–intrapsychic conflicts. These conflicts are formulated in terms of the Core Conflictual Relationship Theme (CCRT) measure developed by Luborsky and Crits-Christoph (1990). CCRT focuses on (a) the wishes and needs of the patient, (b) the responses of others, and (c) the consequent responses of the patient. As Crits-Christoph, Connolly, Azarian, Crits-Christoph, & Shappell (1996) explained,

> Through uncovering the patient's CCRT patterns as manifested in current relationships, past relationships, and the relationship with the therapist, the conflicts contributing to the anxiety symptoms are worked through and better ways of coping with feelings, expressing one's needs, and responding to others are explored. (p. 422)

This treatment has received some initial empirical validation in a treatment development study. Preliminary data on 26 patients with GAD revealed significant change in anxiety, depression, worry, and interpersonal problems.

Other research-oriented, psychodynamic clinicians have attempted to develop a manualized psychodynamic therapy for panic disorder. They call their treatment panic-focused psychodynamic psychotherapy (PFPP; Milrod, Busch, Cooper, & Shapiro, 1997). Whereas traditional psychoanalytic therapies tend to ignore the manifest symptoms of a disorder in favor of an exploration of their underlying, unconscious determinants, PFPP maintains a focus on the symptoms of panic disorder with or without agoraphobia. This therapy can be used as a short-term treatment for the elimination of panic and agoraphobic symptoms or as a longer-term treatment to resolve the panic patient's vulnerability to relapse. To do the latter, however, the therapy must address the unconscious dynamisms that predispose the panic patient to panic symptoms.

PFPP therapy is divided into three phases. Phase I attempts to explore and relieve panic attacks. This exploration may lead the therapist to formulate the unconscious conflicts that may be involved in producing the patient's panic attacks. In my experience, these conflicts typically concern separation, anger, and sexuality. This phase typically takes 12 to 20 weeks of therapy.

In Phase II, the therapist explores in greater detail the thoughts and feelings that produce the patient's panic symptoms and the characterological underpinnings of these symptoms. During this phase, there is a special focus on the transferential reactions of the patient to the therapist. The reduction of the patient's vulnerability to relapse is the goal of this phase of therapy, which is hypothesized to last between 9 months and a year. Phase III, the termination phase, is designed to address the patient's fears of separation and independence.

Critique of Psychodynamic Treatment Models

The recent short-term versions of psychodynamic therapy have begun to pay more attention to the symptoms of an anxiety disorder—a decided plus. This is particularly true for PFPP, which is a specifiable psychodynamic therapy. PFPP possesses a number of strengths and weaknesses. On the positive side, PFPP suggests that (a) the treatment of panic symptoms is critically important, (b) panic attacks are not spontaneous alarms that occur out of the blue and are therefore devoid of psychological meaning, (c) panic attacks reflect underlying unconscious dynamisms that appear to generate panic symptoms, (d) panic symptoms reflect the patient's core issues and self-beliefs that are construed in a catastrophic manner, and (e) the exploration and resolution of these underlying unconscious issues appear to decrease the patient's vulnerability to panic relapse.

The range of unconscious issues as delineated by this approach appears to be limited. The psychoanalytic literature highlights the fact that issues around separation, rage, and sexuality typically underlie panic symptoms. In fact, the range of issues is actually much wider and can involve any issue or affect that is felt to be a potential catastrophe to the individual. When patients enter therapy, these issues are not in their focal awareness. Instead, the panic symptoms seem to occur when the expression of painful and frightening affects surrounding these issues is imminent. This is a decided strength of the psychodynamic model because of the misleading information that has been fostered particularly by the biomedical perspective that the initial panic attack has little to do with psychological meaning.

Another difficulty resides with the psychoanalytic conception of its major process of therapeutic change, the concept of *working through*. Wachtel (1997) has argued that this is a particularly vague concept that is not easily grasped. Working through is viewed as a process by which a patient can ". . . see his conflicts from a variety of perspectives, [a process] of deepening understanding, or presenting the patient with the range of meanings evident in his psychic life, of elaborating insights through repetition, of permitting the ego to gradually absorb new experiences and so on" (pp. 90–91). There is a need to more clearly specify the mechanisms or processes of change in psychodynamic therapy.

A third issue concerns whether there may be more efficient ways of uncovering the implicit meaning of panic than the psychoanalytic conversation. It is a major contention of this book that there are more efficient means of not only uncovering unconscious issues but also modifying them.

The SE treatment for GAD appears to be a promising addition to the treatment armamentarium for GAD. Its focused nature of disorder-specific conflicts is a major strength. Like other dynamic therapies, however, there is insufficient focus on the symptoms of GAD, particularly on the defensive process of worrying. Moreover, all of the same criticisms leveled at PFPP apply as well to SE therapy for GAD.

The Behavioral Treatment Model

The behavioral treatment of anxiety arose as a challenge to the scientific limitations of Freudian psychoanalysis. The early behaviorists viewed psychoanalysis as unscientific at best, quackish at worst (Eysenck, 1960; Wolpe, 1958). By contrast, they argued that the early behavioral therapies were based in laboratory science, which presumably had demonstrated the basic laws of learning, classical, and operant conditioning. Behavioral therapists viewed abnormal or dysfunctional behavior as subject to the same laws of learning as so-called normal behavior. Both prosocial and odd behaviors are learned through either classical or instrumental conditioning processes. Behavioral therapists further assumed that learned behaviors could be unlearned by breaking the associative connection between stimuli and responses. In the case of anxiety disorders, this means that the connection between fear stimuli and fear responses could be severed through a variety of means such as extinction, counterconditioning, or the positive reinforcement of alternative behaviors.

Therapeutic Relationship and Stance

Behavioral therapists have typically argued that developing rapport is a necessary precondition to effective therapy and that the therapist is a socially sanctioned expert in behavioral change processes. It was not until the 1970s, however, that behavioral therapists began to seriously reflect on the role of the therapeutic relationship in the outcome of therapy. An early study by Morris and Suckerman (1974) indicated how the characteristics of the therapist conducting systematic desensitization interacted with its specific procedures. They found that desensitization obtained greater results in reducing the fear of snakes when conducted by a warm therapist than by a cold and aloof one. Goldfried and Davison (1976) pointed out a number of ways in which the therapeutic relationship can affect progress in therapy: (a) the client–therapist interaction may represent a good sample of the client's problem behavior(s); (b) the therapist's personal influence and persuasiveness may enhance the client's cooperation as well as his or her willingness to attempt new or different behaviors outside of the therapeutic situation; (c) the therapist's socially sanctioned role as a healer may enhance the client's expectations of positive results; and (d) the therapist's genuine concern for the client may generally enhance the process of therapy. Currently, behavioral therapists are quite sensitive to the interaction of the therapeutic relationship with the specific therapeutic tasks. However, most research on therapy outcome rarely focuses on the role of the therapeutic relationship in therapy outcome (see, however, the work of Hayes, Strosahl, & Wilson, 1998; Kohlenberg & Tsai, 1995).

Major Techniques

The early behavioral therapies developed out of applications of either classical conditioning or Skinner's operant conditioning theory. The later appearance of social learning theory extended the reach and focus of behavioral therapy and legitimized the analysis of broader psychological events in behavioral therapy (Bandura, 1977). The major techniques of behavioral therapy that were derived from these three behavioral traditions include a variety of procedures designed to break the habitual association between fear stimuli and fear responses. The general strategy has been to decrease unwanted behaviors and increase wanted behaviors. Relaxation strategies have been used as inhibitors of anxiety (Wolpe, 1958). Exposure therapy, with many procedural variations, has emerged as the primary treatment technique in the behavioral treatment of anxiety. Other techniques include punishing the unwanted response and positively reinforcing the desired response.

Behavioral therapy actually has developed along very pragmatic lines (Fishman & Franks, 1997), and creative clinicians have developed a number of performance-based therapeutic techniques without worrying too much about their theoretical inspiration. Thus behavioral rehearsal and problem-solving approaches were developed as active strategies for implementing behavioral change procedures. Rehearsing the desired response during the therapy session is also a frequently used technique to help clients practice the desired response and modify any unwanted associated behaviors. Modern-day behavioral therapists proceed with a functional analysis of the relationships between behavior and the environment, looking for the links among cognition, affect, behavior, and environmental events. The functional analysis guides treatment by pointing the therapist to the specific targets of change and the likely reinforcement paradigm that will bring about change in specific targeted behaviors. It should be noted that a broadly conceived and conducted functional analysis necessarily blurs the boundary between behavioral therapy and CBT. The exploration of cognitive and affective links to targeted behaviors moves behavioral therapy beyond its stated original focus on publicly observable behaviors.

Mechanisms of Change

Proponents of conditioning models of fear response acquisition have argued that conditioned stimuli continue to evoke the conditioned fear response as long as they retain an association with the unconditioned response. But the learned pattern can be unlearned by arranging for the conditioned stimulus to occur in the absence of the unconditioned response to which it is linked so as to eliminate its causal relationship to the fear response. Thus if the conditioned stimulus results in no pain, the learned pattern eventually will be extinguished. Wolpe's systematic desensitization therapy, for example, was based on his research with cats in which a phobic response could be induced and then removed by experimental means. Wolpe labeled the therapeutic mechanism involved in the elimination of anxiety *reciprocal inhibition*. This principle suggested that at least eight different kinds of responses are antagonistic to anxiety, such that if a person responds with one of these eight responses, the anxiety will be eliminated. These responses included, among others, sexual arousal, anger, assertiveness, and relaxation. Wolpe eventually settled on relaxation as the response that was the most practical as well as effective inhibitor of anxiety.

A later model of fear conditioning, Mowrer's two-factor theory, argued that neurotic fear responses (i.e., phobias) were learned by means of classical conditioning and were maintained by avoidance behavior. In this model, fear is viewed as a learned drive that is then reduced by avoidance. To unlearn such a fear response requires the elimination of the avoidance response and the presentation of the conditioned fear stimulus. Because no real harm or pain will come to the individual, the fear response eventually will be extinguished. This is the theoretical underpinning of exposure therapy. Phobic behavior is thought to yield to positively reinforcing approach behaviors and simultaneously extinguishing the consequent anxiety.

Behavioral Therapy Applied to Specific Anxiety Disorders

Specific Phobias. As previously mentioned, behavioral treatments of specific phobias typically involve exposure to the phobic object or situation and the simultaneous use of a specific relaxation strategy. Wolpe's therapy instructed the patient to imagine a series of scenes involving a feared object. These scenes would be arranged in a hierarchy of fearfulness from the least frightening to the most frightening. Patients would begin by imagining the least frightening scene that still induced anxiety and would then use a previously learned relaxation strategy to reduce the anxiety. The imagery trials with a given scene would continue until the patient could imagine the scene without anxiety. At that point, the procedure would move to the next scene in the hierarchy. This would continue until the patient could imagine the most frightening scene in the hierarchy in an anxiety-free state (Wolpe, 1958).

Initially, Wolpe reported a 90% cure rate for phobias with systematic desensitization. But as the cases became more complex, the efficacy figures, although still good, significantly declined. The higher figure seems to apply only to clearly defined single-symptom phobias. Patients with multiple fears and extensive problems in other aspects of their life were less likely to benefit from systematic desensitization (Wolpe, Brady, Serber, Agras, & Liberman, 1973).

Eventually, a number of effective behavioral therapy techniques were developed for phobias, but they all seemed to possess the common factor of exposing the individual—either in imagination or in vivo—to the feared object or situation. Again, the assumption was that such exposure therapies are the treatment of choice for specific phobias, except for the treatment of blood phobia (Öst & Sterner, 1987). Exposure therapies have been useful in the treatment of most anxiety disorders, but it is now clear that they need to be supplemented, usually with relaxation strategies and cognitive therapies.

Social Phobias (Social Anxiety Disorder). Early on, systematic desensitization was used to treat social anxiety as well as other phobias (Wolpe, 1958). In 1971, Goldfried introduced a self-control variation of the desensitization procedure. It used the same desensitization paradigm, but had some significant differences in procedure. Goldfried reconceptualized desensitization as training in coping skills. Desensitization sessions therefore can be seen as providing practice in coping with anxiety. One of the most significant procedural differences was in the construction of the anxiety hierarchy: Instead of a focus on different situations that elicited anxiety, the focus was placed on what it feels like to the client to be tense. As Goldfried (1971) stated it, "The client is being taught to cope with his proprioceptive anxiety responses and cues rather than with situations which elicit the tension" (p. 232).

Agoraphobia. When behavioral therapists first began to treat agoraphobia, they focused on the agoraphobic avoidance behavior. A number of exposure in vivo programs were developed that entailed a gradual movement away from a point of safety toward a feared location (Mavissakalian & Barlow, 1981). Although exposure in vivo was initially found to be effective in increasing the distance that a patient could travel away from his or her point of safety, a number of limitations of this treatment were also uncovered.

One particular variable that was unaffected by exposure in vivo was the accompanying panic attacks. Behavioral therapists began to notice that patients with agoraphobia seemed to be very frightened of specific bodily sensations. Applying the exposure principle to this target was then added to the behavioral treatment. Interoceptive exposure (i.e., exposure to the body sensation) was added to desensitize individuals to these specific bodily sensations. Still, not everyone benefited from exposure therapy and there was typically a fairly high dropout rate for patients with agoraphobia in studies of this treatment (Barlow, 1988).

Obsessive–Compulsive Disorder. Meyer (1966) originally developed the treatment package of exposure and response prevention (EX/RP) for OCD. This treatment combines in vivo exposure to a feared stimulus with subsequent prevention of the compulsive behavior. This combined treatment package compels the patient to experience the anxiety that he or she has been avoiding through ritualization. Prolonged exposure is presumed to reduce anxiety through habituation, whereas response prevention reduces ritualistic behavior through extinction (Sturgis, 1993).

Since Meyer's (1966) initial study, many subsequent studies found that most patients make clinically significant gains with this treatment. Foa and Goldstein (1978) found that EX/RP works particularly well for compulsive behavior. At the end of 10 weekday sessions over the course of 2 weeks, 18 of 21 subjects were completely free of compulsive symptoms. At follow-up, 15 of the 18 successful subjects continued to be asymptomatic. Only 12 of the subjects, however, were free of their obsessions at the end of treatment.

Foa and Kozak (1996) more recently reviewed 12 outcome studies of EX/RP and found that 83% responded to this treatment; in 16 studies reporting long-term outcome, they found that 76% were responders. However, a significant number of patients relapse, perhaps as many as a third of those treated. In addition, an average of 20% drop out of treatment (Sturgis, 1993). It is clear that this efficacious symptom-focused treatment needs to be supplemented.

Social Learning Theory

Bandura's (1977) social learning theory represents a bridge between the earlier behavioral therapies and the later CBTs. His core assumption was that people can observe others behaving and learn without having to perform the observed behaviors. This vicarious learning can produce three kinds of cognitive representations: (a) behavioral possibilities, (b) outcome expectancies, and (c) self-efficacy expectancies. Bandura believed that the latter representation is critical in the development of anxiety and fear. He contended that a person's perception that he or she cannot cope with a potentially aversive situation is the primary mechanism in the development of anxiety. Low self-efficacy expectancies create problems, and improvement in self-efficacy is the critical mechanism in positive therapy changes.

On the basis of his self-efficacy theory, Bandura has used a variety of performance-based treatments to show the importance of self-efficacy expectations in therapeutic change, particularly with patients with agoraphobia and those with a snake phobia (Bandura, Adams, & Beyer, 1977; Bandura, Adams, Hardy, & Howells, 1980). Guided-mastery treatment (Williams, 1990), in particular, has been found to be quite successful with agoraphobia and a variety of specific phobias. This treatment does not focus on exposure per se but rather on the amount of information that a person obtains about his or her ability to cope with challenges in the environment. Instead of being passively exposed to fear stimuli, the individual attempts challenging tasks. Success presumably increases self-efficacy beliefs. Mastery rather than deconditioning is viewed as the primary mechanism of change. A number of studies conducted by Williams and his colleagues demonstrated the superiority of guided mastery over different exposure-based treatments (e.g., Williams & Zane, 1989).

Cognitive–Behavioral Treatment Model

All CBTs assume that "1. Cognitive activity affects behavior. 2. Cognitive activity can be monitored and altered. [and] 3. Desired behavior change may be affected through cognitive change" (Dobson, 2001, p. 4). The early approaches to cognitive therapy focused on the patient's conscious cognitions and self-statements (Meichenbaum, 1977). Cognitive therapists more recently have added a focus on unconscious cognitive schemas that presumably generate the dysfunctional automatic thoughts associated with a given psychological disorder. In the case of anxiety disorders, the relevant schemas relate to perceived, experienced, or imagined dangers in the world (A. T. Beck & Emery, 1985). There are now in existence a fair number of versions of CBT that attempt to directly change cognitive schemas by cognitive means or conduct behavioral procedures to achieve the same ends.

In the CB treatment of any given anxiety disorder, one is likely to find a relaxation strategy to inhibit the anxiety, some form of exposure therapy for the relevant fear stimuli, and cognitive restructuring methods for modifying inaccurate danger-related cognitive schemas and negative thoughts (Barlow, 2000). CB therapists have more recently included affect as a dimension and target of therapeutic change. In fact, this trend is becoming so pronounced that I recommend that the orientation be renamed cognitive–behavioral–affect therapy, or CBAT (Barlow, 2000; Segal, Williams, & Teasdale, 2002; Teasdale & Barnard, 1993).

Therapeutic Relationship and Stance

The therapy is relatively directive; therefore, the therapist role is one of an expert who guides the unfolding of the therapy. The relationship, however, has been described as *collaborative empiricism* (A. T. Beck & Emery, 1985). The therapist and client collaborate on the setting of therapeutic goals and on the means and timing of specific therapeutic tasks. The therapist, for example, often suggests behavioral experiments for the client to test the accuracy of his or her cognitive schemas. Therapeutic empathy is an important skill not only for building rapport but also for helping the therapist understand the subtleties and nuances of the patient's problems.

Major Techniques

Relaxation strategies, such as diaphragmatic breathing (DB) or progressive relaxation, are used to inhibit anxiety. Exposure to the primary fear stimuli is a major technique used in CBT. For example, the technique of worry exposure has recently been added to the protocol for GAD (Brown, O'Leary, & Barlow, 2001). For patients with phobias, exposure is applied imaginally or in vivo to the phobic object or situation. In panic disorder patients, interoceptive exposure is used for the feared body sensations, whereas for patients with OCD, exposure to the obsessional thought is uniformly used. Cognitive techniques, such as the downward arrow technique or Socratic questioning, are often used to explore the nature of the patient's danger cognitions. Cognitive restructuring techniques are used to modify dysfunctional cognitive schemas, and behavioral rehearsal techniques are used to teach new and more effective behaviors.

Mechanisms of Change

Most CBTs for anxiety disorders are based on a realist epistemology that suggests that there is an objective reality against which a person's thought processes can be measured. These therapies necessarily view the cognitions and cognitive processes associated with anxiety disorders as irrational or dysfunctional. Thus the basic goals of these approaches include behavioral change (i.e., confronting fears without—or with minimal—anxiety) and restructuring cognitions and thought processes according to the rational.

The mechanisms of change that are thought to operate in these therapies include the extinction of anxiety by means of counterconditioning, the identification and modification of dysfunctional cognitive schemas by rational methods of disputation and behavioral experiments, the modification of automatic thoughts, the reduction of self-focused attention, and the correction of cognitive errors, again by rational means (Craske & Barlow, 2001).

Recent years have seen the development of constructivist models of cognitive therapy, based in a postmodern epistemology, that reject the assumptions of philosophical realism. These approaches focus on facilitating the inherent meaning-making propensities of human beings. For the constructivist, reality is ultimately unknowable and knowledge claims are without foundation. However, humans all are active participants in the process of coconstructing their realities (Mahoney, 1991). Constructivist therapists focus on the coherence and pragmatic utility of the patient's self-narrative. This process-oriented approach to therapy attempts through an empathic collaboration to help patients puzzle through their own experience so that they can create a more meaningful and coherent self-narrative.

One example of a constructivist cognitive therapy that has been applied to anxiety disorders is the work of Guidano (1991). Guidano starts with the assumption that there are two levels of knowledge processes: an explicit theory of self and a more tacit (and more variable) experience of self. The tacit level of self-awareness seems to be more influential in shaping the person's selective attention to certain themes in the world. A dynamic tension between explicit and tacit layers of self-awareness is postulated as the guiding force in self-knowledge.

Emotional disorders arise as a function of developmental experiences that shape a specific personal cognitive organization (P.C. Org). A P.C. Org is a stable configuration of cognitive–affective structures that represent the individual's current perspective on self and the world. The relationship between P.C. Orgs and psychopathology is expressed by Guidano in the following statement: "Now, the central argument . . . is that *different patterns of organizational closure—structured on the basis of different specific developmental pathways—correspondingly underlie the expression of different clinical patterns*" (1991, p. 113; emphasis added).

One of the disorders that Guidano (1991) has described in terms of specific P.C. Orgs is agoraphobia. This disorder is based in an emotional polarity between "(1) the need for protection from a perceived dangerous world, and (2) the need for freedom and independence in the same world" (p. 139). What is particularly characteristic of this organizational pattern is that the person responds with anxiety to any shift in the balance between the two emotional poles—a loss of protection or a loss of freedom and independence. Guidano believes that a majority of patients with agoraphobia experienced patterns of anxious attachment with parents who lacked emotional warmth and who controlled their children either through frightening stories of a dangerous world or by restricting their autonomy with threats of abandonment.

Another significant characteristic of the underlying P.C. Org of patients with agoraphobia is the tendency to view attachment and separation processes as mutually antagonistic. If one acts independently, one will be abandoned. If one strives for close attachments, one will lose one's independence. There seems to be no gray area between the two emotional poles. Loss of protection evokes intense feelings of loneliness. Loss of independence elicits unbearable feelings of being trapped. Those with agoraphobia, as a consequence, construct an explicit model of self as in control of potentially dangerous interpersonal situations and of emotions that are construed as shaming.

This conceptualization of agoraphobia implies two therapeutic goals: (a) helping the client to achieve a decentered awareness of problematic emotions; this information can be used to restructure the person's explicit view of self and world, and (b) directing the client in a developmental review of the roots of his or her explicit theory of self and how these have prevented a more satisfying and more coherent experience of self and the world (Arciero & Guidano, 2000; Guidano, 1991). The mechanisms of change are increasing self-awareness and reconstruing the self and the world.

Cognitive–Behavioral Therapy Applied to Specific Anxiety Disorders

Specific Phobias. From a CB point of view, maladaptive cognitions are seen as elicitors of anticipatory anxiety and the anxiety a person experiences when faced with the phobic object or situation. Thus they are particularly relevant for the maintenance of specific phobias (Last, 1987). One way in which cognitive mediation of phobic responses may take place is through the exposure-induced negative self-statements based on past learning experiences that then bring on the physiological indicators of fear and avoidance of the phobic object.

If this model is accurate, then the reduction of fear may occur through the reduction of the frequency of negative self-statements. Fewer negative self-statements would produce less physiologically based fear, which in turn would result in less avoidance behavior. This hypothesis has been difficult to empirically validate because most cognitive treatments of specific phobias include exposure. Therefore it is difficult to determine if positive changes in the phobia are due to changes in the associated cognitive processes.

Social Phobias (Social Anxiety Disorder). Rick Heimberg and his colleagues have developed a 12-session group-format CBT for social anxiety disorder. Among the advantages they cite for the group format are (a) learning vicariously, (b) seeing that one is not alone with this type of problem, (c) making a public commitment to change, (d) having others to help correct one's distorted thinking, and (e) having several built-in role-play partners (Turk, Heimberg, & Hope, 2001).

The major treatment techniques, however, include the usual suspects: exposure to fear stimuli and cognitive restructuring. For the exposure treatment, a fear and avoidance hierarchy is developed, containing 10 hierarchically arranged social situations that are feared and avoided. Three role-play exposures are typically carried out in a session. A designated group member role-plays an anxiety-evoking situation with another group member. The situations are individualized and may vary from having a conversation with an unfamiliar person to giving a formal presentation.

The cognitive restructuring procedures include correcting thinking errors, offering disputing questions, and developing rational responses. Two or three automatic thoughts from each group member become the focus of a given treatment session, and each group member receives a list of thinking errors (J. S. Beck, 1995):

> Together the group members identify the thinking errors in each automatic thought, question the automatic thoughts using the disputing questions, and answer the disputing questions to arrive at alternative, more

realistic ways of viewing the situation. The answers to the disputing questions are then summarized into one or two statements that serve as rational responses. (Turk et al., 2001, p. 133)

After each session, homework is given, which involves recording automatic thoughts in anxiety-provoking situations, identifying the thinking errors, questioning the automatic thoughts, and creating rational responses. The authors report that 80% of treatment completers experience meaningful reductions in their social anxiety (Turk et al., 2001).

Panic Disorder With Agoraphobia. CBTs focus on the multifaceted features of this disorder, including the elimination of the panic attacks, the reduction of the anticipatory anxiety, the cognitive restructuring of the catastrophic cognitions that occur when patients with panic disorder experience frightening body sensations, and the elimination of agoraphobic avoidance behavior. Barlow's Panic Control Treatment (PCT) provides a highly structured treatment for panic disorder and agoraphobia. Craske and Barlow (2001) described a 15-session treatment protocol with a basic goal of changing the catastrophic misappraisal of panic attacks and anxiety, modifying conditioned fear reactions to physical cues, and reducing the fear and avoidance of agoraphobic situations. The treatment includes psychoeducation about the nature of panic disorder, breathing retraining, cognitive restructuring of the patient's overestimation of danger and catastrophic thinking, interoceptive exposure to the frightening body sensations, and in vivo exposure to agoraphobic situations.

Craske and Barlow (2001) reported highly encouraging results from a number of studies to suggest that between 80% and 100% of patients are panic free at the end of treatment, and these gains are maintained for at least 2 years. However, they do note the fact that 50% of patients continue to experience substantial symptomatology despite initial improvement. This is particularly true for patients with severe agoraphobia. Similar CBT models of panic disorder developed by D. M. Clark (1986) and A. T. Beck (A. T. Beck & Emery, 1985) have achieved similar results (J. G. Beck, Stanley, Baldwin, Deagle, & Averill, 1994; D. M. Clark et al., 1999).

PCT is an excellent symptom-focused treatment but it concentrates only on the factors that maintain panic disorder. It ignores the implicit meaning of the initial panic attacks. In fact, Craske and Barlow (2001) were quite explicit about ignoring the implicit meaning of these attacks:

> Clients are informed that understanding the reasons why they began to panic is not necessary in order to benefit from treatment, because the factors involved in onset are not necessarily the same as the factors involved in the maintenance of the problem. (p. 30)

Yet, it is my conviction that part of the reason for the significant number of relapses and the continuing symptomatology of many patients is the fact that the implicit meaning of panic has not been addressed.

Obsessive–Compulsive Disorder. The exposure plus response prevention (ERP) behavioral treatment is generally viewed as the treatment of choice for OCD. Foa and Kozak (1986), however, have maintained that cognitive change, particularly the disconfirmation of erroneous beliefs, is an integral part of ERP. Several cognitive therapies that do not include exposure as a component have also been developed. At least one study has shown that rational emotive therapy was as effective as ERP (Emmelkamp, Visser, & Hoekstra, 1988). Beyond this, there is little research on the efficacy of any purely cognitive therapy with OCD.

Generalized Anxiety Disorder. Two major CB treatment programs have been developed for GAD: one by Borkovec and his colleagues, and the other by Barlow and his colleagues. The CBT package developed by Borkovec teaches clients to identify internal and external anxiety cues and to implement new coping skills for the symptoms of the disorder. The treatment involves self-monitoring of worrying and other anxiety symptoms, applied relaxation training, cognitive restructuring for the client's negative thinking, and imagery rehearsal of coping skills (Borkovec & Ruscio, 2001). On average, about 50% of patients with GAD who participate in clinical trials achieve high end-state functioning by the end of treatment (Borkovec & Whisman, 1996).

The program developed by Barlow and his colleagues (Brown et al., 2001) includes self-monitoring, progressive muscle relaxation, cognitive countering of the individual's misinterpretations of situations, and worry exposure. The final technique is a relatively new addition to the CBT armamentarium for GAD. It involves (a) the identification of two or three major areas of worry for the individual, which are then hierarchically ordered in ascending levels of stress, (b) imagery training of pleasant scenes, and (c) self-exposure to one's anxious thoughts while imagining the worst possible outcome for that particular area of worry. The individual moves up each step of the hierarchy only after he or she can vividly imagine the worry with no or low levels of anxiety. The key mechanisms of change for this therapy include (a) the habituation of anxiety, (b) cognitive restructuring of inaccurate thoughts, and (c) worry behavior prevention. To date, there are only promising pilot data in support of this new treatment protocol (Brown et al., 2001).

Critique of Behavioral and Cognitive–Behavioral Models

Because the same issues are raised for behavioral social learning and CB treatments, I have included all three tributaries of the CB river in the same critique. The behavioral and CB perspectives are characterized by clear conceptualizations of treatment targets, well-specified treatment operations, and a commitment to systematic evaluation of therapy outcome. To date, behavioral, social learning, and CB treatments are particularly effective in ameliorating the symptoms of an anxiety disorder. These treatments are very useful in helping individuals gain control over their anxiety symptoms and decatastrophizing individuals' thoughts about the meaning of their symptoms.

As I have shown, most CBT models now postulate underlying, tacit cognitive schemas as the source of anxiety symptoms and the current therapies focus, often very effectively, on the conscious manifestation of these schemas (i.e., automatic negative thoughts and cognitive errors). It is less clear, however, how effective these therapies are in modifying the underlying cognitive schemas. A greater focus is needed on the implicit meaning of anxiety symptoms (e.g., panic attacks), and therapeutic operations need to be developed to access and modify these tacit issues.

A second issue concerns the potential role of emotional processing in the change process. The CB perspective has recently evidenced elasticity in its focus on emotional issues. Foa and Kozak (1996), in particular, have noted the role of emotional processing in changing the fear structures underlying OCD. But, by and large, the CB perspective has not developed a sufficient focus on the role of emotions in the development, maintenance, and amelioration of anxiety disorders.

A third issue involves the lack of focus of research evaluations of the therapeutic process and its contribution to outcome. Most studies of behavioral, social learning, and CB treatments focus primarily on the outcome of specific treatment operations; rarely do they investigate the role of therapist, client, and therapist–client interaction variables. Yet, other research suggests that the interaction between therapist and client contributes more to the outcome variance than do the effects of specific treatments (Lambert, 1992; Orlinsky, Grawe, & Parks, 1994). When these CBT treatments are effective, the specific elements of the change process remain unclear.

Experiential Psychotherapy Model

Perhaps the only experiential model specifically designed for anxiety disorders is the one I developed (Wolfe & Sigl, 1998). The basic assumption underlying this model is that anxiety disorders are based in dangerous self-experience, which in turn depends on the underlying form(s) of self-pathology. A chronic sense of self-endangerment is observable in every anxiety disorder. Although different anxiety disorders reflect variations in the contents of threatening self-experience, they also represent variations in the experiential processes used to stave off the danger.

The goals of the experiential therapy model include the treatment of both the symptoms of specific anxiety disorders and the underlying issues of self-pathology. To effectively treat both the symptoms of an anxiety disorder and the associated underlying issues, I developed a four-stage treatment sequence: (a) establishing the therapeutic alliance, (b) ameliorating the anxiety symptoms, (c) uncovering the deficiencies in immediate self-experiencing, and (d) repairing the underlying self-pathology (see Wolfe, 1989, 1992, 1995, and 2005, and Wolfe & Sigl, 1998, for the evolution of this model).

Therapeutic Relationship and Stance

From the experiential point of view, the therapeutic relationship is viewed as the greenhouse of change. The relationship serves many functions for the patient with an anxiety disorder, the most important of which is the provision of a safe environment in which the patient can explore his or her own experience. Patients need to feel safe, accepted, and understood to explore the difficult terrain of their tender and unspoken thoughts and feelings.

The therapist stance combines the passive following position of the Rogerian person-centered approach with the process-directive position of gestalt therapy. The therapist does not actively try to change the content of the patient's experience. Instead, he or she attempts to facilitate the patient's awareness of his or her experience. The therapist does this by directing the patient's attention to various aspects of his or her in-the-moment experiencing. Such a stance eventually helps patients acknowledge the previously unacceptable aspects of self and the various ways in which one protects one's self from such acknowledgment.

Major Techniques

Although experiential therapists traditionally have not emphasized specific techniques, a number of these are particularly helpful for patients with anxiety disorders. I have developed, for example, a modification of the behavioral techniques of imaginal and interoceptive exposure. Wolfe's focusing technique (WFT; Wolfe 1992, 2005; see also Appendix) involves exposure to the patient's fear stimuli and, instead of waiting for the anxiety to habituate, the patient pays close attention to the thoughts and feelings that automatically arise. This is a rapid and effective technique for accessing the implicit meaning of the patient's specific anxiety.

This focusing technique often brings up internal conflicts between different sides of the self, unfinished business with significant others, and thoughts and feelings that evoke great shame and guilt. Once patients become aware of such issues, a number of specific experiential interventions may be used, including the two-chair dialogue for self-splits, empty-chair work for unfinished business, and empathic affirmation for shame-related thoughts and feelings (L. S. Greenberg et al., 1993). Guided imagery is often used to explore the network of associations that is connected to a specific fear stimulus (Wolfe & Sigl, 1998). Another technique that is often used involves working with metaphors, both therapist-generated and client-generated. Much of the personal reality that we construct for ourselves is metaphoric in nature. Moreover, metaphors are closely associated with our implicit feelings about self, others, and the world. The exploration of a client-generated metaphor often deepens a patient's awareness of the implicit meaning of his or her anxiety, and the alteration of that same metaphor can also lead to a transformation in one's view of self and others (Kopp, 1995).

Mechanisms of Change

The experiential treatment of anxiety contends that change begins with awareness of one's in-the-moment experiencing. Patients with anxiety have difficulty allowing themselves to directly experience their feelings because of their dangerous implications. Instead they shift their attention to cogitating about being anxious. As they begin to allow themselves to contact their in-the-moment experience, they undercut the defensive cogitating. As they allow themselves to explore their experiencing in-depth, they become aware of the implicit meaning of their anxiety symptoms, which usually entails a catastrophically painful view of the self. As they contact these painful feelings and process them, they eventually come to a new understanding of self, a new way of experiencing and of thinking about one's self. Thus the primary mechanism of change involves the emotional processing of painful feelings about the self, which presumably underlie the conscious symptoms of anxiety. Emotional processing transforms the patient's view of self.

Experiential Psychotherapy Applied to Specific Anxiety Disorders

Specific Phobias. The treatment of specific phobias begins with teaching the patient DB or another relaxation strategy. This is necessary because of the fear that is induced by the phobic object or situation. Relaxation training is followed by imaginal exposure, which serves as an experiential rehearsal for in vivo exposure. In addition, WFT, a modified version of imaginal exposure, is used to uncover the implicit meaning of the phobia. The tacit meaning of a phobia is usually some catastrophic psychological situation for the patient that is accompanied by unbearably painful feelings. The in vivo exposure is continued to work on the manifest phobic symptoms, and experiential techniques are used to modify the sense of catastrophe that the person experiences. For example, a young woman named Elaine with a driving phobia discovered through WFT that her fear of driving was connected to a catastrophic conflict she felt regarding her marriage. She felt, emotionally, that the marriage was over, but she was too frightened to live on her own. The image that surfaced, as she imagined pulling out of her driveway, was that she would never come home again. But the image of her on her own brought up a catastrophic level of terror. Through guided imagery, she reduced her fear of every aspect of living autonomously that evoked such high levels of anxiety.

Social Phobias (Social Anxiety Disorder). The experiential treatment of social phobia follows the same basic paradigm: DB training followed by imaginal and in vivo exposure for symptom management, followed by WFT to uncover various problems surrounding the perception and conception of self, followed by the emotional processing of painful and positive messages about the self. Rick's fear of public speaking was based in the self-damaging ridicule he received, beginning in childhood, regarding his mixed Asian and American background. Anything less than a perfect speaking performance left him vulnerable, he believed, to unbearable humiliation. The symptom-focused treatment (i.e., DB and exposure) worked fairly well, but many tacit issues that surfaced through experiential exploration required therapeutic attention. He needed to allow and accept his anger, which was directed at many people both inside and outside his family. He then needed to express that anger through empty-chair work with his biological father who had given him up for adoption. He needed to experiment with, and experience, new ways of expressing his anger that were not so toxic to other people. And he needed to work experientially with the modification of his perfectionistic standards (i.e., through guided imagery and later, role play giving an imperfect but good-enough talk). Moreover, we worked on his staying in touch with his direct experience, which necessarily undercut his tendency to engage in impression management.

Panic Disorder With Agoraphobia. In panic disorder, the focus of exposure shifts to feared body sensations (i.e., interoceptive exposure), but basically the same symptom-focused treatment of DB plus exposure will help an individual gain some control over the symptoms. Jean, a 30-year-old Asian American woman, was diagnosed with panic disorder and agoraphobia. She could drive to and from work, but mostly relied on her husband to get anywhere else. She was very frightened of having pain in her neck and shoulders. The WFT technique revealed a significant amount of anger toward her husband whom she described as a pain in the neck, but there was also incredible rage at her parents for the endless toxic messages they had given her about herself. She was very frightened of focusing on the symptoms of her anxiety because she eventually realized that they were a signal of a storehouse of painful depressive feelings as well as boundless rage. Once, while she was engaged in interoceptive exposure, she described an image of herself as a deformed child struggling to leave a womb.

She also had great fears of being abandoned, which we were able to trace to an incident that occurred when she was 3 years old. Her mother had taken her shopping at a local mall and then absentmindedly drove off without her. These images and memories were difficult for Jean to experience and explore because for her to acknowledge parental deficiencies and cruelty was unbearable. It was somehow easier for her to believe that she was a deformed child who merited such treatment.

The symptom-focused treatment, which concentrated on extending the distance from home that she could drive, was followed by experiential work on allowing and accepting her anger and expressing some of that anger toward the image of each parent in the empty chair. We worked on modulating her anger so that it would not feel so explosive inside her. We also set up a number of behavioral experiments so that she could feel herself acting with more and more autonomy.

Generalized Anxiety Disorder. The key targets of treatment include (a) getting to the direct experience that is being defensively interrupted by worrying, (b) interrupting the defensive interpersonal strategy of impression management by training the patient with GAD to remain centered in his or her immediate experience of the social interaction, and (c) helping the patient allow and accept his or her actual immediate experience of self and others. These goals are realized through DB, exposure to worry thoughts, and imaginal exposure to social interactions in which the patient's attention is primarily on his or her own feelings and reactions of the other person or people. Often patients with GAD interrupt the awareness or expression of anger toward specific people in their lives. Thus, a series of empty-chair sessions may be used to give the patients a chance to express and emotionally process their anger.

Obsessive–Compulsive Disorder. As with all of the other anxiety disorders, treatment initially focuses on the manifest symptoms of the disorder by using experientially modified versions of CB techniques. In the case of OCD, ERP is used. The goal of this treatment is to have patients directly experience the anxiety induced by their obsessive thoughts. But instead of relying on habituation as the mechanism of anxiety reduction, the experiential version of this treatment helps patients to come to understand the implicit meaning of their obsessive thoughts. The self-pathology typically associated with OCD is the belief that one is a bad person because of the mistakes one has made and the harm one has caused one's loved ones.

The experiential work that follows focuses on the reorganization of the self-concept of patients with OCD. These patients often possess perfectionistic standards for behavior that guarantee their failure to live up to them. The work involves the patient allowing and accepting the experience of his or her imperfections, on the one hand, and revising his or her overestimation of the likelihood of causing harm, on the other. One patient, for example, was so fearful of causing harm to his grandchild that, before she would visit, he would carry out a meticulous search of the entire house to make sure there was nothing that she might ingest or otherwise harm herself with. He would carry out these child-proofing activities to such an extent that this ritualistic behavior often took hours. Experiential exploration eventually uncovered the inadvertent harm he had caused another soldier during the Vietnam War that cemented his self-concept as a harmful person. Through guided imagery, we transformed his perspective on that particular incident and therefore on his self-concept as well. At the same time, we worked on discriminating between taking reasonable child-proofing precautions and going to his compulsive extremes. The experiential techniques that are most frequently used with OCD include experiential exploration, focusing, guided imagery, allowing and accepting painful feelings, behavioral rehearsals, and empty-chair and two-chair work.

Critique of Experiential Treatment Model

The experiential treatment model possesses a number of strengths. First, it focuses on a critical piece of effective treatment for anxiety disorders: the role of emotional experiencing. The model suggests that one of the concomitant insights the patient with anxiety acquires in therapy is that anxiety serves as a protective screen against painful emotions. Another insight is that the implicit meaning of anxiety typically concerns painful self-images. But the anxiety itself is painful so the individual automatically shifts his or her attention to cogitating about the symptoms. This self-focused attention is unfortunately a self-defeating distraction of attention away from the direct experience of anxiety.

The experiential treatment model also recognizes that the initial focus on symptom resolution constitutes a process of reconnecting the individual with his or her in-the-moment experience of anxiety. The successful reduction or elimination of anxiety symptoms not only is an important goal in and of itself but also enhances a patient's sense and concept of self, which in turn empowers him or her to explore and resolve the emotional roots of the disorder. Finally, the model argues that the emotional processing of painful self-images is a necessary part of a comprehensive treatment of anxiety disorders.

This model, however, also possesses a couple of weaknesses. Many patients with anxiety disorders are not ready at the outset of therapy to confront their painful emotions. Therapists, therefore, need to focus on different access points (i.e., behavioral or cognitive issues). Behavioral change and cognitive restructuring work can begin the process of modifying painful and negative views of the self (i.e., tacit self-schemas). It is my conviction, however, that transformational change of one's sense and concept of self requires a corrective emotional experience (Alexander & French, 1946).

Biomedical Treatment Model

Because this is a book about psychotherapy integration, I will note only in passing that (a) the major targets of change for pharmacotherapy are synaptic neurotransmitter deficiencies, (b) the pharmacotherapist's primary role is as a supportive dispenser of medication, and (c) the hypothesized mechanism of change is the restoration of the synaptic availability of specific neurotransmitters such as norepinephrine and serotonin. The further assumption is that with the proper neurotransmitter balance in place, amygdala-based danger appraisals can be appropriately integrated with cortex-based appraisals (Cozolino, 2002).

In fact, substantial evidence points to the fact that a number of anxiolytic medications can reduce anxiety and block panic attacks. The selective serotonin reuptake inhibitors, in particular, are coming into prominence especially as panic blockades (Lydiard, Brawman-Mintzer, & Ballenger, 1996).

There is, however, no evidence that any of these medications can transform a person's view of self or resolve any of the conflicts that appear to generate the symptoms of an anxiety disorder.

One other trend that has relevance for the biomedical perspective needs to be mentioned: the effort to connect psychological change with changes in neurobiological processes. Several emerging fields, such as cognitive neuroscience, neuropsychoanalysis, and, most recently, the neuroscience of psychotherapy, are taking this challenge as their central focus. In a recent book, Louis Cozolino (2002) attempted to make the case that psychotherapy produces neurobiological changes. In Cozolino's words,

> all forms of psychotherapy—from psychoanalysis to behavioral interventions—are successful to the extent to which they enhance change in relevant neural circuits. I will also make a case for the notion that the "unscientific" use of language and emotional attunement (for which psychotherapists are often criticized by those in the hard sciences) actually provides the best medium for neural growth and integration. (pp. xiv–xv)

If this hypothesis garners increasing support, it will have profound implications for the way in which we conceptualize psychotherapy and its effects.

COMMON TREATMENT FACTORS

A number of common treatment factors can be abstracted from the treatment perspectives reviewed in this chapter. First, it is the now generally accepted truism that the development of a strong therapeutic alliance is the necessary prerequisite to implementing any specific task of therapy. Every psychotherapeutic approach now recognizes the interconnectedness of relationship factors and tasks in the successful conduct of therapy. The therapeutic relationship is now viewed in all therapy orientations as an integrative common factor in psychotherapy (Horvath & Greenberg, 1994). Some perspectives emphasize the constant monitoring of the therapeutic alliance more than others do, but no perspective ignores its importance.

A second common factor is that the initial treatment focus is typically on the symptoms of an anxiety disorder. Psychodynamic therapies have traditionally bypassed a focus on symptoms and focused instead on the analysis of the genetic roots of a disorder. However, short-term dynamic therapies such as PFPP have been developed that do focus on symptoms early in the therapy (Milrod et al., 1997). Most perspectives now recognize not only that an early focus on symptoms is being responsive to a patient's initial concerns but also that success in this arena may motivate the patient to confront the putative underlying issues that may be generating the symptoms.

A third common factor is that exposure therapy is a necessary—if not sufficient—condition of therapy. Whereas CB therapies use exposure to the conscious fear stimuli, both psychodynamic and experiential therapies attempt to expose patients to the preconscious feelings associated with panic and anxiety symptoms (Craske & Barlow, 2001; Milrod et al., 1997; Wolfe & Sigl, 1998).

A fourth common factor is a work in progress. Increasingly, all perspectives are in the process of developing treatment interventions focused on underlying psychic structures that presumably govern the symptoms of an anxiety disorder. Recent iterations of CBT have increasingly focused on the modification of underlying cognitive schemas or fear structures related to specific anxiety symptoms (e.g., Foa & Franklin, 2001). The experiential approach argues that dysfunctions are rooted in part in maladaptive, tacit emotion schemes (L. S. Greenberg et al., 1993). Psychodynamic therapies have always argued that symptoms were based in unconscious conflicts or character traits (Michels et al., 1985). Although differences do exist in the various conceptualizations of these underlying psychic structures, all therapies, with the exception of the purist versions of behavioral therapy, are now becoming depth-oriented psychotherapies.

These conceptual differences, however, do not obscure the fact that all perspectives are beginning to converge on a focus on underlying dysfunctional self-related issues. Segal and Blatt (1993) have highlighted the importance of dysfunctional self-schemas in both the CB and psychodynamic perspectives. Despite their differences, particularly in how they achieve a similar end, cognitive and dynamic perspectives are coming closer together in their focus on repair of the self. As Segal and Blatt (1993) put it,

> Whether one uses cognitive therapy to explore the consequences of self-referent information processing, or traces the developmental trajectory of repetitive maladaptive behaviors in psychodynamic therapy, the attempt in both cases is to allow for revisions of distortions and/or to bolster or build up a self that is fundamentally lacking in important qualities. (p. 373)

Experiential therapies attempt to make similar changes by still other means. These therapies attempt to enhance a patient's awareness of his or her in-the-moment, organismic experience, which will lead to corrective emotional experiences involving his or her sense and concept of self (Wolfe & Sigl, 1998).

DIFFERENTIATING FACTORS

Despite these similarities, many differences still separate the various therapeutic perspectives. Psychodynamic models focus on underlying unconscious conflicts, characterological issues, and defenses. Except for recent short-term versions of dynamic therapy, most dynamic therapies tend to ignore anxiety symptoms per se. They pay more attention to the in-session interpersonal interaction between therapist and client and on how present behavior links with past patterns of interpersonal relating. The therapist is more passive and less directive in stance than in other therapies (except for the classic Rogerian therapist) and, of course, transference issues are particularly emphasized.

Behavioral models focus primarily on behavioral change. They are not particularly concerned with the meaning of anxiety, whether explicit or implicit. The therapist's stance is one of being the expert and director of therapy. Despite behavioral therapists' common acknowledgment of the importance of therapeutic rapport, they tend to view the therapeutic relationship as important only insofar as rapport is necessary for carrying out the specific techniques of the therapy approach.

The cognitive perspective is more concerned with the explicit and implicit meaning of anxiety, but most treatment is focused on the modification of conscious, irrational interpretations of internal and external stimuli. The therapist's stance is one of collaborating participant, one who negotiates the means and ends of therapy with the patient. The therapist, however, is the director of the therapy, which is more structured than dynamic therapy. Behavioral experiments are suggested to disconfirm the patient's irrational appraisals.

The experiential therapist emphasizes empathic attunement and is a facilitator of the process of experiencing that helps patients to explore their in-the-moment experience. There is a greater focus on conscious awareness, although the theory of dysfunction acknowledges underlying conflicts and assumptions. Imagery techniques are more frequently used in this perspective to uncover the underlying sources of anxiety. Finally, in passing, let me note that biomedical therapies (i.e., anxiolytics and panic medications) apparently reorganize the biochemical underpinnings of the catastrophic meaning making engaged in by the patient.

RATIONALE FOR THE SELECTION OF PARTICULAR DIFFERENTIATING FACTORS

To begin with, nothing in the integrative model of anxiety disorders would disqualify the use of any of the specific techniques embedded in each therapeutic perspective. At different points in therapy, with different patients, it is possible that insight-oriented, behavior-modifying, awareness-enhancing, or schema-modifying techniques might be used with anxiety disorders. By integrating research, evidence, and clinical experience, I arrived at the most relevant factors.

Research Evidence

The research evidence is quite convincing that relaxation training, exposure to fear stimuli, and cognitive restructuring of conscious cognitions are necessary treatment interventions for the reduction of anxiety symptoms. Although it may be possible to reduce anxiety with other techniques, the research evidence is consistent in demonstrating the power of these three interventions to help patients achieve some sense of control over their symptoms of anxiety. Patient variability, however, produces differences in the timing, format, intensity, and duration of exposure, and ultimately in the amount of improvement achieved with it. Patients also have their preferences for specific relaxation techniques. Finally, the details of how one carries out cognitive restructuring must be tailored to the characteristics and interpersonal style of the patient.

The research evidence is useful as far as it goes, but there are several issues that hardly have been addressed by outcome research on anxiety disorders, much less answered. Virtually all of the research that has demonstrated the efficacy of relaxation, exposure, and cognitive restructuring has ignored (a) the role of patient–therapist interaction in the change process and (b) the details of the change process for the individual patient. The conclusion one must draw in the face of the selective focus of research is that whereas the evidence is good that relaxation, exposure, and cognitive restructuring are effective, it is not known why it works. Nor is it known how much the vicissitudes of the therapeutic alliance contribute to the success (and failures) of these interventions. This research is not routinely carried out.

The research evidence is also virtually mute on the internal process of change for the individual patient. It is thought that as a result of exposure, anxiety will habituate, but it is not clear from the available research that this is in fact what happens in successful exposure. Beyond habituation, some theorists propose the necessity of activating tacit fear structures and modifying their misinformation (e.g., Foa & Kozak, 1986), but very little research demonstrates that this characterization of the change process is what actually takes place.

An entirely separate research literature deals with the general contributions of the therapeutic relationship to therapy outcome (Elliott, Greenberg, & Lietaer, 2003; Norcross, 2002; Orlinsky, Grawe, & Parks, 1994). Although not specifically focused on anxiety disorders per se, this research provides much insight into the role that the therapy process plays in successful therapy. A task force was convened by Division 29 of the American Psychological Association to review this process research literature to determine what relationship factors have received empirical support. Among their conclusions was the following: "The therapy relationship acts in concert with discrete interventions, patient characteristics, and clinician qualities in determining treatment effectiveness. A comprehensive understanding of effective (and ineffective) psychotherapy will consider all of these determinants and their optimal combinations" (Norcross, 2002, p. 441).

Stiles and Wolfe (in press) reviewed the relationship factors that seem to be involved in the efficacious treatment of anxiety disorders. They found relatively little research conducted on relationship factors in the treatment of anxiety disorders. This sparse collection of research findings suggests that the relationship factors associated with the successful treatment of anxiety disorders include, among others, a strong therapeutic alliance, empathy, positive regard for the patient, therapist congruence or genuineness, and repairing therapeutic alliance ruptures.

The research is also fairly quiet on the implicit meaning of anxiety symptoms, that is, the role that unconscious processes and contents (including intense, painful emotions) play in the generation of anxiety symptoms. Although theoretical accounts of tacit cognitive schemas are on the increase, there is as yet little evidence regarding effective techniques for their activation and modification. This is particularly true for a patient's tacit, core beliefs about the self. Moreover, there is little research on the underlying painful emotions that may be generating the anxiety symptoms.

Clinical Experience

My clinical experience verifies the necessary but insufficient role that the symptom-focused treatment package of relaxation training, exposure therapy, and cognitive restructuring plays in the treatment of anxiety disorders. This combination can achieve significant clinical benefits, but it cannot produce a comprehensive remission of an anxiety disorder.

My clinical experience leads me to add to the research findings the following propositions:

1. There are unconscious conflicts in anxiety disorders. These can often be identified fairly rapidly by techniques such as WFT.
2. Patients defend against painful emotions related to negative or conflicted self-appraisals associated with the symptoms of an anxiety disorder.
3. Although behavioral change is important, so is the implicit meaning of the anxiety symptoms.
4. Behavioral models underestimate the continuing importance of the therapeutic relationship in catalyzing the specific tasks of therapy.
5. Most cognitive treatments focus primarily on the conscious cognitions that maintain the disorder—those that derive from self-focused attention. Recently, cognitive therapies are focusing more on the patient's affect associated with the dysfunctional thinking, but more work is needed to develop effective emotional-processing techniques.
6. Empathic attunement is a necessary element of effective treatment as is the effort to facilitate the patient's exploration of his or her in-the-moment experiencing.

7. Facilitating a patient's exploration of his or her experiences is a critical element in resolving anxiety disorders.
8. Imagery and metaphoric techniques are very important in eliciting and transforming the implicit meaning of anxiety—the painful self-appraisals.

Unconscious Conflicts in Anxiety Disorders

The application of the imagery probe known as WFT (Wolfe, 2005; see also Appendix) typically uncovers one or more unconscious conflicts associated with anxiety symptoms. These usually entail extremely painful self-appraisals and their accompanying painful emotions. Sometimes these conflicts are of the damned-if-you-do, damned-if-you-don't variety. For example, Elaine, one of the patients with a driving phobia mentioned earlier, possessed a core self-related conflict that involved two extremely unpalatable life options: continuing in a dead marriage that she hated or living on her own, which she dreaded.

Defending Against Painful Emotions

In my experience, anxiety serves as a self-protective screen against painful emotions that will surface into awareness if the patient maintains a constant attentional focus on the anxiety. The automatic shift of attention away from experiencing the anxiety directly to cogitating about the catastrophic implications of being anxious (i.e., self-focused attention) is the first line of defense used against these painful, self-denigrating emotions.

Implicit Meaning of Anxiety

Despite what some CB theorists have said, the implicit meaning of anxiety is a critical feature of these disorders (Craske & Barlow, 2001). These implicit meanings take us quickly to the underlying determinants of an anxiety disorder. These must be identified and treated as well. The idea that the implicit meanings of anxiety and panic relate to negative or conflicted self-appraisals has appeared in specific theoretical models within each of the major psychotherapy perspectives. Psychodynamic, CB, and experiential models of anxiety have recently appeared that focus on negative and conflicted thoughts and feelings about the self as the core locus of these disorders (Guidano, 1991; Milrod et al., 1997; Wolfe & Sigl, 1998). But none of these as yet can be considered representative of the therapy perspective from which each emanates.

Importance of the Therapeutic Relationship

The findings from psychotherapy process research make a significant contribution to an understanding of effective treatment. The therapeutic alliance must be constantly monitored for possible implicit alliance ruptures. Moreover, the meaning of each therapeutic task for the continuing alliance must be constantly gauged. The effectiveness of any given technique depends on the skill with which the therapist implements it and this in turn depends on how well the therapist monitors the vicissitudes of the therapeutic alliance.

Developing Interventions to Modify Core Debilitating Self-Appraisals

However these unconscious psychic structures are conceptualized, it is important to acknowledge their existence and develop interventions that will modify debilitating self-appraisals. It is becoming increasingly clear to representatives of the three psychotherapy perspectives that these psychic structures generate the symptoms of an anxiety disorder. The treatment of symptoms is critically important but a comprehensive and durable therapy should not stop there. The best hope for the continuing remission of anxiety symptoms is the transformation of the patient's core self-appraisals.

Painful Emotions Around the Self

My clinical experience makes clear that by focusing directly on the experience of anxiety (i.e., WFT), the patient eventually comes into contact with painful emotions surrounding catastrophic, negative, or conflicted self-appraisals. The painful emotions typically contacted include anger and rage, shame and humiliation, or defeat and despair. These emotions are so painful that patients avoid these feelings at all costs. Exposure work needs to go beyond just the experience of anxiety. Patients need to allow and accept the painful feelings that the anxiety screens off. Once patients can allow this experience, they become aware of the painful self-appraisals that they do not want to face. If these appraisals are accurate, then therapy focuses on helping patients to do the work necessary to improve their sense and concept of self. If these appraisals are not accurate, which is frequently the case, then the therapeutic work involves correcting the mistaken self-appraisals.

Facilitating the Patient's Experiential Exploration

A critical element in treating anxiety disorders involves facilitating the patient's experiential exploration. Whether this involves exposure to the fear stimulus or to the implicit meaning of the anxiety, a major task of therapy is to help the individual regain the ability to allow and accept his or her direct, in-the-moment experiencing. This is the avenue not only to the underlying core beliefs and images of the self but also to their transformation.

Imagery and Metaphoric Techniques in Transforming Painful Self-Appraisals

Much of a patient's in-the-moment experiencing comes out in images and metaphors. These modalities of self-representation are important because human beings have a natural inclination to develop narratives of their lives (G. S. Howard, 1991). Self-generated narratives are the means by which we make sense of our experience. Several commentators have argued that much of reality is metaphorically structured and that metaphors are (to use a metaphor) the common currency of conversation among people (Kopp, 1995; Lakoff & Johnson, 1981). Imagery techniques and metaphor therapy are often useful in contacting and transforming old images of the self that no longer apply (see case of Peter in chap. 10).

SUMMARY

These then are the factors, based on research evidence and my clinical experience, that I believe are necessary elements of a comprehensive and durable treatment of anxiety disorders. The following is a summary of the common treatment factors and the selected differentiating factors that will be combined into an integrative treatment model.

1. Empathic attunement is needed.
2. A strong therapeutic alliance is developed and constantly monitored.
3. Exposure therapy, relaxation, and cognitive restructuring for symptoms are provided.
4. Patients need to experience the implicit meaning of anxiety, which will lead to the experience of unconscious negative and painful appraisals of self.
5. Anxiety disorders are based in unconscious conflicts and self-appraisals that are extremely painful and negative.
6. These painful and negative self-appraisals need to be identified, accessed, and treated.
7. Although cognitive restructuring may be helpful, changes in core self-appraisals require corrective emotional experiences.
8. Patients defend against these painful emotions and appraisals and these defenses need to be identified and modified.
9. The therapeutic relationship interacts with therapeutic tasks throughout the therapy. Consequently, the therapist must continuously monitor the meaning to the patient of the specific therapy tasks.
10. A major task for the therapist is to facilitate the patient's exploration of his or her experiencing.
11. Imagery and metaphor techniques are very useful in eliciting and transforming painful self-appraisals.

In the next chapter, these elements are woven into an integrative treatment model of the anxiety disorders.

9

AN INTEGRATIVE PSYCHOTHERAPY
FOR ANXIETY DISORDERS

Go to the heart of danger for there you will find safety.
—Ancient Chinese Proverb

This chapter describes an integrative model of psychotherapy for anxiety disorders that synthesizes the best ideas and techniques from the psychodynamic, behavioral, cognitive–behavioral, and experiential psychotherapies. The model defines (a) the goals of therapy, (b) an integrative model of therapeutic change and the various focal points of change, and (c) the phases of treatment and the specific interventions used in each phase.

THE GOALS OF THERAPY

Three sets of goals are associated with this integrative psychotherapy for anxiety disorders: (a) reduction of symptoms, (b) analysis and modification of defenses against painful self-views, and (c) healing the self-wounds. Therapy initially focuses on the reduction of symptoms of a given anxiety disorder. I begin here for several reasons. People often enter into therapy to have their symptoms reduced or eliminated. By beginning with a focus on symptoms, the therapist is honoring the patient's wishes. A second reason is that the reduction of symptoms is likely to bring about fairly rapid therapeutic improvements. An initial focus on behavioral change has been shown to be the quickest route to initial therapeutic success (K. Howard, Kopta, Krause, & Orlinsky, 1986). This research finding comports well with my own clinical experience. A final reason for focusing on symptoms is that patients tolerate work at this level better than they do any in-depth work, particularly in the early stages of therapy. In my view, the in-depth work (i.e., identifying and healing the preconscious self-wounds) is contingent on two prior achievements: the development of a strong therapeutic alliance that will provide sufficient support and safety, and initial success in reducing anxiety symptoms.

The second set of therapeutic goals concerns the identification and modification of psychological defenses against painful self-views. Many of these defenses come into play during the initial phase of therapy, the development of the therapeutic alliance. Several of the patient's interpersonal strategies become apparent in how he or she responds to the initial clinical interviews. Although a wide variety of defensive strategies may make their appearance in therapy, they all share the same goal of interrupting one's in-the-moment experiencing to prevent exposure of one's self-wounds or painful feelings. Avoidance is a defense that all patients with anxiety exhibit. Often avoidance is behavioral but not always. Avoidance may include thoughts and feelings. For example, many patients with generalized anxiety disorder (GAD) monitor their behavior, thoughts, and feelings in an attempt to secure a favorable impression on my part. They do not want to reveal, for example, that they at times feel angry, weak, or intimidated and will go to great lengths to hide such feelings from me and from themselves. Patients with obsessive–compulsive disorder (OCD) often display the defense of isolation, as a way of separating strong feelings from obsessional thoughts. Thus, for example, many such patients experience a violent obsessional thought without any awareness of the anger that drives it. And, of course, the compulsive, ritualistic behavior of patients with OCD represents defenses against the experience of anxiety and its explicit (i.e., obsessional thought) as well as implicit (i.e., self-wound) meaning. Patients with GAD engage in defensive worrying, also as a way of avoiding painful feelings.

A patient's defensive strategies also make their appearance when we attempt the symptom-focused treatment. Often, cognitive–behavioral therapy (CBT) either does not work or takes us only so far. In these instances, I endeavor to ascertain why this very useful treatment does not work. The defensive strategy that prevents CBT from working usually is readily apparent. One way I approach this task is by attempting Wolfe's focusing technique (WFT; Wolfe, 1992, 2005; see also Appendix); if this does not access the underlying self-wounds, I attempt to discover why not. Here the defenses against painful feelings are fairly easy to discover.

To modify these defenses, I begin by acknowledging the patient's prior need for them but then suggest that they no longer aid the patient in adapting to contemporary realities. The particular strategy used to modify a given defense depends on its characteristics and may involve behavioral, cognitive, or emotion-focused techniques. For example, patients who cannot accept their anger but who make clear at an intellectual level that they have issues with a significant other will be invited to engage in some empty-chair work. By imagining the other person sitting in the empty chair in the safety of the therapy situation, a patient might begin to experiment with the experience and expression of anger.

A third set of goals involves the identification and healing of the painful self-wounds. The self-wounds are most frequently identified through WFT. By focusing one's attention on the most salient body location for anxiety, individuals readily contact their painful self-wounds and associated feelings. Once these wounds are accessed, the process of healing may begin. A number of subsidiary goals are associated with this healing process, including (a) enhancing the individual's sense of agency or self-efficacy, (b) increasing the individual's tolerance for emotional experience, particularly negative affects, (c) emotionally processing painful realities, (d) restructuring toxic views of the self, (e) resolving intrapsychic conflicts, (f) resolving discrepancies between self-standards and immediate self-experiencing, (g) increasing the patient's ability to engage in authentic relationships, and (h) engaging in new behaviors to validate the revised self-appraisals.

The elements of the integrative therapy are composed of common treatment factors shared by the various perspectives as well as a selection of differentiating factors based on research evidence and the author's clinical experience. I first present an integrative model of therapeutic change, which addresses the various focal points of change. The general model of change is followed by a description of the various phases of treatment and the specific interventions that are used in each phase.

AN INTEGRATIVE MODEL OF THERAPEUTIC CHANGE

The psychotherapy model presented here posits that change takes place in all three of the traditional foci of treatment: behavior, cognition, and affect. The debate concerning whether insight, behavioral change, or emotional experiencing represents the fundamental mechanism of therapeutic change is a sterile one. Intellectualized insight without behavioral change or corrective emotional experiencing often results in a new way of talking about one's problems, but behavioral change and catharsis without a change in the person's central processing unit (i.e., cognitions, emotional processing, or perspective) is not likely to endure.

Each mechanism, however, seems to point to a particular truth about change. Behavioral change implies a proactive engagement with the world in which one makes a decision to act, implements that decision, and experiences the consequences of that decision. The concept of insight, however, points to the necessity of change in the way we perceive, think, and feel about the world and ourselves. Thus insight implies some kind of cognitive–emotional change in the way in which we construe self and world.

For political as well as theoretical reasons, the various psychotherapy orientations touted one focus of change over the others. Yet all of the foci of change seem important and necessary. What has been sundered by the polemics among psychoanalytic, behavioral, and humanistic therapists needs to be (re)integrated. An integrative concept of change must, on the one hand, involve behavior, cognition, and affect and, on the other, encompass both surface-level and deep-structure change. With respect to the anxiety disorders, this translates into symptom reduction, on the one hand, and the healing of the underlying self-wounds, on the other.

Change in this model begins with the individual directly engaging the world and articulating the resulting emotional and conceptual experience. Doing so can be quite difficult. Patients develop and implement many strategies that prevent them from directly encountering either the outside world or their inner experience. Patients with anxiety disorder, for example, immediately shift their attention from the direct experience of anxiety to cogitating about their anxiety symptoms. Patients with anxiety who can remain anxious when confronting the feared object or situation will eventually begin to experience the disavowed emotions connected to past catastrophic situations. When patients can do this, they come to see that they are actually not being threatened in the present. Once the discrimination between past catastrophe and present reality can be made, patients with anxiety eventually gain a sense of safety in the feared situation. There is therefore a dialectical tension between one's immediate experience of the world and the ideas that one has already stored in memory. The tension that permeates problematic moments and the painful memories that seem ineluctably associated with them are at the heart of the therapeutic modification of anxiety disorders.

In this model, direct experience is a necessary ingredient in the modification of behavior, cognitions, affects, and underlying self-beliefs. Different patients, however, possess different access points for the process of change. For a variety of reasons, patients differ in their comfort level in the initial focus of therapeutic work. Behavioral change is the initial access point for many patients. For some patients, cognitive change is the initial point of access. For a very few patients, therapeutic work may begin with a focus on bringing about corrective emotional experiences (Alexander & French, 1946). Research data and clinical experience both confirm that behavioral change is the simplest and easiest locus of change; cognitive change tends to be more difficult; and changes in the core self are the most difficult to effect and require treatment of the longest duration (K. Howard et al., 1986). Changing core self-beliefs and healing internal wounds require corrective emotional experiences and the emotional processing of painful as well as positive meanings.

My clinical experience also suggests that different change processes may be associated with different foci of change. Behavioral change, for example, can occur with or without changes in the cognitive or emotional realms. Individuals with a phobia can learn to approach their feared object but may continue to experience significant anxiety. People can also rationally reevaluate their beliefs and change them at a cognitive level. This cognitive change may or may not be accompanied by behavioral change. Change at the level of self-belief and self-experiencing, however, appears to require corrective emotional experiences. These experiences necessarily embed cognitive changes and they increase the possibility that any future behavioral change will be experienced as congruent with a revised perspective on the self. Change at this level results in an individual feeling and thinking differently about self and others. In other words, some kind of emotional processing seems to be a necessary ingredient of an enduring change process.

At least four therapy orientations now use the term *emotional processing* or some close variant. A description of the role of emotional processing and its importance for the therapy change process can be found in the behavioral, cognitive–behavioral, experiential, and psychodynamic literature (Alexander & French, 1946; Foa & Kozak, 1986; L. S. Greenberg, Rice, & Elliott, 1993; Rachman, 1980). All of these perspectives provide a model for the resolution of such negative emotions as anger, fear, shame, and despair. Perhaps, as Mahoney (1995) has suggested, corrective emotional experiences lie at the heart of effective psychotherapy, regardless of the theoretical orientation or strategic techniques of the practitioner. If Mahoney is right, then the field does seem to be moving toward a consensus that suggests that the key element in affective change events is the acknowledgment, acceptance, and often expression of emotional pain to the appropriate persons, and the eventual reorganization or restructuring of the person's internal psychic structures that results from such acknowledgment, acceptance, and expression.

All of the perspectives provide indices of unprocessed emotion, that is, cognitive, affective, or behavioral patterns that suggest that specific emotional reactions still affect and influence a person's functioning, usually not for the better. Second, all perspectives, except for the purely behavioral, assume that emotional problems for the most part involve underlying tacit psychic structures. Third, emotional processing involves the restructuring or modification of these tacit structures. Fourth, for emotional processing to take place, these psychic structures must, in some way, be activated—that is, brought into consciousness—before they can be restructured or modified. Finally, the modification of psychic structures involves the presentation of new or discrepant information, which must then be accommodated by these structures.

The psychodynamic conception of the corrective emotional experience clearly involves the activation of unconscious interpersonal psychic structures, which then are presumably modified through the therapist's provision of a different kind of relationship. The experiential conception of emotion scheme, which corresponds in some respects to the idea of cognitive schema, highlights the critical role of affect in terms of both the constituents of the emotion scheme and the processes necessary for the activation and modification of these psychic structures. And the cognitive–behavioral view, as mentioned before, involves the activation and modification of a cognitive–affective psychic structure.

Each perspective, however, also adds important additional components to the phenomenon of emotional processing. Rachman's (1980) behavioral view provides some observable indicators of processed and unprocessed emotion, at least with respect to fear. Foa and Kozak's (1986) cognitive–behavioral perspective provides a general, schematic framework of the nature of emotional processing; the psychodynamic view points to the variety of psychological defenses that people use to interrupt the processing of painful emotional experiences and thereby keep the tacit psychic structures out of awareness (Eagle, 1987); and the view of L. S. Greenberg and his colleagues (L. S. Greenberg et al., 1993) points toward the variety of affective change processes and a number of emotion-focused techniques for resolving these processing difficulties.

There is even an integrative model of emotional processing that suggests that problematic or painful experiences are assimilated into schemas that are developed in the interaction between therapist and client. According to Stiles et al. (1990), the assimilation of problematic experiences is a common change mechanism associated with most, if not all, psychotherapies. They argued that the assimilation process involves several predictable stages: "The client moves from being oblivious, to experiencing the content as acutely painful, then as less distressing, merely puzzling, then understood, and finally as confidently mastered" (Stiles et al., 1990, p. 411).

Every one of these therapies has reported successful results in helping patients to process difficult or painful emotions even though they approach the task in different ways. A question therefore arises: What does it mean that these different therapies can help their patients successfully process painful emotions through different means? One possible answer was suggested previously: that these therapies focus on different therapeutic access points and that different patients are initially reachable at these different points. Some patients prefer to respond to life's challenges through action, others by thinking and planning, and still others through gaining a feel or emotional sense of a problem. Thus a therapist may focus initially on a patient's behavior, cognitions, or emotions. Selecting the wrong initial access point can seriously impede the progress of therapy. For example, I once attempted to use imagery work with a patient with depression who told me, "I am not comfortable with the language of feelings." I then switched to implementing a cognitive–behavioral approach for his depression.

The idea of differing access points is echoed somewhat in Safran and Greenberg's (1991) distinction between top-down versus bottom-up processing. In top-down processing, the therapeutic emphasis is on exploring and challenging tacit rules and beliefs that guide the processing of emotional experience, whereas in bottom-up processing, the therapeutic emphasis is on accessing and intensifying the emotional experience itself. Top-down processing characterizes the access points that psychodynamic and cognitive–behavioral approaches tend to focus on, whereas bottom-up processing characterizes experiential and emotion-focused initial access points.

In the dynamic case, the analysis of defenses and the interpretation of transference may allow the individual to finally process interrupted emotional experience. From the cognitive point of view, it may be necessary to help a client develop new concepts to make sense of emotional experience that had been interpreted as diffuse anxiety or modify dysfunctional beliefs that generate painful emotional experience. In experiential forms of therapy, the intense experience, acceptance, and expression of disavowed feelings appear to lead quite naturally to the modification of the underlying cognitive–affective psychic structure.

If there is merit to this suggestion, then the felicitous matching of therapeutic intervention and access point for different patients becomes an integral part of any successful therapeutic intervention. Regardless of the initial access point for therapy, all of these therapies attempt to do the same thing: activate and modify the tacit emotion-laden irrational idea, the underlying dysfunctional psychic structure. It now may be possible to develop a general model of this fundamental change process. Such a model would be rooted in a number of assumptions:

1. Emotional experiencing and affect regulation are central psychological processes particularly involved in the acquisition and maintenance of personal identity and self-esteem.
2. Psychotherapeutic change at the level of personal identity and self-beliefs necessarily involves changes in the experience of affect.
3. Changes in the experiencing of affect lead to the resolution of specific difficulties in self-related emotional processing.
4. The resolution of emotional processing difficulties leads to a revised view of self, others, self-with-others, the world, and the future.
5. These changes can be achieved through relational, behavioral, cognitive, and emotion-focused approaches.
6. Different approaches will be more effective for different patients because of their differing preferred styles of processing information.

Such an approach possesses great flexibility because it recognizes that the achievement of emotional processing may be obtained by a variety of means applied to different access points. Such an integrative approach can more easily be tailored to individual differences in patients because it acknowledges the patently obvious but challenging fact that patients have learned to use different strategies for dealing with life's difficulties and therefore will not initially be amenable to other strategies for change.

Thus far, I have attempted to map the patient's internal process of change. Another critical dimension of change, however, involves the interpersonal processes that tend to foster the intra-individual change process. Here is found yet another factor that all perspectives share. All therapeutic change is predicated on the development of a strong, supportive nonjudgmental therapeutic alliance. The consensually validated importance of the therapeutic relationship in the change process is a true integrative common factor in all forms of therapy (Gelso & Hayes, 1998; Norcross, 2002).

As the therapeutic relationship evolves, however, many of the issues emphasized by the psychodynamic therapeutic orientation come into play. Even when the patient attempts to carry out the specific tasks of therapy, the alert therapist will observe the patient's transferential feelings. Therapists will also note their own countertransference toward the patient. Sometimes these feelings can interrupt—if not totally undermine—the successful completion of specific therapeutic tasks. One of my patients experiencing frequent panic attacks was carrying out Wolfe's focusing technique. She maintained a strict attentional focus on the sensation of light-headedness, which was the primary prodrome of her panic attacks. As she continued to focus, she began to experience an image of herself being sexually abused. She immediately shut down the image and began to express an enormous degree of rage that she now felt toward me for confronting her with these memories. She made it clear that she was not ready to face these horrible recollections and stormed out of my office in a huff. It was obvious to me that I had not provided enough safety in the therapeutic relationship to allow her to undertake such a harrowing imaginal probe. As the previous example illustrates, monitoring the therapeutic alliance is particularly important when a therapist attempts to implement a specific therapeutic task (such as exposure therapy). These tasks possess both explicit and implicit meaning to the patient, and these meanings may aid or impede therapeutic progress.

In regard to the specific interventions that are typically used and the typical sequence in which they are used, the treatment of anxiety disorders initially focuses on symptomatic change to give the patient a sense of control over the anxiety symptoms. Relaxation strategies, exposure to the feared object or situation, and cognitive restructuring are the first line of treatment for anxiety symptoms once the therapeutic relationship is solid enough to support this harrowing work. This cognitive–behavioral treatment attempts to reconnect patients to their direct experience of the world while it simultaneously attempts to change their threat-laden interpretations of that experience. Once patients have some control over their symptoms, they may opt to explore and modify the underlying determinants of their anxiety disorder.

A deeper level of change is achieved by having patients confront, experience, and ultimately revise the extremely painful self-views they morbidly fear. This work may be done by (a) analyzing and gently confronting patients' defenses against direct experience and (b) conducting experiential work that allows patients to emotionally process their feared self-views. Socratic questioning and other cognitive techniques are very useful in helping patients contact their self-wounds, and behavioral experiments are then designed to help patients enact a new sense of self. It is, however, my conviction that the experiential work will most likely produce the corrective emotional experiences that lead to the reorganized perception and conception of self. The experiential interventions that are frequently used include the empty-chair dialogue, the two-chair dialogue, guided imagery, focusing, and the use of transforming metaphors.

FOUR PHASES OF AN INTEGRATIVE PSYCHOTHERAPY FOR ANXIETY DISORDERS

There are four primary phases for this integrative approach to treating anxiety disorders. The first phase is to establish a therapeutic alliance, the second is to treat the symptoms of the disorder, and the third is to elicit the tacit self-wounds so they may be healed during the final phase. I discuss the details of these four phases in this section.

Phase I: Establishing the Therapeutic Alliance

All effective psychotherapy is predicated on the establishment of a secure, safe, and solid therapeutic alliance. Before any specific intervention can have its desired effect, a working alliance between therapist and patient must be developed. This mandated initial phase of psychotherapy with patients with anxiety is often characterized by a difficult beginning because of their self-protecting interpersonal style. The life histories of patients with anxiety disorder are replete with experiences of betrayal, empathic failures, mistreatment, and difficulties with attachment. Thus, the negotiation of trust is typically the first task of therapy. From the first session onward, the therapist typically encounters fears of trusting, humiliation, and being known. The process of repairing the wounded self begins here by attempting to enhance the client's ability to trust both the therapist and him- or herself, and by desensitizing the client's fear of being known.

Often, the process of negotiating this trust can be completely nonverbal. One patient who possessed an intense fear of being trapped (one symptom in an agoraphobia complex) entered my office for the first time and was unable to sit down. Instead, he paced my office as he recounted the most superficial aspects of his problems. When I invited him to sit, he said it felt unsafe to do so. I then invited him to take a walk with me around the medical complex in which my office was situated. As we walked, he felt an increasing sense of comfort and was able to relate many aspects of his problems of which he was ashamed. Eventually, we returned to my office and he sat down. He experienced no further difficulties in either sitting or talking with me about his problems.

This example, in fact, illustrates a frequently occurring phobogenic conflict in patients with agoraphobia: the conflict between being free and being secure. Each pole of this conflict possesses both a positive and a negative valence. Freedom connotes autonomy and isolation; security connotes being cared for and being controlled. With such patients, therapists will be called on to pass specific tests of trustworthiness, as I was in the example presented previously (Friedman, 1985; Weiss & Sampson, 1986). These tests embed the following questions: Can therapists care for without controlling patients with agoraphobia? By the same token, can therapists allow patients to function autonomously without abandoning them? Unless therapists pass such tests, patients with agoraphobia cannot make use of any of the therapeutic techniques and tasks, including imaginal or in vivo exposure. The first therapeutic task, then, is for therapists to establish their trustworthiness, and for patients to experience and accept this trustworthiness.

Because of past disillusionments and resultant fears of disappointment, patients may find it difficult to acknowledge and accept the therapist's care and concern. Part of the alliance-building phase of therapy involves identifying the various strategies by which patients interrupt their immediate experience of the therapist's trustworthiness. As these defenses are identified and found to be inapplicable in the present context, patients may begin to experience the therapist's trustworthiness. The resurrection of immediate experiencing will lead to a corrective emotional experience regarding the dependability of a significant other.

The direct experiencing of the therapist's trustworthiness indirectly contributes to the rebuilding of patients' sense of self-efficacy. With the therapist as ally, patients feel more confident of their ability to face the anxiety-inducing objects or situations and to endure the automatically occurring anxiety. The provision of a safe relationship that is empathic, genuine, and nonjudgmental serves as a therapeutic bulwark against which patients lean as they negotiate the specific tasks of therapy (Rogers, 1957). The process of maintaining a safe environment in which patients can carry out the difficult work of facing their fears is a constant challenge throughout the course of psychotherapy. Perls (1965) once referred to the therapy situation as a *safe emergency*, a phrase that captures the task of facing terror in the safety of the therapy relationship.

For this reason, the therapist must constantly monitor the meaning that the patient constructs of each specific task of therapy as he or she carries it out. On occasion, patients may construct a negative meaning about the work the therapist is asking them to undertake. They may not share their growing negative feelings but instead continue to comply with the therapist's directives. In this instance, unspoken alliance ruptures may be developing (Safran, 1993). The therapist needs to stay on top of these potential ruptures or the specific task of therapy will become counterproductive (Safran, Muran, & Samstag, 1994). The patient's level of trust in both the therapist and the therapeutic work must be monitored throughout the course of psychotherapy.

Phase II: Treating the Symptoms of an Anxiety Disorder

By the third or fourth session—although it may take longer—most patients are ready to begin Phase II of treatment. This phase focuses on the symptom layer of the disorder, which typically includes the bodily symptoms of anxiety and the obsessive catastrophic cogitating about the symptoms. The primary task of this phase is to help the patient achieve some measure of control over the anxiety symptoms. The vast majority of patients with anxiety possess initial access points in the behavioral and cognitive realm. Thus I usually begin with a baseline assumption that a CB treatment will be effective in the treatment of the symptoms of an anxiety disorder. In those rare cases in which this assumption is not borne out, I may begin with psychodynamic or experiential interventions. For example, a patient may resist the treatment because its nature or manner of presentation activates unconscious conflicts regarding authority. Beutler and Consoli (1992) have labeled this characteristic as *reactance*. Patients who possess a high level of reactance tend to resist directives from any authority, including therapists. Such patients possess a different initial access point, one that calls for psychodynamic or experiential interventions even for the surface-level work.

For the symptom-focused treatment presented here, I have drawn liberally from the treatments developed by Barlow and his colleagues for panic disorder and agoraphobia (Craske & Barlow, 2001), Foa and her colleagues for OCD (Foa & Franklin, 2001), Heimberg and his colleagues for social anxiety disorder (Turk, Heimberg, & Hope, 2001), and Borkovec and his colleagues for GAD (Borkovec & Ruscio, 2000). The core of all of these treatment programs involves a combination of relaxation training, exposure to fear stimuli, and cognitive restructuring. The symptom phase of treatment typically begins with teaching the patient a specific relaxation strategy. I usually begin with diaphragmatic breathing. Most—but not all—patients seem to like this form of relaxation. Some patients automatically begin to cogitate about their breathing and the technique results in increased anxiety (Heide & Borkovec, 1983). If diaphragmatic breathing does not work out, I try progressive relaxation (Jacobson, 1929). If that also does not work out, I collaborate with the patient to discover or develop a relaxation strategy that might work. I typically augment diaphragmatic breathing with imagery-based relaxation. This might entail asking the patient to imagine a safe, comforting, or highly enjoyable setting and to place him- or herself there while continuing the slow breathing (Wolfe, 2005).

Once a patient is comfortable with a particular relaxation strategy, therapy then shifts to imaginal or interoceptive exposure. In imaginal exposure, patients focus on a graduated hierarchy of scenes of ascending fearfulness that involve the anxiety-inducing objects or situations. Patients with OCD are asked to imagine or think their obsessional thoughts, but are not allowed to engage in the anxiety-reducing ritualistic response. In interoceptive exposure, patients are asked to simulate the body sensations that frighten them. For example, a patient who fears the sensation of light-headedness would be asked to breathe rapid shallow breaths until he or she just begins to experience light-headedness. Exposure therapy is typically practiced for about 20 to 30 minutes of a session. In vivo exposure for agoraphobic avoidance behavior is usually carried out for a longer period, usually 60 minutes at a time. This technique involves having the patient travel to a feared destination, usually a place where he or she once experienced a panic attack. As with the imaginal exposure, in vivo exposure is carried out in graduated steps. A patient with a driving phobia, for example, might be asked to drive a mile, then two miles, and so on.

The third component of the symptom-focused treatment is cognitive restructuring. This intervention attempts to modify the threat-laden appraisals and catastrophic interpretations that occur as the patient engages in exposure therapy. Patients are taught to reframe their catastrophic thoughts as hypotheses. The downward arrow technique (J. S. Beck, 1995) is used to elicit the kinds of anticipated catastrophes that patients predict as they move through a descending hierarchy of catastrophic possibilities. Other identified thinking errors (e.g., overestimation of threat) are countered with alternate possible interpretations and an analysis of evidence for each hypothesis.

Phase III: Eliciting the Tacit Self-Wounds

The combination of relaxation training, exposure, and cognitive restructuring provides substantial reduction in anxiety and changes in conscious catastrophic thoughts. Although patients are usually not completely symptom-free, they feel that they have gained significant control over their anxiety symptoms. Patients are now at a decision point. For some patients, the therapy is complete. They have received what they came for and are ready to terminate the therapy. Many other patients, however, wish to explore the roots of their anxiety and are willing to undergo a shift in therapeutic focus and technique. The therapeutic goal of Phase III is to elicit the tacit self-wounds and the feared catastrophes and emotions associated with them.

The major technique used during Phase III is WFT, a modified form of imaginal exposure (Wolfe & Sigl, 1998).

Patients are first told to relax and to engage in the previously taught diaphragmatic breathing for about 2 minutes. During this induction process, patients are primed to allow themselves to be open to whatever thoughts or feelings may arise during the exercise. Patients are subsequently instructed to focus all of their attention on the anxiety-inducing cue and simply to notice whatever thoughts, feelings, or images appear. As a thought, feeling, or image emerges, the patient is instructed to report his or her experience. Sometimes patients report their experience as it happens, in a manner similar to free association. At other times, they respond after a period of silent experiencing, as happens in eye movement desensitization and reprocessing (Shapiro, 1995).

In the case of phobias, patients are asked to imagine the phobic object or situation. Patients with panic disorder, however, are asked to identify the most prominent bodily sites of anxiety or fearful bodily sensations and to maintain a strict attentional focus on these sites. For patients with OCD, the strict attentional focus is on the obsessive thought that is causing anxiety. Typically, within one or two sessions, this procedure results in the appearance of several thematically related emotion-laden images. It usually takes longer with patients with panic disorder because they have great difficulty contacting emotion-laden imagery. Despite this, however, the procedure is almost uniformly successful in eliciting the catastrophic imagery reflecting a specific self-wound.

The imagery is imbued with themes of conflict and catastrophe that the patient is helpless to prevent or terminate. These memories of self-endangerment reflect specific self-wounds. For example, memories of parental betrayal may shape a painful view of one's self as unwanted, unlovable, or unworthy, which in turn produces fears of abandonment. These memories are usually accompanied by powerful and painful emotions, which also become fear stimuli.

This technique often segues into a guided-imagery procedure that allows the patient and me to explore the network of interconnected ideas, feelings, and associations that constitute the implicit meaning of anxiety. One patient, for example, who experienced the generalized subtype of social phobia possessed two core fears: humiliation and social ostracism. He was afraid, for example, that he could not respond appropriately, in general, but particularly to mistreatment. I had him imagine being mistreated. He imagined that he would say nothing, which made him angry with himself. He knew he couldn't hide the anger, because it was readily displayed in the tightness of his mouth and in his perpetual scowl. He assumed that people saw his anger and thought it was directed at them. He imagined that they would ostracize him for his irrationality. He was also afraid that he would not express anger appropriately: too little and he felt like a wimp, too much and he feared people would retaliate. He went on to imagine that the person to whom he inappropriately expressed anger would then convince others to avoid him because of his irrational anger. His role model was John Wayne, who he believed could handle any situation without expressing any emotion. Therefore, he would become very angry with himself if another person successfully elicited an unwanted feeling. The self-wound sequence, as expressed in imagery, was as follows: Mistreatment leads to frustration, helplessness, and anger, which leads him to conclude that he is a bad person, which elicits fear that he will be rejected and he will become an isolated outcast. The guided-imagery work uncovered his core self-wound: his belief that he was not worthy of human companionship.

One interesting feature of applying WFT with patients with an anxiety disorder is that whereas consciously their fears are often about physical destruction, the tacit catastrophic imagery is most often about psychological destruction. The image of psychological destruction is usually associated with a specific self-wound. The goals of the modified imaginal exposure depart somewhat from the original behavioral version. The experience of anxiety is not only for the purpose of learning that the feared disaster will not take place or that the anxiety will habituate but also for uncovering the underlying self-wound and its associated felt catastrophes.

Although WFT and guided imagery are the major techniques for eliciting self-wounds, they also may be elicited on occasion through interpretive insight-oriented techniques. Socratic questioning also has been successful, on occasion, in pursuing a fear to its ultimate catastrophic end, which will reveal the specific self-wound in question. Whether one initially uses imagery, interpretation, or questioning depends on what is determined to be the most acceptable or congenial access point for the patient. I usually proceed on a trial-and-error basis for determining a patient's access point because when a patient does not comply with—or benefit from—a particular kind of intervention, the therapist obtains a great deal of diagnostic information about the patient's defenses or conflicts. The failure of a particular type of intervention is critically important information that the therapist then uses in selecting more promising interventions.

Phase IV: Healing the Self-Wounds

The healing of the activated self-wounds involves a variety of interventions, focused on a number of separate but interrelated goals. For self-wounds to heal, the following processes must be set in motion: (a) identifying and modifying the patient's defenses against painful experiencing, (b) enhancing the patient's self-efficacy (Bandura, 1977), (c) increasing tolerance for painful emotions, (d) emotionally processing painful realities, (e) modifying toxic self-appraisals, (f) resolving catastrophic conflicts, (g) resolving discrepancies between self-standards and immediate self-experiencing, (h) increasing the patient's willingness to engage in authentic relationships, and (i) engaging in new behaviors to validate the revised self-appraisals.

Identifying and Modifying the Patient's Defenses Against Painful Experiencing

Often, this fourth phase of therapy begins with the identification of the patient's defenses against emotional and visceral experience. This is done in conjunction with the application of Wolfe's focusing technique. As previously mentioned, a core element of all anxiety disorders is the automatic shift of attention from the anxiety to cogitating about its implications. Cogitation typically increases the severity of anxiety while prolonging its duration. Symptom-focused treatments (i.e., CBT), by and large, focus on reducing or eliminating the anxiety associated with cogitation. One patient, for example, began to cogitate about the implications of his anxiety symptoms as he attempted to carry out the focusing technique. The implications spun off into other implications, all of which made his anxiety worse while protecting him from the underlying feelings. Being anxious meant that he is unstable, socially unpleasant, and unable to perform optimally in his career. These thoughts produced more anxiety, which in turn generated the implications that there must be some basic flaw in his makeup because he was staying anxious for so long. As he became aware of this defense, he began working on allowing the experience of feelings that underlie his anxiety. This was followed by work to transform his self-appraisal as mentally ill and defective.

Another common defense involves patients who shift out of the task altogether. Once patients contact a painful feeling during focusing, they may begin to talk about something entirely unrelated to the task. The task will remind them of some story that they must share at that moment with the therapist. One of my patients with OCD has a million stories that seem to appear just as he is contacting a painful reminder of his mortality, a concept that terrifies him.

All of these defenses protect the patient with anxiety from the same phenomenon—the experience of intensely painful feelings. The fear of feelings is desensitized gradually, which then allows the patient to engage in the imagery techniques previously described. For example, one patient whose panic attacks began right after the death of his father was frightened of the focusing technique because he sensed that his panic and anxiety protected him from feelings that would negate his ego ideal of being a nice guy. With gradual desensitization, he eventually was able to experience and imaginally express intense rage toward his father, as well as grief and despair over the loss. It is interesting to note that this phase of treatment highlights the interplay of uncovering techniques and behavioral interventions in the modification of psychological defenses.

Enhancing a Person's Sense of Self-Efficacy

The enhancement of the patient's self-efficacy actually begins with Phase II, the symptomatic treatment phase, but continues throughout the entire duration of therapy. The symptom-focused treatment supplies the patients with a number of coping skills for reducing anxiety. By achieving some control over their anxiety symptoms, patients begin to feel more confident and hopeful not only about beating their disorder but also about solving other major difficulties in their lives. Patients' self-efficacy increases as they begin to allow themselves to experience and accept their tacit fears and disavowed emotions. Cognitive restructuring aids the process by consciously modifying the negative self-appraisals regarding their ability to achieve certain outcomes or goals in their lives. Behavioral experiments in which they actually solve a basic difficulty in their lives provide patients with the most tangible evidence of their self-efficacy.

Concerns about self-efficacy, however, also appear during the Phase IV work of healing self-wounds. Focusing and imagery probes often indicate that patients with anxiety disorders doubt their ability to cope with a broad range of life's difficulties. For example, many people develop panic disorder during a transitional phase in their life when they experience a terrible sense of dread about the resulting life changes. Patients, for example, have experienced panic attacks when they first go away to college, start a new job, get pregnant for the first time, lose their spouse, move to a new neighborhood, or discover that they have a life-changing chronic illness. A patient who had a driving phobia for 16 years achieved some gains with in vivo exposure therapy, but the therapy was insufficient. He had grave doubts about living and functioning alone. We shifted into a more insight-oriented therapy that led to the discovery that part of his dependency was an attempt to punish his parents for their neglect when he was a child. Armed with this insight, we began a behaviorally oriented skills training program that gradually led to an increase in his confidence that he could live alone. During the behavioral therapy, we monitored his feelings as he increasingly experienced himself as a capable, mature, and autonomous adult. In addition, we conducted family therapy sessions that gave him an opportunity to express his anger to his parents and likewise to absorb their responses to him. The implicit rule of silence that guided this family's interactions for years was thereby broken.

Increasing Tolerance for Painful Emotions

Because it appears to be the case that many, if not most, anxiety disorders are based in a fear of intensely painful self-related feelings, the ability to tolerate such feelings becomes a necessary part of the healing process. A staple of L. S. Greenberg et al.'s (1993) process–experiential therapy is the technique of allowing and accepting one's disavowed emotions. L. S. Greenberg and Safran (1987) gave an eloquent justification for emotion-focused techniques:

People in therapy need to learn that fear isn't weak, that pain won't kill, and that anger isn't necessarily bad; and that rather than being signs of weakness, of losing control, or of being unable to cope, these emotions can facilitate problem resolution. (p. 188)

As patients see that they can experience painful feelings without falling apart, they acquire a new sense of self-efficacy. Many patients find that experiencing these painful, disavowed feelings is actually less painful than the anxiety and panic. The process of allowing and accepting can be done in degrees. If the pain is too much, the patient stops the experiential exploration and carries out a favorite relaxation strategy. Wachtel (1997) has likened this process to exposure therapy in which the fear stimulus is the disavowed emotion. Like other forms of exposure therapy, it can be done gradually and under the patient's control. For example, over the course of several sessions, a patient with agoraphobia finally allowed in the rage that she had suppressed for years toward her parents for their overprotectiveness, on the one hand, and their intrusive hypercriticalness, on the other.

Emotionally Processing Painful Realities

It was suggested in chapter 6 that in most instances the self-wounds that generate the symptoms of an anxiety disorder are associated with an inability to accept a number of existential realities that human beings cannot avoid. People lose loved ones, careers, and physical abilities. People get confused about how much to trust others and how much freedom versus security they wish to have in their lives. People sometimes are trapped in bad relationships or life situations and they discover that they are fundamentally alone. People also fail, become ill, and know that eventually they will die. Each of these realities is painful to accept and assimilate. Patients with anxiety disorders are terrified of one or more of these inexorable realities. They seem unable to accept the unavoidable.

Guided-imagery work is particularly useful in helping patients to emotionally process and assimilate the painful facts of their lives. I ask patients to imagine the ontological given that terrifies them and to notice and express the feelings that automatically arise. Patients then imagine the implications of accepting reality and express those. Finally, patients work to develop ways of coping with the reality that they fear. Occasionally, merely expressing sadness or anger over an inevitable reality may be enough to reduce a patient's fear. One patient with a social phobia began to feel less anxious about public speaking once he acknowledged to himself that he was lacking in certain public speaking skills. He took the initiative to learn some of the missing skills and his speaking performance significantly improved. More to the point, however, he approached the task of speaking with minimal anxiety instead of the terror that used to accompany his talks. This patient came to realize that much of his anxiety was generated by a need to present himself as the leading expert on whatever topic about which he was speaking, which he thought was necessary to win the audience's approval. By accepting what his speaking abilities truly were, he undercut the impression management strategy that had the paradoxical effect of keeping him highly anxious.

Another patient with GAD began to have panic attacks after the death of her spouse. Focusing revealed her inability to accept her husband's death, which had prevented her from grieving. I had her imagine first the scenes leading up to her husband's death, then the funeral. Later, I had her remember many specific episodes from their life together. The grief brought sobs, but the anxiety and panic disappeared.

Modifying Toxic Self-Appraisals

Another aspect of the healing of self-wounds involves the modification of toxic self-appraisals. These appraisals are usually the product of severe and repeated criticism from primary caregivers and other significant people in a patient's life. Toxic self-appraisals present, I believe, the most difficult challenge to any form of psychotherapy. My typical clinical experience in working with patients with anxiety is that they can achieve significant control over their anxiety symptoms in a couple of months, but it may take them 1 to 3 years to change some of the underlying, toxic self-appraisals.

The work of changing self-appraisals begins with their identification and the experience of the associated painful emotions. Appraisals of inadequacy, being unwanted, or not measuring up usually are associated with scorching experiences of humiliation and shame. These emotions are so painful that they are to be avoided at all costs. Anxiety occurs whenever a patient is about to contact these painful emotions. The experience of these painful feelings not only reduces or eliminates the anxiety but also allows the individual to more clearly assess the validity of these painful self-views. To the extent there is truth in these self-views, the individual begins to plan and implement steps to remedy the perceived deficiencies. To the extent they are found to be invalid, these self-views are challenged and modified.

Resolving Catastrophic Conflicts

Although toxic self-appraisals may appear as single unitary experiences, they often are experienced as catastrophic self-splits. The experience of these self-splits possesses a damned-if-you-do, damned-if-you-don't quality (Wolfe, 1989). Many patients with agoraphobia, for example, believe that if they are married, they will see themselves as trapped, and if they are not, they see themselves as alone and isolated. Either experience of self is excruciatingly painful. An individual with a social phobia possesses a variation of the same conflict. He discovers that he possesses a deep-seated emotional belief that if people are not interested in him, he is worthless and he will be miserable and alone for the rest of his life. But if people are interested in him, they do not really know him and are therefore not to be trusted.

Often these conflicts become apparent in guided-imagery work or in the appearance of a client-generated metaphor. Conflict resolution involves the creation of a synthesis between incompatible aims. A synthesis is often necessary because each side of the conflict usually possesses a value important to the patient. Although patients often wish to destroy one side of the conflict, they are encouraged through two-chair work to have the two sides dialogue and listen to one another.

The steps involved in resolving conflict include (a) identifying the poles of the conflict, (b) using the two-chair technique to heighten the experience of each pole, (c) beginning a dialogue between the two poles to create a synthesis, and (d) making a provisional decision to take specified steps toward change. Once a decision has been made regarding specific behavioral changes, the next step is to take action and allow one's immediate experience to inform the patients of the results of the change steps taken. Successful outcomes from these self-fashioned choices increase the likelihood of a change in dysfunctional self-representations and increase the patients' ability to accept their immediate in-the-moment emotions.

Catastrophic conflicts often involve a self-split, in which the patient simultaneously holds two incompatible views of the self (L. S. Greenberg et al., 1993). The manifestation of one side of the split threatens the other, and the result is a feeling of paralysis. We have already mentioned Elaine (see chap. 8), the patient who experienced a split between her failed-marital-partner self and her autonomous-but-alone self. Focusing revealed the following dilemma: If she drove away from home, she would never come back to her husband because she doubted she could change her lifeless marriage. This, however, would mean she was a failure. But leaving her husband would mean that she would have to function autonomously, which she believed she was currently unable to do. In this instance, a two-chair dialogue between the two self-views allowed her to integrate these seemingly opposed self-appraisals. She began to realize that her fear of functioning autonomously was based in an unwillingness to give up the convenience of having her husband assume responsibility for many tasks that she knew she could perform (or learn to perform). She also began to realize that the marriage was beyond saving and that she needed to accept partial responsibility for its failure. A brief stint of marital therapy that supplemented the two-chair work also validated her realization that she no longer wanted to stay in the marriage.

Resolving Discrepancies Between Self-Standards and Immediate Self-Experiencing

In the course of development, human beings internalize a collection of self-standards to guide their behavior. These self-guides (Higgins, 1987) comprise a number of beliefs about the way the individual ought to behave. As such, they serve a regulatory function for our behavior. When our experience deviates from our stored self-guides, we experience painful emotions

(Strauman, 1994). Strauman and Higgins (1993) suggested that discrepancies between self-guides and the person's actual experience produce different emotional responses. For example, discrepancies between the actual self and the ought self-guides (i.e., the way the self is supposed to be) seem to be related to social anxiety, whereas discrepancies between the actual self and the ideal self-guides produce depressive emotions. Strauman and Higgins (1993) viewed these self-guides as cognitive structures; however, my clinical experience suggests that (a) they are cognitive–affective structures and (b) they influence the development of virtually all anxiety disorders.

One of the most efficacious techniques for resolving such discrepancies is the two-chair dialogue between the self-guide and the perplexing immediate experiencing. For example, one patient possessed the self-guide of never getting angry. She was, however, experiencing significant anger at the moment. Until she allowed the anger to surface, she experienced anxiety and even panic whenever she got close to anger. Allowing the anger, however, caused her a painful dilemma because her experience seemed to nullify her self-guide. By personifying the self-guide and the discrepant experiencing and having the two sides engage in a dialogue, the patient has an opportunity to eliminate the discrepancy. The therapist neither prejudges nor predetermines the outcome of this dialogue. As a result of the dialogue, the patient may conclude that (a) the self-guide is too rigorous or inappropriate for the patient's current life functioning and therefore needs revision, (b) the experience is outside the bounds of acceptability and will be discouraged, or (c) some compromise solution will be generated that honors the significant concerns of both the self-guide and the discrepant experiencing. The previously-mentioned patient with panic disorder engaged in a dialogue between the self-guide of never getting angry and the experience of being enraged at her husband. She concluded that she had good and sufficient reason to be angry and that her anger did not disqualify her from considering herself a nice person. On the other hand, it was important that the anger be expressed appropriately. This two-chair work, by the way, was preliminary to her doing some empty-chair work in which she expressed her anger at her husband, who she imagined was sitting in the empty chair.

Increasing Patients' Willingness to Act Authentically in Relationships

Patients with an anxiety disorder keep secrets. Typically, patients feel shameful about one or more aspects of their person and they do not want other people to know. Consequently, they develop an inauthentic style of relating to others. Their lack of authenticity, however, lends power to their secrets, which in turn increases their anxiety regarding the prospect of their being exposed. As exemplified in the case of Glen, individuals with a public speaking phobia often feel they are imposters. In fact, they believe they are not as bright or gifted as they would like others to think. To protect their secret, they adopt the pose of all-knowing experts. Whenever they approach the task of giving a talk, their anxiety rapidly rises. For example, an individual loses focus on the task at hand and instead cogitates about the reaction of members of the audience if they discover his or her limitations as an intellect and as a speaker.

The therapeutic task is to help patients accept their limitations (and their strengths) and to be willing to selectively share their secrets with people they trust. By accepting themselves, they undercut any power that their secrets may have in keeping them anxious. Very often such patients do not even reveal that they are in therapy to the people closest to them. Often, the first authenticity assignment is to let someone they trust know that they are in therapy. If their confidant proves to be trustworthy with this information, patients are then encouraged to share a little more. This process needs to be in the complete control of the patient. The patient must decide when and how much to reveal. The selective sharing of secrets, however, does reduce interpersonal anxiety.

Engaging in New Actions That Validate the Revised Self-Appraisals

In the final stage of treatment, when patients are in the process of revising their self-views, they will undertake new actions that reinforce and validate the new self-view. Those with a public speaking phobia, for example, are now encouraged to seek out speaking opportunities, not to show themselves that they can control their anxiety but to validate their new view of self as a confident and relaxed speaker. Patients with OCD develop a sense of self that is characterized by a new sense of confidence that they can tolerate whatever emotions arise as a result of disturbing thoughts; and they know as well that to think a thought does not automatically lead to acting the thought out. Patients with panic disorder come to believe in their ability to tolerate the emotions and associated meanings that underlie the heretofore-frightening body sensations. Agoraphobic avoidance becomes meaningless because these patients now are cognizant of the actual source of their panic attacks.

SUMMARY

From these pieces of the treatment model, a prototypical pattern of change can be delineated. It begins with patients developing a sense of control over their anxiety symptoms. The second step is for patients to come to understand their defenses against painful self-related experiencing. Step 3 is for patients to contact the painful emotions and their associated self-wounds and to differentiate the painful self-views that are based in fact from those that are based in the inaccurate but toxic opinions that they have internalized from significant people in their lives. Step 4 involves patients learning to tolerate and emotionally process the painful realities of their lives and to begin to develop a remediation plan to transform their liabilities into strengths.

Step 5 involves resolving the catastrophic conflicts that have maintained the painful self-views. Step 6 involves the self-empowering expressiveness that comes from confronting people in their lives that have harmed, betrayed, humiliated, or traumatized them. This is initially done imaginatively (e.g., empty-chair work) and later, if possible and necessary, the patients may confront these people in actuality. Step 7 involves engaging in other new actions that validate the revised view of self.

The change process, as I have seen it unfold with my patients, appears to involve a shuttling back and forth between old ways of thinking, feeling, and enacting the self and the new ways of thinking, feeling, and behaving that are learned in therapy. The old patterns are never completely erased. Instead, they are eventually replaced by the new patterns, which are built, as it were, on top of the old. After much oscillation, the new patterns become consolidated. Under conditions of severe stress, however, it is not impossible for the patient to revert to old ways of thinking, feeling, and enacting the self.

With this model as the prototype, the next chapter describes how the model is applied to the specific anxiety disorders. Some of these cases follow the prototypical pattern but others do not; in the latter case, I show how and why they deviate from the prototype.

10

THE INTEGRATIVE THERAPY APPLIED TO SPECIFIC ANXIETY DISORDERS

Head—This is one of the scrapes into which you are ever leading us. You must look forward before you take a step that may interest our peace.

Heart—Let the gloomy monks, sequestered from the world, seek unsocial pleasures in the bottom of his cell. Had they ever felt the solid pleasure of one generous spasm of the heart, they would exchange for it all the frigid speculations of their lives.

Head—Do not bite at the bait of pleasure til you know there is no hook beneath it. The art of life is the art of avoiding pain.

Heart—Leave me to decide when and where friendships are to be contracted. We have no rose without its thorn; no pleasure without its alloy.

—Thomas Jefferson (1786; A dialogue between his head and heart, written upon falling in love with Maria Cosway)

To describe the application of the integrative therapy model to specific anxiety disorders, I return to the cases described in chapter 7. In each of these cases, with regard to the specific interventions, the patient's initial access point is determined through the clinical interview. In every one of the cases presented, the patient was found to initially prefer behavioral and cognitive interventions. This should not be particularly surprising because these were well-educated individuals who preferred a direct approach to fixing their anxiety problem. In fact, the vast majority of patients prefer a sequence of interventions that moves from behavioral to cognitive and eventually to psychodynamic and experiential interventions. Preceding the specific interventions, of course, is a relationship-building phase that depends more on Rogerian and psychodynamic concepts of empathy (Bohart & Greenberg, 1997).

JIM: A CASE OF MULTIPLE SPECIFIC PHOBIAS

In chapter 7, I presented an integrative etiological model of Jim's multiple specific phobias, which included fears of flying, traveling on the subway, elevators, and relational commitment. I had suggested that these phobias were thematically linked by a damaged sense of self-efficacy. Jim did not believe that he or his efforts made any difference in his life. He felt powerless, unable to move his life in any desired direction, and totally at the mercy of the actions of others. He therefore felt trapped in an airplane because he was at the mercy of the pilot's actions. But he also felt trapped on subways, in elevators, and in his relationships.

The first phase of therapy always involves establishing a solid therapeutic alliance. Jim and I connected easily, which was surprising because of his usual lack of trust of people he does not know well. The solid connection that we had forged allowed the treatment to move quickly to the alleviation of the phobic symptoms. This phase of treatment began with my teaching Jim diaphragmatic breathing (DB). His initial homework assignment was to practice DB twice per day. Jim quickly gained facility in carrying out the technique and found it generally useful in the reduction of tension.

The second technique used during the symptom alleviation phase of the treatment involved imaginal exposure. We divided the plane trip into 11 steps that included his (a) making plane reservations, (b) traveling to the airport, (c) checking his baggage, (d) sitting at the gate, (e) entering the plane, (f) sitting on the plane, (g) experiencing the plane taxiing to its take-off position, (h) feeling the plane take off, (i) climbing to cruising altitude, (j) adjusting to cruising altitude, (k) experiencing turbulence, and (l) experiencing the plane landing. Jim was then instructed to imagine the first step in this sequence and to use DB to reduce whatever anxiety emerged. When he no longer experienced anxiety imagining the first image, he moved to the next image in the sequence. An interesting facet of this treatment was that we had to desensitize Jim to other images that spontaneously occurred during his imagining of a particular image. For example, when he entered the plane, he avoided looking at the other passengers because he did not want to know how crowded the plane really was. We had to add the image of his looking around and taking in all of the passengers on the plane.

The imaginal exposure phase of treatment was conducted for seven sessions; Jim then felt ready to begin in vivo exposure. He began by making reservations for a short flight in 3 weeks. He did this with very little anxiety. During the interim, he practiced going to the airport and sitting near the ticket counter. He used DB to reduce the ensuing anxiety. In addition, we also addressed his fear of riding the Metro. Because he experienced the same symptoms on the subway as he did on a plane, we agreed that he would use riding the Metro not only as a treatment target in its own right but also as a rehearsal for flying. Jim started right in with in vivo exposure. Because the Metro made frequent stops, it was easy to arrange the exposure treatment in small sequential steps. He began by going just one stop, progressed to two, and so on until he was able to take a complete subway ride from his home in a Northern Virginia suburb into Washington, DC.

At the scheduled time, Jim took a 1-hour flight to his destination and the 1-hour flight back. He was ecstatic that he was able to do this, but at the same time was apprehensive about a transcontinental flight that he was scheduled to take for work the very next month. We continued the imaginal exposure as a rehearsal for the longer trip. Jim took the trip as scheduled to California but he experienced a significant amount of anxiety during that trip, primarily because of an unusual amount of turbulence on both legs of the trip. Upon his return, we focused imaginal exposure on the experience of turbulence. This work appeared to help him during his subsequent flights.

Although Jim now felt he had enough control over his symptoms that he no longer needed to avoid flying, he still was not completely free of anxiety in anticipation of and during the flights. We were now at a decision point. He could terminate therapy, or continue it with a focus on exploring the underlying determinants of his several phobias. He chose the latter option and we shifted our therapeutic gears.

I asked Jim to pick one of the contexts in which he felt trapped and to focus his attention on that scene and notice what thoughts and feelings automatically arose. He chose the commitment context and began to imagine having lunch with his girlfriend, Nina, whom he described as being a strong feminist. He imagined that he inadvertently used sexist language during the lunch and she reamed him out. He began to get anxious, experiencing the usual feelings of tightness in his chest. I asked him to keep his attention on the tight-chest sensations and notice the feelings that come up. He began to experience anger and then hurt. I asked him to engage in empty-chair work. He imagined Nina sitting in the empty chair and began to express these feelings to her. He told her that he was hurt that she criticized him for his inadvertent language and thought she was making too much of a slip of the tongue. As he did, he began to feel a little less helpless and panicky. He associated to a similar critical point in his relationship with a previous girlfriend. Again, she had criticized him and this resulted in the same tightness in his chest. By using Wolfe's focusing technique (WFT; Wolfe 1992, 2005; see also Appendix), he became clear that he was hurt and angry but very frightened of fully experiencing these feelings and expressing them to her. As he expressed these feelings in the guided-imagery exercise or through empty-chair work, his felt sense of helplessness and panic continued to decrease.

During the next session, we did empty-chair work with his mother. He became terribly frightened as he tried to express the inexpressible—the hurt and anger he felt regarding her domineering behavior toward him. During this exercise, he subsequently put Nina back in the empty chair and found himself spontaneously asking Nina a question that he had never asked her: Why was she so offended by his gender faux pas? Once he began to allow himself to experience and express his feelings, the dialogue with Nina went deeper and into many other directions, all of which promised his getting to know her better.

Jim then wanted to try to tell Nina in person how he felt and to ask her why she was offended. Jim, however, took a very unfortunate tack. He did ask Nina why she was so offended but then added that his therapist wanted to know. Nina was understandably furious and proceeded to ream him out. This set him back and it took several sessions before he was able to restart the dialogue with Nina. In the meantime, we did guided-imagery work around his relationship with his mother and his fear of the concept of marriage. The felt meaning of marriage was that he will always have to give in and will not be able to express himself.

As the actual dialogue between Jim and Nina improved, her spontaneous displays of affection increased. However, her intimate aggressiveness felt to Jim like she had an unquenchable need to be close, and closeness frightened him. In imagery, we rehearsed their meeting and on how and what about his feelings he wanted to communicate. Intellectually, he was now aware of a characteristic interpersonal pattern. He avoided closeness to protect himself from being in a position in which he stifled his complaints out of a fear of hurting her and eventually losing her. We continued imagery work around Nina's spontaneous affection, which generated in him a fear of being overwhelmed. He used the metaphor of being steamrolled. We worked with the metaphor and how he could possibly stop the steamroller. I had him imagine that he could accept the affection and closeness but could say no to Nina when he needed to. Similarly, he imagined her telling him that she loved him. She actually did this frequently, and it stimulated his fear of being controlled.

As he gained some ability in imagery to differentiate between accepting her affection and defining his boundaries, he gained confidence in the relationship. Over time, he was increasingly able to allow himself to know what he was feeling and share it with Nina. They went on vacation together for the first time, and both had a very good time. After this, the focusing and guided-imagery work made Jim less anxious.

Over the next 6 months, however, a number of setbacks and false starts occurred, all because of his fear of letting Nina know how he really felt. During the subsequent 6 months of work, Jim showed improvement in his ability to allow and accept his feelings and to express them to Nina. As he did, he felt less trapped. With the decline of his feeling trapped, he found it easier to fly, travel on a subway, and get in an elevator. By the time we terminated, Jim had made great progress in all of his phobic contexts.

This case, I believe, illustrates that specific phobias, which we used to refer to as simple phobias, are not so simple. The underlying determinants of specific phobias can be quite complex. If these can be identified and alleviated, I believe that the optimistic findings reported in the literature on symptom-focused treatments (i.e., cognitive–behavioral therapy [CBT]) will be extended. An integrative psychotherapy for complex anxiety disorders promises to be more comprehensive and durable. This is the promise that needs to be empirically evaluated.

GLEN: A CASE OF SOCIAL PHOBIA

I did not have as easy a time establishing a therapeutic alliance with Glen as I did with Jim. Because shame was a central issue in his social phobia, Glen allowed access to his most tender experience at a very slow pace. He was very concerned about my opinion of him; he was particularly concerned about being an interesting enough patient. Perhaps the first rupture in our alliance came when he noticed my becoming heavy-lidded while he was talking. I had had insufficient sleep the night before, and I was struggling to be alert for Glen. His response was telling. Without a hint of sarcasm, he said, "I am sorry that I am not a more interesting patient today." As I describe, this response spoke volumes about his family history, a history filled with shaming responses from his father and uncle. His response was also a major clue as to the implicit meaning of his panic attacks and anticipatory anxiety. Although he assumed a deferential stance with me during the therapy hour, he frequently went home angry. His being able to finally allow himself to express his anger toward me for my virtually nodding off while he talked was a significant indication of therapeutic progress.

After several sessions during which Glen described the nature of his problem(s) and the implications that his public speaking fears possessed for both his career and personal well-being, he was ready to participate in the symptom management phase of treatment. We began with my explaining the rationale of my integrative psychotherapy and segued into my teaching him DB. The breathing technique became his most important tool for coping with anxiety. He used it frequently and successfully.

One of the key features of his anxiety process was that in anticipation of giving a talk, he would cogitate about the audience's likely reaction to his having a panic attack. While his attention was focused on the audience, he could not focus on the task at hand, which was giving the talk. Thus, I taught Glen to retrain his attention away from cogitation toward a focus on what he wanted to communicate to the audience. By focusing his attention on the content of his talk, he gradually was able to reduce his anxiety. A third technique involved his preparing short talks during which he could use both DB and attention retraining as coping skills. Eventually he rehearsed with me the actual talk he was planning to give.

Attention retraining in conjunction with DB provided significant relief to Glen, and it convinced him that he could control the level of his anxiety both before and during his talk. One mark of this progress was that before therapy he would begin to cogitate and obsess a month before he had to give a talk. After about 12 sessions, he did not start cogitating until a day or so before the talk. He also clearly experienced the reciprocal relationship with respect to anxiety between focusing his attention on the talk and cogitating.

With these improvements in the management of his anxiety symptoms, Glen wanted to explore the roots of his anxiety. We began with imaginal probes using WFT. I asked him to imagine having a panic attack while giving a speech and to notice the feelings and thoughts that arose. He began to experience intense feelings of humiliation and began to harshly criticize himself for being weak and pathetic. He also imagined the audience coming to his aid and being sympathetic. This also humiliated him because it made him feel weak and needy. As we continued the probe, he began to encounter feelings of being an intellectual imposter and thoughts that he really is not as intelligent as he would like others to think.

When we explored the network of images associated with his self-perceived level of intelligence, we found that he possessed a split in his self-view. One view was that he is very bright; the other view is that he is an intellectual imposter. I asked him to engage in a two-chair dialogue between the two self-views to help him integrate these two perspectives. This work helped him to entertain the possibility that he was smart enough to be successful in his field. As he began to assimilate this self-view, his public speaking anxiety decreased.

The most difficult challenge in working at this level with Glen was the attempt to modify the shameful connotations of panic. If he were to have a panic attack while giving a talk, Glen would harshly condemn himself as pathetic, weak, and an intellectual fraud. He would then imagine his colleagues revising their good opinion of his abilities and his being paralyzed by the resulting shame. The imagery probes revealed that the harsh, condemning voices originally belonged to his mean-spirited uncle and his disappointed father. His father in particular, Glen believed, was disappointed that Glen was not a better athlete and that he was not a star achiever in traditional masculine endeavors. These kinds of experiences and memories produced in Glen a core self-wound that he was not a good enough athlete, man, husband, and academic. For Glen to panic was to confront this unbearably painful view of himself as "not enough."

In our efforts to heal this self-wound, we encountered a number of obstacles along the way. One of these involved his relationship with his father. Glen was very angry and hurt about the fact that his father rarely listened to him. A core memory involved Glen trying to have a conversation with his father and the latter having his face in a newspaper. At the same time, however, Glen was unable to tell his father about his achievements. I asked Glen to do some empty-chair work with his father. I asked Glen to tell him about his achievements and to also tell him that in some ways he had surpassed what his father had been able to achieve in his life. This request terrified

Glen. He could not do it. He was afraid that such declarations would deeply hurt his father. In fact, Glen was afraid that he might permanently damage his father psychologically. This fear was still prominent in Glen's mind despite the fact that his father had been dead for many years. Thus Glen had constructed a conflict of the damned-if-you-do, damned-if-you-don't kind. He was in pain because he continued to believe that his father was disappointed in Glen's achievements, but he could not own those achievements in his father's presence for fear that his father would be shattered.

Because his father was long dead, Glen could not confront his father in actuality. Instead, we engaged in work to restructure his memories of their relationship. Glen worked very hard during the empty-chair procedure to tell his father that he had made a success of his career and of his life. Eventually, he was able to do this comfortably and to subsequently imagine his father responding with the following statement: "I always knew you would be, but it was difficult for me to tell you how much I respected you and how proud of you I really am." These, by the way, were the actual words his father uttered on his deathbed. The empty-chair work resulted in Glen feeling less conflicted about owning and accepting his very real competence.

A major defensive process that he used to avoid facing his own self-recriminations was impression management. He attempted to present himself as a superstar academic who should be considered one of the leading authorities in his field. He desperately wanted his colleagues to view him in such a manner. However, Glen was painfully aware of the gap between how he actually felt about himself and the image that he was trying to project. Awareness of this gap produced significant anxiety. With this interpersonal strategy, Glen strongly believed that having a panic attack during his presentation would clearly unmask him for the fraud that he believed he was.

To modify this defensive tendency, Glen engaged in imagery exercises in which he had a panic attack and told his audience that he has a problem with public speaking. This letting go of his secret began the process of undermining his impression management strategy. We continued to work on accepting whatever his abilities are and to do the best he can. I encouraged him to tell someone he trusts that he is in therapy because he has a public speaking problem. As Glen became more and more willing to risk these disclosures, he discovered just how much his secrets were helping to keep him anxious.

Glen began to realize that the impression management strategy was yoked to his tendency to constantly compare himself with other academics. Attention retraining was reintroduced to help him replace social comparisons with intrinsic motivations. Consequently, we worked on keeping his focus on the task of delivering his ideas and on why he considered his ideas useful or important rather than on the constant self-diminishing comparisons with other academics. This combination of self-acceptance and attention retraining went some distance toward reducing his anxiety about speaking in general. Over time, he was virtually anxiety free when he had to prepare and give a talk.

Another aspect of the self-acceptance strategy involved his experiencing the feelings connected with acceptance of his limitations. When he tried to face the fact that he might not be as intelligent as he would like others to think, he experienced a great deal of sadness and pain. Through the emotional acceptance of his limitations, Glen was able to come to the realization that despite his limitations, he was still intelligent enough to make contributions to his field that will be respected and valued by his colleagues.

A final piece of the therapeutic work concerned reframing the meaning of panic per se. Even after our work on self-acceptance, attention retraining, and allowing and accepting the feelings associated with the acceptance of one's limitations, Glen still found the idea of panicking unbearably humiliating. To address this problem we took two different tacks. The first was to have Glen experience the fact that he can survive the experience of being humiliated. This approach was based on the safe assumption that humiliation is an ontological given: We all experience it. We all can survive it. The second tack was to redefine panic as a problem that represents one small item of his being. It is a problem that he currently is living with and trying to solve, but the fact that he has panic attacks does not represent a total characterization of his personhood. By the end of therapy, Glen had made some headway in redefining panic's meaning, but he was still quite uncomfortable with the idea. The healing of his self-wounds continued and he could approach the task of giving a talk with much greater self-confidence and with much less apprehension that he will be viewed as a pathetic imposter if he should happen to have a panic attack.

JOAN: A CASE OF PANIC DISORDER WITH AGORAPHOBIA

Joan was a somewhat shy and very guarded individual. She had difficulty sharing her problems with me. Her reticence was due to her embarrassment and difficulty in trusting others. Anything that I said that sounded like criticism to Joan hurt her deeply and resulted in an extended period of silence. I had to take special pains in the way I worded my questions and comments. It took several sessions before Joan felt any degree of safety with me.

A major expression of Joan's agoraphobia involved her inability to drive her car beyond routine trips to the grocery store. It was even difficult for her to drive her children to school and pick them up. Therefore extending her driving radius became the first goal of therapy. One of the complicating features of her fear of driving had to do with her fear of bodily sensations. She was afraid that if she began to feel any of them, she would become lightheaded and fearful of losing control of the car. I began the symptom phase of the treatment by teaching her DB, which she found very useful. Once she had gained facility with DB, I introduced a technique known as awareness training. This technique involves asking the patient to focus on different parts of her body and notice whether she feels tense or relaxed. If she experienced tension or anxiety while focusing on any part of the body she was to use DB to reduce some of the tension and anxiety. Awareness training was basically a warm-up for interoceptive exposure, which involved asking Joan to focus attention on the body sensations that frighten her. The two sensations that were particularly terrifying to Joan were light-headedness and tightness in her chest. I asked her to try to produce the light-headedness by spinning around and the chest tightness by holding her breath. As she experienced these sensations, she carried out DB to reduce her anxiety.

Once she saw that she could control the level of anxiety with her breathing, she was ready to engage in imaginal exposure of her driving her car beyond her current safety zone. The imaginal exposure produced some of the same frightening sensations, and Joan used DB to calm herself down. After a few sessions of imaginal exposure, she was then ready for in vivo exposure. We developed a graduated program in which she would drive one mile the first day, two miles the second day, and so on. If she experienced the frightening sensations, she was to use DB to calm herself down.

The in vivo therapy was assigned as homework and at each subsequent session, we discussed how she did and fine-tuned the program if any problems emerged. After about 2 weeks, Joan felt that she could drive anywhere, because she was confident that she could now control her anxiety before it reached the level of a panic attack.

Joan decided to remain in therapy to resolve the underlying issues that she sensed were there. The next phase of therapy began with WFT in which she focused on the two fearful sensations that caused her the greatest anxiety: light-headedness and the sensation of tightness in her chest. Unlike in imaginal exposure, Joan was instructed to maintain a strict attentional focus on the sensation and to notice what thoughts and feelings automatically arose. As she focused on being light-headed, Joan began to recall a visit years ago to an elderly relative who was living in a nursing home. While making her way to her relative's room, she noticed several elderly people confined to their wheelchairs, unable to control their movements or their bowels. This awful sight made her very light-headed, and eventually she had a panic attack— the first she could remember having. Since that time, Joan had been fearful of her body failing her. If she began to feel light-headed, she became afraid of either having another panic attack or of losing control of her body.

When she focused on the sensation of tightness in her chest, she began to experience first a trickle of anger and later, full-blown rage directed at her husband. The rage, however, contradicted her self-image as a nice, agreeable person who does not get angry. It turned out that she had many reasons to be angry with her husband. Chief among these was his making the unilateral decision to move from a middle-class neighborhood where she felt comfortable to an upper-middle-class neighborhood where she knew no one and in which she felt uncomfortable.

At this point, I invited her to engage in some empty-chair work to confront her husband with her anger. When she attempted this, she kept interrupting herself because she was "not the kind of person who gets angry." Yet she also knew how angry she really was. Before we could continue with the empty-chair work, I invited her to digress and engage in a two-chair dialogue between the part of her that actually felt angry and the part of her who felt she ought not to be angry. Just as Strauman and Higgins' (1993) research has shown, a split between the actual self and the ought self produces anxiety. And this was clearly the case with Joan. She engaged in a two-chair dialogue between the actual and ought selves. The goal of such a dialogue is for each side to hear the other and to see if the person can forge a synthesis of the two conflicting views. Joan arrived at an emotionally acceptable conclusion: By appropriately expressing anger, she did not forfeit her claim to being a nice person. The synthesizing of the two views of self allowed her to reengage with the empty-chair work. She was able to express, albeit somewhat tentatively, some of the anger she felt toward her husband. We then supplemented this experiential technique with the behavioral technique of assertiveness training. This involved Joan selecting a number of issues that she needed to discuss with her husband. We rehearsed these discussions in session. In addition, I used Socratic questioning to help her challenge her original conception of self as the easygoing doormat. Eventually, she was able to initiate a discussion with her husband about her complaints.

The experience of being appropriately assertive with her husband was quite effective in healing the self-wound of feeling powerless and inadequate. There appeared to be at least three steps to this healing process: (a) healing the conflict between two seemingly incompatible views of the self, (b) allowing and expressing her actual feelings to her husband, and (c) proactively negotiating with her husband to get her needs met. Actually, the work of healing self-wounds involved cognitive, behavioral, and experiential techniques.

We next addressed her self-representations as inferior to the people in her new neighborhood. As previously mentioned, one of the reasons she was so angry with her husband was because of their move. Now she had to face her discomfort with this well-heeled group of women that she was beginning to meet in the neighborhood. One woman in particular became the focal point and trigger of her inferiority feelings. This woman became the convenient icon of upper-middle-class snootiness in Joan's mind. An empty-chair dialogue with this woman helped Joan deflate this woman's image in her mind. In subsequent sessions, I learned that they had actually become friends.

Joan was making great progress in therapy, but several months into the work, she appeared to have a setback. She began to experience the chest-tightening sensation, which as before triggered her anxiety, fear of panic, and fear of having a heart attack. We turned once again to WFT. While Joan maintained a strict focus on the sensation of her chest tightening, she began to experience intense sadness and despair about her recent miscarriage. Up to this point, Joan had not allowed herself to grieve her loss. We spent several sessions focusing on grief work. We used guided imagery to allow Joan to (a) imagine what her unborn child's life might have been like, (b) relive the experience of her pregnancy, and (c) say good-bye to the fetus. The emotional processing of this loss led to the surcease of her chest tightening and the associated anxiety.

After 14 months of therapy, Joan was no longer having panic attacks, nor did she get particularly anxious about any body sensation. Moreover, she was feeling much better about herself and better able to take control of her life and to make her wishes known, particularly to her husband.

PETER: A CASE OF PANIC DISORDER WITHOUT AGORAPHOBIA

Peter's therapy began with our having a difficult time establishing the therapeutic alliance. He was a physician who was initially reluctant to share his problems with me, a mere psychologist. At the outset, he seemed to view me with a mixture of hope and disdain. He felt great shame as he began to tell me of his weakness. Peter saw the world completely in terms of winners and losers. He was accustomed to viewing himself as a winner. Now he was beginning to see himself as a loser and this self-perception caused him great pain.

His sense of desperation trumped his feelings of contempt and he was eventually able to tell me the story of his initial panic attacks and how frightening they were. He now was quite fearful of having another attack. Because he had explicitly expressed an interest in cognitive–behavioral therapy, we began with the general package of DB, interoceptive exposure, and cognitive restructuring. The panic process for him began with the sensation of tightness in the chest, which he interpreted (i.e., through cogitation) as a sign of an impending heart attack. This conclusion produced a very high level of anxiety that eventually culminated in a panic attack. After teaching him DB, I moved quickly into interoceptive exposure. The exposure technique was focused on the sensation of tightness in his chest. The cognitive restructuring technique helped Peter see that nothing catastrophic would take place even if he had a panic attack. Moreover, the DB was an effective anxiety reducer; whenever he experienced the chest-tightening sensation, he could successfully use DB to reduce his cogitative anticipatory anxiety. The combined CBT package helped Peter gain sufficient control over his anxiety and markedly reduce his fear of having a panic attack. However, he still had an occasional panic attack.

Peter was very interested in trying to understand the roots of his anxiety disorder. We therefore began with some imaginal probes. We used WFT; the initial focal point was Peter's tightness-of-chest sensation. I asked him to notice any thought, image, or feeling that might spontaneously arise as he carried out the focusing technique. As he focused on the tightness in his chest, he began to see himself as an old man. His idyllic family life was coming to an end with his elder son's entrance into college so far away from home. We explored the imagery associated with his family life. From Peter's point of view, it was an almost perfect life, which included work he cared about, a wife he loved, and two young sons with whom he was deeply involved. As he put it, his bubble burst when his son left home. This was an undeniable sign that he was indeed aging. Another sign was the multiple injuries he sustained to his leg while playing tennis. Until he was injured, he was playing tennis competitively and this too was a sign that he was still young.

As Peter became aware of their implicit meaning, his panic attacks—and fear of panic—completely disappeared. However, he fell into a depression as he contacted his fear and shame of growing old. He felt like he was a loser in life, an old man who had little left to live for, and this self-perception generated the extremely painful feelings of dread and shame. The fact that he still had a wife and an adolescent son remaining at home did little to cheer him. He tried to play tennis again and reinjured his leg. This sent him deeper into his depression. At this point, Peter started taking Zoloft for his depression.

Over the course of the next 10 weeks, Peter's depression lessened, but he was still troubled by the image of getting older. We began to work on his feelings of shame and its connection to his *vertical logic* (i.e., seeing the world as composed of only winners or losers). First we worked on his being able to tolerate some feelings of shame and humiliation. I suggested that these feelings were inevitable in this life, that we all experience them at some point, and that they will not crush him. The work we did might be viewed as an exposure paradigm in which the anxiety hierarchy was composed of gradually ascending doses of painful feelings (Wachtel, 1997).

Next, I began to challenge his vertical logic and its relevance to his life. Because his goal was to make a new life for himself that fit him and his family, it was difficult to see the functional value of thinking of the world in terms of winners and losers. This cognitive challenge had no immediate effect but was to become important later in the therapy.

During one session, Peter stated he wished he could stop time. This statement generated an image in my mind of Peter standing on a ledge of a giant clock, pushing with all of his might against the minute hand. I shared this image with him and I asked him to imagine it too. Once he had the image in mind, I asked him to push against the minute hand as hard as he could. He imagined this scene and noticed that no matter how hard he tried he could not stop time. I then asked him to imagine riding on the minute hand and going with it rather than trying to hold it back. As he imagined this scene, he brightened and then a moment later became excited. "Yes, that's it," he said. "I can go with the flow of time."

The transformation of this metaphor (Kopp, 1995) was a clear turning point in Peter's therapy. It is difficult to explain why this metaphor at this point in therapy had such meaning for Peter, but it was undeniably powerful. We began working toward his adding back the various pieces of his life that he had let fall by the wayside. He began to play tennis again, but was more careful about doing his stretching exercises beforehand. He began to focus on his younger son who was entering high school and developing into an excellent baseball player. Baseball became a passion that they both shared and Peter went to all of his son's baseball games. Our therapy work turned next toward an exploration of his marriage and of his feelings toward his wife. After rehearsing some conversations with his wife through empty-chair work, he began to initiate a discussion with her about where to take their relationship now that their parental duties would soon end. They began to explore new interests and, as he said, "get reacquainted." They remembered that they always wanted to travel and began to plan a number of exotic trips.

We turned next to his work as a physician and brainstormed about pathways to revitalizing his interest in his work. He found a research project on which he could collaborate. He began to attend workshops on cutting-edge technologies and developments in his field. He associated himself with a local university as a member of the clinical faculty and tried teaching for the first time. He found he loved it. Peter was able to effect changes in each area of his life. As he experienced the proactive power of his initiative, he knew he was living life to the fullest. He began to feel good about himself again, even though he had discarded the irrelevant vertical logic of winners and losers. He no longer needed to strive for winning and avoid losing. He needed only to find his unique place in the world and to live life according to his own individual values and needs.

Peter has been panic free for 10 years. More important, he has truly enjoyed his life for the past 10 years. He feels good about himself, his family, and the choices that he has made in his life at home and at work. By healing the self-wound that he was somehow inferior to many of his physician colleagues or that he was shamefully losing in the imaginary competition of life, Peter regained the ability to enjoy his life, free of panic attacks and of the despair and shame that generated them.

The reader may ask why Peter did not develop the typical agoraphobic avoidance behavior. This is not an easy question to answer. Clum and Knowles (1991) implied that patients with panic disorder who do not become avoidant are probably experiencing less severe panic attacks; on the other hand, Craske and Barlow (1988) implied that nonavoidant patients with panic disorder have not developed avoidance as a response style, have had more mastery experiences, and have less need for secondary gain. What does seem clear, however, is that Peter never associated the location of his panic attacks with its cause. He seemed to sense that issues below the surface of his awareness were generating the tightness in his chest and his panic attacks.

DON: A CASE OF GENERALIZED ANXIETY DISORDER

Don's conflict about seeing me was apparent from the beginning of therapy. He seemed to be sending me a double message. On the one hand, he did not want to reveal very much about himself to me, but, on the other, he seemed to want me to extract details from him. He was very guarded but very eager for me to get to know him. His ability to trust me developed very slowly. His guarded and oppositional tendencies informed me that he possessed a differing order of access points than did many patients with an anxiety disorder. Instead of beginning with a symptom-focused CBT approach, I decided to work through our developing relationship. An important aspect of the therapeutic process involved my feeding back to him my reactions to his style of relating to me. From the psychoanalytic point of view, this would be viewed as the analysis of defenses. I suggested to him, for example, that he seemed to hold himself on a tight leash. He seemed to monitor his reactions very closely, apparently afraid that I would see all of the bad feelings he carried inside of him. I wondered aloud whether he was in conflict in all of his relationships. He seemed to me to want to be close to people but was afraid of what they would think when they discovered his malevolent side.

As we explored what he considered to be his malevolent side, it became clear that he was very uncomfortable with the experience of anger and dreaded the possibility of ever expressing any. He was convinced that the expression of anger would lead to his being rejected. As our exploration continued, we learned that Don came from a family whose implicit norms precluded the expression of anger. For any family member to be angry with another family member was tantamount to betrayal.

The psychodynamic probing eventually made it clear to him that he perceived himself as a malevolent person because of his anger. He would never be loved because of this defect. To hide this wound from others, he constantly monitored and tailored his behavior to what he thought others wanted from him. But he feared causing pain to others as much as he feared people hurting his feelings. Thus he tended to avoid people to protect himself from uncomfortable interactions. He felt he lived in a catch-22 world because he experienced shame and humiliation when he related to people and when he avoided them. Because he was so frightened of his anger, he believed that if he ever expressed it, it would destroy the other person.

As Don became clear about the nature of his self-wound and how his anxiety functioned as a signal of either his forbidden anger or his unbearable shame, we began to work experientially and behaviorally to begin the process of healing. The only person he could allow himself to be angry at was himself for being afraid of his feelings. The psychodynamic work had also uncovered a self-split between the angry Don and the part of him that was very critical of his anger. Several months into the therapy, Don had developed enough trust in me and in the therapy process to consider the experiential work. He willingly engaged in a two-chair dialogue between his angry and critical self. This work resulted in Don developing a less harsh view of his anger, as long as he expressed the anger appropriately.

Much of Don's implicit anger was directed at his parents for the toxic messages they had given him about his anger. I asked Don to engage in empty-chair work with each parent. With my support, he was able to gingerly express some dismay at each parent's treatment. Because of the previous two-chair work, Don was able to reframe his anger as a normal response to a feeling of being unjustly criticized. We also did work on appropriate assertiveness and on how to express an issue that he might have with a particular individual. We role-played the difference between yelling at someone and appropriately expressing a grievance.

The next facet of therapy focused on romantic relationships. Don was very frightened of women, but at the same time wanted very much to have a girlfriend. There was a young woman at work that Don was interested in but too frightened to ask out. She seemed friendly enough to him, but the thought that she might turn him down was painfully humiliating. He was given a homework assignment to ask her out. During the session, however, we broke the task down into smaller steps: (a) finding out her number, (b) deciding on a date, (c) dialing the phone, (d) engaging in preliminary chitchat, and (e) asking her out. We rehearsed each step first in imagery and then in role-play. I played the role of the fetching young woman (to the best of my ability). Subsequent to these rehearsals, Don's homework was to ask her out. She accepted and Don noted that he was simultaneously delighted and terrified. It was at this point that I taught him DB to help him with his anxiety.

This young woman did in fact become his girlfriend and our sessions began to revolve around an exploration of his feelings as they emerged in the relationship and the development of an authentic communication style. He was conflicted about expressing tender feelings as well as feelings of annoyance. We engaged in role-plays to rehearse his participation in their first fight. The process of change for Don alternated between positive steps in which he began to handle difficult situations differently than before and regressive steps in which he fell back into old patterns of impression management and not telling his girlfriend how he really felt. His tendency to hide his true feelings from his girlfriend always produced anxiety. We used WFT so that he could see that the anxiety kept him from experiencing his two most feared emotions, anger and shame.

This case illustrates, among other things, that the sequence of specific interventions is largely dependent on the patient's acceptable access points. The transactions that took place between us during the first phase of the treatment made it clear to me that Don would initially resist a cognitive–behavioral approach. I therefore had to shift gears and stay with an insight-oriented approach. This allowed Don to see in his interactions with me his general style of relating to others, its defensive nature, and what it was he was defending against. This work also strengthened his trust in me. The enhanced alliance then made it possible for us to begin the experiential and cognitive–behavioral interventions that were not feasible earlier in therapy. By the end of therapy, Don had increased his tolerance for painful feelings, had reframed their meaning in less catastrophic terms, and was able to interact more authentically with the important people in his life. Don continued his oscillating pattern of change, which involved several missteps and a regressive return to old patterns leading to increased anxiety. At 1-year follow-up, his anxiety was minimal and he experienced fewer episodes of his past dysfunctional patterns of interaction. Although his self-wounds had healed substantially, Don had work left to do before he could be fully confident in himself, his ability to communicate his authentic feelings, and his new self-view as someone who was neither defective nor inferior.

SPENCER: A CASE OF OBSESSIVE–COMPULSIVE DISORDER

The first phase of therapy with Spencer was marked by the usual difficulties in trusting that therapists typically encounter with patients who have an anxiety disorder. Most patients experience some shame about their problems and thus are vigilant regarding any judgmental behavior from a therapist. Spencer was reluctant to share the full extent of his ritualistic behavior because it sounded crazy to him. I told him that he had a specific disorder but that he was not psychotic or mad in the colloquial sense of the term. His fear of being crazy had an obvious source. His mother experienced severe mental illness for most of her life. She had been hospitalized on several occasions and had made several suicide attempts. I therefore had to remain cognizant of my language and its potential to inadvertently wound Spencer (Wachtel, 1993). He clearly viewed me as someone with the power to render an absolute judgment on his mental status. He actually had the fantasy that I would lock him up in a mental institution and throw away the key.

Once Spencer developed a certain amount of trust in me and in the therapy process, we embarked on a program of exposure plus response prevention (ERP). Developed by Edna Foa and her colleagues (Foa & Franklin, 2001), ERP is a 3-week inpatient program. Using ERP in an outpatient setting, however, presents some different challenges. Although some of the work was carried out during the therapy sessions, much of it was to be self-initiated outside of therapy. I therefore had no control over whether the patient would carry out the critical response prevention portion of the treatment. Much of the initial good work with this intervention took place in-session because of Spencer's erratic attempts to carry it out on his own. ERP involves exposing the patient to the anxiety-inducing obsessional thoughts and images and preventing him from carrying out his temporary-relief-giving rituals. I taught Spencer DB, which he was to substitute for the rituals.

After four sessions of ERP, Spencer had benefited significantly from the cognitive–behavioral intervention. His ritualizing significantly decreased. But several sessions later, he began to complain that he was having bad days with his symptoms. The bad days were correlated with heavy drinking, pain over the loss of a girlfriend, ruminations about his ability to cope with life, and criticizing himself. He had a particularly bad day when his mother had to be hospitalized again. In other words, the occurrence of his obsessional thoughts correlated with high stress. We then supplemented the ERP with stress management techniques. In addition to DB, we worked on his pacing himself better at work and taking time-outs during the day to do DB to shift his attention away from distracting self-criticisms and back to the tasks at hand. The stress management techniques were helpful and Spencer's symptoms of obsessive–compulsive disorder (OCD) began to lessen again. I also put him on an alcohol reduction program, and he found that as he reduced his drinking, his OCD symptoms lessened.

Spencer began to feel that he had some tools with which to cope with his OCD symptoms. At this point, he was very interested in exploring the roots of his disorder. I began this exploration by having Spencer conjure up his obsessional thoughts and use WFT. The first obsession on which he focused was the thought and image of smashing his girlfriend in the face. As he kept a strict attentional focus on his obsession, he began to notice that he was becoming enraged at her. Until this point, he had not associated his obsession with his being angry at his girlfriend. As he stayed with the experience of rage, he began to recall situations in which he felt humiliated by her behavior. For example, when they were at parties together, she could be an outrageous flirt. He construed her flirtatiousness as an attempt to humiliate him. This would lead to an argument and they would break up for a few days. Still, the thought of hurting her terrified him because he equated thought with action. Spencer learned this thought–action fusion, which is characteristic of patients with OCD (Shafran, Thordarson, & Rachman, 1996), through the religious teachings of his church which equate a sinful thought with a sinful act. Working metaphorically, I asked him to imagine a wall. On one side was the violent fantasy or thought; on the other was the violent act. As long as he stayed on the fantasy or thought side of the wall, he need not worry. I then asked him to imagine the thought while carrying out DB and then to imagine the wall between thought and action. Spencer found this helpful. The next step was to explore the violent image to learn what the underlying feeling was and to attempt to understand why he was so angry. In this way, he learned how humiliated he felt when his girlfriend flirted with other men.

Once he allowed the experience of rage, I asked him to participate in empty-chair work. He imaginatively placed his girlfriend in the empty chair and began to tell her why he was so upset. This imaginative act reduced his anxiety. He was learning another way to deal with his anger. We continued with WFT. As he continued the focusing, he encountered his fear of isolation associated with his girlfriend rejecting him and his fear of being trapped if she made too many demands. These fears made him ashamed, as did his fear of being a loser. While contemplating the image of being alone, Spencer recalled that when he was three years old, his mother went next door while Spencer was asleep. He woke up and found her missing. He thought that she was gone for good. In response to this thought, he had what was probably his first panic attack. In the present, however, Spencer's fear of being alone meant being without a woman. Spencer found the shame resulting from this image almost impossible to bear.

As Spencer was now able to allow in the feelings that he feared, we began to work cognitively to modify the catastrophic meanings he had imputed to his core issues. I reframed the states of being alone and being in a committed relationship as developmental milestones. He first had to learn how to be alone before he could be successful in a relationship and then he would need to learn how to be in a relationship in which he could be committed and still preserve a significant degree of his autonomy. These developmental achievements would directly address his core bipolar fears of being alone and isolated or being committed and trapped.

He decided to take a break from his girlfriend and to spend some time without female companionship. Spencer found this to be a very painful and lonely but helpful time. During this period, we worked cognitively and emotionally on reframing his interpretation of being alone. Being alone was reconstrued as an optional lifestyle, one that he might or might not choose. If he was to choose a mate, we discussed the importance of doing so on the basis of a goodness-of-fit criterion rather than out of a desperate need to avoid the feared status of being alone.

As a result of the period of spending time with himself, Spencer located his core values. He also discovered that although he preferred to be with someone, he could nevertheless get along very well on his own.

SUMMARY

All six of these cases illustrate how the core catastrophic fears of patients with anxiety disorders typically involve the ineluctable dilemmas of a human life. These existential givens are challenges that we all face. My clinical experience has convinced me that patients with anxiety disorders have not been able to take the challenge head-on. They have instead developed dysfunctional defenses against confronting these challenges and the feelings that they evoke. Usually these defenses were developed in childhood and represented the best responses that a child could create to deal with overwhelming trauma, chaos, or disillusionment. These defensive strategies, however, are no longer necessary or functional, however difficult they may be to give up.

The symptoms of anxiety manifested in each of these disorders all appear to relate to a terrifying apprehension that some overwhelming catastrophe will occur. The various categories of anxiety disorders can be differentiated in part by (a) the kinds of conscious cognitive concerns that are prototypical for each disorder, (b) the nature of the implicit meanings associated with different disorders, and (c) the types of cognitive–affective defenses that are erected against the feared experiences. The integrative psychotherapy under consideration here attempts to address the similarities and differences among the various anxiety disorders by means of a flexible application of interventions derived from the major psychotherapeutic perspectives. In addition to the differences that characterize these disorders, this integrative therapy takes into account the personality characteristics of the individual patient in developing an individually tailored sequence of interventions. Such issues as patients' most comfortable access point and their typical cognitive style become primary determinants of that sequence. The next chapter discusses future directions in the development of this integrative psychotherapy.

11

FUTURE DIRECTIONS
AND A FINAL SUMMARY

May you never cease your quest after the truth; and may you always be
spared the company of those who are absolutely convinced they found it.
                                          —Reverend John Porter (1981)

Two interrelated integrative models have been presented for anxiety
disorders: an etiological theory and a treatment model. Both of these models
have synthesized the best ideas from the various extant models of anxiety
disorders. The self-wound model of anxiety disorders highlights a person's
subjective struggle with his or her own self-experience, that is, his or her self-
perception and self-conception. The classic psychodynamic paradigm of signal anxiety, I believe, is basically correct. Anxiety is a signal that the usual
defenses against unbearably painful views of the self are failing. The catastrophic self-view may, in fact, be true, and the individual, in a frantic effort
to avoid this possibility, experiences the protest of anxiety. The anxiety, however, is itself extremely painful. Consequently, people develop cognitive–
affective defenses against such self-perceptions as well as behavioral strategies to support these defenses. These defenses protect against awareness of
the painful self-view, but they begin to lose their effectiveness under stress.
When the defenses become stressed, people experience anxiety and panic as
the self-view is about to be contacted.

The difficulties associated with anxiety disorders are compounded by
the fact that the usual response to the painful experience of anxiety is to

automatically shift one's attention to one's self being anxious and to experience negative thoughts and feelings about one's anxiety. This process of obsessively cogitating about one's anxiety (or seeing one's self as anxious) both intensifies and prolongs the experience of anxiety. Many if not most of the symptoms associated with a given anxiety disorder derive from the process of catastrophic cogitation. The cognitive perspective in particular presents a very useful schematic description of this process.

A final area of concern is the way patients with anxiety deal with painful emotions: they fear them. Shame and humiliation, anger and rage, and hopelessness and despair are the implicit emotions that most often appear if a patient can remain focused on his or her anxiety. These emotions are associated with the unbearable self-views, that is, the self-wounds that I hypothesize are the ultimate source of the various anxiety disorders. These emotions need to be experienced, evaluated, and processed. If they reflect an accurate self-assessment, then work must begin on repairing these deficiencies. If, however, they are based on inaccurate self-assessments, then the therapeutic work needs to focus on their modification.

DERIVING INTEGRATIVE TREATMENT INTERVENTIONS FROM THE ETIOLOGICAL THEORY

Although each of the integrative models represents a synthesis of the various perspectives on the etiology of anxiety disorders on the one hand, and on the treatment of anxiety disorders on the other, it is also possible to derive virtually the same treatment interventions in the same sequence from the etiological theory. The etiological theory suggests a layered conception of anxiety disorders, which allows treatment to be divided into surface and depth work. It is possible to successfully treat the symptoms of an anxiety disorder without modifying the underlying self-wounds. Such success provides better ways of controlling the level of anxiety without dealing with its source. Such results tend to leave individuals with significant residual anxiety or vulnerable to relapse. This is *surface work*.

The *depth work*, however, involves another realm: the emotional processing of painful beliefs about the self. It is my contention that the durable alleviation of the symptoms and sources of an anxiety disorder is based in the emotional processing of painful beliefs about the self. Whereas the surface work makes liberal use of cognitive–behavioral techniques, the depth work may use interventions from all of the major therapeutic perspectives discussed within. Imagery techniques such as Wolfe's focusing technique (1992; 2005; see also Appendix) are used to identify the self-wounds and allow the experience of painful emotions. These can be supplemented by psychodynamic interpretations and cognitive techniques such as the downward arrow technique. Because relationship issues are so often interconnected with the underlying determinants of an anxiety disorder, the therapeutic relationship serves as a living laboratory for helping the therapist and patient to understand and modify the patient's dysfunctional relationship strategies. Interpretive strategies and emotional-processing techniques are also useful here. Behavioral strategies are then used to test out the viability of new ways of viewing the self. Although cognitive and behavioral strategies are important and necessary elements of the change process, the key change process in depth work is emotional processing.

EMOTIONAL PROCESSING IS THE KEY TO DEPTH WORK

One of the major theses of this book is that although surface-level symptom change can be achieved through behavioral change or alterations in one's pattern of cognitive processing, changes in one's core self-beliefs necessarily require the emotional processing of painful realities. The experience and expression of previously ignored emotional information can facilitate change in people's sense and concept of self by confronting them with irrefutable information about previously disowned emotions and behavioral tendencies. Individuals who possess a core self-belief that they are incapable of being angry, for example, begin to revise this self-concept once they allow and access irrefutable affective evidence to the contrary. The key to the effective processing of painful emotions is acknowledging and accepting the painful feelings, and eventually expressing them to the appropriate persons. Such a process can effect a change in one's perspective toward one's self and also toward the other person(s).

It is ironic that despite the protracted polemics among pundits of different therapeutic points of view, changes in emotional-processing difficulties can be—and have been—brought about by relational, behavioral, cognitive, and emotion-focused approaches. Some approaches are more effective for some patients because of differences in comfort levels with different ways of processing information. Although these preferences may vary across different individuals, they may also vary within the same individual at different periods of the therapeutic enterprise. My integrative therapy provides the flexibility of interventions that will map well with the enormous heterogeneity that exists among individuals even within a given diagnostic category such as anxiety disorders.

CHALLENGES IN APPLYING AN
INTEGRATIVE PSYCHOTHERAPY

Apart from the usual challenges of conducting psychotherapy, a number of unique challenges accompany the application of an integrative therapy.

I mention three of these here because of the frequency with which they appear in work with patients with an anxiety disorder: (a) switching therapeutic stances, (b) finding the proper sequence of interventions, and (c) the complication of comorbidity.

Switching Therapeutic Stances

One of the most important challenges of using technical procedures from different therapy orientations is the necessity of switching therapeutic stances. If therapy is begun from a psychodynamic point of view, for example, the therapist assumes a passive, nondirective listening stance. The therapist follows the lead of the patient and reacts to whatever communications he or she is willing to express. When the therapist later attempts to use a cognitive–behavioral technique, his or her therapeutic stance necessarily becomes more active, directive, and structured. The sudden switch may take the patient by surprise and some patients may have difficulty accepting this dramatic change. This reality argues strongly for orienting the patient at the outset of therapy about the various phases that the therapy process may take. Even with this orientation, some patients may find the transition difficult. Integrative therapists need to make the switch as smooth as possible. It is imperative for therapists to monitor the meaning that such changes have for the patient to prevent a therapeutic alliance rupture.

Finding the Proper Sequence of Therapeutic Interventions

Most models of integrative psychotherapy define a set of decision rules with respect to when the therapist uses a specific technique. In the integrative therapy under consideration, I have suggested that patients have different levels of comfort with behavioral, cognitive, and emotion-focused interventions (i.e., therapeutic access points). For the surface or symptom layer of an anxiety disorder, I have suggested that behavioral and cognitive techniques tend to be better tolerated early in therapy. Emotion-focused and interpretive, dynamic interventions are better tolerated later in therapy when therapist and client agree to explore the underlying determinants of an anxiety disorder. However, as previously mentioned, there are great individual differences in comfort levels with different therapeutic access points and these must be determined on a case-by-case basis. A further decision rule is based on the type of emotional-processing difficulty that emerges within a therapy session (L. S. Greenberg, Rice, & Elliott, 1993). For example, patients who experience a painful conflict between two compelling but incompatible sides of the self may benefit from a two-chair dialogue. Patients with unexpressed feelings toward a loved one are exhibiting a marker for some empty-chair work. If the patient is not yet ready to participate in any emotion-focused work, then the therapist may attempt a more psychodynamic interpretive intervention focused on these conflicts.

The Problem of Comorbidity

As mentioned in chapter 2, patients with a particular anxiety disorder typically have other disorders as well. They may have other anxiety disorders, other Axis I disorders, or one or more Axis II disorders. These additional disorders complicate and perhaps impede the treatment of their anxiety disorders. If an anxiety disorder, however, is presented as the patient's primary concern, it is important to initially focus therapy on the presenting problems. The additional disorders, however, will limit, if not undermine, the treatment of the anxiety disorder. In monitoring the progress of the treatment of the anxiety disorder, the therapist usually observes clues as to why the therapy is not working or works only up to a certain point. It may be an alliance rupture that reflects the patient's typical interpersonal problems. It may be that the patient has difficulty letting go of his or her usual defenses against painful emotions. Or it may be that the symptom-reduction work brings up a core intrapsychic conflict that must be addressed before additional progress can be made. Whatever the reason, the therapist must stay empathically attuned to the patient so that he or she can observe these clues and be ready to flexibly adjust the treatment to deal with the patient's concerns that prevent the patient from making further progress in the treatment of his or her anxiety disorder.

FUTURE DIRECTIONS

I would like to discuss some possible directions for research on this integrative approach. First I address the basis on which I have founded my approach, and then I offer some potential ways to examine the approach empirically.

Empirical Evidence for the Integrative Models

Although this approach is a work in progress, I have used it for 15 years with significant success in a private practice setting. There have been significant failures as well and I do not want to give the impression that this approach always works. In my practice, I have found several recurring reasons for failure. The chief reason why depth work does not succeed is fear of experiencing painful emotions. Many patients come to a decision point regarding whether they want to do the work to change their underlying painful views of the self and decide it is too difficult. Other reasons for failure include (a) the extreme tenacity of shame-based self-beliefs, (b) emotional conflicts around the implications of change, and (c) logistical reasons that interrupt the therapy before its completion (e.g., insurance coverage runs out).

To date, no efficacy studies have been conducted on the treatment, although they are needed. I am in no position to carry these out myself, but I hope that some readers may be interested in mounting pilot studies and clinical trials on this approach. One of the major challenges that researchers face, however, is that this integrative psychotherapy has not been manualized. Although I have expressed reservations elsewhere regarding what can be learned from the investigation of manualized therapies in a randomized clinical trial, I do see the trial as one piece in the puzzle of empirical evaluation (Goldfried & Wolfe, 1996, 1998; Wolfe, 1994).

However, a number of complications are involved in manualizing this and any other integrative psychotherapy. First of all, manualizing an integrative therapy presents an additional layer of complexity to the task of treatment standardization. In addition to the problems that inhere in standardizing the specific interventions, one must also standardize the sequence of their application. The four-phase model goes some distance toward achieving standardization in the sequencing of interventions, but there will be great variability because of the different styles of information processing that patients with the same anxiety disorder bring to therapy.

Another research-related complication inheres in the fact that this conceptualization of anxiety disorders goes beyond their characterization in the *Diagnostic and Statistical Manual of Mental Disorders* (4th ed.; American Psychiatric Association, 1994). In addition to the cluster of symptoms that compose the *DSM*-defined syndromes, I am concerned with the cognitive–affective defenses and self-wounds that appear to be associated with different anxiety disorders. In many instances, the self-wounds may be the same across different anxiety disorders, but the cognitive–affective defenses may differ. In other instances, the self-wounds differentiate the anxiety disorders. In addition, most patients whom I see with anxiety disorders meet criteria for comorbidity. These patients are comorbid not only for other Axis I disorders but also for Axis II disorders or their combination. In other words, I typically see complex cases of anxiety disorder.

As I mentioned in chapter 2, the *DSM* definition of anxiety disorders sheds no light on the interactions of Axis I and II pathology. The self-wound model attempts to spell out the processes observed in patients with an anxiety disorder that link the surface manifestation of anxiety symptoms with their underlying determinants. I have attempted to show, for example, the connection between the maladaptive interpersonal scenarios that are often found in personality disorders (i.e., vicious circles and self-fulfilling prophecies) and the somatic and cognitive manifestations of anxiety symptoms.

A final complication in conducting efficacy studies on anxiety disorders is that the existing literature primarily involves symptom-focused treatments that are studied for a relatively brief period. Typically, efficacy studies involve a treatment length of 12 to 16 sessions. In perhaps the largest clinical trial ever conducted on the treatment of anxiety disorders, Barlow's panic control treatment was compared with imipramine in the treatment of panic disorders. Patients were treated weekly for 3 months (12 sessions). Those who responded to treatment were then seen monthly for 6 months (Barlow, Gorman, Shear, & Woods, 2000). Although this treatment was quite useful for the symptoms of panic disorder, it would not be sufficient for modifying the underlying self-wounds.

The treatment phase of an efficacy study of this model is likely to require at least a year, although the modification of a painful self-wound could take as long as 3 years. But even studying one therapy for a year would be enormously expensive. Including an adequately designed follow-up study would ratchet up the cost significantly more. Although I value empirical research and would like to see this treatment evaluated, formidable obstacles are associated with this task.

A Research-Informed Rather Than an Evidence-Based Perspective

In the introduction to the book, I described this integrative model as research-informed rather than evidence-based. Evidence-based therapies are those that have been supported by at least two independent efficacy studies, that is, randomized clinical trials. There are, however, a number of limitations to these studies that make it difficult to directly translate these treatments into clinical practice.

Limitations of Efficacy Studies as a Primary Source of Treatment Validation

Evidence-based therapies draw their support from efficacy studies. The assumption that many psychotherapy researchers make is that a therapist can directly apply a therapeutic approach that has been found efficacious in randomized clinical trials to a patient with the investigated disorder (Chambless, 1996). But it is precisely because of the methodological rigor that characterizes these studies that their findings are difficult to generalize to real-world patients. Such methodological requirements as random assignment to treatment, fixed number of sessions, and manualization of the operations of therapy ensure the integrity of the studied treatment (i.e., the treatment's internal validity) but, at the same time, decrease its relevance and generalizability to real-world patients (i.e., the treatment's external validity). The dilemma of psychotherapy efficacy studies is the inherent inverse relationship between the two forms of validity: As one increases, the other decreases. Efforts are now being made to supplement efficacy studies with *effectiveness studies*. Effectiveness studies represent the application of evidence-based treatments to real-world settings (Seligman, 1995). My sense of this nascent effort is that there is as yet no acceptable solution to the internal–external validity dilemma.

It has also been my conviction that efficacy research and the more recent effectiveness research address only half of what makes psychotherapy successful. These studies virtually ignore the contribution of relationship factors to successful psychotherapy. However, reviews of the psychotherapy outcome literature reveal that only 5% to 15% of the outcome variance can be attributed to specific techniques of therapy (Lambert, 1992; Wampold, 2001). Relationship factors account for as much if not more of the outcome variance than do particular treatments (Norcross, 2002).

The Task Force on Empirically Supported Therapy Relationships was created by Division 29 (the Division on Psychotherapy) of the American Psychological Association to supplement the work of the Division 12 Task Force on Empirically Validated Treatments (Chambless et al., 1996; Task Force on Promotion and Dissemination of Psychological Procedures, 1995). The work of the Division 29 task force culminated in the publication of *Psychotherapy Relationships That Work* (Norcross, 2002). By examining the literature on psychotherapy process and its relationship to therapy outcome, the task force produced a list of relationship factors that were demonstrably effective, including therapeutic alliance, empathy, and goal consensus and collaboration, and a group of factors that were promising and probably effective, including positive regard, congruence and genuineness, feedback, repair of alliance ruptures, self-disclosure, management of countertransference, and the quality of relational interpretations (Norcross, 2002, p. 441). The report also presented a list of conclusions regarding the empirical evidence on customizing the therapy relationship to individual patients on the basis of patient behaviors or qualities. It has been found, for example, that patients who possess high resistance respond better to self-control treatments and minimal therapist direction, whereas patients with low resistance improve in a more structured therapy conducted by more directive therapists (Beutler & Consoli, 1992). Taking into account a patient's level of resistance and functional impairment is demonstrably effective as a means of customizing therapy, whereas taking into account a patient's coping style, stage of change, and expectations (among other factors) is promising and probably effective as a means of customizing therapy. The report concluded with 19 recommendations that included general recommendations, practice recommendations, training recommendations, research recommendations, and policy recommendations. The final practice recommendation is particularly germane to the themes of this book: "Concurrent use of empirically supported relationships *and* empirically supported treatments tailored to the patient's disorder and characteristics is likely to generate the best outcomes " (Norcross, 2002, p. 442).

Supplemental Research Designs Are Needed

Efficacy research, effectiveness research, and research on the process of therapeutic change need to be supplemented by more in-depth research on the individual case. Although individual case studies have been a major source of data for clinicians since Sigmund Freud's time, their scientific value has always been in doubt. However, systematic studies of individual cases have recently appeared in the literature as an alternative source of scientific information (Barlow & Hersen, 1984; Jones, 1993; Rice & Greenberg, 1984; Stiles, 1993, 2003). The systematic single-case investigation is now believed to be particularly useful for treatment development and for testing specific clinical hypotheses (Jones, 1993).

Stiles (2003), for example, defined scientific research as a process of comparing ideas with observations. Using a goodness-of-fit criterion for evaluating theoretical ideas, Stiles argued that the numerous observations that can be made of an individual case over the course of a long-term therapy can either increase or decrease confidence in a specific theoretical idea or clinical hypothesis. As Stiles put it in the following:

> For a variety of familiar reasons (selective sampling, low power, potential investigator biases etc.), the increase (or decrease) in confidence in any one theoretical statement may be very small. That is, isolated descriptive statements drawn from a case study can't be confidently generalized. Nevertheless, because many statements are examined, the increase (or decrease) in confidence in the theory may be comparable to that stemming from a statistical hypothesis-testing study. A few systematically analyzed cases that match a theory in precise and unexpected detail may give people considerable confidence in the theory as a whole. . . . (p. 4)

Still another alternative approach to aggregating data about the benefits of psychotherapy was recently proposed by Fishman (2000). He suggested that the American Psychological Association sponsor a new, electronic *Journal of Pragmatic Case Studies* that would begin the process of building "databases of systematic, rigorous solution-focused case studies" (Abstract, ¶ 1). Fishman suggested that such a database would represent a pragmatic integration of efficacy and effectiveness research.

Although single case studies can enhance the information that clinicians can obtain from psychotherapy research, they are still left with the problem of translating research findings into clinical practice. The translation problem is one that has been virtually ignored by the field and, in my view, is a major reason why clinicians do not find the research literature as relevant to their work as psychotherapy researchers hope and believe they should. From the clinician's perspective, however, the findings of psychotherapy research still provide insufficient information regarding how to treat a specific individual (Fensterheim & Raw, 1996).

Translating current research findings into clinical practice guidelines is problematic because the research does not take into account several issues that the practicing therapist confronts daily. Psychotherapy research, particularly as it pertains to patients with anxiety disorders, has not adequately addressed the implicit meaning of anxiety symptoms, the identification and modification of a patient's cognitive–affective defenses against painful emotional experience, and the modification of the underlying self-wounds that appear to be the ultimate source of anxiety symptoms. Nor has it verified with any precision exactly how a painful experience is emotionally processed, although there are some very promising models (L. S. Greenberg et al., 1993; Stiles, 2002). Moreover, the real-world patient may meet criteria for several disorders simultaneously and in addition may be experiencing a number of life crises that significantly stress him or her (Goldfried & Wolfe, 1998; Wolfe, 1994). Finally, there are differences in the contexts in which a research patient and a real-world patient undergo psychotherapy.

Consequently, I use the findings from the research literature as far as they take me. But because of the reasons stated earlier, I supplement the research findings with my clinical experience. For these reasons, I refer to my integrative perspective as research-informed rather than evidence-based. I use an iterative process of applying research-based interventions and relationship factors while making adjustments with an individual patient as my experience and empathic attunement with the patient suggest. As I have written elsewhere, this is how I have approached the development of this integrative perspective from the beginning (Wolfe, 2001a, 2004).

APPLICATION OF THE INTEGRATIVE PERSPECTIVE TO OTHER DISORDERS

I have focused exclusively on using this approach with one set of common disorders. In this section I address the possibility of using this integrative approach with other disorders. There is not enough space to cover every conceivable aspect of therapy for these disorders, but I touch on the key points for using this approach in other ways and provide some examples of its use.

Posttraumatic Stress Disorder

The reader may have noticed a significant omission in my consideration of anxiety disorders: the absence of posttraumatic stress disorder (PTSD). This disorder was not considered for the simple reason that I lack sufficient experience in treating individuals who meet criteria for PTSD. Yet I excluded this disorder with great reluctance because I believe that the integrative perspective presented here not only is applicable to PTSD but also promises to be very effective in its treatment. Several of my students have described the application of various aspects of my integrative model to PTSD in their dissertations.

Ouseley (1999), for example, applied an earlier version of my integrative model to conceptualize and treat a Vietnam War veteran who had symptoms of PTSD for 30 years. However, this 48-year-old African American, whom Ouseley called Mr. James Patient, also met criteria for major depression, recurrent, severe type; panic disorder with agoraphobia; polysubstance dependence, in early remission; and personality disorder, not otherwise specified, but with dependent and paranoid features. Mr. Patient had experienced numerous horrific war experiences during his tour of duty in Vietnam. These experiences precipitated his PTSD symptoms, which included nightmares, intrusive thoughts, avoidant behavior, and an exaggerated startle response. Mr. Patient also experienced panic attacks that were connected to flashbacks of his Vietnam experiences. In addition, he experienced panic attacks unrelated to his war experiences, developed agoraphobic behaviors in an attempt to limit his panic attacks, and was quite worried about their reoccurrence. Subsequently, he developed phobic-like reactions to wooded areas and Asian American storeowners. In addition to his other difficulties, Mr. Patient, who lived with his mother, exhibited marked passive-dependent traits.

Ouseley based the selection and sequencing of his treatment interventions on my integrative model. He used behavioral, cognitive, experiential, and psychodynamic interventions during the course of Mr. Patient's treatment. As Ouseley succinctly put it:

> Several sessions were spent developing a sense of trust, utilizing empathic attunement and other nondirective techniques. Cognitive–behavioral, experiential, and dynamic interventions were then used. The behavioral component of therapy consisted of guided-imagery, desensitization, deep muscle relaxation, and other stress management techniques. The cognitive component focused on cognitive restructuring of trauma-related guilt issues and homework. Experiential interventions were then used to facilitate the emotional processing of traumatic events. Last, psychodynamic interventions from an object relations perspective were initiated to deal with Mr. Patient's underlying dependent personality pathology. (p. 33)

One of the most difficult aspects of Mr. Patient's PTSD was his inability to process an excruciatingly painful event from the war. Thirty years later, he was still having nightmares involving a little boy who had been boobytrapped by the Viet Cong. The boy approached a group of American soldiers saying he wanted to shine their shoes. Mr. Patient could tell he was loaded with explosives and made the decision to shoot the little boy. The memory of that killing has haunted him ever since. At one point in the therapy, Ouseley invited Mr. Patient to engage in some empty-chair work by imaginatively placing the little boy in the empty chair. The goal of this work was for Mr. Patient to finally say good-bye to the little boy. Ouseley first asked the patient to describe the incident so he could get it fresh in his mind. The patient started describing what was going on about an hour before the boy showed up. Eventually, the boy began walking toward the American soldiers with a box under his arm crying out "Shoeshine! Shoe shine!" Mr. Patient looked at his very muddy boots and thought this a strange request. He told the boy to go away, but the boy continued to approach the soldiers. Finally, Mr. Patient shot him and the boy died. On the one hand, Mr. Patient was relieved that he did not die; on the other hand, shooting and killing a little boy was traumatic.

Ouseley then invited Mr. Patient to engage in some empty-chair work and asked the patient to imagine the little boy sitting across from him. Here is a brief excerpt:[1]

C-21: Well, I don't know who sent you or what, but you was coming towards me, I felt the gun . . . and I reacted. . . .

T-21: Go, go ahead and tell him what you now feel about his leader sending him to his death.

C-22: I apologize for that man sending you, I don't know whether you (nervous chuckle) would have taken an ass whipping or something. I didn't want to kill you (with emphasis). I'm sure you didn't want to die, me either.

T-22: Tell him you wish that he had a chance to have lived out his life like you had.

C-23: I wish you had a chance to live, grew up, really, jus thankful that I grew up, I wasn't (muffled crying) you put me in a situation where I believe I had no choice.

T-23: Tell him what you've come to believe about him not having any choice in this.

C-24: I realize now that you probably ain't had a choice in it neither, you were told to do something and probably was scared to say no or whatever, but made you responsible (muffled crying) . . . my side. They should be taking the blame for this.

T-24: Um hmm. Go on.

C-25: Like you—I had no choice but to do as I had to do, and as you see now and between me and you, yep.

T-25: I'd like you to look in that boy's eyes right now. What would you like to tell him?

C-26: Rest in peace. One day the god that you pray to has got you in his arms and you sleeping as well.

---

[1]The C and the T in the transcript stand for client and therapist, respectively. The numbers represent the line in the transcript. Hence, C-21 represents line twenty-one of the client's statements.

T-26: Now, can you say "I forgive myself for this event."

C-27: I forgive myself for this event.

T-27: And it is time to move on.

C-28: Forget this and move on.

T-28: You have your grandchildren.

C-29: That are put by God in my life (crying and sighs). (There is a long pause between therapist and client.)

T-29: I want you to imagine that little boy is gone back to his god, is no longer in the room and that to the extent possible this matter is closed. (Another long pause.) How do you feel?

C-30: How do I feel? I feel a little better, at least I know now you made me think of the different ways, you know, you know I use to think it might come back on me too hard. I know now I got control of it.

This episode was one among many that plagued Mr. Patient and helped produce his recurrent nightmares and intrusive thoughts. In subsequent sessions, it became clear that for the first time in 30 years Mr. Patient was not having the nightmares or flashbacks associated with this incident. It appeared that the empty-chair work allowed him to emotionally process this painful episode and bring it to closure.

In general, the integrative treatment gave Mr. Patient behavioral tools to cope with intrusive thoughts when they occurred, revised his inappropriate guilty thoughts, altered specific negative self-representations such as that he was a hopeless and helpless loser, and improved his sense of self-efficacy. In addition, he learned that he could survive the experience of painful emotions and use these experiences to his benefit. Last, he began to be more proactive in his life and well on his way to independent living while still remaining responsive to his mother's needs. This case example suggests that the self-wound model and the integrative treatment derived from it may be applicable to patients who meet criteria for PTSD. However, a great deal more work is necessary before one could feel confident in the efficacy and effectiveness of this treatment approach with PTSD. That is one of the future directions that I hope to pursue in the development and expansion of this treatment model.

Depression

Another area in which I plan to apply the integrative perspective is the category of mood disorders. Major depressive disorder, in particular, has been the subject of significant theoretical consideration by virtually all of the perspectives considered here (Blatt & Bers, 1993; L. S. Greenberg, Watson, &

Goldman, 1998; Segal & Muran, 1993). Segal and Muran, for example, based their cognitive–behavioral perspective on depression in negative or depressogenic self-schemas, which usually involve an interconnected set of tacit cognitive structures whose content involves global, stable, and negative evaluations of the self. Depression in this view results from experiences of failure to control events. Individuals react to these experiences with thoughts and feelings of helplessness and hopelessness, which eventually develop into generalized expectations of failure and inadequacy.

Blatt and Bers (1993) present a psychodynamic view of the sense of self in depression. In their more phenomenological view of the self, they view a disrupted sense of self as fundamental in depression. They suggest that the senses of self that are disrupted include self-reflectivity, the capacity to tolerate and integrate affective experiences, and a sense of personal agency. In the type of depression that they call *self-critical depression*, there are negative feelings about the self, a sense of guilt, and feelings of hopelessness. Individuals experiencing this subtype of depression tend to describe themselves as cold and unnurturing and as having difficulties relating to others.

In dependency-based depression, one's sense of self is depleted, impaired, or only partially developed. There is limited reflectivity, feelings are warded off, and a distorted sense of agency is typically expressed in symptoms. Dependency-based depressive experiences are more often enacted in a search for gratification and less often expressed verbally. If no one is around to gratify one's impulses, the person feels depleted, abandoned, or unloved.

According to the process-experiential model of L. S. Greenberg and his colleagues (1998), depression results from the activation of a person's "emotionally based, powerless, hopeless, weak/bad self-organization" (p. 231). This self-organization is composed of an interconnected set of negative, self-related emotion schemes. L. S. Greenberg and colleagues maintained that this self-organization is more than just a negative view of self, others, and the world. Rather, it involves a deeply insecure sense of self, encoded from life's experience as weak, unprotected, and unable to cope or an encoded sense of self as worthless, bad, incompetent, and inadequate. Experiences of loss and abandonment incline the individual toward a dependent type of depression, whereas experiences of invalidation incline him or her toward a self-critical type of depression.

The similarities to the psychodynamic model are striking even in its attempt to go beyond the cognitive view of negative self-schemas. However, L. S. Greenberg et al. (1998) maintained that in self-critical depressions, it is the "intensity of contemptuous affect accompanying the negative view of self" (p. 231) more than just the negative view of self that is the critical variable in eliciting the bad sense of self. They also suggested that the nonresilient reaction of panic and powerlessness eventually leads to the emotional collapse of the self. The depressive self-organization is triggered by a specific emotional experience of loss or failure. "It is the whole integrated emotional meaning of an event, rather than thoughts alone, that govern depressive functioning" (p. 232). Moreover, depression also involves a process of secondary self-criticism—for being depressed. Thus, on top of feeling bad, the depressed individual chastises him- or herself for being depressed and feeling bad. This idea is very close to my notion of cogitation and the concept of self-focused attention.

The reader may hear echoes, as I do, of the self-wound model that I have presented. These models present many of the same theoretical threads: (a) damaging life experiences leading to (b) painful views of the self that generate (c) a secondary process of feeling bad about feeling bad (i.e., cogitation), which in turn increases the intensity of the contemptuous self-related affect. The difference between how these elements manifest themselves in depression as compared with anxiety disorders involves the acceptance of the validity of these painful views instead of experiencing apprehension and fear that they might be true. It is the resigned acceptance that one is basically flawed that separates the experience of depression from the experience of anxiety which is characterized by frantic efforts by means of anxiety symptoms and other defenses to protect one's self from facing the possibility that one is basically flawed. The anxious apprehension (Barlow, 2000) routinely seen in anxiety disorders is a protest against the catastrophe that one would experience if these painful views of self were true. Clinical support for this notion derives from the fact that several of the patients with anxiety whom I have treated fell into depression once they became aware of the implicit meaning of their anxiety and panic. Patients are usually panic free and experiencing low anxiety at this point, and their therapy concentrates its focus on the remediation of one's painful self-beliefs. I hope to expand the self-wound model and the integrative treatment model to depressive disorders in the near future.

THE ROLE OF MARITAL AND FAMILY THERAPIES

The one major therapeutic perspective that was not incorporated into my integrative treatment model is marital and family therapy. Although it is clear from the etiological model that significant interpersonal consequences result from a patient's efforts to cope with his or her anxiety symptoms, I have not systematically included this treatment modality in my integrative perspective. Since the inception of the psychotherapy integration movement there have been a number of attempts to develop an integration of individual and marital or family therapy. Most notable among these are the models presented by Pinsof (1995) and Wachtel (1997). Pinsof's model is basically a technically eclectic one in which decision rules are provided for when and under what circumstances a therapist would use one of the pure-form individual therapies and when he or she would use one of the many forms of marital and family therapy.

Wachtel (1997), in a later edition of his classic theoretical integration of psychodynamic and behavior therapies, attempts to integrate a relational perspective into his evolving integrative theory. His cyclical psychodynamic theory, as mentioned before, focuses on the circular causal relationships between an individual's intrapsychic patterns, the behaviors that they give rise to, and the reactions of others to these behaviors, which often reinforce the dysfunctional intrapsychic expectations. As Wachtel put it:

> Like other psychodynamic theories, cyclical psychodynamics emphasizes a person's unconscious wishes, fears, fantasies, expectations, conflicts, images of self and other, and so on. Rather than viewing these as part of an "inner world" separated from the daily world of lived experience, however, cyclical psychodynamic formulations lead us to look at how the internal state (wishes, fears, fantasies, expectations, conflicts) both leads to and results from the network of concrete experiences with others that constitutes the structure of daily life. Such an approach is acutely attentive to the details and subtleties of intrapsychic processes but conceptualizes those processes in a way that highlights their connection to the systems of mutual interaction that give form and tone to a person's life structure. (1997, p. 372)

From this perspective, marital and family therapy become arenas in which the therapist can view the behavioral manifestations of the intrapsychic assumptions of each participant, the reactions of the other participants to these behaviors, and the interpretations of other family members' reactions given by each participant. These therapy formats are clear venues for observing circular causality in action. Once the *vicious* and *virtuous cycles*, as Wachtel calls them, have been observed, then systemic principles of change can aid in modifying the dysfunctional intrapsychic conflicts, fantasies, fears, and expectations.

My own clinical work, however, only occasionally has included marital therapy as an adjunct to my individual work with patients with an anxiety disorder. I earlier mentioned the case of a patient with a driving phobia whose implicit meaning clearly indicated that she was at a painful choice point with respect to her marriage. It required a series of marital therapy sessions for her to finally decide that, despite her terror of living alone, she no longer wanted to be in the marriage. On other occasions, I have worked with couples in which one member experienced agoraphobia to help the other spouse become less of an enabler. In most of these cases, the husband's loving attentiveness was reinforcing his wife's agoraphobic avoidance behavior. To theoretically incorporate the results of these treatments into my integrative perspective is one more task that lies in the future.

A FINAL SUMMARY

This book is an ambitious one. It attempts to synthesize several major perspectives on anxiety disorders, the theory of their development, and the principles of their amelioration. The integrative model places self-perception and self-conception at the center of its focus. This is not an invitation for people to become self-absorbed. On the contrary, the integrative etiological model suggests that self-preoccupation is a response to severe stress, whether that stress emanates from outside or within the individual. The characterization of the healthy self, as described in chapter 5, describes a person who is relatively unfocused on self. The person with a healthy self is one who experiences a background level of confidence and security that allows the individual to (a) act on one's intentions, (b) experience one's reactions to what is happening to one's self in the world, and (c) tolerate a certain amount of painful feelings. When people feel overwhelmed by what is happening to them and by the painful feelings these events generate, they develop dysfunctional ideas about themselves and the world in which they live as well as dysfunctional defenses against the pain produced by what they see and feel.

Herein lies the seedbed of a developing anxiety disorder. Although genetics may play a role in sensitizing some people more than others to stress, I believe it is clinically naïve to suppose that an unmediated biological diathesis can fully explain the origins and trajectory of an individual's anxiety disorder. Human beings are much too human for that to be the case. Human beings are more than just biological entities, and our very human capacities give us an edge up on other species in terms of our ability to generate accurate insights, on the one hand, and catastrophic scenarios, on the other. For one thing, our complex symbolic capacities, although based in neurobiological processes, are far too complex to be sufficiently explained by our current understanding of the workings of the brain.

This integrative psychotherapy attempts to move beyond my earlier experientially based treatment model and therefore one step closer to a more seamless psychotherapeutic integration (Wachtel, 1991). It capitalizes on the best theoretical ideas, clinical strategies, and specific techniques gleaned from the extant treatment perspectives. This model recognizes individual differences and, with the concept of access point, provides an algorithm for directing the treatment sequencing according to patient differences on this variable. The depth and flexibility embedded in this integrative perspective have led—at least within the context of my unsystematic clinical practice— to more comprehensive and durable therapeutic benefits than have the mainstream, single-modality therapies for anxiety disorders. But I am speaking as one psychotherapist. It is time to subject this model to more critical and systematic scrutiny to determine whether this integrative perspective possesses theoretical coherence, efficacy, and effectiveness when conducted by other therapists treating a broader range of individuals with complex anxiety disorders.

APPENDIX:
WOLFE'S FOCUSING TECHNIQUE

Wolfe's focusing technique in some respects is a modification of imaginal exposure. After a brief induction period of slow, diaphragmatic breathing, the patient is asked to maintain a strict attentional focus on the primary body location of his or her anxiety. The patient is then instructed to notice whatever thoughts or feelings automatically arise during the focusing. The following are the specific steps to this procedure:

1. The patient is asked to begin normal breathing while focusing on the sensations of his or her breathing. The patient is instructed to notice how it feels and how it sounds when he or she inhales and exhales.
2. The patient is then asked to switch to slow, diaphragmatic breathing and to continue focusing on the breathing sensations.
3. The patient is instructed to give him- or herself permission to be open to whatever thoughts or feelings may arise during this procedure.
4. The patient is then asked to imagine that his or her attention is like a beacon of light and to shine the light (i.e., focus all of one's attention) on the primary location on the body where he or she experiences anxiety and to notice what automatically arises.
5. The patient is reassured that it is all right if nothing comes up.
6. If nothing comes up, the therapist might ask, "Is there a problem in your current life or relationships that is causing you stress?" The patient is then asked to imagine the problem or person.
7. Whether through focusing on the body sensations or on the problem image, it is expected that the feared catastrophe with its associated painful feelings will emerge.
8. The patient is encouraged to stay with the imagery and experience the feelings, which helps him or her to contact the tacit self-wound.
9. The image is experienced as the patient contacts the entire network of associated images and feelings.
10. The images that emerge then become the focus of guided-imagery work later in the therapy session or in subsequent sessions.

11. The goal of the imagery work is to heighten the patient's awareness of the implicit meanings of his or her anxiety, particularly the underlying self-wounds and associated feelings.
12. At the conclusion of the imagery work, the therapist and patient step back from the direct experiencing work and discuss a more conceptual understanding of the focusing process.

REFERENCES

Alexander, F., & French, T. M. (1946). *Psycho-analytic therapy: Principles and applications*. New York: Ronald.

American Psychiatric Association. (1952). *Diagnostic and statistical manual of mental disorders*. Washington, DC: Author.

American Psychiatric Association. (1968). *Diagnostic and statistical manual of mental disorders* (2nd ed.). Washington, DC: Author.

American Psychiatric Association. (1980). *Diagnostic and statistical manual of mental disorders* (3rd ed.). Washington, DC: Author.

American Psychiatric Association. (1987). *Diagnostic and statistical manual of mental disorders* (3rd ed., rev.). Washington, DC: Author.

American Psychiatric Association. (1994). *Diagnostic and statistical manual of mental disorders* (4th ed.). Washington, DC: Author.

American Psychiatric Association. (2000). *Diagnostic and statistical manual of mental disorders* (4th ed., text revision). Washington, DC: Author.

Andreasen, N. (1984). *The broken brain. The biological revolution in psychiatry*. New York: HarperCollins.

Arciero, G., & Guidano, V. F. (2000). Experience, explanation, and the quest for coherence. In R. A. Neimeyer & J. D. Raskin (Eds.), *Constructions of disorder: Meaning-making frameworks for psychotherapy* (pp. 91–117). Washington, DC: American Psychological Association.

Arieti, S. (1978). *On schizophrenia, phobias, depression, psychotherapy and the farther shores of psychiatry*. New York: Brunner/Mazel.

Arieti, S. (1979). New views on the psychodynamics of phobias. *American Journal of Psychotherapy, 33*, 82–95.

Arnold, M. (1960). *Emotion and personality* (Vols. 1–2). New York: Columbia University Press.

Bandura, A. (1969). *Principles of behavior modification*. New York: Holt, Rinehart & Winston.

Bandura, A. (1977). Self-efficacy: Toward a unifying theory of behavioral change. *Psychological Review, 84*, 191–215.

Bandura, A. (1978). The self-system in reciprocal determinism. *American Psychologist, 33*, 344–358.

Bandura, A. (1982). The assessment and predictive generality of self-percepts of efficacy. *Journal of Behavior Therapy and Experimental Psychiatry, 13*, 195–199.

Bandura, A. (1986). *Social foundations of thought and action: A social cognitive theory*. Englewood Cliffs, NJ: Prentice-Hall.

Bandura, A., Adams, N. E., & Beyer, J. (1977). Cognitive processes mediating behavior change. *Journal of Personality and Social Psychology, 35*, 125–139.

Bandura, A., Adams, N. E., Hardy, A., & Howells, G. (1980). Tests of the generality of self-efficacy theory. *Cognitive Therapy and Research, 4,* 39–66.

Barlow, D. H. (1988). *Anxiety and its disorders.* New York: Guilford Press.

Barlow, D. H. (2000). Unraveling the mysteries of anxiety and its disorders from the perspective of emotion theory. *American Psychologist, 55,* 1247–1263.

Barlow, D. H., Gorman, J. M., Shear, M. K., & Woods, S. W. (2000). Cognitive-behavioral therapy, imipramine, or their combination for panic disorder: A randomized controlled trial. *Journal of the American Medical Association, 283,* 2529–2536.

Barlow, D. H., & Hersen, M. (1984). *Single case experimental designs: Strategies for studying behavior change* (2nd ed.). New York: Pergamon Press.

Barlow, D. H., & Wolfe, B. E. (1981). Behavioral approaches to anxiety disorders: Report on NIMH–SUNY, Albany Research Conference. *Journal of Consulting and Clinical Psychology, 49,* 191–215.

Baumeister, R. F. (1991). *Escaping the self.* New York: Basic Books.

Beck, A. T. (1976). *Cognitive therapy and the emotional disorders.* New York: International Universities Press.

Beck, A. T., & Emery, G. (with Greenberg, R.). (1985). *Anxiety disorders and phobias: A cognitive perspective.* New York: Basic Books.

Beck, A. T., Freeman, A., & Associates. (1990). *Cognitive therapy of personality disorders.* New York: Guilford Press.

Beck, J. G., Stanley, M. A., Baldwin, L. E., Deagle, E. A., & Averill, P. M. (1994). Comparison of cognitive therapy and relaxation training for panic disorder. *Journal of Consulting and Clinical Psychology, 62,* 818–826.

Beck, J. S. (1995). *Cognitive therapy: Basics and beyond.* New York: Guilford Press.

Bednar, R. L., & Peterson, S. R. (1995). *Self-esteem: Paradoxes and innovations in clinical theory and practice* (2nd ed.). Washington, DC: American Psychological Association.

Beitman, B. D., Basha, I. M., DeRosear, L., Flaker, G., & Mukerji, V. (1987). Comparing panic disorder uncomplicated and panic disorder with agoraphobia in cardiology patients with atypical and nonanginal chest pain. *Journal of Anxiety Disorders, 1,* 301–312.

Bellack, A. S., & Hersen, M. (1979). *Research and practice in social skills training.* New York: Plenum Press.

Berzoff, J., Flanagan, L. M., & Hertz, P. (1996). *Inside out and outside in.* Northvale, NJ: Jason Aronson.

Beutler, L. E. (1983). *Eclectic psychotherapy: A systematic approach.* Elmsford, NY: Pergamon Press.

Beutler, L. E., & Clarkin, J. F. (1990). *Systematic treatment selection: Toward targeted therapeutic interventions.* New York: Brunner/Mazel.

Beutler, L. E., & Consoli, A. J. (1992). Systematic eclectic psychotherapy. In J. C. Norcross & M. R. Goldfried (Eds.), *Handbook of psychotherapy integration* (pp. 264–299). New York: Basic Books.

Billett, E. A., Richter, M. A., & Kennedy, J. L. (1998). Genetics of obsessive-compulsive disorder. In R. P. Swinson, M. M. Antony, S. Rachman, & M. A. Richter (Eds.), *Obsessive-compulsive disorder* (pp. 181–206). New York: Guilford Press.

Blashfield, R. K. (1991). Models of psychiatric classification. In M. Hersen & S. M. Turner (Eds.), *Adult psychopathology and diagnosis* (pp. 3–22). New York: Wiley.

Blasi, A. (1988). Identity and the development of the self. In D. K. Lapsley & F. C. Power (Eds.), *Self, ego, and identity* (pp. 226–242). New York: Springer-Verlag.

Blatt, S. J., & Bers, S. A. (1993). The sense of self in depression: A psychodynamic perspective. In Z. V. Segal & S. J. Blatt (Eds.), *The self in emotional distress: Cognitive and psychodynamic perspectives* (pp. 171–210). New York: Guilford Press.

Bohart, A. C. (1993). Experiencing: The basis of psychotherapy. *Journal of Psychotherapy Integration, 3,* 51–67.

Bohart, A. C., & Greenberg, L. S. (1997). Empathy: Where are we and where do we go from here? In A. C. Bohart & L. S. Greenberg (Eds.), *Empathy reconsidered: New directions in psychotherapy* (pp. 419–449). Washington, DC: American Psychological Association.

Borkovec, T. D., Alcaine, O. M., & Behar, E. (2004). Avoidance theory of worry and generalized anxiety disorder. In R. G. Heimberg, C. L. Turk, & D. S. Mennin (Eds.), *Generalized anxiety disorder: Advances in research and practice* (pp. 77–108). New York: Guilford Press.

Borkovec, T. D., & Castonguay, L. G. (1998). What is the scientific meaning of empirically supported therapy? *Journal of Consulting and Clinical Psychology, 66,* 136–142.

Borkovec, T. D., & Roemer, E. (1995). Perceived functions of worry among generalized anxiety disorder subjects: Distraction from more emotionally distressing topics? *Journal of Behavior Therapy and Experimental Psychology, 26,* 25–30.

Borkovec, T. D., & Ruscio, A. M. (2001). Psychotherapy for generalized anxiety disorder. *Journal of Clinical Psychiatry, 62,* 37–45.

Borkovec, T. D., & Whisman, M. A. (1996). Psychological treatment for generalized anxiety disorder. In M. R. Mavissakalian & R. F. Prien (Eds.), *Long-term treatments of anxiety disorders* (pp. 171–199). Washington, DC: American Psychiatric Association.

Bouton, M. E., Mineka, S., & Barlow, D. H. (2001). A modern learning theory perspective on the etiology of panic disorder. *Psychological Review, 108,* 4–32.

Bowers, K. S. (1977). Hypnosis: An informational approach. *Annals of the New York Academy of Sciences, 296,* 222–237.

Bowers, K. S., & Meichenbaum, D. (1984). *The unconscious reconsidered.* New York: Wiley.

Bowlby, J. (1973). *Attachment and loss: Vol. 2. Separation, anxiety, and anger.* New York: Basic Books.

Bowlby, J. (1988). Developmental psychiatry comes of age. *American Journal of Psychiatry, 145,* 1–10.

Breger, L., & McGaugh, J. L. (1965). A critique and reformulation of "learning theory" approaches to psychotherapy and neuroses. *Psychological Bulletin, 63*, 338–358.

Broughton, J. M. (1986). The psychology, history, and ideology of the self. In K. S. Larsen (Ed.), *Dialectics and ideology in psychology* (pp. 128–164). Norwood, NJ: Ablex Publishing.

Brown, T. A., Barlow, D. H., & Liebowitz, M. R. (1994). The empirical basis of generalized anxiety disorder. *American Journal of Psychiatry, 151*, 1272–1280.

Brown, T. A., O'Leary, T. A., & Barlow, D. H. (2001). Generalized anxiety disorder. In D. H. Barlow (Ed.), *Clinical handbook of psychological disorders* (3rd ed., pp. 154–208). New York: Guilford Press.

Bruch, M. A., & Heimberg, R. G. (1994). Differences in perception of parental and personal characteristics between generalized and nongeneralized social phobics. *Journal of Anxiety Disorders, 8*, 155–168.

Bruner, J. (1990). *Acts of meaning: Four lectures on mind and culture*. Cambridge, MA: Harvard University Press.

Cannon, W. B. (1929). *Bodily changes in pain, hunger, fear and rage* (2nd ed.). New York: Appleton-Century-Crofts.

Carr, A. T. (1974). Compulsive neurosis: A review of the literature. *Psychological Bulletin, 81*, 311–318.

Carrera, F., III, & Adams, P. L. (1970). An ethical perspective on operant conditioning. *Journal of the American Academy of Child Psychiatry, 9*, 607–623.

Chambless, D. L. (1996). In defense of dissemination of empirically supported psychological interventions. *Clinical Psychology: Science and Practice, 3*, 230–235.

Chambless, D. L., Sanderson, W. C., Shoham, V., Bennett-Johnson, S., Pope, K. S., Crits-Christoph, P., et al. (1996). An update on empirically validated therapies. *Clinical Psychologist, 49*, 5–18.

Charney, D. S., & Heninger, G. R. (1986). Abnormal regulation of noradrenergic function in panic disorders. *Archives of General Psychiatry, 43*, 1042–1054.

Churchland, P. S. (1986). *Neurophilosophy: Toward a unified science of the mind/brain*. Cambridge, MA: MIT Press.

Clark, D. M. (1986). A cognitive approach to panic. *Behaviour Research and Therapy, 24*, 461–470.

Clark, D. M. (1997). Panic disorder and social phobia. In D. M. Clark & C. G. Fairburn (Eds.), *Science and practice of cognitive behavior therapy* (pp. 121–153). New York: Oxford University Press.

Clark, D. M., Salkovskis, P. M., Hackmann, A., Wells, A., Ludgate, J., & Gelder, M. (1999). Brief cognitive therapy for panic disorder: A randomized controlled trial. *Journal of Consulting and Clinical Psychology, 67*, 583–589.

Clark, D. M., & Wells, A. (1995). A cognitive model of social phobia. In R. G. Heimberg, M. R. Liebowitz, D. A. Hope, & F. R. Schneier (Eds.), *Social phobia: Diagnosis, assessment, and treatment* (pp. 69–93). New York: Guilford Press.

Clark, L. A., Watson, D., & Mineka, S. (1994). Temperament, personality, and the mood and anxiety disorders. *Journal of Abnormal Psychology, 103*, 103–116.

Clum, G. A., & Knowles, S. L. (1991). Why do some people with panic disorders become avoidant? A review. *Clinical Psychology Review, 11*, 295–311.

Connor, K. M., & Davidson, J. R. T. (1998). Neurobiological and pharmacotherapeutic perspectives. *Biological Psychiatry, 44*, 1286–1294.

Cooley, C. H. (1902). *Human nature and the social order*. New York: Scribner.

Cooper, S. H. (1993). The self construct in psychoanalytic theory: A comparative view. In Z. V. Segal & S. J. Blatt (Eds.), *The self in emotional distress* (pp. 41–67). New York: Guilford Press.

Cowley, D. S., & Roy-Byrne, P. P. (1991). The biology of generalized anxiety disorder and chronic anxiety. In R. M. Rapee & D. H. Barlow (Eds.), *Chronic anxiety: Generalized anxiety disorder and mixed anxiety-depression* (pp. 52–75). New York: Guilford Press.

Cozolino, L. (2002). *The neuroscience of psychotherapy*. New York: Norton.

Craske, M. G., & Barlow, D. H. (1988). A review of the relationship between panic and avoidance. *Clinical Psychology Review, 8*, 667–685.

Craske, M. G., & Barlow, D. H. (2001). Panic disorder and agoraphobia. In D. H. Barlow (Ed.), *Clinical handbook of psychological disorders* (3rd ed., pp. 1–59). New York: Guilford Press.

Crits-Christoph, P., Connolly, M. B., Azarian, K., Crits-Christoph, K., & Shappell, S. (1996). An open trial of brief supportive-expressive psychotherapy in the treatment of generalized anxiety disorder. *Psychotherapy, 33*, 418–431.

Crits-Christoph, P., Crits-Christoph, K., Wolf-Palacio, D., Fichter, M., & Rudick, D. (1995). Brief supportive-expressive psychodynamic therapy for generalized anxiety disorder. In J. P. Barber & P. Crits-Christoph (Eds.), *Dynamic therapies for psychiatric disorders (Axis I)* (pp. 43–83). New York: Basic Books.

Crook, J. H. (1980). *The evolution of human consciousness*. Oxford, England: Oxford University Press.

Curtis, R. C. (1991). *The relational self*. New York: Guilford Press.

Cushman, P. (1990). Why the self is empty. *American Psychologist, 45*, 599–611.

Damasio, A. R. (1994). *Descartes' error: Emotion, reason and the human brain*. New York: Putnam.

Darwin, C. R. (1965). *The expression of emotions in man and animals*. Chicago: University of Chicago Press. (Original work published 1872)

Davison, G. C. (1976). Homosexuality: The ethical challenge. *Journal of Consulting and Clinical Psychology, 44*, 157–162.

DeCharms, R. (1987). Personal causation, agency and the self. In P. Young-Eisendrath & J. A. Hall (Eds.), *The book of the self: Person, pretext, and process* (pp. 17–41). New York: New York University Press.

Dewey, J. (1929). *The quest for certainty*. Boston: Minten, Balch.

Diamond, D. B. (1985). Panic attacks, hypochondriasis, and agoraphobia: A self-psychology formulation. *American Journal of Psychotherapy, 39*, 114–125.

Dixon, N. F. (1981). *Preconscious processing*. New York: Wiley.

Dobson, K. S. (2001). *Handbook of cognitive-behavioral therapies* (2nd ed.). New York: Guilford Press.

Dugas, M. J., Freeston, M. H., Ladouceur, R., Rheaume, J., Provencher, M., & Boisvert, J. M. (1998). Worry themes in primary GAD, secondary GAD, and other anxiety disorders. *Journal of Anxiety Disorders, 12,* 253–261.

Duval, S., & Wicklund, R. A. (1972). *A theory of objective self-awareness.* New York: Academic Press.

Eagle, M. N. (1987). The psychoanalytic and the cognitive unconscious. In R. Stern (Ed.), *Theories of the unconscious and theories of the self* (pp. 155–189). New York: Analytic Press.

Edelman, G. (1992). *Bright air, brilliant fire: On the matter of the mind.* New York: Basic Books.

Edelson, M. (1985). Psychoanalysis, anxiety and the anxiety disorders. In A. H. Tuma & J. D. Maser (Eds.), *Anxiety and the anxiety disorders* (pp. 633–644). Hillsdale, NJ: Erlbaum.

Elliott, R., Davis, K. L., & Slatick, E. (1998). Process-experiential therapy for post-traumatic stress difficulties. In L. S. Greenberg, J. C. Watson, & G. Lietaer (Eds.), *Handbook of experiential psychotherapy* (pp. 249–271). New York: Guilford Press.

Elliott, R., Greenberg, L. S., & Lietaer, G. (2003). Research on experiential psychotherapies. In M. Lambert, A. Bergin, & S. Garfield (Eds.), *Handbook of psychotherapy and behavior change* (5th ed., pp. 493–539). New York: Wiley.

Emmelkamp, P. M. G., Visser, S., & Hoekstra, R. J. (1988). Cognitive therapy vs. exposure *in vivo* in the treatment of obsessive-compulsives. *Cognitive Therapy and Research, 12,* 103–114.

Epstein, S. (1973). The self-concept revisited or a theory of a theory. *American Psychologist, 28,* 404–416.

Epstein, S. (1991). Cognitive-experiential self-theory: An integrative theory of personality. In R. C. Curtis (Ed.), *The relational self: Theoretical convergences in psychoanalysis and social psychology* (pp. 111–137). New York: Guilford Press.

Erdelyi, M. H., & Goldberg, B. (1979). Let's not sweep repression under the rug: Toward a cognitive psychology of repression. In J. F. Kihlstrom & F. J. Evans (Eds.), *Functional disorders of memory* (pp. 355–402). Hillsdale, NJ: Erlbaum.

Eysenck, H. J. (1959). Learning theory and behavior therapy. *British Journal of Medical Science, 105,* 61–75.

Eysenck, H. J. (Ed.). (1960). *Behaviour therapy and the neuroses.* New York: Pergamon Press.

Eysenck, H. J. (1967). *The biological basis of personality.* Springfield, IL: Charles C Thomas.

Eysenck, H. J., & Rachman, S. (1977). *The causes and cures of neuroses.* London: Routledge & Kegan Paul.

Fairbairn, W. R. D. (1952). *An object-relations theory of the personality.* New York: Basic Books.

Feather, B. W., & Rhoads, J. M. (1972a). Psychodynamic behavior therapy: 1. Theory and rationale. In J. Marmor & S. M. Woods (Eds.), *The interface between the psychodynamic and behavioral therapies* (pp. 293–309). New York: Plenum Press.

Feather, B. W., & Rhoads, J. M. (1972b). Psychodynamic behavior therapy: 2. Clinical aspects. In J. Marmor & S. M. Woods (Eds.), *The interface between the psychodynamic and behavioral therapies* (pp. 313–330). New York: Plenum Press.

Fensterheim, H., & Raw, S. D. (1996). Psychotherapy research is not psychotherapy practice. *Clinical Psychology: Science and Practice, 3,* 168–171.

Fishman, D. B. (2000, May 3). Transcending the efficacy versus effectiveness research debate: Proposal for a new, electronic "Journal of Pragmatic Case Studies." *Prevention & Treatment, 3,* Article 8. Retrieved November 8, 2004, from http://journals.apa.org/prevention/volume3/toc-may03-00.html

Fishman, D. B., & Franks, C. M. (1997). The conceptual evolution of behavior therapy. In P. L. Wachtel & S. B. Messer (Eds.), *Theories of psychotherapy: Origins and evolution* (pp. 131–180). Washington, DC: American Psychological Association.

Foa, E. B., & Franklin, M. E. (2001). Obsessive-compulsive disorder. In D. H. Barlow (Ed.), *Clinical handbook of psychological disorders* (3rd ed., pp. 209–263). New York: Guilford Press.

Foa, E. B., & Goldstein, A. (1978). A continuous exposure and complete response prevention in the treatment of obsessive-compulsive neurosis. *Behavior Therapy, 9,* 821–829.

Foa, E. B., & Kozak, M. J. (1985). Treatment of anxiety disorders: Implications for psychopathology. In A. H. Tuma & J. D. Maser (Eds.), *Anxiety and the anxiety disorders* (pp. 421–452). Hillsdale, NJ: Erlbaum.

Foa, E. B., & Kozak, M. J. (1986). Emotional processing of fear: Exposure to corrective information. *Psychological Bulletin, 99,* 20–35.

Foa, E. B., & Kozak, M. J. (1996). Psychological treatment of obsessive-compulsive disorder. In M. R. Mavissakalian & R. P. Prien (Eds.), *Long-term treatments of anxiety disorders* (pp. 285–309). Washington, DC: American Psychiatric Press.

Foa, E. B., & Tillmanns, A. (1980). The treatment of obsessive-compulsive neurosis. In A. Goldstein & E. B. Foa (Eds.), *Handbook of behavioral interventions: A clinical guide* (pp. 416–500). New York: Wiley.

Ford, D. H., & Urban, H. B. (1998). *Contemporary models of psychotherapy: A comparative analysis* (2nd ed.). New York: Wiley.

Frances, A. J., & Cooper, A. M. (1981). Descriptive and dynamic psychiatry: A perspective on the DSM-III. *American Journal of Psychiatry, 138,* 1198–1202.

Frances, A. J., & Dunn, P. (1975). The attachment–autonomy conflict in agoraphobia. *International Journal of Psycho-Analysis, 56,* 435–439.

Freud, A. (1946). *The ego and the mechanisms of defense.* New York: International Universities Press.

Freud, S. (1955a). Analysis of a phobia in a five-year-old boy. In J. Strachey (Ed. & Trans.), *The standard edition of the complete psychological works of Sigmund Freud* (Vol. 10, pp. 5–149). London: Hogarth Press. (Original work published 1909)

Freud, S. (1955b). Notes upon a case of obsessional neurosis. In J. Strachey (Ed. & Trans.), *The standard edition of the complete psychological works of Sigmund Freud* (Vol. 10, pp. 155–318). London: Hogarth Press. (Original work published 1909)

Freud, S. (1958). The disposition to obsessional neurosis: A contribution to the problem of choice of neurosis. In J. Strachey (Ed. & Trans.), *The standard edition of the complete psychological works of Sigmund Freud* (Vol. 12, pp. 317–326). London: Hogarth Press. (Original work published 1913)

Freud, S. (1959). The ego and the id. In J. Strachey (Ed. & Trans.), *The standard edition of the complete psychological works of Sigmund Freud* (Vol. 19, pp. 3–66). London: Hogarth Press. (Original work published 1923)

Freud, S. (1959). Inhibitions, symptoms, and anxiety. In J. Strachey (Ed. & Trans.), *The standard edition of the complete psychological works of Sigmund Freud* (Vol. 20, pp. 87–172). London: Hogarth Press. (Original work published 1926)

Freud, S. (1962a). The neuro-psychoses of defense. In J. Strachey (Ed. & Trans.), *The standard edition of the complete psychological works of Sigmund Freud* (Vol. 3, pp. 43–61). London: Hogarth Press. (Original work published 1894)

Freud, S. (1962b). On the grounds for detaching a particular syndrome for neurasthenia under the description "anxiety neurosis." In J. Strachey (Ed. & Trans.), *The standard edition of the complete psychological works of Sigmund Freud* (Vol. 3, pp. 85–117). London: Hogarth Press. (Original work published 1894)

Freud, S. (1963). A reply to criticisms on the anxiety neurosis. In Philip Rieff (Ed. &Trans.), *Freud: Early psychoanalytic writings* (pp. 119–135). New York: Collier Books. (Original work published 1895)

Freud, S. (1966). Project for a scientific psychology. In J. Strachey (Ed. & Trans.), *The standard edition of the complete psychological works of Sigmund Freud* (Vol. 1, pp. 295–397). London: Hogarth Press. (Original work published 1895)

Freud, S. (1975). Three essays on the theory of sexuality. In J. Strachey (Ed. & Trans.), *The standard edition of the complete psychological works of Sigmund Freud* (Vol. 7, pp. 125–243). London: Hogarth Press. (Original work published 1905)

Friedman, S. (1985). Implications of object relations theory for the behavioral treatment of agoraphobia. *American Journal of Psychotherapy, 34,* 525–540.

Fyer, A. J., Mannuzza, S., Chapman, T. F., Liebowitz, M. R., & Klein, D. F. (1993). A direct interview family study of social phobia. *Archives of General Psychiatry, 50,* 286–293.

Fyer, A. J., Mannuzza, S., Chapman, T. F., Martin, L. Y., & Klein, D. F. (1995). Specificity in familial aggregation of phobic disorders. *Archives of General Psychiatry, 52,* 564–573.

Gabbard, G. O. (1992). Psychodynamic psychiatry in the "decade of the brain." *American Journal of Psychiatry, 149,* 991–998.

Gabbard, G. O. (1994). *Psychodynamic psychiatry in clinical practice: The DSM-IV edition.* Washington, DC: American Psychiatric Press.

Gelso, C. J., & Hayes, J. A. (1998). *The psychotherapy relationship: Theory, research, and practice.* New York: Wiley.

Gendlin, E. T. (1962). *Experiencing and the creation of meaning.* Glencoe, IL: The Free Press.

Gendlin, E. T. (1978). *Focusing.* New York: Bantam Books.

Gill, M. M. (1984). Psychoanalysis and psychotherapy: A revision. *International Review of Psychoanalysis, 11,* 161–179.

Gold, J. R., & Stricker, G. (1993). Psychotherapy integration with character disorders. In G. Stricker & J. R. Gold (Eds.), *Comprehensive handbook of psychotherapy integration* (pp. 323–336). New York: Plenum Press.

Goldfried, M. R. (1971). Systematic desensitization as training in self-control. *Journal of Consulting and Clinical Psychology, 37,* 228–234.

Goldfried, M. R. (1980). Toward the delineation of therapeutic change principles. *American Psychologist, 35,* 991–999.

Goldfried, M. R., & Davison, G. C. (1976). *Clinical behavior therapy.* New York: Wiley.

Goldfried, M. R., & Padawer, W. (1982). Current status and future directions in psychotherapy. In M. R. Goldfried (Ed.), *Converging themes in psychotherapy* (3–49). New York: Springer Publishing Company.

Goldfried, M. R., & Robins, C. (1983). Self-schema, cognitive bias, and the processing of therapeutic experiences. In P. C. Kendall (Ed.), *Advances in cognitive-behavioral research and therapy* (Vol. 2, pp. 33–80). New York: Academic Press.

Goldfried, M. R., & Wolfe, B. E. (1996). Psychotherapy practice and research: Repairing a strained alliance. *American Psychologist, 51,* 1007–1016.

Goldfried, M. R., & Wolfe, B. E. (1998). Toward a more clinically valid approach to therapy research. *Journal of Consulting and Clinical Psychology, 66,* 143–150.

Goldstein, A. J., & Chambless, D. L. (1978). A reanalysis of agoraphobia. *Behavior Therapy, 9,* 47–59.

Goleman, D. (1997). *Emotional intelligence.* New York: Bantam Books.

Gorman, J. M., Liebowitz, M. R., Fyer, A. J., & Stein, J. (1989). A neuroanatomical hypothesis for panic disorder. *American Journal of Psychiatry, 146,* 148–161.

Greenberg, J., & Mitchell, S. (1983). *Object relations in psychoanalytic theory.* Cambridge, MA: Harvard University Press.

Greenberg, L. S. (2002). *Emotion-focused therapy: Coaching clients to work through their feelings.* Washington, DC: American Psychological Association.

Greenberg, L. S., Rice, L. N., & Elliott, R. (1993). *Facilitating emotional change: The moment-by-moment process.* New York: Guilford Press.

Greenberg, L. S., & Safran, J. D. (1987). *Emotion in psychotherapy.* New York: Guilford Press.

Greenberg, L. S., Watson, J. C., & Goldman, R. (1998). Process-experiential therapy of depression. In L. S. Greenberg, J. C. Watson, & G. Lietaer (Eds.), *Handbook of experiential psychotherapy* (pp. 227–248). New York: Guilford Press.

Greenson, R. (1967). *The technique and practice of psycho-analysis.* New York: International Universities Press.

Greenwald, A. (1992). New look 3: Unconscious cognition reclaimed. *American Psychologist, 47*, 766–779.

Guidano, V. F. (1991). *The self in process*. New York: Guilford.

Guntrip, H. (1968). *Schizoid phenomena, object relations and the self*. London: Hogarth Press.

Harris, G. (1948). Neural control of the pituitary gland. *Physiological Review, 28*, 139–179.

Harter, S. (1999). *The construction of the self. A developmental perspective*. New York: Guilford Press.

Hayes, S. C., Strosahl, K. S., & Wilson, K. G. (1998). *Acceptance and commitment therapy*. New York: Guilford Press.

Heide, F. J., & Borkovec, T. D. (1983). Relaxation-induced anxiety: Paradoxical anxiety enhancement due to relaxation training. *Journal of Consulting and Clinical Psychology, 51*, 171–182.

Heimberg, R. G., & Becker, R. E. (2001). *Nature and treatment of social fears and phobias*. New York: Guilford Press.

Herman, J. L. (1993). *Trauma and recovery*. New York: Basic Books.

Higgins, E. T. (1987). Self-discrepancy: A theory relating self and affect. *Psychological Review, 94*, 319–340.

Horney, K. (1945). *Our inner conflicts: A constructive theory of neurosis*. New York: Norton.

Horowitz, M. J. (1988). *Introduction to psychodynamics: A synthesis*. New York: Basic Books.

Horvath, A. O., & Greenberg, L. S. (1994). *The working alliance: Theory, research, and practice*. New York: Wiley.

Howard, G. S. (1991). Culture tales: A narrative approach to thinking, cross-cultural psychology, and psychotherapy. *American Psychologist, 46*, 187–197.

Howard, K., Kopta, M., Krause, M., & Orlinsky, D. E. (1986). The dose–effect relationship in psychotherapy. *American Psychologist, 41*, 149–164.

Howard, W. A., Murphy, S. M., & Clarke, J. C. (1983). The nature and treatment of fear of flying: A controlled investigation. *Behavior Therapy, 14*, 557–567.

Ingram, R. E. (1990). Self-focused attention in clinical disorders: Review and a conceptual model. *Psychological Bulletin, 107*, 156–176.

Jacobs, W. J., & Nadel, N. (1985). Stress induced recovery of fears and phobias. *Psychological Review, 92*, 512–531.

Jacobson, E. (1929). *Progressive relaxation*. Chicago: University of Chicago Press.

James, W. (1890). *Principles of psychology* (Vols. 1–2). New York: Holt.

Johnson, F. (1985). The western concept of self. In A. J. Marsella, G. DeVos, & F. L. K. Hsu (Eds.), *Culture and self* (pp. 91–138). London: Tavistock.

Johnson, M. (1987). *The body in the mind: The bodily basis of meaning, imagination, and reason*. Chicago: University of Chicago Press.

Johnson, M. R., & Lydiard, R. B. (1995). The neurobiology of anxiety disorders. In M. H. Pollack & M. Otto (Eds.), *Psychiatric clinics of North America* (pp. 681–725). Philadelphia: W. B. Saunders.

Jones, E. E. (1993). Introduction to special section: Single-case research in psychotherapy. *Journal of Consulting and Clinical Psychology, 61*, 371–372.

Kagan, J., Reznick, J. S., & Snidman, N. (April, 1988). Biological bases of childhood shyness. *Science, 240*, 167–171.

Karen, R. (1992, February). Shame. *The Atlantic Monthly*, 40–70.

Kaufman, G. (1985). *Shame: The power of caring.* Cambridge, MA: Schenkman Books.

Kernberg, O. (1976). *Object relations theory and clinical psychoanalysis.* New York: Jason Aronson.

Kihlstrom, J. F. (1984). Conscious, subconscious, unconscious. In K. S. Bowers & D. Meichenbaum (Eds.), *The unconscious reconsidered* (pp. 149–211). New York: Wiley.

Kihlstrom, J. F. (2002). To honor Kraepelin . . . : From symptoms to pathology in the diagnosis of mental illness. In L. E. Beutler & M. L. Malik (Eds.), *Rethinking the DSM: A psychological perspective* (pp. 279–303). Washington, DC: American Psychological Association.

Kihlstrom, J. F., Barnhardt, T. M., & Tataryn, D. J. (1992). The psychological unconscious: Found, lost, and regained. *American Psychologist, 47*, 788–791.

Klein, D. F. (1981). Anxiety reconceptualized. In D. F. Klein & J. G. Rabkin (Eds.), *Anxiety: New research and changing concepts* (pp. 235–263). New York: Raven Press.

Klein, D. F. (1993). False suffocation alarms, spontaneous panics, and related conditions. *Archives of General Psychiatry, 50*, 306–315.

Klein, G. S. (1976). *Psychoanalytic theory: An exploration of essentials.* New York: International Universities Press.

Klerman, G. L. (1978). The evolution of a scientific nosology. In J. C. Shershow (Ed.), *Schizophrenia: Science and practice* (pp. 99–121). Cambridge, MA: Harvard University Press.

Kohlenberg, R. J., & Tsai, M. (1995). Functional analytic psychotherapy: A behavioral approach to intensive treatment. In W. O'Donohue & L. Krasner (Eds.), *Theories of behavior therapy: Exploring behavior change* (pp. 637–658). Washington, DC: American Psychological Association.

Kohut, H. (1977). *Restoration of the self.* New York: International Universities Press.

Kohut, H. (1978). *The search for the self.* New York: International Universities Press.

Kohut, H. (1979). The two analyses of Mr. Z. *International Journal of Psychoanalysis, 60*, 3–27.

Kopp, R. R. (1995). *Metaphor therapy: Using client-generated metaphors in psychotherapy.* New York: Brunner/Mazel.

Kosslyn, S. M. (1980). *Image and mind.* Cambridge, MA: Harvard University Press.

Kraepelin, E., & Diefendorf, A. R. (1907). *Clinical psychiatry; a textbook for students and physicians* (7th ed.). New York: Macmillan. (Original work published 1904)

Lakoff, G., & Johnson, M. (1981). *Metaphors we live by*. Chicago, IL: University of Chicago Press.

Lambert, M. J. (1992). Psychotherapy outcome research: Implications for practice of integrative and eclectic therapies. In J. C. Norcross & M. R. Goldfried (Eds.), *Handbook of psychotherapy integration* (pp. 94–129). New York: Basic Books.

Last, C. (1987). Simple phobias. In L. Michelson & M. Ascher (Eds.), *Anxiety and stress disorders* (pp. 176–190). New York: Guilford Press.

Lazarus, A. A. (1992). Multimodal therapy: Technical eclecticism with minimal integration. In J. C. Norcross & M. R. Goldfried (Eds.), *Handbook of psychotherapy integration* (pp. 231–263). New York: Basic Books.

Leahy, R. L. (2003). *Cognitive therapy techniques: A practitioner's guide*. New York: Guilford Press.

LeDoux, J. (1996). *The emotional brain*. New York: Simon & Schuster.

Levin, J. D. (1992). *Theories of the self*. Washington, DC: Hemisphere Publication Services.

Linehan, M. M. (1993). *Cognitive-behavioral treatment of borderline personality disorder*. New York: Guilford Press.

Luborsky, L. (1984). *Principles of psychoanalytic psychotherapy: A manual for supportive-expressive treatment*. New York: Basic Books.

Luborsky, L., & Crits-Christoph, P. (1990). *Understanding transference: The core conflictual relationship theme method*. New York: Basic Books.

Lydiard, R. B., Brawman-Mintzer, O., & Ballenger, J. C. (1996). Recent developments in the psychopharmacology of anxiety disorders. *Journal of Consulting and Clinical Psychology, 64*, 660–668.

Mahoney, M. J. (1974). *Cognition and behavior modification*. Cambridge, MA: Ballinger.

Mahoney, M. J. (1985). Psychotherapy and human change processes. In M. J. Mahoney & A. Freeman (Eds.), *Cognition and psychotherapy* (pp. 3–48). New York: Plenum Press.

Mahoney, M. J. (1991). *Human change processes: The scientific foundations of psychotherapy*. New York: Basic Books.

Mahoney, M. J. (1995). Emotionality and health: Lessons from and for psychotherapy. In J. W. Pennebaker (Ed.), *Emotion, disclosure, and health* (pp. 241–253). Washington, DC: American Psychological Association.

Markus, H., & Nurius, P. (1986). Possible selves. *American Psychologist, 41*, 954–969.

Markus, H., & Wurf, E. (1987). The dynamic self-concept: A social psychological perspective. *Annual Review of Psychology, 38*, 299–337.

Marshall, J. R. (1996). Comorbidity and its effects on panic disorder. *Bulletin of the Menninger Clinic, 60*, A32–A53.

Mavissakalian, M., & Barlow, D. H. (Eds.). (1981). *Phobia: Psychological and pharmacological treatment*. New York: Guilford Press.

May, R. (1979). *The meaning of anxiety*. New York: Washington Square Press.

McFall, M. E., & Wollersheim, J. P. (1979). Obsessive-compulsive neurosis: A cognitive-behavioral formulation and approach to treatment. *Cognitive Therapy and Research, 3*, 333–348.

McLemore, C. W., & Benjamin, L. S. (1979). Whatever happened to interpersonal diagnosis? A psychosocial alternative to DSM-III. *American Psychologist, 34*, 17–34.

McNally, R. J. (1994). *Panic disorder: A critical analysis.* New York: Guilford Press.

Mead, G. H. (1934). *Mind, self, and society.* Chicago: University of Chicago Press.

Meichenbaum, D. H. (1977). *Cognitive-behavior modification: An integrative approach.* New York: Plenum Press.

Melzack, R. (1989). Phantom limbs, the self, and the brain. *Canadian Psychology, 30*, 1–14.

Messer, S. B. (1992). A critical examination of belief structures in integrative and eclectic psychotherapy. In J. C. Norcross & M. R. Goldfried (Eds.), *Handbook of psychotherapy integration* (pp. 130–168). New York: Basic Books.

Messer, S. B. (2001). Empirically supported treatments: What's a non-behaviorist to do? In B. D. Slife, R. N. Williams, & S. H. Barlow (Eds.), *Critical issues in psychotherapy: Translating new ideas into practice* (pp. 3–19). Thousand Oaks, CA: Sage.

Messer, S. B., Sass, A. L., & Woolfolk, L. R. (Eds.). (1988). *Hermeneutics and psychological theory.* Rutgers, NJ: Rutgers University Press.

Meyer, V. (1966). Modification of expectations in cases with obsessional rituals. *Behaviour Research and Therapy, 4*, 273–280.

Michels, R., Frances, A. J., & Shear, M. K. (1985). Psychodynamic models of anxiety. In A. H. Tuma & J. D. Maser (Eds.), *Anxiety and the anxiety disorders* (pp. 595–618). Hillsdale, NJ: Erlbaum.

Milrod, B., Busch, F. N., Cooper, A. M., & Shapiro, T. (1997). *Manual of panic-focused psychodynamic psychotherapy.* Washington, DC: American Psychiatric Press.

Mitchell, K. R., & Orr, T. E. (1974). Note on treatment of heterosexual anxiety using short-term massed desensitization. *Psychological Reports, 35*, 1093–1094.

Morris, R. J., & Suckerman, K. R. (1974). Therapist warmth as a factor in automated systematic desensitization. *Journal of Consulting and Clinical Psychology, 42*, 244–250.

Mowrer, O. H. (1939). Stimulus response theory of anxiety. *Psychological Review, 46*, 553–565.

Mowrer, O. H. (1960). *Learning theory and behavior.* New York: Wiley.

Nathanson, D. L. (Ed.). (1987). *The many faces of shame.* New York: Guilford Press.

Neisser, U. (1976). *Cognition and reality.* San Francisco: Freeman.

Nemiah, J. (1981). A psychoanalytic view of phobias. *American Journal of Psychoanalysis, 41*, 115–120.

Norcross, J. C. (Ed.). (2002). *Psychotherapy relationships that work.* New York: Oxford University Press.

Noyes, R., Clancy, J., Garvey, M., & Anderson, D. J. (1987). Is agoraphobia a variant of panic disorder or a separate illness? *Journal of Anxiety Disorders, 1*, 3–13.

Obsessive–Compulsive Cognitions Working Group. (1997). Cognitive assessment of obsessive-compulsive disorder. *Behaviour Research and Therapy, 35*, 667–681.

Ogilvie, D. M., & Ashmore, R. D. (1991). Self-with-other representation as a unit of analysis in self-concept research. In R. C. Curtis (Ed.), *The relational self: Theoretical convergences in psychoanalysis and social psychology* (pp. 282–314). New York: Guilford Press.

Orlinsky, D. E., Grawe, K., & Parks, B. K. (1994). Process and outcome in psychotherapy—Noch einmal. In A. E. Bergin & S. L. Garfield (Eds.), *Handbook of psychotherapy and behavior change* (4th ed., pp. 270–376). New York: Wiley.

Öst, L.-G., & Sterner, U. (1987). Applied tension: A specific behavioral method for treatment of blood phobia. *Behaviour Research and Therapy, 25*, 25–29.

Ouseley, F. A. (1999). *Integrative treatment for anxiety disorders with comorbid Axis II psychopathology—A case study.* Unpublished manuscript, Argosy University, Washington, DC.

Pasnau, R. O. (Ed.). (1984). *Diagnosis and treatment of anxiety disorders.* Washington, DC: American Psychiatric Association.

Pavlov, I. (1928). *Conditional reflexes* (G. V. Anrep, Trans.). London: Oxford University Press.

Perls, F. (1965). Gestalt therapy. Part II. In E. Shostrom (Producer & Director), *Three approaches to psychotherapy* [Motion picture]. Santa Ana, CA: Psychological Films.

Piaget, J. (1966). *Judgment and reasoning in the child.* Totowa, NJ: Littlefield, Adams. (Original work published 1924)

Pine, F. (1990). *Drive, ego, object, and self.* New York: Basic Books.

Pinsof, W. M. (1995). *Integrative problem-centered therapy: A synthesis of family, individual, and biological therapies.* New York: Basic Books.

Polkinghorne, D. E. (1988). *Narrative knowing and the human sciences.* Albany: State University of New York Press.

Pribram, K. H. (1986). The cognitive revolution and mind/brain issues. *American Psychologist, 41*, 507–520.

Pylyshyn, Z. W. (1984). *Computation and cognition.* Cambridge, MA: MIT Press.

Rachman, S. (1977). The conditioning theory of fear-acquisition: A critical examination. *Behaviour Research and Therapy, 15*, 375–387.

Rachman, S. (1980). Emotional processing. *Behaviour Research and Therapy, 18*, 51–60.

Rachman, S. (1993). A critique of cognitive therapy for anxiety disorders. *Journal of Behavior Therapy and Experimental Psychiatry, 24*, 279–288.

Rapee, R. M. (1991). The conceptual overlap between cognition and conditioning in clinical psychology. *Clinical Psychology Review, 11*, 193–203.

Rauch, S. L., & Jenike, M. A. (1997). Neural mechanisms of obsessive-compulsive disorder. *Current Review on Mood and Anxiety Disorders, 7*, 84–94.

Redmond, D. E. (1985). Neurochemical basis for anxiety and anxiety disorders: Evidence from drugs which decrease human fear or anxiety. In A. H. Tuma & J. D. Maser (Eds.), *Anxiety and the anxiety disorders* (pp. 533–555). Hillsdale, NJ: Erlbaum.

Reiser, M. F. (1984). *Mind, brain, body: Toward a convergence of psychoanalysis and neurobiology*. New York: Basic Books.

Reiss, S. (1987). Theoretical perspectives on the fear of anxiety. *Clinical Psychology Review, 7,* 585–596.

Rescorla, R. A. (1988). Pavlovian conditioning: It's not what you think it is. *American Psychologist, 43,* 151–160.

Rice, L. N., & Greenberg, L. S. (Eds.). (1984). *Patterns of change.* New York: Guilford Press.

Rogers, C. R. (1957). The necessary and sufficient conditions of psychotherapeutic personality change. *Journal of Consulting Psychology, 21,* 95–103.

Rogers, C. R. (1961). *On becoming a person.* Boston: Houghton Mifflin.

Rosenbaum, J. F., Biederman, J., Pollock, R. A., & Hirshfeld, D. R. (1994). The etiology of social phobia. *Journal of Clinical Psychiatry, 55*(Suppl. 6), 10–16.

Rosenbaum, R., & Dyckman, J. (1995). Integrating self and system: An empty intersection? *Family Process, 34,* 21–44.

Rossi, E. L. (1986). *The psychobiology of mind-body healing: New concepts of therapeutic hypnosis.* New York: Norton.

Safran, J. D. (1993). Breaches in the therapeutic alliance: An arena for negotiating authentic relatedness. *Psychotherapy, 30,* 11–24.

Safran, J. D., & Greenberg, L. S. (Eds.). (1991). *Emotion, psychotherapy, and change.* New York: Guilford Press.

Safran, J. D., Muran, J. C., & Samstag, L. W. (1994). Resolving therapeutic alliance ruptures: A task analytic investigation. In A. O. Horvath & L. S. Greenberg (Eds.), *The working alliance: Theory, research and practice* (pp. 225–255). New York: Wiley.

Safran, J. D., & Segal, Z. V. (1991). *Interpersonal process in cognitive therapy.* Northvale, NJ: Jason Aronson.

Salkovskis, P. M. (1985). Obsessive-compulsive problems. A cognitive-behavioral analysis. *Behaviour Research and Therapy, 25,* 571–583.

Salovey, P., & Mayer, J. D. (1990). Emotional intelligence. *Imagination, Cognition, and Personality, 9,* 185–211.

Salter, A. (2000). *The case against psychoanalysis.* New York: HarperCollins.

Salzman, L. (1980). *Treatment of the obsessive personality.* New York: Jason Aronson.

Segal, Z. V., & Blatt, S. J. (1993). The self as a vantage point for understanding emotional disorder. In Z. V. Segal & S. J. Blatt (Eds.), *The self in emotional distress: Cognitive and psychodynamic perspectives* (pp. 371–377). New York: Guilford Press.

Segal, Z. V., & Muran, J. C. (1993). A cognitive perspective on self-representation in depression. In Z. V. Segal & S. J. Blatt (Eds.), *The self in emotional distress: Cognitive and psychodynamic perspectives* (pp. 131–163). New York: Guilford Press.

Segal, Z. V., Williams, J. M. G., & Teasdale, J. D. (2002). *Mindfulness-based cognitive therapy for depression*. New York: Guilford Press.

Seligman, M. E. P. (1971). Phobias and preparedness. *Behavior Therapy, 2,* 307–320.

Seligman, M. E. P. (1995). The effectiveness of psychotherapy: The *Consumer Reports* study. *American Psychologist, 50,* 965–974.

Shafran, R., Booth, R., & Rachman, S. (1992). The reduction of claustrophobia II—Cognitive analyses. *Behaviour Research and Therapy, 30,* 75–85.

Shafran, R., Thordarson, D. S., & Rachman, S. (1996). Thought action fusion in obsessive-compulsive disorder. *Journal of Anxiety Disorders, 5,* 379–391.

Shapiro, F. (1995). *Eye movement desensitization and reprocessing: Basic principles, protocols, and procedures*. New York: Guilford Press.

Shear, M. K., Cooper, A. M., Klerman, G. L., Busch, F. N., & Shapiro, T. (1993). A psychodynamic model of panic disorder. *American Journal of Psychiatry, 150,* 859–866.

Shevrin, H., & Dickman, S. (1980). The psychological unconscious: A necessary assumption for all psychological theory? *American Psychologist, 35,* 421–434.

Sinha, S. S., Mohlman, J., & Gorman, J. M. (2004). Neurobiology. In R. G. Heimberg, C. L. Turk, & D. S. Mennin (Eds.), *Generalized anxiety disorder: Advances in research and practice* (pp. 187–216). New York: Guilford Press.

Smith, M. B. (1978). Perspectives on selfhood. *American Psychologist, 33,* 1058–1063.

Sperry, R. W. (1988). Psychology's mentalist paradigm and the religion/science tension. *American Psychologist, 43,* 607–613.

Spitzer, R. L. (1980). Introduction. In *Diagnostic and statistical manual of mental disorders* (3rd ed., pp. 1–12). Washington, DC: American Psychiatric Association.

Stampfl, T. G., & Levis, D. J. (1967). Essentials of implosive therapy. *Journal of Abnormal Psychology, 72,* 496–503.

Stern, D. N. (1985). *The interpersonal world of the infant*. New York: Basic Books.

Stiles, W. B. (1993). Quality control in qualitative research. *Clinical Psychology Review, 13,* 593–618.

Stiles, W. B. (2002). Assimilation of problematic experiences. *Psychotherapy, 38,* 462–465.

Stiles, W. B. (2003). *When is a case study scientific research?* Unpublished manuscript.

Stiles, W. B., Elliott, R., Llewelyn, S. P., Firth-Cozens, J. A., Margison, F. R., Shapiro, D. A., & Hardy, G. (1990). Assimilation of problematic experiences by clients in psychotherapy. *Psychotherapy, 27,* 411–420.

Stiles, W. B., & Wolfe, B. E. (in press). Relationship contributions to the treatment of anxiety disorders: Empirically supported principles. In L. G. Castonguay & L. E. Beutler (Eds.), *Principles of therapeutic change that work*. New York: Oxford University Press.

Stopa, L., & Clark, D. M. (1993). Cognitive processes in social phobia. *Behaviour Research and Therapy, 31,* 255–267.

Strauman, T. J. (1994). Self-representations and the nature of cognitive change in psychotherapy. *Journal of Psychotherapy Integration, 4,* 291–316.

Strauman, T. J., & Higgins, E. T. (1988). Self-discrepancies as predictors of vulnerability to distinct syndromes of chronic emotional distress. *Journal of Personality, 56*, 685–707.

Strauman, T. J., & Higgins, E. T. (1993). The self construct in social cognition: Past, present, and future. In Z. V. Segal & S. J. Blatt (Eds.), *The self in emotional distress: Cognitive and psychodynamic perspectives* (pp. 3–40). New York: Guilford Press.

Sturgis, E. T. (1993). Obsessive-compulsive disorders. In P. B. Sutker & H. E. Adams (Eds.), *Comprehensive handbook of psychopathology* (2nd ed., pp. 129–144). New York: Plenum Press.

Sullivan, H. S. (1953). *The interpersonal theory of psychiatry*. New York: Norton.

Sulloway, F. J. (1979). *Freud: Biologist of the mind*. New York: Basic Books.

Swann, W. (1990). To be adored or to be known: The interplay of self-enhancement and self-verification. In R. M. Sorrentino & E. T. Higgins (Eds.), *Handbook of motivation and cognition* (Vol. 2, pp. 408–480). New York: Guilford Press.

Task Force on Promotion and Dissemination of Psychological Procedures. (1995). Training in and dissemination of empirically-validated psychological treatments. *The Clinical Psychologist, 48*, 3–23.

Teasdale, J. D., & Barnard, P. (1993). *Affect, cognition, and change*. Hove, England: Erlbaum.

Thoresen, C. E. (1974). Behavioral means and humanistic ends. In M. J. Mahoney & C. E. Thoresen (Eds.), *Self-control: Power to the person* (pp. 308–322). Monterey, CA: Brooks/Cole.

Turk, C. L., Heimberg, R. G., & Hope, D. A. (2001). Social anxiety disorder. In D. H. Barlow (Ed.), *Clinical handbook of psychological disorders* (pp. 114–153). New York: Guilford Press.

Van Dyke, P., & Harris, R. B. (1982). Phobia: A case report. *American Journal of Clinical Hypnosis, 24*, 284–287.

Varela, F., Thompson, E., & Rosch, E. (1992). *The embodied mind: Cognitive science and human experience*. Boston: MIT Press.

Wachtel, P. L. (1977). *Psychoanalysis and behavior therapy*. New York: Basic Books.

Wachtel, P. L. (1991). From eclecticism to synthesis: Toward a more seamless psychotherapeutic integration. *Journal of Psychotherapy Integration, 1*, 43–54.

Wachtel, P. L. (1993). *Therapeutic communication: Principles and effective practice*. New York: Guilford Press.

Wachtel, P. L. (1997). *Psychoanalysis, behavior therapy, and the relational world*. Washington, DC: American Psychological Association.

Wachtel, P. L. (2001). An (inevitably) self-deceiving reflection on self-deception. In M. R. Goldfried (Ed.), *How therapists change: Personal and professional reflections* (pp. 83–101). Washington, DC: American Psychological Association.

Wampold, B. E. (2001). *The great psychotherapy debate: Models, methods, and findings*. Hillsdale, NJ: Erlbaum.

Watson, J. B., & Morgan, J. J. B. (1917). Emotional reactions and psychological experimentation. *American Journal of Psychology, 28*, 163–174.

Watson, J. B., & Raynor, R. (1920). Conditioned emotional reactions. *Journal of Experimental Psychology, 3*, 1–14.

Weinberger, J. (1993). Common factors in psychotherapy. In G. Stricker & J. R. Gold (Eds.), *Comprehensive handbook of psychotherapy integration* (pp. 43–56). New York: Plenum Press.

Weiss, J., & Sampson, H. (1986). *The psycho-analytic process.* New York: Guilford Press.

Weitzman, B. (1967). Behavior therapy and psychotherapy. *Psychological Review, 74*, 300–317.

Westen, D. (1985). *Self and society.* Cambridge, NY: Cambridge University Press.

Westen, D. (1991). Cultural, emotional, and unconscious aspects of the self. In R. Curtis (Ed.), *The relational self: Theoretical convergences in psychoanalysis and social psychology* (pp. 181–210). New York: Guilford Press.

Westen, D. (1992). The cognitive self and the psychoanalytic self: Can we put our selves together. *Psychological Inquiry, 3*, 1–13.

Williams, S. L. (1990). Guided mastery treatment of agoraphobia: Beyond stimulus exposure. *Progress in Behavior Modification, 26*, 89–121.

Williams, S. L., & Zane, G. (1989). Guided mastery and stimulus exposure treatments for severe performance anxiety in agoraphobics. *Behaviour Research and Therapy, 27*, 237–245.

Wilson, M. (1993). DSM-III and the transformation of American psychiatry: A history. *American Journal of Psychiatry, 150*, 399–410.

Wolfe, B. E. (1989). Phobias, panic and psychotherapy integration. *Journal of Integrative and Eclectic Psychotherapy, 8*, 264–276.

Wolfe, B. E. (1992). Self-experiencing and the integrative treatment of the anxiety disorders. *Journal of Psychotherapy Integration, 2*, 29–43.

Wolfe, B. E. (1994). Adapting psychotherapy outcome research to clinical reality. *Journal of Psychotherapy Integration, 4*, 160–166.

Wolfe, B. E. (1995). Self pathology and psychotherapy integration. *Journal of Psychotherapy Integration, 5*, 293–312.

Wolfe, B. E. (2000). Toward an integrative theoretical basis for training psychotherapists. *Journal of Psychotherapy Integration, 10*, 233–246.

Wolfe, B. E. (2001a). The integrative experience of psychotherapy integration. In M. R. Goldfried (Ed.), *How therapists change: Personal and professional reflections* (pp. 289–312). Washington, DC: American Psychological Association.

Wolfe, B. E. (2001b). A message to assimilative integrationists: It is time to become accommodative integrationists: A commentary. *Journal of Psychotherapy Integration, 11*, 123–131.

Wolfe, B. E. (2003). Knowing the self: Building a bridge from basic research to clinical practice. *Journal of Psychotherapy Integration, 13*, 83–91.

Wolfe, B. E. (2005). Integrative psychotherapy of the anxiety disorders. In J. C. Norcross & M. R. Goldfried (Eds.), *Handbook of psychotherapy integration* (2nd ed., pp. 263–280). New York: Oxford University Press.

Wolfe, B. E., & Sigl, P. (1998). Experiential psychotherapy of the anxiety disorders. In L. S. Greenberg, J. C. Watson, & G. Lietaer (Eds.), *Handbook of experiential psychotherapy* (pp. 272–294). New York: Guilford Press.

Wolitzky, D. L., & Eagle, M. N. (1997). Psychoanalytic theories of psychotherapy. In P. L. Wachtel & S. B. Messer (Eds.), *Theories of psychotherapy: Origins and evolution* (pp. 39–96). Washington, DC: American Psychological Association.

Wolpe, J. (1958). *Psychotherapy by reciprocal inhibition.* Stanford, CA: Stanford University Press.

Wolpe, J. (1973). *The practice of behavior therapy.* New York: Pergamon Press.

Wolpe, J., Brady, J. P., Serber, M., Agras, W. S., & Liberman, R. P. (1973). The current status of systematic desensitization. *American Journal of Psychiatry, 130,* 961–965.

Wolpe, J., & Rowan, V. C. (1988). Panic disorder: A product of classical conditioning. *Behaviour Research and Therapy, 26,* 441–450.

Wurmser, L. (1981). *The mask of shame.* Baltimore: Johns Hopkins University Press.

Yalom, I. (1980). *Existential psychotherapy.* New York: Basic Books.

Young, J. E. (1990). *Cognitive therapy for personality disorders: A schema-focused approach.* Sarasota, FL: Professional Resources Exchange.

Zohar, J., & Insel, T. R. (1987). Obsessive-compulsive disorder: Psychobiological approaches to diagnosis, treatment, and pathophysiology. *Biological Psychiatry, 22,* 667–687.

AUTHOR INDEX

Jacobs, W. J., 48
Jacobson, E., 201
James, W., 82
Jenike, M. A., 50
Johnson, F., 82, 100
Johnson, M., 87n, 96, 98n, 128, 189
Johnson, M. R., 47, 48
Jones, E. E., 241

Karen, R., 114
Kaufman, G., 114
Kennedy, J. L., 50
Kernberg, H., 101
Kihlstrom, J. F., 16, 21, 75
Klein, D. F., 14, 18, 21, 33, 48, 50, 63, 77,
    143, 158
Klein, G. S., 91
Klerman, G. L., 16, 32, 77
Knowles, S. L., 143, 225
Kohlenberg, R. J., 166
Kohut, H., 56, 101, 163
Kopp, R. R., 177, 189, 225
Kopta, M., 192
Kosslyn, S. M., 98n
Kozak, M. J., 39, 44, 45, 72, 73, 75, 77, 112,
    159, 169, 175, 176, 185, 195, 196
Kraepelin, E., 16
Krause, M., 192

Lakoff, G., 96, 128, 189
Lambert, M. J., 176, 240
Last, C., 173
Lazarus, A. A., 8, 11
Leahy, R. L., 73, 75
LeDoux, J., 48, 77, 128
Levin, J. D., 81
Levis, D. J., 6
Liberman, R. P., 168
Liebowitz, M. R., 50, 146
Lietaer, G., 185
Linehan, M. M., 110
Luborsky, L., 35, 163
Lydiard, R. B., 47, 48, 181

Mahoney, M. J., 36, 72, 82, 84, 96, 109, 171,
    195
Markus, H., 82, 85, 102
Marshall, J. R., 142
Mavissakalian, M., 168
May, R., 14, 57, 146
Mayer, J. D., 104
McFall, M. E., 44

McGaugh, 36, 69
McLemore, C. W., 22
McNally, R. J., 19
Mead, G. H., 82, 135
Meichenbaum, D., 21
Meichenbaum, D. H., 170
Melzack, R., 83, 86, 87
Messer, S. B., 10, 11, 56
Meyer, J., 169
Michels, R., 14, 35, 161, 183
Milrod, B., 33, 77, 163, 182, 183, 187
Mineka, S., 38, 112
Mitchell, K. R., 41
Mitchell, S., 163
Mohlman, J., 50
Morgan, J. J. B., 36
Morris, R. J., 166
Mowrer, O. H., 13, 14, 36, 40, 43, 44
Mukerji, V., 143
Muran, J. C., 201, 246
Murphy, S. M., 23, 128

Nadel, N., 48
Nathanson, D. L., 114
Neisser, U., 98
Nemiah, J., 31
Norcross, J. C., 185, 198, 240
Noyes, R., 143
Nurius, P., 102

Obsessive-Compulsive Cognitions Working
    Group, 45
Ogilvie, D. M., 101
O'Leary, T. A., 171
Orlinsky, D. E., 176, 185, 192
Orr, T. E., 41
Öst, L.-G., 168
Ouseley, F. A., 243

Padawer, W., 7
Parks, B. K., 176, 185
Pasnau, R. O., 15
Pavlov, I., 74
Perls, F., 200
Peterson, S. R., 103, 104, 116
Piaget, J., 135
Pine, F., 91
Pinsof, W. M., 247
Polkinghorne, D. E., 82
Pribram, K. H., 86
Pylyshyn, Z. W., 98n

SUBJECT INDEX

in obsessive–compulsive disorders, 150–152

and panic disorder, 225

in psychoanalytic perspective, 30–31

and response to failure, 116

and self-esteem, 103

in social phobia, 135

in specific phobias, 128–129

case study on, 133

of undesirable information, 90–91

Awareness training, 221

Bandura's social learning model, 36–37, 45, 72, 169–170

Beck's cognitive model, 38–39

Behavioral approach and behaviorists

on affect, 76

on agoraphobia, 42–43

on anxiety, 57

on anxiety disorders, 36–38, 62, 63

and damaged or deficient self, 110

on fear and anxiety, 14

in integrative etiological model, 123

and meaning, 56

and specific phobias, 126

for surface work, 236

and unconscious processes, 74, 76, 97

Behavioral avoidance, 118–119

Behavioral change

as access point, 194

as focus of change process, 193, 195

and psychodynamic approach, 162

Behavioral and cognitive–behavioral perspectives on anxiety disorders, 35–39

and differentiation of various disorders, 46

and specific disorders, 39–46

Behavioral inhibition, 49

Behavioral rehearsals, 180

Behavioral therapy (treatment model), 165–167

for agoraphobia, 18, 168–169

and anxiety reactions, 63–64

critique of, 175–176

as different from other models, 184

and emotional processing, 195, 196

in rapprochement with psychoanalysis, 7

as specifically targeted at behavioral change, 8

and specific anxiety disorders, 167–169

and symptoms of anxiety disorder, 158, 175

and therapeutic relationship, 165–166, 184, 186

Behavioral treatment model (therapy), 165–167

Betrayal, 114

Biological diathesis, 31, 32, 33, 43, 249

Biologically vulnerable self, 108

Biological perspective

on etiology of anxiety disorders, 66–67

of Freud, 56

Biological reductionism, of Freud, 26

Biomedical perspective on anxiety disorders, 46–48, 78

on affect and emotion, 77

and agoraphobia, 18

on anxiety, 14

and differentiation of various disorders, 51

on etiology of anxiety disorders, 67–68

focus of, 158

and meaning, 56

on nature of anxiety disorders, 47, 63

and relation of panic attack to psychological meaning, 164

and specific disorders, 48–50

in unconscious or preconscious, 76

Biomedical treatment model, 181–182

and catastrophic meanings, 184

Bohart's critique of cognitive perspective, 73–74

Brain structures, in biological models of phobias, 48–49, 50

Bridge phobia, case example of (Trent), 3–4, 127

Bruner, Jerome, 57

Catastrophe, feared

in case study (generalized anxiety disorder), 149–150

in case study (panic disorder with agoraphobia), 142

in case study (panic disorder without agoraphobia), 144

in case study (social phobia), 137

eliciting of, 202

in Wolfe's focusing technique, 251

See also Endangered self; Self-endangerment

Catastrophic associations

distinguishing of from present reality, 194

in specific phobias, 126, 129
in unconscious or preconscious, 76
Catastrophic cogitation, 234
Catastrophic cognitions, 123
Catastrophic conflicts, in unconscious emotional beliefs, 78
Catastrophic danger
in anxiety disorder, 106
in obsessive–compulsive disorder, 151
resolving of, 208–209
Catastrophic fears, and dilemmas of life, 230
Catastrophic imagery or fantasy, 33
from imaginal exposure therapy, 4–5
tacit (from WFT), 204
and unconscious conflicts, 6
Catastrophic interpretation of anxiety, 52
Catastrophic meaning of anxiety symptoms, 23
anxiety disorders as anticipation of, 24, 70–71
biochemical underpinnings of, 184
in case study (panic disorder with agoraphobia), 141
Catastrophizing, 158
Ceiling effect, 5
Change, integrative model of, 193–199, 211–212
Classical conditioning, 36, 39–40, 42, 68, 69, 166
Claustrophobia, 40
in case studies, 130, 141
Clinical experience
and integrative psychotherapy model, 159–161
on techniques for treatment model, 186–189
Clinical interview, access point determined in, 213
Clinical relevance, in narrowing of psychiatric gaze (DSMs), 21, 22
Clinical researchers, and practitioners, 10
Cogitation, 89–90, 93, 133, 178, 234
anxiety from, 205
in case study (panic disorder with agoraphobia), 142
in case study (multiple specific phobias), 133
in case study (social phobia), 217–218
information yielded by, 91–93
in integrative treatment approach, 111
in maintenance of anxiety disorder, 117–118

direct experience of anxiety escaped through, 117, 194
obsessive or repetitive, 88, 135
in panic process, 132, 140
and secondary self-criticism in depression, 247
worry as, 147–148
Cognitive approaches or perspective, 71–74, 78
access points for, 197
and affect, 77
and basic biological variables, 71
and catastrophic cogitation, 234
in depth work, 234
in integrative etiological model, 123
for surface work, 236
Cognitive avoidance, 46, 119
Cognitive–behavioral perspective, 37. See also Behavioral and cognitive–behavioral perspectives on anxiety disorders
on anxiety disorders, 36–38, 62, 63
on anxiety disorders, 36–38, 62, 63
and cognitive schemas, 74–75
and deep-structure schemas, 110
on depression, 246
and fear structures or schemas, 72
focus of, 158
and language of self-representation, 83
and psychic structure, 196
and reflexive focus on fear, 79
Cognitive–behavioral treatment model, 170–173
and anxiety associated with cogitation, 205
in case study (generalized anxiety disorder), 228
in case study (PTSD treatment), 243
critique of, 175–176
and emotional processing, 195, 196
exposure used in, 182–183
as focusing on self, 187
optimistic findings on, 216–217
and specific anxiety disorders, 173–175
and surface work, 234
and symptomatic change, 198–199, 201
and underlying psychic structures, 183
Cognitive change, as access point, 194
Cognitive–experiential self theory of Epstein, 92
Cognitive model of panic disorder, 73, 111

Cognitive models of learning, and mediational models, 36
Cognitive psychology, Bruner on, 57
Cognitive restructuring of conscious cognitions, 184–185, 186, 189, 198, 202
    in case study (panic disorder without agoraphobia), 223
    for enhancing self-efficacy, 206
    in symptom phase of treatment, 201
Cognitive schema, 37, 163, 176
Cognitive science *versus* psychoanalysis, on unconscious, 75
Cognitive therapies
    and affect, 186
    constructivist models of, 171–172
    as different from other models, 184
    and negative self-beliefs, 83
    and self-with-other representations, 101
    as specifically targeted at cognitive changes, 8
Collaborative empiricism, 170–171
Common factors approach, 7–8
Comorbidity, 23–24
    as frequently found, 238
    problem of, 237
Compulsive rituals, in obsessive–compulsive disorders, 151. *See also* Rituals
Conceptualizing, and experiencing, 94
Conditioned anxiety, 43
Conditioning
    classical, 36, 39–40, 42, 68, 69, 166
    cognitive processes in, 71
    operant (instrumental), 36, 40, 69, 166
    in specific phobias, 127
    and unconscious processes, 74
Conditioning model of fear acquisition or response, 69–71, 78, 167
Conditioning theory(ies)
    changes in, 68–69
    of panic disorder, 42–43
Conflict(s)
    catastrophic, 208–209
    emotional, 237–238
    between freedom and security, 200
    resolving of, 193
    around the self, 109–110
    standard *versus* standard or standard *versus* wishes, 100
    unconscious, 6, 75, 147, 161, 163, 183, 186, 187, 189
Conflict resolution, 209
Confused or conflicted self, 109–110

Consciousness, and behavioral perspective, 35
Constructivist therapy, 171–172
Cooley, Charles H., 82, 83, 135
Coping
    with failure or rejection, 116
    and self-esteem, 103
Coping abilities or skills
    in etiology of anxiety, 64
    imagery rehearsal of, 175
    for reducing anxiety, 201
Core Conflictual Relationship Theme (CCRT) method, 34–35, 163
Corrective emotional experience, 189, 195, 195–196, 199
    as access point, 194
    and therapist's trustworthiness, 200
Countertransference, 198
Cultural patterning, of identity, 100–101
Cyclical psychodynamic theory, 248

Darwin, Charles, on anxiety, 13, 63
DB. *See* Diaphragmatic breathing
Death and dying, fear of, 108, 116, 129, 130
Defense mechanisms (defenses), 233
    analysis of
        in case study (generalized anxiety disorder), 226
        in psychodynamic approach, 161, 162, 197
    analysis and confrontation of, 199
    analysis and modification of (as goal of therapy), 191, 192–193
    as cognitive avoidance, 119
    in differentiating various categories of disorder, 231, 238
    against dilemmas of human life, 231
    and Freud on anxiety disorders, 27, 29, 29–30
    and Freudian paradigm, 28
    identifying and modifying, 189, 204, 205
    in modern psychoanalytic conception, 33
    in panic disorder, 157–158
    in psychodynamic models of anxiety disorders, 30–31, 35
    as self-image protective processes, 120–121, 122
    from sense of shame, 114
    and therapist's trustworthiness, 200
Denial, as cognitive avoidance, 119

Dependency-based depression, 246
Depression
    in case study (panic disorder without
        agoraphobia), 145, 224
    integrative approach for, 245–247
Depth work, 234
    conditions for success of, 192
    and emotional processing, 235
    reasons for failure in, 237
Desegregation, psychotherapy, 7–8
Desensitization, 166, 205
    in case study (PTSD treatment), 243
    for social anxiety, 168
    systematic, 6
        Wolpe's systematic desensitization
            therapy, 167, 167–168
Developmental perspective, in narrowing of
        psychiatric gaze (DSMs), 21, 22
Dewey, John, 135
*Diagnostic and Statistical Manual of Mental
    Disorders* (1st ed.) (*DSM–I*), 14, 15
*Diagnostic and Statistical Manual of Mental
    Disorders* (2d ed.) (*DSM–II*), 15–16
*Diagnostic and Statistical Manual of Mental
    Disorders* (3d ed.) (*DSM–III*), 9, 16–
    17
    on anxiety disorders, 17–19
    on generalized anxiety disorder, 19–20,
        50
    on obsessive–compulsive disorders, 20
    on phobias, 19
*Diagnostic and Statistical Manual of Mental
    Disorders* (3d ed., revised) *DSM–III–
    R*, 9
    on anxiety disorders, 17–19
    on generalized anxiety disorder, 19–20
    on obsessive–compulsive disorders, 20
    on phobias, 19
*Diagnostic and Statistical Manual of Mental
    Disorders* (4th ed.) (*DSM–IV*), 6
    anxiety disorders in, 9, 17–19, 238
    anxiety neurosis symptoms in, 28
    on generalized anxiety disorder, 19–20
    multiaxial approach to classification in,
        23
    on obsessive–compulsive disorders, 20
    on panic disorder, 139
        with agoraphobia, 142
    on phobias, 19
    and psychoanalysis, 34
    and psychodynamic clinicians, 163
    on traumatic experience, 113

*Diagnostic and Statistical Manual of Mental
    Disorders* (4th ed., text revision)
    (*DSM–IV–TR*), 14
    on anxiety disorder, 160
Dialectic, between experiencing and concep-
    tualizing, 94, 194
Dialogue. *See* Two-chair dialogue
Diaphragmatic breathing (DB), 171, 201,
    203
    in case studies, 214, 217, 221, 223, 227,
        229
    for generalized anxiety disorder, 180
    for panic disorder with agoraphobia, 179
    for specific phobias, 178
    in Wolfe's focusing technique, 203, 251
Diathesis, biological or neurobiological, 30,
    31, 32, 33, 43, 71, 249
Diathesis stress model, 28–29
Disaffected and isolated self, 109
Disavowed emotions, 158
Disputing questions, 173. *See also* Socratic
    questioning
Don (case study, generalized anxiety disor-
    der), 149–150, 226–228
Dorothy (case example, driving phobia), 126
Downward arrow technique, 171, 202, 234
Driving phobia
    in case study (Joan), 141, 220–221
    examples of, 4, 70, 122, 126, 129, 159,
        178, 206, 209, 248
    in vivo exposure for, 202
Drugs. *See* Medications, antianxiety
Dryden, John, quoted, 105
*DSM. See at Diagnostic and Statistical Manual
    of Mental Disorders*
DSM classification system, 20–24

Eclecticism, 6
    technical, 7–8
Effectiveness studies, 239–240
Efficacy studies, 238, 238–239
    limitations of, 239
Einstein, Albert, quoted, 3
Elaine (case example, driving phobia), 178,
    209
Embodied self, 87
Emotion(s)
    defending against pain of, 186, 187
    disavowed, 158
    fear of (GAD), 147
    and self-wounds, 234
    tolerating pain of, 206

and symptom-focused treatment, 201
Genetics
 and anxiety disorder, 65, 112, 122, 294
  development of, 63
 and specific phobias, 49
Genetic vulnerabilities, in biomedical view
 of anxiety disorders, 48
Gestalt therapy, 51, 177. *See also* Experiential therapies
Glen (case study, social phobia), 136–138,
 210, 217–220
Grief work, in case study (panic disorder with
 agoraphobia), 223
Group-format CBT, for social anxiety disorder, 173–174
Guided imagery, 177, 203, 204, 207
 in case study (multiple specific phobias),
  130
 in case study (PTSD treatment), 243
 as experiential intervention, 199
 for obsessive–compulsive disorder, 180
 in Wolfe's focusing technique, 251
Guided-mastery treatment, 170
Guilt, and self-esteem struggle, 76

Healthy self, 249
Height phobias, and fear of loss of control, 3
Helplessness, anxiety as, 37–38, 63
Heredity
 in Freud's view of anxiety neurosis, 28–
  29
 See also Genetics
Hippocampus, 48, 49
Humanistic–existential view, and meaning
 of anxiety, 57
Humanistic values, and behaviorists, 38
Human reflexivity, 87–88
Humiliation
 attentional focus away from, 90
 in case study (generalized anxiety disorder), 149–150
 in case study (panic disorder with agoraphobia), 142
 in case study (social phobia), 179, 218,
  220
 as given of life, 220
 in obsessive–compulsive disorder, 151
  case study, 229, 230
 and self-esteem struggle, 76
 as self-wound, 109, 234
 in social phobia example, 203
 in specific phobias, 129

"I." *See* Self
Idealized image, 120
Identity, 99–100
 affect as necessary to change in, 197
 confusion or conflict about, 109
 cultural patterning of, 100–101
 and self-wounds, viii
 and values, 100
Image, idealized, 120
Imagery, 188–189, 189
 in case study (bridge phobia), 4
 catastrophic
  from imaginal exposure therapy, 4–
   5
  and unconscious conflicts, 6
 catastrophic associations from, 126
 in emotional processing, 96
 guided, 130, 177, 180, 199, 203, 204,
  207, 243, 251
 self-wounds identified by, 234
Imagery dialogue
 in case study (panic disorder without
  agoraphobia), 145
 See also two-chair work
Imagery training, 175
Imaginal exposure therapy, 160, 177, 202
 for bridge phobia patient, 3–4
 in case study (multiple specific phobias),
  214, 215
 in case study (panic disorder with agoraphobia), 221
 catastrophic imagery from, 4–5
 in experiential psychotherapy, 178, 180,
  184
 and trustworthiness tests, 200
 WFT as, 177, 203, 204, 251
Imipramine, 18, 239
Implicit (preconscious) meaning of anxiety,
 viii, 9, 22, 106, 187, 189, 203
 and Wolfe's focusing technique, 252
Implicit meaning of anxiety symptoms, 21,
 22–23, 186
 research deficient on, 241–242
Impression management, 103, 118–119, 119
 in general anxiety disorder, 148
  treatment of, 180
 in social phobia, 135–136
  case studies, 138, 179, 219
   example of public speaking phobia,
    208
Inadequate or incompetent self, 108–109
Individual case studies, 241

theoretical considerations in support of, 158–159

treatment models contributing to, 161
behavioral, 165–169
biomedical, 181–182
cognitive–behavioral (CBT), 170–176
experiential, 176–181
psychodynamic, 161–165
social learning theory, 169–170

Integrative model of self, 83, 84, 104
and attentional focus in self-knowledge, 90–93
experiencing, symbolizing and construing in, 88–90
and human reflexivity, 87–88
and mind–body problem, 86–87
organism, person and self in, 84–86
self-knowledge development processes in, 93–98

Integrative model of therapeutic change, 193–199, 211–212

Intellectualization, 120–121. *See also* Cogitation

Intentionality
and anxiety disorder, 67
causes and meanings in understanding of, 57
and subject's stance, 84

Interoceptive exposure, 169, 171, 177, 179, 202
in case study (panic disorder with agoraphobia), 221, 223

Interpersonal behavior, negative cycles of, 119–120

Interpersonal consequences
in case study (panic disorder without agoraphobia), 145–146
in case study (social phobia), 138
in case study (specific phobias), 134
in generalized anxiety disorder, 148–149
of obsessive–compulsive disorder, 152
of panic disorder with agoraphobia, 140–141

Interpersonal focus, in narrowing of psychiatric gaze (DSMs), 22

Interpersonal schemas, 101

Interpretation, in psychodynamic therapy, 162

Intersubjectivity, and human reflexivity, 88

In vivo exposure therapy, 3, 202
for agoraphobia, 168–169

case example of, 178
in case study (multiple specific phobias), 214
in case study (panic disorder with agoraphobia), 221
and trustworthiness tests, 200

Isolation, as defense, 192

James, William, 82, 83, 89
Jean (case example, panic disorder with agoraphobia), 179
Jefferson, Thomas, quoted, 213
Jim (case study, multiple specific phobias), 129–134, 213–217
Joan (case study, panic disorder with agoraphobia), 141–142, 220–223
Journal of Pragmatic Case Studies, 241
Journal of Psychotherapy Integration, 7

Klein, D. F., 18
Knowing, 73
experiential, 74
Kraepelin, Emil, 16

Language, reflexivity of (Mead), 82–83
Learning theories, 35–36, 46
Lewin, Kurt, quoted, 125
Little Albert (case example on classical conditioning), 36
Little Hans (Freudian case study), 29
Looking-glass self, 82

Magical thinking, in obsessive–compulsive disorders, 150
Mahoney, Michael J., 61
Manualizing, 10, 238
Marital and family therapies, and integrative treatment model, 247–248
Masculinity, in case study (social phobias), 137
Mayonnaise phobia, 127
Mead, George H., 82–83, 89, 135
Meaning(s)
anxiety disorders and problem of, 24
and cognitive psychology (Bruner), 57
and constructivist models of cognitive therapy, 171–172
and defenses, 120
and developmental perspective, 22
and emotional processing, 95, 96
felt, 89, 91
and Freud on anxiety, 56

isolation as defense in, 192
maintenance processes in, 150–152
   case study, 153
and modern psychoanalytic perspective,
   34
as projection, 119
ruminative thinking of, 65
shame anxiety in, 115
and symptom-focused treatment, 201
and validation of revised self-appraisals,
   211
Ontological givens. *See* Existential givens of
   life
Openness to experience, 102
Operant (instrumental) conditioning, 36, 40,
   69, 166
Organism, 84
Organismic experience
   bypassing of, 94
   and positive self-knowledge, 102

Painful emotions
   attentional focus away from, 90
   defending against, 186, 187
   tolerance for, 206–207
   See also Emotion(s)
Painful or traumatic experience, 65
Panic anxiety (panic attack), 15
   from experience of self-wounds, 107
Panic Control Treatment (PCT), 174
Panic disorder
   biological hypotheses for, 49–50
   bodily sensations in, 68
   catastrophic cognitions in, 123
   clinical trial on treatment of, 239
   cognitive–behavioral therapy for, 171
   cognitive model of, 73, 111
   DSM–III classification of, 18
   in *DSM–III* and *DSM–IV*, 18–19
   eclectic approach for, 6
   eliciting tacit self-wounds in, 203
   examples of, 5, 108
   experiential perspective on, 54
   and fear structure, 46
   Freud on, 31–32
   and genetic vulnerability, 48
   modern psychodynamic conception of,
     32–33
   and symptom-focused treatment, 201
   symptoms of, 157
   and validation of revised self-appraisals,
     211

Panic disorder with agoraphobia, 139
   and agoraphobia as distinction, 143
   behavioral models of, 42–43
   case study on (Joan), 141–142, 220–223
   cognitive–behavioral therapy for, 174
   cognitive models of, 43
   DSM–III classification of, 18
   experiential therapy for, 179
   maintenance process in, 139–140
   and social phobia, 142
Panic disorder without agoraphobia, 142
   case study of (Peter), 143–146
   DSM–III classification of, 18
Panic-focused psychodynamic psychotherapy
   (PFPP), 163–164, 182
Panic process
   in case study (panic disorder with ago-
     raphobia), 141
   in case study (panic disorder without
     agoraphobia), 144
   in case study (social phobia), 136
   in case study (specific phobias), 132
Parloff, M. B., 6
   quoted, 157
Patient, access point of. *See* Access point of
   patient
Patients, individual differences among. *See*
   Individual differences
Pavlov, Ivan, 68, 74. *See also* Classical con-
   ditioning
Perseveration, 89
Person(hood), 84–85
   versus self, 85
Personal cognitive organization (P.C. Org),
   172
Personal meaning, of anxiety symptoms, 22–
   23
Person-centered therapy, 51. *See also* Expe-
   riential perspective on anxiety dis-
   order
Perspective taking, 135
Peter (case study, panic disorder without ago-
   raphobia), 143–146, 223–226
PFPP (panic-focused psychodynamic psycho-
   therapy), 163–164, 182
Pharmacological dissection, 18
Pharmacotherapy, 181–182
   and integrative psychotherapy, 9
Phobias
   and change process, 195
   cognitive–behavioral therapy for, 171
   deeper issues related to, 4

and therapeutic relationship, 198
and underlying psychic structures, 183
Psychopathology, and self, 83
Psychosocial model of mental illness, 14–15
Psychotherapy
    combined with behavioral therapy (bridge phobia), 4
    research-informed, 10, 11
Psychotherapy desegregation, 7–8
Psychotherapy integration, 7
    and anxiety disorders, 8
    assimilative integration in, 11
    See also Integrative model of psychotherapy for anxiety disorders
Psychotherapy integration movement, 247
Psychotherapy Relationships That Work, 240
Psychotherapy theories, self in, 83–84
PTSD (posttraumatic stress disorder), integrative approach for, 242–245
Public-speaking phobia (type of social phobia)
    case study on (Glen), 136–138
    examples of, 4–5, 73, 108, 109, 178–179, 207–208
    inauthenticity in, 210–211

Rational emotive therapy,175
Rationalization, as cognitive avoidance, 119
Rational system, experiential system compared with, 92
Reactance, 201
"Reaction," 15
Reaction formation, 30
Reality
    and self-esteem, 103
    See also Existential givens of life
Reciprocal inhibition, 69–70, 167
Reductionism (biological), of Freud, 26
Reflection, 89
Reflexivity, 85, 87–88
Rehearsals, behavioral, 180
Rejection
    response to, 115–116
    and self-esteem, 103
    See also Humiliation
Relapses, and implicit meaning of panic, 174
Relationship factors in psychotherapy process, 240. See also Therapeutic alliance; Therapeutic relationship
Relaxation response, and Wolpe, 167
Relaxation strategies or training, 166, 171, 175, 178, 184, 189, 198

in CB treatment, 170
and clinical experience, 186
in symptom phase of treatment, 201–202
Repression, 158
    Freud on, 27
Research, on psychotherapy process, 11, 239–242
Research findings
    for selection of techniques in treatment model, 184–186
    on treatment for anxiety disorders, 159
Research-informed psychotherapy, 10, 11
Responsibility, causes and meanings in understanding of, 57
Rick (case example, public speaking phobia), 178
RIGS (representations of interactions that have become generalized), 101
Rituals
    in case study (obsessive–compulsive disorder), 228, 229
    and behavioral therapy, 169
    in obsessive–compulsive disorder, 150, 151
    case studies, 153, 180
Rodent phobia (example), 5
Role model, self-aspirations from, 102
Role-plays, in case study (generalized anxiety disorder), 227
Role–relationship models, 101
Romantic relationships
    in case study (generalized anxiety disorder), 150, 227
    in case study (multiple specific phobias), 131, 132, 215–216
    inhibited by list of requirements (example), 93
    See also Significant others

Safe emergency, therapy situation as, 200
Schema-based models of anxiety, 72–73
Schemas
    cognitive, 37, 163, 176
    in cognitive–behavioral view, 74–75
    and cognitive therapy, 73
    deep-structure, 110
    interpersonal, 101
    self-schema, 181, 183
Schemes, emotion, 75–76, 196
SE (supportive–expressive) treatment for GAD, 163, 165

Secondary emotional reaction, 52–53
Secrets, selective sharing of, 211
Selective serotonin reuptake inhibitors, 181
Self, 81, 85
    and agency, 133
    and anxiety reactions, 78
    biologically vulnerable, 108
    as common focus, 183
    confused or conflicted, 109–110
    directly experienced senses of, 91
    disaffected or isolated, 109
    early psychological theories of, 81–83
    embodied, 87
    endangered, 132
    in experiential therapy, 178
    and external perspective, 135
    and felt meanings, 91
    healthy, 249
    inadequate or incompetent, 108–109
    integrative model of, 83, 84–98, 104,
    necessary elements in account of, 83
    and opinions of others, 115
    painful emotions around, 188
    and person, 85
    in psychotherapy theories, 83–84
    relationship with, 84
    revised perspective on, 195, 199, 235
    and self-wounds, viii
    shamed, defective or humiliated, 109
    as social object (in social phobia), 41
    as subject and as object, 93–94
Self-appraisals
    debilitating or painful, 188, 189
    revised, 193
        validation of, 211
    toxic, 193, 208
Self-assessments, 102
    therapeutic work following from, 234
Self-awareness, 135
    explicit and tacit layers of, 172
Self-beliefs
    affect as necessary to change in, 197
    changes in, 235
    construction of, 98–99
    from emotional processing, 96
Self-concept
    development of, 98–99
        as social phenomenon, 98, 99
    and skill learning, 90
Self-critical depression, 246
Self-deception, and response to failure, 116
Self-efficacy expectations or beliefs

and Bandura on anxiety disorders, 37,
    38
in case study (multiple specific phobias),
    214
enhancing of, 193, 206
lack of, 64, 72
rebuilding of, 200
from toleration of painful emotions,
    207
Self-endangerment, 52, 71, 106, 121
    and experiential model, 176
    and obsessive–compulsive disorder, 54–
    55
    in panic disorder, 139
    and self-wounds, 107–108, 203
    in social phobias, 134–135
    in specific phobias, 127, 128, 132–133
Self-esteem, 102–103
    and response to existential givens, 115
    struggle for, 76
Self-evaluation
    defenses as protection against, 121
    and social phobia, 135
Self-experiencing
    in case study (panic disorder without
        agoraphobia), 145
    in case study (social phobia), 136–137
    in case study (specific phobias), 132–
        133
    versus self-standards, 193, 209
Self-exposure to anxious thoughts, 175
Self-focused attention, 64, 68, 79, 111, 187
    and experiential model, 181
    and ruminative thinking, 65
    and secondary self-criticism in depres-
        sion, 247
    in social phobias, 135
Self-fulfilling prophecy, 238
    in generalized anxiety disorder, 34
    in social phobia (case study), 135
Self-guide, in example, 210
Selfhood
    causes and meanings in understanding
        of, 57
    and historical changes, 100
Self-knowledge
    attentional focus in, 90–93
    contents of, 98–102
    development of, 93
        through direct experience and
            through cogitation, 93–95
    and emotional processing, 95–98

Spencer (case study, obsessive–compulsive disorder), 152–153, 228–230
Stance, 84
Stance, therapist. *See* Therapist stance
Standards, and identity, 100
Stern, Daniel, 81
Strategy(ies) of patients with anxiety disorders, 122, 125, 194
    agoraphobia as, 42
    behavioral, 233
    impression management, 103, 118–119, 135–136 (*see also* Impression management)
    after symptom reduction, 160
    See also Cogitation; Defense mechanisms
Stress
    failure of defenses under, 233
    from self-preoccupation, 249
    and Wolfe's focusing technique, 251
Stress management
    in case study (obsessive–compulsive disorder), 229
    in case study (PTSD treatment), 243
Subjective experience
    and biological processes, 86–87
    Freud on, 56
    and neurobiological systems, 66–67
    struggle with, 121
Subjectivity, as embodied, 87
Substantial self, 82
Suffocation sensitivity, 33
Supportive–expressive (SE) treatment for GAD, 163, 165
Surface work, 234
Symbolic capacities, 249
Symbolic themes, 128
Symptom-focused treatment, 10
Symptom reduction
    as goal of therapy, 191–192, 194
    in-depth work contingent on, 192
    intrapsychic conflict as blocking, 237
    and treatment effect, 159
Symptoms of anxiety or anxiety disorder, 8, 157, 231
    and behavioral therapists, 158, 175
    catastrophic meaning of, 23
    change of as initial focus, 198–199
    and cognitive–behavioral treatment, 175
    as common focus, 182
    in experiential treatment, 181

    implicit meaning of, 21, 22, 186
        research deficient on, 241–242
    and psychodynamic approach, 158, 160–161, 164
    and social learning, 175
    treating of (Phase II of psychotherapy model), 201–202
    treatments for, viii, 159
    unconscious associations of, 21

Tacit processes, 21. *See also* Unconscious
Tacit psychic structures
    and emotional processing, 195, 196
    self-schemas, 181
Tacit self-wounds, eliciting of (Phase III of psychotherapy model), 202–204
Targets of change, 157
    for behavioral therapy, 167
    in panic disorder, 157–158
Task Force on Nomenclature and Statistics, 16, 17
Technical eclecticism, 7–8
Technological development, and individualism, 100
Termination of therapy, 202
    patient's decision point on (case study), 215
Terminology, of self-wound hypothesis, 110
Theoretical integration, 7, 8
Therapeutic alliance, 158, 176, 182, 189, 198
    in case study (multiple specific phobias), 214
    in case study (panic disorder without agoraphobia), 223
    in case study (social phobia), 217
    and changes in therapeutic stance, 236
    and defenses, 192
    in-depth work contingent on, 192
    establishment of (Phase I of psychotherapy model), 199–201
    monitoring of, 187, 198
    and research findings, 186
    and uncovering of unconscious meanings, 21
    See also Therapeutic relationship
Therapeutic change, integrative model of, 193–199, 211–212
Therapeutic intervention
    and access points, 197
    sequence of, 213, 228, 231, 236–237, 238, 249

See also Integrative model of psychotherapy for anxiety disorders; Treatment
Therapeutic process, in case study (generalized anxiety disorder), 226
Therapeutic relationship, 160, 161, 162, 182,
189, 235
and behavioral therapists, 165–166,
184, 186
in case study (generalized anxiety disorder), 226, 227
in case study (obsessive–compulsive disorder), 228
and clinical experience, 187–188
collaborative empiricism as, 170–171
emotional self-assessment as guidelines
for, 234
from experiential point of view, 177
object relations and self-psychology approaches on, 162–163
research lacking on, 176
and research literature, 185–186
See also Therapeutic alliance
Therapist congruence, 186
Therapist stance, 177
in behavioral models, 184
switching of as challenge, 236
Thinking *versus* perceiving and experiencing, 74
Thinking errors, correcting of (CBT), 173–
174, 202
Thought–action fusion, in case study (obsessive–compulsive disorder), 229
Tolerance for emotional experience, 193
Tolerance for painful emotions, 206–207
Toxic messages, 115, 134
in generalized anxiety disorder, 146–147
case study, 227
from significant others, 114
Toxic self-appraisals or view of self
modifying of, 208
restructuring of, 193
Transduction, 66–67
Transference, 97, 160
analysis of, 161, 162
and emotional processing, 197
Transforming metaphors, 199
Trauma (traumatic experiences), 65, 113–
114
and experiential frame of reference, 64
as related to other sources of self-
wounds, 116

as relative to individual, 52, 113
See also Posstraumatic stress disorder
Treatment(s)
all foci necessary to, 193
and comorbidity, 237
surface work and depth work in, 234
symptom-focused, viii, 10
See also Integrative model of psychotherapy for anxiety disorders; Therapeutic intervention
Treatment integration
pharmacotherapy and integrative psychotherapy as, 9
See also Psychotherapy integration
Trent (bridge phobia patient), 3–4, 127
Trustworthiness, therapist's establishment of,
200
Twin studies, on obsessive–compulsive disorder, 50
Two-chair dialogue, 177, 199
between actual and ought selves (case
study, panic disorder with agoraphobia), 222
in case study (generalized anxiety disorder), 227
in case study (social phobia), 218
in conflict resolution, 209
example of, 210
for obsessive–compulsive disorder, 180
patients suitable for, 236
Two-factor theory of Mowrer, 36, 40, 43, 167
cognitive–perceptual extension of, 45

Uncertainty, intolerance of, 46
Unconscious
and anxiety disorders, 74–76
in cognitive–behavioral GAD model,
46
in development of self-knowledge (information processing), 97–98
and Freud on anxiety disorders, 27, 28
and implicit meanings of symptoms, 186
and modern psychoanalytic perspective,
31, 33
in narrowing of psychiatric gaze (*DSMs*),
21
as unobserved by clinical assessment, 21
in panic-focused psychodynamic psychotherapy, 164
Unconscious conflicts, 186, 187, 189
and catastrophic imagery, 6
in generalized anxiety disorder, 147

ABOUT THE AUTHOR

Barry E. Wolfe, PhD, is currently in full-time private practice. He is also president and CEO of the Center for Training in Psychotherapy Integration, which is focused on training practicing therapists in integrative approaches to psychotherapy. He was formerly a senior consultant for training at Washington Assessment and Therapy Services. Between 1994 and 2003, Dr. Wolfe was professor of clinical psychology at the American School of Professional Psychology of Argosy University, Washington, DC. There he taught several psychotherapy courses in Argosy's PsyD program. Dr. Wolfe was the first faculty member hired at the Virginia campus of the American School of Professional Psychology when it opened in the fall of 1994. Before that, Dr. Wolfe was associated with the National Institute of Mental Health for 24 years where he served in several different capacities, all relating to the support and conduct of psychotherapy research. He served as project officer on many grants that evaluated the efficacy of new behavioral, cognitive–behavioral, experiential, marital, and psychodynamic therapies.

For the past 30 years, Dr. Wolfe has been in private practice in the Bethesda–Rockville area, where he specializes in the treatment of anxiety and mood disorders, marital therapy, and therapy for life transitions. Dr. Wolfe is a founding member of the Society for the Exploration of Psychotherapy Integration, an organization devoted to the development of the best approaches to psychotherapy, independent of theoretical orientation. A native of Washington, DC, Dr. Wolfe completed his undergraduate work at Howard University in 1963 and received his PhD from the University of Florida in 1970.

Dr. Wolfe is the author of over 50 publications on psychotherapy, psychotherapy integration, psychotherapy research, as well as a variety of other topics. He was also a coeditor of *Treatment of Panic Disorder: A Consensus Development Conference* (American Psychological Association, 1994).